Register Your Book
at ibmpressbooks.com/ibmregister

Upon registration, we will send you electronic sample chapters from two of our popular IBM Press books. In addition, you will be automatically entered into a monthly drawing for a free IBM Press book.

Registration also entitles you to:

- Notices and reminders about author appearances, conferences, and online chats with special guests

- Access to supplemental material that may be available

- Advance notice of forthcoming editions

- Related book recommendations

- Information about special contests and promotions throughout the year

- Chapter excerpts and supplements of forthcoming books

Contact us

If you are interested in writing a book or reviewing manuscripts prior to publication, please write to us at:

Editorial Director, IBM Press
c/o Pearson Education
800 East 96th Street
Indianapolis, IN 46240

e-mail: IBMPress@pearsoned.com

Visit us on the Web: ibmpressbooks.com

WebSphere Business Integration Primer

IBM Press

The developerWorks® Series

The IBM Press developerWorks Series represents a unique undertaking in which print books and the Web are mutually supportive. The publications in this series are complemented by their association with resources available at the developerWorks Web site on ibm.com. These resources include articles, tutorials, forums, software, and much more.

Through the use of icons, readers will be able to immediately identify a resource on developerWorks which relates to that point of the text. A summary of links appears at the end of each chapter. Additionally, you will be able to access an electronic guide of the developerWorks links and resources through ibm.com/developerworks/dwbooks that reference developerWorks Series publications, deepening the reader's experiences.

A developerWorks book offers readers the ability to quickly extend their information base beyond the book by using the deep resources of developerWorks and at the same time enables developerWorks readers to deepen their technical knowledge and skills.

For a full listing of developerWorks Series publications, please visit: **ibmpressbooks.com/dwseries**.

DB2® Books

DB2® Universal Database V8 for Linux, UNIX, and Windows Database Administration Certification Guide, Fifth Edition
Baklarz and Wong

Understanding DB2®
Chong, Liu, Qi, and Snow

High Availability Guide for DB2®
Eaton and Cialini

DB2® Universal Database V8 Handbook for Windows, UNIX, and Linux
Gunning

DB2® SQL PL, Second Edition
Janmohamed, Liu, Bradstock, Chong, Gao, McArthur, and Yip

DB2® for z/OS® Version 8 DBA Certification Guide
Lawson

DB2® Universal Database V8.1 Certification Exam 700 Study Guide
Sanders

DB2® Universal Database V8.1 Certification Exam 703 Study Guide
Sanders

DB2® Universal Database V8.1 Certification Exams 701 and 706 Study Guide
Sanders

DB2® Universal Database for OS/390
Sloan and Hernandez

The Official Introduction to DB2® for z/OS®, Second Edition
Sloan

Advanced DBA Certification Guide and Reference for DB2® Universal Database v8 for Linux, UNIX, and Windows
Snow and Phan

DB2® Express
Yip, Cheung, Gartner, Liu, and O'Connell

Apache Derby—Off to the Races
Zikopoulos, Baklarz, and Scott

DB2® Version 8
Zikopoulos, Baklarz, deRoos, and Melnyk

On Demand Computing Books

Business Intelligence for the Enterprise
Biere

On Demand Computing
Fellenstein

Grid Computing
Joseph and Fellenstein

Autonomic Computing
Murch

Rational® Software Books

Software Configuration Management Strategies and IDM Rational® ClearCase®, Second Edition
Bellagio and Milligan

Implementing IBM® Rational® ClearQuest®
Buckley, Pulsipher, and Scott

Project Management with the IBM Rational Unified Process
Gibbs

IBM Rational® ClearCase®, Ant, and CruiseControl
Lee

Visual Modeling with Rational Software Architect and UML
Quatrani and Palistrant

WebSphere® Books

IBM® WebSphere®
Barcia, Hines, Alcott, and Botzum

IBM® WebSphere® Application Server for Distributed Platforms and z/OS®
Black, Everett, Draeger, Miller, Iyer, McGuinnes, Patel, Herescu, Gissel, Betancourt, Casile, Tang, and Beaubien

Enterprise Java™ Programming with IBM® WebSphere®, Second Edition
Brown, Craig, Hester, Pitt, Stinehour, Weitzel, Amsden, Jakab, and Berg

IBM® WebSphere® and Lotus
Lamb, Laskey, and Indurkhya

IBM® WebSphere® System Administration
Williamson, Chan, Cundiff, Lauzon, and Mitchell

Enterprise Messaging Using JMS and IBM® WebSphere®
Yusuf

More Books from IBM Press

Irresistible! Markets, Models, and Meta-Value in Consumer Electronics
Bailey and Wenzek

Service-Oriented Architecture Compass
Bieberstein, Bose, Fiammante, Jones, and Shah

Developing Quality Technical Information, Second Edition
Hargis, Carey, Hernandez, Hughes, Longo, Rouiller, and Wilde

Performance Tuning for Linux® Servers
Johnson, Huizenga, and Pulavarty

RFID Sourcebook
Lahiri

Building Applications with the Linux Standard Base
Linux Standard Base Team

An Introduction to IMS™
Meltz, Long, Harrington, Hain, and Nicholls

Search Engine Marketing, Inc.
Moran and Hunt

Can Two Rights Make a Wrong?
Insights from IBM's Tangible Culture Approach
Moulton Reger

Inescapable Data
Stakutis and Webster

WebSphere Business Integration Primer

Process Server, BPEL, SCA and SOA

developerWorks® Series

Ashok Iyengar

Vinod Jessani

Michele Chilanti

IBM Press
Pearson plc
Upper Saddle River, NJ • Boston • Indianapolis • San Francisco
New York • Toronto • Montreal • London • Munich • Paris • Madrid
Capetown • Sydney • Tokyo • Singapore • Mexico City
ibmpressbooks.com

IBM Press Program Managers: Tara Woodman, Ellice Uffer

Cover design: IBM Corporation

Associate Publisher: Greg Wiegand
Marketing Manager: Kourtnaye Sturgeon
Publicist: Heather Fox
Acquisitions Editor: Katherine Bull
Development Editor: Ginny Bess
Managing Editor: Gina Kanouse
Designer: Alan Clements
Project Editor: Anne Goebel
Copy Editor: Gayle Johnson
Indexer: Erika Millen
Senior Compositor: Gloria Schurick
Manufacturing Buyer: Dan Uhrig

Published by Pearson plc
Publishing as IBM Press

IBM Press offers excellent discounts on this book when ordered in quantity for bulk purchases or special sales, which may include electronic versions and/or custom covers and content particular to your business, training goals, marketing focus, and branding interests. For more information, please contact:

U.S. Corporate and Government Sales
1-800-382-3419
corpsales@pearsontechgroup.com

For sales outside the U.S., please contact:

International Sales
international@pearsoned.com

Safari BOOKS ONLINE ENABLED — This Book Is Safari Enabled

Library of Congress Cataloging-in-Publication Data

Iyengar, Ashok.

WebSphere business integration primer : Process server, BPEL, SCA, and SOA / Ashok Iyengar, Vinod Jessani, and Michele Chilanti.

p. cm.

ISBN 0-13-224831-X

1. WebSphere. 2. Middleware. 3. Enterprise application integration (Computer systems) 4. Systems migration. I. Jessani, Vinod. II. Chilanti, Michele. III. Title.

QA76.76.M54I94 2007

005.1—dc22

2007041648

ISBN-13: 978-0-13-224831-0
ISBN-10: 0-13-224831-X

Text printed in the United States on recycled paper at R.R. Donnelley in Crawfordsville, Indiana.
First printing December 2007

*This book is dedicated to the two people I miss the most—
my dad, Shri Bindiganavale Govindaswamy Iyengar,
and my best friend, Ramesh Raheja.*

—*Ashok Iyengar*

Contents

Foreword   xxv

Acknowledgments   xxix

About the Authors   xxxi

Introduction   xxxiii

Chapter 1   Business Integration   1

Business Integration Challenge   1
Service-Oriented Architecture   3
SOA Lifecycle   5
Business Integration Programming Model   7
     Service Component Architecture   7
BPEL (Now Called WS-BPEL)   8
Service Data Objects   8
Closing the Link   9
Links to developerWorks   9

Chapter 2   Business Integration Architecture and Patterns   11

Business Integration Scenarios   12
Business Integration: Roles, Products, and Technical Challenges   12
     Clear Separation of Roles   13
     A Common Business Object Model   13
     The Service Component Architecture (SCA) Programming Model   14
     Tools and Products   14
The Business Object Framework   14
     Working with the IBM Business Object Framework   16

Service Component Architecture   16
    The SCA Programming Model: Fundamentals   19
    Invoking SCA Components   19
    Imports   20
    Exports   20
    Stand-alone References   21
Business Integration Patterns   21
    Data Exchange Patterns   21
Business Processes   23
Qualifiers   23
Closing the Link   24
Links to developerWorks   25

Chapter 3   Business Orchestration   27

Business Processes   27
BPEL   28
    Partner Links   29
    Variables   29
    Activities   29
    Expression Language   33
    Correlation Set   33
    Scope   33
    Fault Handler   33
    Compensation Handler   34
    Event Handler   34
BPEL Extensions   35
Short-Running and Long-Running Processes   35
    Transaction Characteristics of Processes   36
    Versioning BPEL Processes   37
BPEL and SCA   38
Closing the Link   38
Links to developerWorks   39

Chapter 4   WebSphere Integration Developer   41

Installing WID   41
Working with WID   42
Business Integration Solution Building Blocks   43
    Modules   43

Mediation Modules   43
Libraries   44
Creating Projects and Other Artifacts   44
Creating a Library   44
Creating a Simple Business Object   46
Creating a Nested Business Object   49
Creating an Interface   50
Creating a Module   52
Process Editor   54
Assembly Editor   57
Binding Information   59
Visual Snippet Editor   61
Exporting Modules   64
Exporting Modules as EAR Files   64
Exporting Modules as serviceDeploy Files   65
Exporting Modules as Project Interchange Files   66
Testing Modules and Components   67
Module and Component Testing   67
Test Servers   68
Integration Test Client   70
Logging and Troubleshooting   71
Eclipse Shell Sharing   72
Closing the Link   72
Links to developerWorks   73

Chapter 5   WebSphere Process Server   75

WebSphere Process Server in a Nutshell   76
Introduction to WPS Functional Content   77
WPS Infrastructure   79
Business Process Choreographer (BPC)   81
Terminology and Topology   82
Profiles   82
Cells and Nodes   83
Installing WPS   85
WPS Administration   85
Starting and Stopping WPS   86
Key Steps in Creating a WPS Cell   87

WPS Clustered Topologies   87
    Cluster   87
    Clustering WPS Components   89
    Clustering the SI Bus   90
Topology Choices   92
    Single-Server Topology   92
    Single-Cluster Topology   92
    Single-Cluster Topology with Partitioned Destinations   93
    Multiple-Cluster Topologies   94
Closing the Link   97
Links to developerWorks   98

Chapter 6   Business Processes   99

Sample Application   99
Working with a Short-Running Business Process   102
    Creating a Short-Running Process   102
    Adding Reference Partners   103
    Invoking a Partner Operation   104
    Using an Assign Activity   105
    Using a Choice Activity   106
    Using the Visual Snippet Editor for the Choice Branch   106
    Defining a Fault   107
Working with a Long-Running Business Process   108
    Creating a Long-Running Process   108
    Empty Action   109
    Using a Human Task   109
    Using the While Loop   111
Advanced BPEL Features   113
    Adding a Scope   114
    Fault Handlers   114
    Receive Choice   116
    Correlation Sets   117
    Events   120
Closing the Link   122
Links to developerWorks   123

Chapter 7   Business Maps and Business Rules   125

Supporting Services   125
   Maps   126
   Relationships   126
   Selectors   126
   Mediation Flows   126
Mapping   126
   Data Maps   127
   Interface Maps   127
   Relationships   127
A Mapping Scenario   129
Implementing Maps   132
   Creating the Data Map   132
   Creating the Interface Map   135
Relationships   138
A Relationship Scenario   138
   Relationship Editor   139
   Relationship Manager   141
Business Rules   142
   Decision Tables   143
   Rulesets   143
A Decision Table Scenario   143
   Creating a Rule Group   144
   Administering Business Rules   149
   Exporting the Rules   151
Selectors   152
Mediation   153
Closing the Link   154
Links to developerWorks   154

Chapter 8   Business State Machines, Human Tasks, and Web Services   155

Business State Machines   155
State Transition Diagram of the Order Process   156
Implementing the Order Business State Machine   158
   The Order Business State Machine Interface   158
   Creating the Order BSM   159
   Completing the Assembly Diagram   164
   Deploying and Running the BSM   165

Human Tasks   166
    Participating Human Task   166
    Originating Human Task   166
    Pure Human Task   166
    Administrative Human Task   167
    Ad Hoc Task   167
User Interface   168
    User Interface Generator in WID   168
Web Services   171
Working with Web Services in WID   172
    Importing the WSDL file   172
    Testing and Using the WSDL File   175
    Importing Inline WSDL Files   177
    Publishing WSDL Files   178
Closing the Link   179
Links to developerWorks   179

Chapter 9   Business Integration Clients   181

Business Process Choreographer (BPC)   181
Business Process Choreographer Explorer   182
Working with the BPC Explorer   183
    Starting a Process Instance   185
    Claiming and Working on a Task   186
    Viewing the Business Process   187
Observing Versus Monitoring   189
Common Event Infrastructure (CEI)   190
    Common Base Event (CBE)   190
    Enabling CEI in WebSphere   191
    CEI Monitoring   192
Business Process Choreographer Event Collector   193
Business Process Choreographer Observer (BPCO)   193
    Installing BPCO   194
    Enabling Logging for the BPCO   195
Working with the Observer   196
Closing the Link   197
Links to developerWorks   198

Chapter 10   Business Integration Services Management   199

Security   199
    WebSphere Security   200
    Enabling WebSphere Global Security   200
    Steps to Enable Global Security in WebSphere   201
    Configuring Security Using an LDAP Server   203
    Mapping Security Roles for the BPC Applications   206
    Securing WPS Access to Databases and Messaging   208
Logging and Tracing   210
    Tracing User Applications   212
    Installation Log Files   213
Message Logger   213
    Message Logger Usage   214
    Steps to Versioning a Process in WID   214
    Recommendations for Versioning BPEL Processes   216
Closing the Link   217
Links to developerWorks   217

Chapter 11   Business Integration Programming   219

SCA Programming Model   219
    Programmatic Use of SCA: Java References   220
    Programmatic Use of SCA: WSDL References   223
    Declarative Use of SCA: Qualifiers   227
Event Sequencing in WPS   229
    Adding Event Sequencing Qualifier   230
Business Graphs and Programmatic Manipulation of Business Objects   232
    Programmatically Manipulating Business Objects   232
APIs or SPIs   237
    Business Flow Manager APIs   238
    APIs Used to Initiate a Business Process   239
    Packaging the Client Application   241
    Human Task Manager APIs   242
Visual Programming   242
    The Setup   243
    Creating the Custom Visual Snippet   243
Closing the Link   249
Links to developerWorks   249

Chapter 12   WebSphere Adapters   251

Adapters   252
Adapter Architecture   254
   Common Client Interface   255
   Service Provider Interface   255
   Outbound Processing   255
   Inbound Processing   256
   Enterprise Discovery   256
   Resource Adapter Archive Files   257
Working with an Adapter   258
   Create the JDBC Outbound Adapter Component   258
   Test the Adapter   264
FTP, Flat File, and Email Adapters   266
SAP Adapter   266
   SAP Adapter Installation   267
Siebel Adapter   267
   Siebel Adapter Installation   268
Custom Adapters   268
   Starting the Adapter Project in WID   269
Closing the Link   271
Links to developerWorks   271

Chapter 13   Business Modeling   273

Installing WebSphere Business Modeler   274
Business Modeling Terms and Concepts   274
Working with WebSphere Business Modeler   276
Business Process Diagrams   280
Business Measures   281
Working with the Business Model   282
   Business Items   282
   Importing a Business Item   284
   Business Process Model   285
   Exporting a Business Item   288
   Business Measures   290
   Business Simulation   291
Closing the Link   293
Links to developerWorks   293

Chapter 14   Business Monitoring   295

Business Activity Monitoring   296
Installing WebSphere Business Monitor   298
Installing WebSphere Business Monitor Development Toolkit   298
Working with WebSphere Business Monitor   301
KPIs   302
Dashboards   302
Monitor Models   303
Working with MME   305
    The Scenario   305
    Enabling CEI Logging   307
    Generating the Monitor Model   308
    Creating a Trigger   310
    Creating a Counter   311
    Creating a Metric   313
    Creating Dimensions and Measures   314
    Creating a KPI   315
    Deploying and Testing the Monitor Model   316
Closing the Link   318
Links to developerWorks   319

Chapter 15   Enterprise Service Bus and Service Registry   321

WebSphere Service Registry and Repository (WSRR)   322
Installing WSRR   324
    Governance Lifecycle   325
Working with WSRR   326
    Loading Documents   327
    Making a Document Governable   329
    Transitioning the State of a Governed Object   330
    Searching for Documents   331
WSRR and WID   332
Enterprise Service Bus (ESB)   335
WebSphere Enterprise Service Bus   336
WESB Terminology   337
    Mediation   337
    Mediation Module   337
    Mediation Flow Component   340

Mediation Flow   340
Mediation Primitive   340
Installing WESB   342
Working with WESB   343
WESB and WID   344
Creating a Mediation Module   344
Deploying the Mediation Module   345
Checking the Bus   347
Closing the Link   348
Links to developerWorks   348

Appendix A   WebSphere Process Server Installation   349

Installing WebSphere Process Server   349
Creating a Profile   353
Installing WPS Silently   358
Creating Additional Profiles Silently   359
WPS Installation Folder   359
Uninstalling WPS   360

Appendix B   WebSphere Integration Developer Installation   361

Installing WebSphere Integration Developer   361
WID Usage   364
Updating WID   366

Appendix C   WebSphere Business Modeler Installation   367

Installing WebSphere Business Modeler   367
Stand-alone Installation   367
WID Plug-in Installation   369

Appendix D   WebSphere Business Monitor Installation   373

Installing WebSphere Business Monitor   373
Installing WebSphere Business Monitor Development Toolkit   380

Appendix E   WebSphere Service Registry and Repository Installation   385

Installing WSRR   385
Installing the WSRR Eclipse Plug-in in WID   388

Appendix F   WebSphere Adapter Toolkit Installation   393

Installing WebSphere Adapter Toolkit   393
    Using RPU   393
    Using Product CDs   394
Verifying the WAT Eclipse Plug-in in WID   395

Index   397

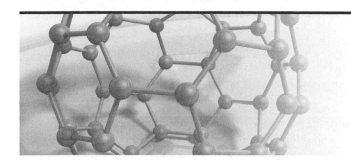

Foreword

When we originally set out to build Version 6.0 of the WebSphere® Business Integration (WBI) portfolio, Service-Oriented Architecture (SOA) and Business Process Management (BPM) were relatively new concepts with only early deployments. While a number of standards-based J2EE-based servers had anchored a pretty well-defined application server market, a wide variety of products and technologies, each with different technological roots, attempted to solve application integration, business integration, process management, and other related middleware problems.

At IBM®, we found ourselves with myriad products in the integration space as well. A strong messaging history with WebSphere MQ and WebSphere Message Broker anchored one key aspect of part of our integration strategy—connectivity. On the other end was WBI-Server Foundation (WBI-SF) as a strategic process engine, sporting an early version of the BPEL specification and built on the WebSphere Application Server Foundation. We also had MQ-Workflow and CrossWorlds'® Interchange Server (ICS) centered traditional workflow and advanced application integration, respectively. Each of these solutions had different development tools and different runtime execution architectures. A package suite called WBI Server 4.x, in fact, had MQ-Workflow (MQWF), Message Broker, and CrossWorlds' ICS all bundled in a single offering, providing choice (and maybe some confusion) to all customers wanting a WBI solution. These offerings were complemented by a set of adapters that came with the CrossWorlds acquisition as well as a WBI Modeler and WBI Monitor product that was an early view of BPM, with relatively strong affinity to MQ-Workflow.

The strategy within IBM's Software Group was focused around the WebSphere Application Server runtime and building out our portfolio of middleware using that strong and robust foundation. The new mission of the WBI team was to offer an integration solution that held the combined capabilities of WBI-SF, CrossWorlds' ICS, and MQWF, built upon the WebSphere Application Server Foundation. The foundation was to be counted upon for things such as configuration, administration, workload management, high availability, and security. The idea was that this consolidated solution could provide an end-to-end set of integration capabilities. Customers would have fewer runtimes to manage if they needed to solve various middleware problems.

In the early days, we knew of this work as WBI Server Version 6.0. Through a variety of marketing and naming actions, this was renamed the WebSphere Process Server (WPS). So while WPS serves as a broad-spectrum integration server that goes beyond process, the name WPS has persisted.

One of the key goals of WPS and the associated development tools named WebSphere Integration Developer (WID) was to enable the creation and composition of solutions without mandatory coding and the complexity involved in traditional programming-language-based development. This paradigm would then allow a broader set of engineers, with less-intense J2EE skills and, in some cases, very limited Java skills, to contribute and build out solutions. This was and still is a clarifying and influencing premise of the product directions.

To make this objective become reality, it was clear from the early going that just putting some fancy editors on top of a J2EE programming model wouldn't be sufficient. Service Component Architecture (SCA) was invented and produced to provide a service invocation model and a service composition model that would abstract away many of the details associated with specific infrastructure tasks. While SCA, along with Service Data Object (SDO) as a consistent way to deal with data, helped solve the WBI challenge, there was a bigger plan behind SCA and SDO. These technologies, in conjunction with web services and related standards, would come to form the basis of IBM's SOA strategy.

As Business Process Management (BPM) has evolved, we have also evolved our integration products to support a BPM model. Our WebSphere Business Modeler and WebSphere Business Monitor products provide WPS with the complementary function needed for a complete BPM solution. Built on the same fundamentals as the rest of the WebSphere portfolio (Monitor is based on WebSphere Application Server, and Modeler is built on Eclipse), these products have evolved to provide first-class support for processes and services running WPS (and other environments).

WebSphere Process Server and the related WBI products started rolling out in 2005. Since then, a number of interesting things have occurred. We've seen the WBI products used for many new projects, some starting from BPM needs and requirements, while others have started from more technical roots centered around connectivity and application integration. The WBI product set has become the anchor of our SOA and BPM efforts. This has all happened at the same time as customers have begun migrating from the earlier WBI server—namely, MQ-Workflow, CrossWorlds' ICS, and WBI-SF.

At the same time, the Enterprise Service Bus (ESB) movement has come alive. In December of 2005, IBM released the WebSphere Enterprise Service Bus (WESB) product. This product is intended to provide ESB capabilities to a broad range of customers. Architecturally, the same foundational technology that makes up WPS is in WESB. In fact, there's enough software inside of every WPS to allow it to be an ESB.

The book you are about to read does a great job of providing the foundational concepts necessary to succeed with the WBI Version 6-based products, irrespective of whether you intend to capitalize on SOA or BPM opportunities or to meet other integration challenges that you face. The concepts are elaborated upon and supported by deep explanations of the various features and functions of WPS and the related products. Examples and patterns are used to demonstrate how real solutions can be constructed from the capabilities available.

Eric Herness
IBM Distinguished Engineer
WBI Chief Architect

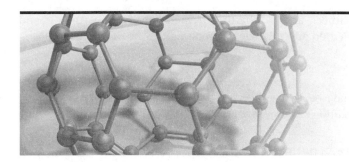

Acknowledgments

The authors would like to say a special thank you to Chris Tomkins and Kirk Davis for reviewing the initial manuscript. Our deep gratitude to the subject matter experts who reviewed individual chapters: David Waldron, Joseph "Lin" Sharpe, Madhu Channapatna, Sunita Chacko, Arnauld Desperts, Eric Erpenbach, Venkata "Vishy" Gadepalli, and Russ Butek. Your constructive criticism, attention to the technical details, and insights were invaluable and did a lot to improve the content of the book. But most of all, your enthusiasm and willingness to help review the material is what stands out.

We would also like to thank members of the Bringup Lab in Rochester, Minnesota and the WebSphere Business Integration development team and the WebSphere Enablement team for answering questions and allowing us to bounce ideas off them.

Special thanks to Tara Woodman, the point person in the IBM Press program at IBM, for her consistent support. Todd Martin got things rolling during the nascent stages.

Thanks to the talented staff at Pearson Education Publishing. Thanks to Greg Wiegand for managing it all through the turbulent times at Pearson; and to Gayle Johnson and Anne Goebel for doing a marvelous job of copy editing. Thank you to Carol Serna, the developerWorks editor, for providing the dW links.

Finally, we owe it to Ginny Bess, our development editor, for making this book happen. She stepped into a tough situation but did a masterful job of editing the draft manuscript.

Hats off to our managers and Distinguished Engineers at IBM for being so supportive. And above all, a special thank-you to Eric Herness for his vision and direction.

Ashok Iyengar:

Thanks to my family—Radha, Sameer, and Siddharth, for their unwavering support and patience; and to my coauthors—Vinod and Michele, for making this book a reality.

Vinod Jessani:

I want to thank my family, who have been incredibly supportive of me during this endeavor. My wife, Robin, and kids, Allison and Andrew, were really understanding and patient while I went through this effort.

I would also like to thank the folks on the IBM WebSphere Process Server daily call, who provided a lot of ideas and thoughts that helped when we wrote the book.

Finally, I would like to thank my coauthors, Ashok and Michele, whose incredible drive and enthusiasm spurred me on to do my part.

Michele Chilanti:

The sense of accomplishment one can derive from writing a book is, I think, somehow related to the arduousness of getting to the end of the path. But, unlike certain mountain climbers who claim for themselves all the credit for their endeavors (like that toxic friend of yours always does), authors must acknowledge that, without the help of a long list of people, they would have never made it.

In my case, the complete list would be a remarkably long one. I'll mention only a few of those who supported me, sincerely hoping not to hurt the feelings of anyone of the many I had to omit.

I'd like to start with my coauthors, Ashok and Vinod. It's because of their dedication, spirit of initiative, and enthusiasm that I wrote my part.

To my management team—in particular, Sam Kaipa and Ken McCauley—I thank you for your encouragement.

To my family—my son, Maurizio, and my wife, Rosa—thank you for helping me with your support and, as always, with your great patience.

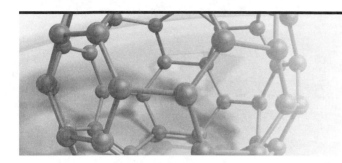

About the Authors

Ashok Iyengar is a Senior Software Engineer at IBM based in San Diego. He holds an MS degree in computer science from North Dakota State University, Fargo. He has worked in the IT industry for more than 22 years. For the past couple of years, he has worked extensively with the WebSphere Business Integration platform doing proofs-of-concept, pilots, and architecture design. In his spare time, he loves to write. Among his works is the popular *WebSphere Portal Primer* by IBM Press.

Vinod Jessani is a Senior Software Engineer with the IBM WebSphere Enablement Team in San Diego. He has more than 15 years of experience in distributed systems and online transaction processing systems. As a senior member of the WebSphere Enablement team, he leads pre-sales types of activities, including pilots, proofs-of-concept, and technical presentations that involve the WebSphere Business Integration Server and WebSphere development tools. He has a master's degree in computer applications from the University of Poona, India.

Michele Chilanti is a Consulting IT Specialist with IBM Software Services. In his current position, he consults on a daily basis with IBM customers worldwide, helping them in their J2EE and WebSphere Business Integration development and deployment projects. During his career with IBM, he has held a number of technical positions that have exposed him to a wide variety of the IBM product portfolio and computing platforms. He regularly speaks at IT conferences worldwide and has authored a number of IBM and external technical publications.

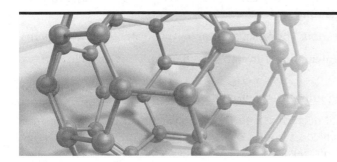

Introduction

This book addresses the needs of those who intend to create process-centric business integration solutions based on standards. It is targeted toward people and organizations that want to understand business integration—the technologies and the issues. Having worked in this area for the past few years, the authors provide real-life deployment examples, end-to-end solutions, and best practices from the field.

Even though this book discusses business integration in general, it uses IBM's WebSphere Business Integration product suite as the vehicle to convey the ideas and solutions necessary for business integration and provides real examples. Organizations using or intending to use WebSphere Business Integration technologies will find this book valuable. This book is also useful to IT professionals who are approaching business integration projects for the first time.

This book describes the emergence of Service-Oriented Architecture (SOA) and introduces Service Component Architecture (SCA). With this programming paradigm, this book covers concepts such as Business Objects, Business Process Execution Language (BPEL)-based process choreography, mediation, data mapping, relationships, dynamic selectors, business rules, and back-end adapters. Core to each of the capabilities, the IBM WebSphere Process Server runtime includes a dramatic simplification of the programming model for writing business integration applications.

This book discusses both process (the functional flow of processing) and data (information used in processing) integration solutions. Basic workflows, document flows, and complex long-running business flows are considered for process integration, and common data integration solutions, such as a canonical object hub, are discussed. The importance of Web Services is also highlighted.

From a programming perspective, there is extensive coverage of SCA, the SCA Interaction Model, business graphs, and the business object framework. This book also covers installation, setup, administration, tuning, and usage of the WebSphere software. In addition, there are tips and recommendations for best practices.

Chapters 1, 2, and 3 introduce the various concepts, terminology, and architectural patterns.

Chapter 4 introduces WebSphere Integration Developer (WID), which is an Eclipse-based integrated development environment.

Chapter 5 presents IBM's Java-based runtime—WebSphere Process Server.

Chapters 6, 7, and 8 are a technical deep dive into the various components of a business integration solution. There are detailed examples of how to create a BPEL-based business process, Business Rules, Business Maps, Business State Machines, and much more.

Chapters 9 and 10 talk about the various business integration clients and discuss the importance of security and logging.

Chapter 11 touches on all the programming aspects that a software developer would encounter in a business integration solution.

Chapter 12 stands by itself, because it discusses business integration adapters that are used to connect to back ends and the challenges of implementing them.

Chapters 13 and 14 are primers on Business Modeling and Business Monitoring. The concepts are explained using WebSphere Business Modeler and WebSphere Business Monitor.

Chapter 15 looks at Enterprise Service Bus and Service Registry, two items that are becoming the cornerstones of all business integration solutions.

So whether you are an IT manager, an IT architect, a business integration project manager in a large enterprise, or a technical lead or developer in a small or medium-sized company, we hope you find this book useful in understanding business integration issues and SOA technologies.

Chapter 1

Business Integration

Business integration is the discipline that enables companies to identify, consolidate, and optimize business processes. The objective is to improve productivity and maximize organizational effectiveness. Interest in business integration has become more acute as companies merge and consolidate, and as they grow a legacy of disparate information assets. These assets often lack consistency and coordination, thus giving rise to "islands of information."

As we go through this book, you will notice that business integration has strong links to BPM and SOA. Although there is no question that SOA stands for Service-Oriented Architecture, BPM is sometimes thought of as Business Process Modeling. We think of it as an abbreviation for Business Process Management, which is a better choice, because it covers a broader scope of activities. One of the goals of this book is to highlight the many facets you must be aware of to achieve business integration in an enterprise. Some of those facets are business modeling, architecture, development, governance, and patterns.

This chapter explains some of the terms and concepts related to SOA in general and to business integration in particular. This book is not based on any particular version of a product, but we will use software to illustrate the concepts.

Business Integration Challenge

With its pervasiveness and the vast array of connectivity options it offers, information technology (IT) is arguably the premier vehicle for achieving true business integration within large organizations. Depending on the nature of the company and the extent of the integration needs, business integration poses different requirements for IT departments. Some projects may deal with only a few aspects, whereas some larger projects may encompass many of these requirements. Here are some of the most common aspects of business integration projects:

A.1.1

- **Application integration** is a common requirement. The complexity of application integration projects varies from simple cases, in which you need to ensure that a small number of applications can share information, to more complex situations, in which transactions and data exchanges need to be reflected simultaneously on multiple application back ends. Complex application integration often requires complex unit-of-work management as well as transformation and mapping.
- **Process automation** is another key aspect that ensures that activities performed by an individual or organization systematically trigger consequential activities elsewhere. This ensures the successful completion of the overall business process. For example, when a company hires an employee, payroll information has to be updated, appropriate actions need to be taken by the security department, the necessary tools need to be given to the employee, and so on. Some activities in a process might capture human input and interaction, whereas others might script back-end systems and other services in the environment.
- **Connectivity** is an abstract, yet critical, aspect both in a company and in terms of business partners. By connectivity, we mean both the flow of information between organizations or companies and the ability to access distributed IT services.

Some of the technical challenges of business integration implementations can be summarized as follows:

- Dealing with different data formats and therefore not being able to perform efficient data transformation
- Dealing with different protocols and mechanisms for accessing IT services that may have been developed using very different technologies
- Orchestrating different IT services that may be geographically distributed or offered by different organizations
- Providing rules and mechanisms to classify and manage the services that are available (governance)

As such, business integration encompasses many of the themes and elements that are also common to SOA. IBM's vision of business integration builds on many of the same foundational concepts that are found in SOA. One of the immediate consequences of this vision is that business integration solutions may require a variety of products for their realization. IBM provides a portfolio of tools and runtime platforms to support all the various stages and operational aspects.

To paraphrase IBM's vision of business integration, it should enable companies to define, create, merge, consolidate, and streamline business processes using applications that run on a SOA IT infrastructure. Business integration work is truly role-based. At the macro level, it involves modeling, developing, governance, managing, and monitoring business process applications. With the help of proper tools and procedures, it enables you to automate business processes involving people and heterogeneous systems, both inside and outside the enterprise. One of the key aspects of business integration is the ability to optimize your business operations so that they are efficient, scalable, reliable, and flexible enough to handle change.

Business integration requires development tools, runtime servers, monitoring tools, a service repository, toolkits, and process templates. Because there are so many aspects to business integration, you will find that you have to utilize more than one development tool to develop a solution. These tools enable integration developers to assemble complex business solutions. A server is a high-performance business engine or service container that runs complex applications. Management always wants to know who is doing what in the organization, and that is where monitoring tools come into play. As enterprises create these business processes or services, governance, classification, and storage of these services becomes critical. That function is served by a service repository. Specific toolkits to create specialized parts of the solution, such as connectors or adapters to legacy systems, are often required.

Business integration is not based on a single product. It involves almost everybody and all business aspects within an organization and across organizations. Business integration encompasses many of the services and elements in the SOA reference architecture, which is covered in the next section.

Service-Oriented Architecture

SOA has generated a large buzz in the IT industry. Without doubt, it is one of the most important and interesting concepts that has swept the IT landscape in recent years. According to industry analyst firm Gartner Group, by 2008, more than 60 percent of enterprises will use SOA as the guiding principle when creating mission-critical applications and processes. SOA has many entry points; one of them is by way of business integration. Beware that this is not as easy as some people profess it to be. The idea of integration seems simple, but there are many things to take into account, and some rigorous steps are necessary to achieve true business integration. That is the thrust of this book—showing you what you must be aware of to achieve business integration in an enterprise.

A.1.2

Some view SOA as a component model, whereas others view it as application architecture. A component model describes the tight coupling between components and their containers in a child-parent relationship, but SOA is all about loosely coupled services that act more as peers with each other. This book views SOA as an integration architecture based on the concept of services. So what is a service? A service is a software application that provides a specific function. Another way to state this is that a service is a repeatable task within a business process. Business and infrastructure functions are broken into their component parts and then are provided as services. The individual service, or a composite service made up of a collection of these, delivers application functionality to end-user applications or to other services. These services typically are described in terms of the interface they expose, independent of the way in which they are implemented. Web services, for example, use the Web Service Description Language (WSDL) to describe the service interface. A business process is composed of a number of these so-called loosely coupled software services.

A business process can be as simple as a credit check. Or it can be an elaborate process such as building the wing of a plane, comprising a number of smaller services that may in turn be implemented as other business processes. Regardless of how complex the process, one or more of these business processes defined in a high-level language such as BPEL (Business Process Execution Language) are put together or orchestrated together to form SOA. SOA is not tied to a specific technology and can be implemented in one or more technologies, such as Web services, Remote Method Invocation (RMI), Object Request Broker (ORB), or Service Component Architecture (SCA). The other parts of a SOA include a service registry and repository to store the definitions of these services, some form of a user service or interface, and, naturally, the business logic and data that are used to implement these services.

In IBM's view of SOA, the Enterprise Service Bus (ESB) is the central component of the architecture, and it enables services to interact. The service registry and repository play a major role in storage and governance of those services. That gives rise to the SOA reference architecture, illustrated in Figure 1.1. It has the following services:

- **Partner Services** provide the document, protocol, and partner management capabilities required for your business to interact with your external partners and suppliers.
- **Business Application Services** provide runtime utility services, based on a robust, scalable, and secure services environment, that are required for new business applications.
- **Access Services** provide the ability to connect to existing applications, legacy systems, and enterprise data stores.
- **Interaction Services** provide the human aspect of services by enabling collaboration among people, processes, and information. They deliver IT functions and data to end users based on their roles and preferences.
- **Process Services** are the main set of services that help orchestrate and automate business processes.
- **Information Services** manage diverse data and content in a unified manner. They provide the capabilities required to federate, replicate, and transform data sources that may be implemented in a variety of ways.

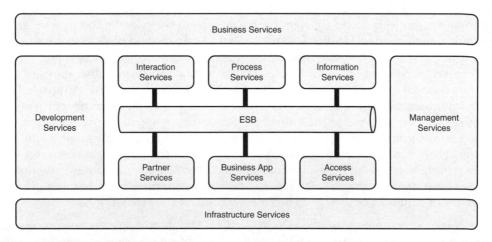

Figure 1.1 SOA reference architecture

These core services are supported by the following:

- **Infrastructure Services** are the underlying services that help optimize throughput, availability, and utilization of the functional services.
- **Business Services** support enterprise business processes and goals through the various functional services.
- **Development Services** provide an integrated environment for designing and creating solution assets.
- **Management Services** help manage and secure services, applications, and resources.

The ESB, at the core of the SOA, is responsible for providing the low-level interconnectivity capabilities required to leverage the services implemented across the entire architecture, such as transport services, event services, and mediation. The main point of such an architecture is that it is a vendor-neutral way of looking at and planning the set of services that go into building a SOA. Therefore, SOA can be seen as an approach to defining business integration architecture based on the concept of a service. A service can be either fine-grained or coarse-grained. The granularity of a service refers to the scope of functionality a service exposes. Providing basic data access is an example of a fine-grained service. Providing rudimentary operations can be considered slightly more coarse-grained. Business services that provide the most value are coarse-grained services that are constructed from lower-level services, components, and objects that meet specific business needs. The goal of SOA can be described as bringing the benefits of loosely coupled objects and data encapsulation to integration at the enterprise level.

SOA Lifecycle

IBM views the SOA lifecycle as consisting of four phases: Model, Assemble, Deploy, and Manage, as shown in Figure 1.2. This lifecycle is used to deliver end-to-end business integration

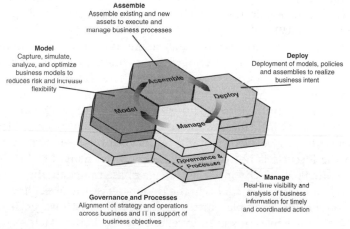

Figure 1.2 SOA lifecycle

solutions. We use this lifecycle throughout the book while mapping each step to the IBM product that can be used to perform the activity involved.

Even though the SOA lifecycle is a continuum, it typically begins with the modeling step and continues clockwise through the assembly, deployment, and management steps. After the steps have been completed, feedback from these steps is used to refine the model and begin the cycle again. Notice that the lifecycle is layered on top of a set of governance processes that ensure compliance and control across the whole SOA. (See Chapter 15, "Enterprise Service Bus and Service Registry," for a more detailed discussion of how SOA Governance is achieved using the service registry.) Here is a brief explanation of the four phases:

- **Model:** In this phase, more often than not lines-of-business people capture the business design and create an encoded model based on the goals, assumptions, and specifications of the business processes. Business executives like to measure key performance indicators (KPIs), such as which resources are being heavily utilized or what the customers are buying. The model also captures KPIs and metrics that are important measurements for the business. In addition, you build what-if simulation models. These and other modeling concepts are explained in Chapter 11, "Business Integration Programming."
- **Assemble:** The business design is communicated to the IT organization so that business processes, services, and related activities can be defined. During this phase, you also search for existing assets that can be reused. These existing assets should be rendered as services for assembly into composite applications. An example of a reusable asset is a Web service contained in the service registry that performs creditworthiness verification of loan applicants.
- **Deploy:** In the Deploy stage, everything comes to fruition. In this stage, IT personnel strive to resolve application resource dependencies, operational conditions, and access constraints. The hosting environment or server is set up, and the application built in the assemble phase is actually deployed. In addition to making sure the interaction logic, business process flows, and all the services perform correctly, you have to ensure the application's reliability, availability, serviceability, usability, and installability (RASUI).
- **Manage:** Whether it is to address management as a whole or to monitor performance of specific requests and noting the timeliness of service responses, in this phase, the line-of-business people get involved. The IT people may manage the system by administering and securing the applications, resources, and users and performing routine maintenance. But it is the line-of-business people who typically monitor the usage of the business processes involved and track bottlenecks so that future capacity can be predicted and fed back into the model. The progression through the lifecycle is not entirely linear. In fact, changes to KPIs in the Model phase are often fed directly into the Manage phase to update the operational environment. In addition, constraints in the Deploy phase can affect how business logic or components are assembled in the Assemble phase. However, from a business integration perspective, this is an excellent way to know where you stand in the integration cycle.

Business Integration Programming Model

There are many technologies and so many ways to represent or interact with data that achieving integration is no easy task. If you take the three aspects of a programming model—data, invocation, and composition—and apply some of the new paradigms of a A.1.3 services-based approach, the new programming model for SOA starts to emerge. First, we see that data is primarily represented by Extensible Markup Language (XML) and is programmed with Service Data Objects (SDOs) or through native XML facilities such as XPath or XSLT (Extensible Stylesheet Language Transformation). Second, service invocation maps to SCA. Finally, composition is embodied in process orchestration using BPEL. The third aspect, composition, is that BPEL typically is used for dynamic composition of services, whereas the SCA modules provide the static composition of services. Both are needed. Figure 1.3 shows the three aspects of this new programming model, known as the SOA invocation model.

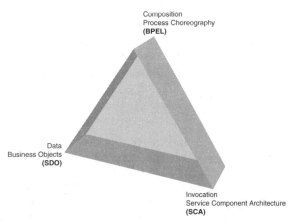

Figure 1.3 SOA invocation model

Service Component Architecture

In addition to providing a consistent syntax and mechanism for service invocation, the SCA is the invocation framework that provides a way for developers to encapsulate service implementations in reusable components. It enables developers to define interfaces, implementations, and references in a technology-agnostic way, giving you the opportunity to bind the elements to whichever technology you choose. SCA separates business logic from infrastructure so that application programmers can focus on solving business problems.

In the WebSphere environment, the SCA framework is based on the Java™ 2 Platform, Enterprise Edition (J2EE) runtime environment of WebSphere Application Server. SCA is described in detail in Chapter 2, "Business Integration Architecture and Patterns," where you will learn about Service Imports, Service Exports, and Standalone References. These are the building blocks that can be used in an integration solution. The later chapters describe the supporting services, such as Selectors, Relationships, Maps, and Mediation Flows. They also cover service components such as Business Processes, Human Tasks, Business State Machines, and Business Rules. The same framework with a subset of this overall capability, targeted more specifically at the connectivity and application integration needs of business integration, is available in WebSphere Enterprise Service Bus (WESB).

BPEL (Now Called WS-BPEL)

Business Process Execution Language (BPEL) is an XML-based language for the formal specification of business processes and business interaction protocols. BPEL extends the Web Services interaction model and enables it to support business transactions. Previously it was known as Business Process Execution Language for Web Services, or BPEL4WS. The OASIS standards body shortened it to BPEL in 2003. Quite often you will see it called WS-BPEL or Web Services for BPEL. Information on OASIS can be found at www.oasis-open.org.

A process that is defined in BPEL consists of activities; partner links; variables; correlation sets; and compensation, event, and fault handlers. BPEL is covered in depth in Chapter 3, "Business Orchestration." You can get more information about the BPEL specification at http://docs.oasis-open.org/wsbpel/2.0/wsbpel-specification-draft.html.

Service Data Objects

As a software entity, an object is a software bundle that is used to model real-world entities. There are various kinds of objects: business objects, ASP objects, web objects, data objects. In the business integration space, it is best to start with Service Data Objects (SDOs). Actually, SDO is a framework for data application development that includes architecture and an associated application programming interface (API). SDO unifies data representation across disparate data stores, simplifies the J2EE data programming model, and supports and integrates XML. Most important, it is the common data model for SOA because it provides a layer of abstraction.

With the SDO framework, you do not need to be familiar with a technology-specific API to access and use data. You need to know only one API—the SDO API. It lets you work with data from multiple data sources, including relational databases, entity Enterprise Java Bean (EJB) components, XML pages, Web services, Java Server Pages (JSP), the J2EE Connector Architecture (JCA), and more. It provides both a dynamic (loosely typed) and static (strongly typed) data API. SDO does not stop at data abstraction. It also incorporates a number of J2EE patterns and best practices, making it easy to incorporate proven architecture and designs into your applications. Information about the SDO framework can be obtained from www.jcp.org/en/jsr/detail?id=235.

Closing the Link

We have discussed SOA and how it can be used to facilitate business integration. We have also
explained how standards such as SCA, SDOs, and WS-BPEL help facilitate SOA. Business components and services are the basic building blocks that are used to achieve business integration.   A.1.4

If SOA is implemented carefully and correctly, it helps reduce IT costs and improve systems
agility, thereby maximizing your return on investment (ROI). Like all other software solutions, successful SOA implementations may realize some or all of these benefits, but this
largely depends on the quality and relevance of the system architecture and design. We also
know that service reuse is one of the main drivers of SOA. But beware of some of the common pitfalls of SOA and business integration in general. Following these principles can
increase your chances of success:

- Focus on using open standards. Do not get locked into SOA vendor offerings that
  are proprietary in nature.
- Do not equate Web services, which is a set of standards, with SOA, which is archi-
  tecture.
- Start small, but avoid very fine-grained services.
- Institute a governance system sooner rather than later.
- When integrating legacy systems, know the technical constraints of your legacy
  system.

This chapter introduced the SOA lifecycle. IBM's WebSphere Process Server introduced SCA
and makes heavy use of SDOs through the business object API. The SOA lifecycle was born
from these beginnings and serves as a key foundation of IBM's SOA strategy today. Now that
we have defined most of the terminology and concepts, the remaining chapters describe
how IBM's BPM product suite can help you perform each step in the SOA lifecycle.

Links to developerWorks

A.1.1   www.ibm.com/developerworks/websphere/zones/businessintegration/

A.1.2   www.ibm.com/developerworks/websphere/zones/soa/

A.1.3   www.ibm.com/developerworks/webservices/library/ws-soa-whitepaper/

A.1.4   www.amazon.com/Service-Oriented-Architecture-SOA-Compass-
         developerWorks/dp/0131870025/ref=sr_1_1/102-3279043-
         7910568?ie=UTF8&s=books&qid=1178715952&sr=1-1

Chapter 2

Business Integration Architecture and Patterns

A typical business integration project involves coordinating several different IT assets, potentially running on different platforms, and having been developed at different times using different technologies. Being able to easily manipulate and exchange information with a diverse set of components is a major technical challenge. It is best addressed by the programming model used to develop business integration solutions.

This chapter explores the fundamentals of the business integration programming model. It introduces the Service Component Architecture (SCA) and discusses patterns related to business integration. Patterns seem to permeate our lives. Sewing patterns, think-and-learn patterns for children, home construction patterns, wood-carving patterns, flight patterns, wind patterns, practice patterns in medicine, customer buying patterns, workflow patterns, design patterns in computer science, and many more exist.

Patterns have proven successful in helping solution designers and developers. Therefore, it is not surprising that we now have business integration patterns or enterprise integration patterns. In the referenced literature, you will find a wide array of patterns that are applicable to business integration, including patterns for request and response routing, channel patterns (such as publish/subscribe), and many more. Abstract patterns provide a template for resolving a certain category of problems, whereas concrete patterns provide more specific indications of how to implement a specific solution. This chapter focuses on patterns that deal with data and service invocation, which are at the foundation of the programming model of the IBM software strategy for WebSphere business integration.

A.2.1

Business Integration Scenarios

Enterprises have many different software systems that they use to run their business. In addition, they have their own ways of integrating these business components. The two most prevalent business integration scenarios are as follows:

- **Integration broker:** In this use case, the business integration solution acts as an intermediary located among a variety of "back-end" applications. For example, you might need to ensure that when a customer places an order using the online order management application, the transaction updates relevant information in your Customer Relationship Management (CRM) back end. In this scenario, the integration solution needs to be able to capture and possibly transform the necessary information from the order management application and invoke the appropriate services in the CRM application.
- **Process automation:** In this scenario, the integration solution acts as the glue among different IT services that would otherwise be unrelated. For example, when a company hires an employee, the following sequence of actions needs to occur:
  - The employee's information is added to the payroll system.
  - The employee needs to be granted physical access to the facilities, and a badge needs to be provided.
  - The company might need to assign a set of physical assets to the employee (office space, a computer, and so on).
  - The IT department needs to create a user profile for the employee and grant access to a series of applications.

  Automating this process is also a common use case in a business integration scenario. In this case, the solution implements an automated flow that is triggered by the employee's addition to the payroll system. Subsequently, the flow triggers the other steps by creating work items for the people who are responsible for taking action or by calling the appropriate services.

In both scenarios, the integration solution needs to do the following:

- Work with disparate sources of information and different data formats, and be able to convert information between different formats
- Be able to invoke a variety of services, potentially using different invocation mechanisms and protocols

Throughout this book, we illustrate how the foundational programming model of IBM's WebSphere Process Server (WPS) addresses these requirements.

Business Integration: Roles, Products, and Technical Challenges

Successful business integration projects require a few basic ingredients:

- A clear separation of roles in the development organization to promote specialization, which typically improves the quality of the individual components that are developed
- A common business object (BO) model that enables business information to be represented in a canonical format
- A programming model that strongly separates interfaces from implementations and that supports a generic service invocation mechanism that is totally independent of the implementation and that only involves dealing with interfaces
- An integrated set of tools and products that supports development roles and preserves their separation

The following sections elaborate on each of these ingredients.

Clear Separation of Roles

A business integration project requires people in four collaborative, but distinctly separate, roles:

- **Business analyst:** Business analysts are domain experts responsible for capturing the business aspects of a process and for creating a process model that adequately represents the process itself. Their focus is to optimize the financial performance of a process. Business analysts are not concerned with the technical aspects of implementing processes.
- **Component developer:** Component developers are responsible for implementing individual services and components. Their focus is the specific technology used for the implementation. This role requires a strong programming background.
- **Integration specialist:** This relatively new role describes the person who is responsible for assembling a set of existing components into a larger business integration solution. Integration developers do not need to know the technical details of each of the components and services they reuse and wire together. Ideally, integration developers are concerned only with understanding the interfaces of the services that they are assembling. Integration developers should rely on integration tools for the assembly process.
- **Solution deployer:** Solution deployers and administrators are concerned with making business integration solutions available to end users. Ideally, a solution deployer is primarily concerned with binding a solution to the physical resources ready for it to function (databases, queue managers, and so on) and not with having a deep understanding of the internals of a solution. The solution deployer's focus is quality of service (QoS).

A Common Business Object Model

As we discussed, the key aspects of a business integration project include the ability to coordinate the invocation of several components and the ability to handle the data exchange among those. In particular, different components can use different techniques to represent business items such as the data in an order, a customer's information, and so on. For example, you might have to integrate a Java application that uses entity Enterprise Java Beans

(EJBs) to represent business items and a legacy application that organizes information in COBOL copybooks. Therefore, a platform that aims to simplify the creation of integration solutions should also provide a generic way to represent business items, irrespective of the techniques used by the back-end systems for data handling. This goal is achieved in WPS and WebSphere Enterprise Service Bus (WESB) thanks to the *business object framework*.

The business object framework enables developers to use XML Schemas to define the structure of business data and access and manipulate instances of these data structures (business objects) via XPath or Java code. The business object framework is based on the Service Data Object (SDO) standard.

The Service Component Architecture (SCA) Programming Model

The SCA programming model represents the foundation for any solution to be developed on WPS and WESB.

SCA provides a way for developers to encapsulate service implementations in reusable components. It enables you to define interfaces, implementations, and references in a technology-agnostic way, giving you the opportunity to bind the elements to whichever technology you choose.

There is also an SCA client programming model that enables the invocation of those components. In particular, it enables runtime infrastructures based on Java—such as IBM's WebSphere Process Server, BEA's WebLogic Server (with its Aqualogic product family), and Oracle's Application Server (part of Oracle's Fusion Middleware family)—to interact with non-Java runtimes. SCA uses business objects as the data items for service invocation.

Tools and Products

IBM's WebSphere Integration Developer is the integrated development environment that has all the necessary tools to create and compose business integration solutions based on the technologies just mentioned. These solutions typically are deployed to the WPS or, in some cases, to the WESB—the products that are at the center of this book.

Now that you understand the key ingredients of business integration solutions, let's take a look at the business object framework, at SCA, and at some of the key patterns, processes, and qualifiers in more detail.

The Business Object Framework

The computer software industry has developed several programming models and frameworks that enable developers to encapsulate business object information. In general, a BO framework should provide database independence, transparently map custom business objects to database tables, and bind business objects to user interfaces. Of late, XML schemas are perhaps the most popular and accepted way to represent the structure of a business object.

From a tooling perspective, WebSphere Integration Developer (WID) provides developers with a common BO model for representing different kinds of entities from different domains. At development time, WID represents business objects as XML schemas. At run-time, however, those same business objects are represented in memory by a Java instance of an SDO. SDO is a standard specification that IBM and BEA Systems have jointly developed and agreed on. IBM has extended the SDO specification by including some additional services that facilitate the manipulation of data within the business objects. We'll discuss some of these later in this chapter.

Before we get into the BO framework, let's look at the basic types of data that get manipulated:

- **Instance data** is the actual data and data structures, from simple, basic objects with scalar properties to large, complex hierarchies of objects. This also includes data definitions such as a description of the basic attribute types, complex type information, cardinality, and default values.
- **Instance metadata** is instance-specific data. Incremental information is added to the base data, such as change tracking (also known as change summary), context information associated with how the object or data was created, and message headers and footers.
- **Type metadata** is usually application-specific information, such as attribute-level mappings to destination enterprise information system (EIS) data columns (for example, mapping a BO field name to a SAP table column name).
- **Services** are basically helper services that get data, set data, change summary, or provide data definition type access.

Table 2.1 shows how the basic types of data are implemented in the WebSphere platform.

Table 2.1 Data Abstractions and the Corresponding Implementations

Data Abstraction	Implementation
Instance data	Business object (SDO)
Instance metadata	Business graph
Type metadata	Enterprise metadata
	Business object type metadata
Services	Business object services

Working with the IBM Business Object Framework

As we mentioned, the WPS BO framework is an extension of the SDO standard. Therefore, business objects exchanged between WPS components are instances of the *commonj.sdo.DataObject* class. However, the WPS BO framework adds several services and functions that simplify and enrich the basic *DataObject* functionality.

To facilitate the creation and manipulation of business objects, the WebSphere BO framework extends SDO specifications by providing a set of Java services. These services are part of the package named *com.ibm.websphere.bo*:

- **BOFactory:** The key service that provides various ways to create instances of business objects.
- **BOXMLSerializer:** Provides ways to "inflate" a business object from a stream or to write the content of a business object, in XML format, to a stream.
- **BOCopy:** Provides methods that make copies of business objects ("deep" and "shallow" semantics).
- **BODataObject:** Gives you access to the data object aspects of a business object, such as the change summary, the business graph, and the event summary.
- **BOXMLDocument:** The front end to the service that lets you manipulate the business object as an XML document.
- **BOChangeSummary and BOEventSummary:** Simplifies access to and manipulation of the change summary and event summary portion of a business object.
- **BOEquality:** A service that enables you to determine whether two business objects contain the same information. It supports both deep and shallow equality.
- **BOType and BOTypeMetaData:** These services materialize instances of *commonj.sdo.Type* and let you manipulate the associated metadata. Instances of *Type* can then be used to create business objects "by type."

Chapter 4, "WebSphere Integration Developer," introduces the facilities that WID provides to enable you to quickly formulate your object definitions.

Service Component Architecture

A.2.2

SCA is an abstraction you can implement in many different ways. It does not mandate any particular technology, programming language, invocation protocol, or transport mechanism. SCA components are described using Service Component Definition Language (SCDL), which is an XML-based language. You could, in theory, create an SCDL file manually. In practice, you're more likely to use an integrated development environment (IDE) such as WebSphere Integration Developer to generate the SCDL file.

An SCA component has the following characteristics:

- It wraps an implementation artifact, which contains the logic that the component can execute.
- It exposes one or more interfaces.

- It can expose one or more references to other components. The implementation's logic determines whether a component exposes a reference. If the implementation requires invoking other services, the SCA component needs to expose a reference.

This chapter focuses on the SCA implementation that WPS offers and the WID tool that is available to create and combine SCA components. WPS and WID support the following implementation artifacts:

- Plain Java objects
- Business Process Execution Language (BPEL) processes
- Business state machines
- Human tasks
- Business rules
- Selectors
- Mediations

SCA separates business logic from infrastructure so that application programmers can focus on solving business problems. IBM's WPS is based on that same premise. Figure 2.1 shows the architectural model of WPS.

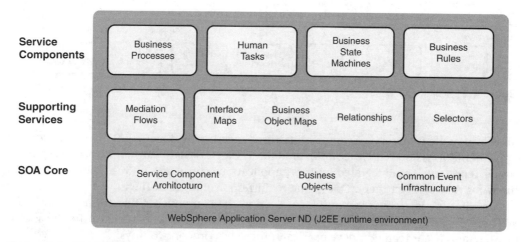

Figure 2.1 Architectural model for WPS

In the WebSphere environment, the SCA framework is based on the Java 2 Platform, Enterprise Edition (J2EE) runtime environment of WebSphere Application Server. The overall WebSphere Process Server framework consists of SOA Core, Supporting Services, and the Service Components. The same framework with a subset of this overall capability, targeted more specifically at the connectivity and application integration needs of business integration, is available in WESB.

The interface of an SCA component, as illustrated in Figure 2.2, can be represented as one of the following:

- A Java interface
- A WSDL port type (in WSDL 2.0, port type is called interface)

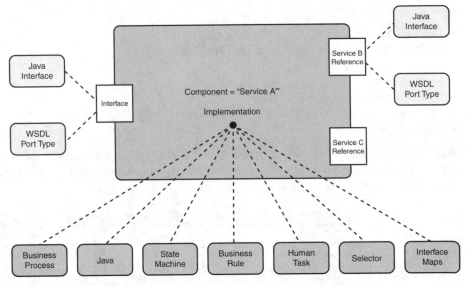

Figure 2.2 SCA in WPS

An SCA module is a group of components wired together by directly linking references and implementations. In WID, each SCA module has an *assembly diagram* associated with it, which represents the integrated business application, consisting of SCA components and the wires that connect them. One of the main responsibilities of the integration developer is to create the assembly diagram by connecting the components that form the solution. WID provides a graphical Assembly Editor to assist with this task. When creating the assembly diagram, the integration developer can proceed in one of two ways:

- **Top-down** defines the components, their interfaces, and their interactions before creating the implementation. The integration developer can define the structure of the process, identify the necessary components and their implementation types, and then generate an implementation skeleton.
- **Bottom-up** combines existing components. In this case, the integration developer simply needs to drag and drop existing implementations onto the assembly diagram.

The bottom-up approach is more commonly used when customers have existing services that they want to reuse and combine. When you need to create new business objects from scratch, you are likely to adopt the top-down approach. Chapter 4 introduces the various wizards in WID and lays out the six phases of creating a simple module using the top-down approach.

The SCA Programming Model: Fundamentals

The concept of a software *component* forms the basis of the SCA programming model. As we mentioned, a component is a unit that implements some logic and makes it available to other components through an interface. A component may also require the services made available by other components. In that case, the component exposes a *reference* to these services.

In SCA, every component must expose at least one interface. The assembly diagram shown in Figure 2.3 has three components—C1, C2, and C3. Each component has an interface that is represented by the letter I in a circle. A component can also refer to other components. References are represented by the letter R in a square. References and interfaces are then linked in an assembly diagram. Essentially, the integration developer "resolves" the references by connecting them with the interfaces of the components that implement the required logic.

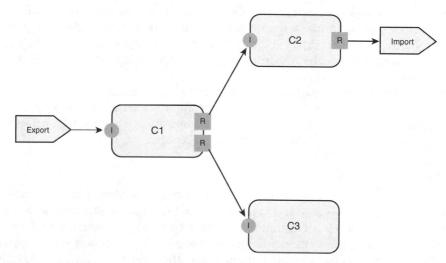

Figure 2.3 Assembly diagram

Invoking SCA Components

To provide access to the services to be invoked, the SCA programming model includes a *ServiceManager* class, which enables developers to look up available services by name. Here is a typical Java code fragment illustrating service lookup. The ServiceManager is used to obtain a reference to the BOFactory service, which is a system-provided service:

```
//Get service manager singleton
ServiceManager smgr = new ServiceManager();
//Access BOFactory service
BOFactory bof =(BOFactory)
        mgr.locateService("com/ibm/websphere/bo/BOFactory");
```

Developers can use a similar mechanism to obtain references to their own services by specifying the name of the service referenced in the *locateService* method. We illustrate in more detail the usage of the SCA programming model in Chapter 11, "Business Integration Programming." For the time being, we want to emphasize that after you have obtained a reference to a service using the *ServiceManager* class, you can invoke any of the available operations on that service in a way that is independent of the invocation protocol and the type of implementation.

SCA components can be called using three different invocation styles:

- **Synchronous invocation:** When using this invocation style, the caller waits synchronously for the response to be returned. This is the classic invocation mechanism.
- **Asynchronous invocation:** This mechanism allows the caller to invoke a service without waiting for the response to be produced right away. Instead of getting the response, the caller gets a "ticket," which can be used later to retrieve the response. The caller retrieves the response by calling a special operation that must be provided by the callee for this purpose.
- **Asynchronous invocation with callback:** This invocation style is similar to the preceding one, but it delegates the responsibility of returning the response to the callee. The caller needs to expose a special operation (the callback operation) that the callee can invoke when the response is ready.

Imports

Sometimes, business logic is provided by components or functions that are available on external systems, such as legacy applications, or other external implementations. In those cases, the integration developer cannot resolve the reference by connecting a reference to a component containing the implementation he or she needs to connect the reference to a component that "points to" the external implementation. Such a component is called an *import*. When you define an import, you need to specify how the external service can be accessed in terms of location and the invocation protocol.

Exports

Similarly, if your component has to be accessed by external applications, which is quite often the case, you must make it accessible. That is done by using a special component that exposes your logic to the "outside world." Such a component is called an *export*. These can also be invoked synchronously or asynchronously.

Stand-alone References

In WPS, an SCA service module is equivalent to a J2EE EAR file and contains several other J2EE submodules. J2EE elements, such as a WAR file, can be packaged along with the SCA module. Non-SCA artifacts such as JSPs can also be packaged together with an SCA service module. This lets them invoke SCA services through the SCA client programming model using a special type of component called a stand-alone reference.

The SCA programming model is strongly declarative. Integration developers can configure aspects such as transactional behavior of invocations, propagation of security credentials, whether an invocation should be synchronous or asynchronous in a declarative way, directly in the assembly diagram. The SCA runtime, not the developers, is responsible for taking care of implementing the behavior specified in these modifiers. The declarative flexibility of SCA is one of the most powerful features of this programming model. Developers can concentrate on implementing business logic, rather than focusing on addressing technical aspects, such as being able to accommodate asynchronous invocation mechanisms. All these aspects are automatically taken care of by the SCA runtime. The declarative aspects of SCA programming are discussed in Chapter 11.

Business Integration Patterns

Patterns help architects, designers, and developers use a common vocabulary to efficiently describe their solutions. This section discusses patterns at the business integration level, which fall into two classes: intraenterprise and interenterprise. These break down into Enterprise Application Integration (EAI) scenarios and business-to-business (B2B) scenarios. The EAI patterns deal mainly with application integration and database replication, whereas the B2B patterns deal with data exchange and process integration.

Another classification of business integration or Enterprise Integration Pattern is based on messaging architectures and messaging specifications such as Java Messaging Service (JMS) and Web services. The common categories in this case are channel patterns, endpoint patterns, routing patterns, system management patterns, and transformation patterns.

A.2.3

Data Exchange Patterns

A data exchange pattern is a rather simple pattern that is predicated on an agreement to use a common data format. The idea behind the SDO standard is to enable Java applications to support the following three common data exchange patterns. Actually, these are mechanisms that you can implement using different design patterns:

- The Plain Business Object pattern
- The Disconnected Object pattern
- The Event pattern

The Plain Business Object Pattern

The Plain Business Object pattern, also known as the Document pattern, is the most common data exchange mechanism. A client component populates a business object and then submits the object to a service by invoking a specific operation. Chapter 4 discusses defining and using plain business objects.

The Disconnected Object Pattern

The Disconnected Object pattern or the Transfer Object pattern is another common data exchange mechanism. Its primary purpose is to minimize the amount of time an application needs to be connected to the back end when making changes to an object. It extends the Transfer Object pattern of the Model-View-Controller architecture.

The Disconnected Object pattern enables an application to get hold of data from a back-end system and manipulate the data without requiring a connection to the back end. Then the application makes the changes persistent in a separate transaction that involves connectivity with the back end. The pattern extends this concept by introducing a mechanism to track the changes made to the business object or to any of the business objects contained by that business object.

In the Disconnected Object pattern, a system uses the change history in addition to the information stored in the object itself. The mechanism to track changes is called a business graph (BG), and it essentially includes four things:

- A *copy of the business object data* that can be manipulated even when no connection exists to the repository that holds the business object itself
- A *change history*, which stores the values of the business object before any manipulation occurred (for example, the original values), with an indication of the operations that modified the state of the business object
- An *event summary*, which contains the identifiers of objects affected by a change and event information recording the actual data involved in the business transaction
- A *verb*, which specifies the kind of operation that was performed (for example, a create or delete operation)

The Event Pattern

The Event pattern is the data exchange mechanism used when an event is produced by an EIS and is injected into WPS through an adapter. Typically, an adapter captures an event that occurred in a back-end system and creates the appropriate business object within WPS. For instance, in a travel reservation application that maintains profiles for travelers, a user might add a new airline company to the list of preferred airlines in his or her traveler's profile. Using the event pattern, that operation is captured as an "update" event that involves a certain traveler ID and a certain airline ID. The appropriate business objects will be materialized in WPS for the benefit of the business processes that can manipulate them.

The Event pattern makes use of the "delta image" information, which is a recording of what was changed in the original object. In our example, the addition of an airline to the list of preferred airlines would be the delta image. The Event pattern becomes important when you design complex relationships between different back ends, especially in integration scenarios that require keeping information about equivalent entities, managed by different applications, synchronized.

> **Object Mapping Pattern**
>
> Every so often, you will hear the term GBO and ASBO. GBO stands for Generic Business Object, and ASBO stands for Application-Specific Business Object. This terminology did not catch on, but we see ASBO-to-GBO and GBO-to-ASBO patterns all the time in business integration solutions.

Many patterns have limitations, which are overcome by the use of a complementary or associated pattern. The Process Integration pattern takes the limitations raised by the Data Exchange pattern and addresses them by providing Business Process Integration (BPI) services. The common underlying entity in both cases is the exchange of XML-based documents, which permits richer, more complex relationships.

Business Processes

Business processes—specifically, BPEL-based business processes—form the cornerstone of service components in the SCA. Whether it is a simple order approval or a complex manufacturing process, enterprises have always had business processes. A business process is a set of activities, related to the business, that are invoked in a specific sequence to achieve a business goal. In the business integration world, a business process is defined using some kind of markup language.

These business processes can invoke other supporting services or contain other service components such as business state machines, human tasks, business rules, or data maps. And, when deployed, these processes can either get done quickly or run over a long period of time. Sometimes, these processes can run for years.

Like most components in the J2EE world, business processes run in a container. In IBM's WebSphere platform, this specific container is called the Business Process Choreographer, which we talk about in Chapter 9, "Business Integration Clients." The container or the BPEL engine provides all the services and process lifecycle requirements.

Qualifiers

In a word, qualifiers are rules. Qualifiers define how much management should be provided by WPS for a component at runtime. A process application communicates its QoS needs to the WPS runtime environment by specifying service qualifiers. The qualifiers govern the interaction between a service client and a target service. Qualifiers can be specified on service component references, interfaces, and implementations and are always external to an implementation. The different categories of qualifiers include the following:

- Transaction, which specifies the way transactional contexts are handled in an SCA invocation
- Activity session, which specifies how Activity Session contexts are propagated. An Activity Session extends the concept of transaction, to encompass a number of related transactions.
- Security, which specifies the permissions
- Asynchronous reliability—rules for asynchronous message delivery

SCA allows these QoS qualifiers to be applied to components declaratively (without requiring programming or a change to the services implementation code). This is done in WID. Table 2.2 lists the different types of qualifiers, along with their qualifying values. Usually, you apply QoS qualifiers when you are ready to consider solution deployment. Look for more details about QoS, especially event sequencing, in Chapter 11.

Table 2.2 Adding References to the Application Deployment Descriptor

Name	Qualifier Values
Reference qualifiers	Asynchronous reliability Suspend transaction Asynchronous invocation Suspend activity session
Interface qualifiers	Event sequencing Join activity session Join transaction Security permission
Implementation qualifiers	Activity session Transaction Security identity

Closing the Link

Imports, exports, references, and so on are new terms in this whole new paradigm called the Service Component Architecture (SCA), which was introduced in this chapter. From the developer's perspective, services are packaged in a service module, which is the basic unit of deployment and administration in an SCA runtime.

Service imports are used in a service module to use external services that are not part of the module itself (for example, services exported by other modules, stateless session EJBs, Web services, EIS services, and so on). External services that are referenced by import declarations are valid targets of service wires. The import binding definition does not need to be finalized at development time. Aspects such as the actual endpoint of services to invoke can be late-bound at deployment, administration, or even runtime. Service exports, on the other hand, are used to offer services from the service module to the outside world, such as services for other service modules or as Web services.

The following chapters build on these concepts and use the tooling and runtime examples to fully explain SCA. It is imperative that you understand the SCA model, because it forms the basis of business integration discussed in this book. It is beneficial to reiterate that patterns are not inventions or edicts; they are harvested from repeated experiences from and use by practitioners. Business integration does not always involve business processes, but in a lot of cases, business processes form the centerpiece of integration.

 ## Links to developerWorks

A.2.1   www.ibm.com/developerworks/podcast/websphere/ws-soa2progmod.html

A.2.2   www.ibm.com/developerworks/websphere/library/techarticles/0610_redlin/
0610_redlin.html

A.2.3   www.ibm.com/developerworks/websphere/techjournal/0508_simmons/
0508_simmons.html

Chapter 3

Business Orchestration

Business integration at the most basic level is process integration, which involves various back-end systems. For example, an order fulfillment process could interact with a credit verification system and a shipping system to complete an order. Using a markup language, business integration addresses such issues and makes it easy for business to integrate various disparate back-end systems.

This chapter presents Web Services Business Process Execution Language (WS-BPEL or just BPEL for short). We do not get into the semantics of whether it is business orchestration, service orchestration, business choreography, or service choreography. The ensemble is made up of Web Services, BPEL would be the script, and a runtime server would coordinate the various interactions. As pointed out in Chapter 2, "Business Integration Architecture and Patterns," WebSphere Process Server (WPS) is the runtime we use to illustrate the concepts and explain the business integration capabilities.

A.3.1

Business Processes

Everything from a simple order approval to a complex manufacturing process can be described as a business process. A *business process* can be thought of as a set of activities, related to the business, invoked in a specific sequence to achieve a particular business goal. Such business processes can involve steps performed by machines and humans. They can be either short-running (for example, a funds transfer process that transfers funds between accounts) or long-running (for example, an order fulfillment process). In the computing world, we typically use a metalanguage or markup language, such as BPEL, to describe a business process.

Service components such as *business state machines, business rules,* and *data maps* are the building blocks of service composition. Business processes use these service components by invoking them to perform some of the activities in the process. Business processes—specifically, BPEL-based business processes—form the cornerstone of composition for service components in the Service Component Architecture (SCA).

BPEL

BPEL is a Web Services Orchestration specification that is defined by the Organization for the Advancement of Structured Information Standards (OASIS), an international nonprofit consortium that drives the development and adoption of e-business standards. BPEL is an XML-based language for the formal specification of business processes and business interaction protocols. The language provides constructs that allow you to build business processes by composing and coordinating access to other services.

A.3.2

In addition to being a Web services standard itself, BPEL leverages other Web services standards:

- **WSDL (Web Services Description Language):** All external services that are invoked by a BPEL process are defined using a WSDL. In addition, a BPEL process is itself described using a WSDL. Given that a BPEL process is defined by a WSDL, it can be invoked as a service by other BPEL processes.
- **XML (Extensible Markup Language):** Business processes in BPEL are defined using an XML-based language. This language describes the logic of a business process and its interaction with its partners.
- **XPath (XML Path Language):** BPEL supports the use of XPath for writing expressions and queries. The BPEL language provides logic constructs for conditional execution and looping. The XPath language is used to build expressions used by these constructs.
- **XML Schema:** BPEL supports the use of variables in business processes. These variables can be described using XML Schema.

The BPEL interaction model is built on top of the Web services interaction model, which essentially supports stateless and synchronous interactions. BPEL extends the Web services interaction model by providing support for stateful and asynchronous interactions. Whereas a Web services interaction is meant to be short-running and last a few seconds or, at most, a few minutes, BPEL process interactions can be long-running and could last days or even years.

The BPEL language facilitates the creation of a business process by providing capabilities to invoke one or more services in a well-defined way. To support the composition of services, the BPEL language provides a number of key concepts. Before we explain some of the concepts, Figure 3.1 shows a BPEL process. The process starts at the top, with a Receive, flows sequentially down, and finishes with a Reply.

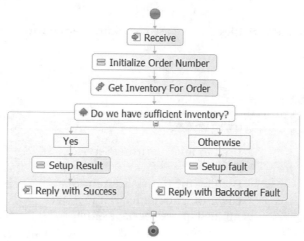

Figure 3.1 BPEL process

Partner Links

Most BPEL processes interact with external services, and BPEL processes in turn are called by clients. BPEL refers to these services and clients as *partners*. For a process to be able to interact with a partner, it needs to contain information about that partner. The BPEL construct, *partnerLink*, makes the definition of a partner available to a BPEL process.

There are two types of partnerLinks:

- partnerLinks that define services that are invoked by the process. In WPS, these are referred to as *reference partners*.
- partnerLinks that define the BPEL process so that clients can invoke it. In WPS, these are called *interface partners*. Every BPEL process defines at least one interface partner.

Variables

A BPEL process can define variables that hold state information for the process between activities. In addition, variables allow the creation of request messages that are used in service invocation and to hold response messages that are returned from invoked services.

Activities

Activities represent the steps in a BPEL process. We classify these BPEL activities into three main categories: *Service Activities*, *Structured Activities*, and *Fault Activities*. The various activities are described in the following tables. The last column in the table shows icons specific to WebSphere Integration Developer (WID), which is the integrated development environment (IDE) that can be used to create and test BPEL processes.

Service Activities

Service Activities include activities that are used to communicate with partners, as shown in Table 3.1.

Table 3.1 Service Activities

Activity Name	Description	WID Icon
Invoke	Used to invoke partner services.	
Receive	Used by the process to wait for a client to send it a request message. All BPEL processes have either a *Receive* (or a *Pick*) as the first activity in the process.	
Reply	Used to send a response message to the client that sent it a corresponding request message.	
Assign	Used to manipulate variables in the process.	
Empty	These serve as placeholders for other activities. They perform no task but help in designing a process that gets implemented later.	

Structured Activities

Structured Activities, described in Table 3.2, group other activities and provide logic constructs such as if-then-else and looping.

Table 3.2 Structured Activities

Activity Name	Description	WID Icon
Switch	This structured activity evaluates the conditions on two or more control paths. The first one that cvaluates to true is followed. If no path evaluates to true, the *otherwise* path is chosen. In WID, this is called a *Choice* activity.	
Pick	A structured activity that halts the process to wait for a client to send it one of the many request messages it is waiting for. Then it follows the path based on the first message it receives. In WID, this is called a *Receive Choice*.	
While	A structured activity that executes one or more nested activities as long as specific conditions are met.	
Wait	Stops a process for a specified period of time.	
Sequence	A structured activity that contains other activities that are ordered in a single control path.	
Scope	Use this to act as a behavioral container for one or more activities in the BPEL process. The process as a whole is contained in a single global scope, and other scopes can be nested within it.	

continues

Table 3.2 Structured Activities (continued)

Activity Name	Description	WID Icon
Flow	A structured activity that contains other activities separated into individual control paths to be executed concurrently. In WID, this is also known as a *Parallel* activity.	

Fault Activities

Fault Activities, described in Table 3.3, include activities that are used to deal with error conditions also known as faults.

Table 3.3 Fault Activities

Activity Name	Description	WID Icon
Terminate	Used to halt the execution process without compensation or fault handling.	
Throw	Used to generate a fault from inside the business process.	
Re-throw	Can be used inside a fault handler to re-throw the fault that the handler is currently handling.	
Fault Handler	When a fault occurs in a process, use this element to find another way to complete the process.	
Catch	Use this element to intercept and deal with a specific kind of fault. It is used in an appropriate fault handler and usually is the first element in the control path.	
Catch All	Use this element to intercept and deal with a fault that is not caught by an associated Catch element.	

Expression Language

BPEL supports XPath as an expression language by default. BPEL processes can use it to evaluate expressions used by its logic and data-manipulation activities. For example, it can be used in the *While* and *Switch/Case* activities to evaluate conditions and in the *Assign* activity to initialize or update process variables.

A.3.3

Expression Language

In addition to XPath, WebSphere Process Server also supports the use of Java as an expression language. Additionally, WPS provides a *Snippet* activity in which you can write Java code as part of your business logic. This enables you to perform complex operations as part of the process. The examples in Chapter 6, "Business Processes," show the use of Java in a BPEL process.

Correlation Set

Given the long-running nature of some BPEL processes, they can have more than one running instance at any point in time. Each of these running instances needs a unique key so that messages sent to the BPEL process can be directed to the correct instance. In a tightly coupled object-oriented system, you can use the object's instance identifier (OID) as the object's key. However, in the Web services world, this does not work well, because services are loosely coupled, so this method would require a dependency on passing OIDs with messages.

To facilitate long-running, stateful interactions, BPEL uses key fields in the messages that are exchanged between services. For example, a message that contains an order number that is sent to an order fulfillment business process can be used to identify a particular instance of that process. Given that different messages can be sent to a business process for the different operations it supports, a process can have more than one key field. A collection of such key fields is called a *correlation set*.

Scope

BPEL provides the ability to create *scopes*, which are the grouping of activities within a process. The purpose of a scope is to provide a context in which the group of activities is executed. Scopes allow you to associate *Fault*, *Compensation*, and *Event Handlers* with it. These handlers are active when the process executes activities within that scope. Scopes and their associated handlers can be nested. Additionally, every BPEL process has an implicit global scope.

Fault Handler

When a business process is executed, errors can occur while invoking services or even when executing logic in the process itself. These errors are called *faults*. BPEL provides a way for processes to handle faults by associating Fault Handlers with scopes in the process. *Fault*

Handlers declare the faults that can be addressed and contain one or more activities that are executed when a corresponding fault is generated. Faults halt the execution of activities in the current scope and cause the Fault Handler at that scope to execute. If no Fault Handler is defined at that scope, or the handler does not handle that particular fault, the fault is re-thrown (passed on) and dealt with at its parent scope.

Compensation Handler

Because BPEL processes can be long-running, the different activities executed in the process run in their own unit of work and finish independently of subsequent activities in the process. When a business process receives a fault, there can be a need to undo some of the activities that were previously completed. These undo activities are specified in BPEL using a Compensation Handler. A *Compensation Handler* is associated with a scope and can contain one or more activities that get executed when an unhandled fault is generated in the scope for which it is defined.

Event Handler

After a BPEL process starts, it can block for messages from a client by executing a *Receive* or *Pick* activity. However, the use of *Receive* and *Pick* means that the process can act on those messages only when it reaches that point in the process. In BPEL 2.0, the *Pick* activity is also known as *Receive Choice*.

To be responsive to asynchronous events, the BPEL specification allows a process to define Event Handlers. An *Event Handler*, which is associated with a scope, declares the asynchronous messages it can receive and contains one or more activities that are executed when a corresponding event message is received.

Figure 3.2 shows a BPEL process in IBM's WID. It highlights the key BPEL concepts that were just discussed.

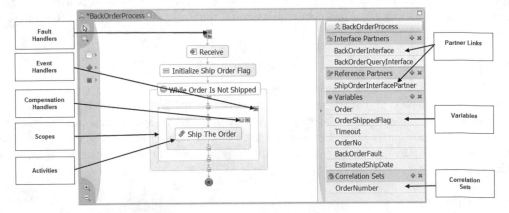

Figure 3.2 BPEL process in WID

BPEL Extensions

BPEL as a language is good at executing a set of activities that occur over time and that interact with internal and external services. But BPEL, like all languages, has limitations. It does
not account for humans in a process, so there are no concepts for roles and inboxes, as in a
workflow. Additionally, BPEL does not support business processes that evolve during their
execution, branching out to incorporate new activities and entities. Finally, it does not have
native support for business activity monitoring (BAM), because there is no data model for
measurement and monitoring.

To alleviate some of these limitations, vendors have proposed extensions. For example, SAP
AG has proposed BPEL4People to incorporate human initiators, approvers, and managers in
BPEL processes. Natively, the process service and the collaborating services are all Web services. However, IBM has proposed the BPELJ extension, allowing for a mix of Java services
and Web services. IBM has proposed the following extensions to BPEL, some of which have
been accepted and will be incorporated into the next version of BPEL:

A.3.4

- Human tasks activities to support human interaction with the process
- Support for Java as an expression language
- Business relevance flags that determine which events are recorded in the audit log
- Explicit checkpointing that supports multiple activities in a single transaction
- Time-outs for activities
- validFrom timestamps for process model versioning

Short-Running and Long-Running Processes

WebSphere Process Server supports two types of processes: short-running and long-running.
Occasionally you will see the terms microflows and macroflows to describe short-running
processes and long-running processes, respectively. The type of process determines the activities the process can perform.

A *short-running* business process has the following characteristics:

- Completes in a short period of time
- Runs in a single transaction
- Its state is transient and is not persisted to a database in between activities
- Should invoke only synchronous services and other short-running subprocesses

A *long-running* process has the following characteristics:

- Can run for hours, days, or even years
- May run as several transactions
- Invokes synchronous and/or asynchronous services
- Stores each intermediate process state, which makes the process forward-
  recoverable
- Involves human interaction or wait activities

Transaction Characteristics of Processes

As stated earlier, one of the differences between a short-running process and a long-running process is its transactional characteristics. As shown in Figure 3.3, all the activities in a short-running process are executed in a single transaction. Services that are invoked by a short-running process may or may not participate in that process's transaction. Services that participate in a short-running process's transaction are automatically rolled back if the process's transaction is rolled back. However, if they do not participate in the transaction, they stay committed.

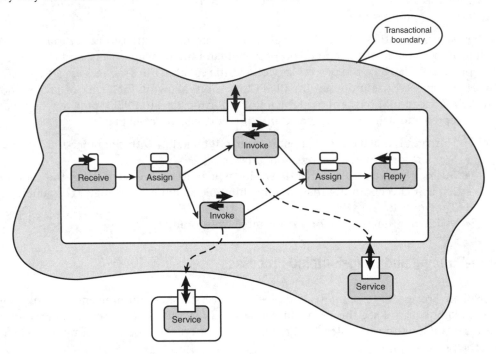

Figure 3.3 Transactions in a short-running process

Figure 3.4 illustrates transactions in a long-running process. Each activity is executed in its own transaction, with the process engine storing the state of the process in a database between activities. The failure and rollback of any one of those transactions does not affect any previously committed transactions. As a result, services that are invoked in a previously committed transaction remain untouched.

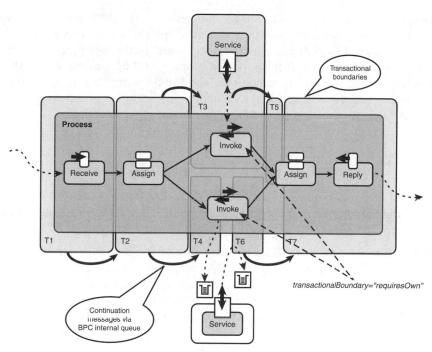

Figure 3.4 Transactions in a long-running process

Global Transaction

A global transaction is a unit of work in which the activities of multiple services (such as *Resource Managers*) are coordinated by an external *transaction coordinator* that is responsible for ensuring that all the services either complete successfully or roll back. For a Resource Manager to be able to participate in such a transaction, it needs to support the two-phase commit protocol. Not all Resource Managers support this protocol. Additionally, long-running processes execute each of their activities in separate transactions. In these cases, services cannot be automatically rolled back by the transaction coordinator.

To undo the changes in these cases, you can use BPEL's Compensation Handler feature.

Versioning BPEL Processes

As you have seen, long-running processes can run for a very long time. However, businesses might have a need to update their business process periodically to meet changing requirements. For example, a company might need to update how claims processing is done at the beginning of each year.

All existing process instances are serviced by the version of the BPEL process that was used to create them. New process instances are created using the latest version of the process. Runtime servers use different approaches to "switch over" to the new process instance. WPS uses a timestamp-based approach to support versioning of BPEL processes such that different versions of a process with the same name and interface can be active concurrently by using different *validFrom* timestamps. Chapter 10, "Business Integration Services Management," discusses versioning of BPEL processes in greater detail.

BPEL and SCA

We introduced Service Component Architecture (SCA) in Chapter 1, "Business Integration." Because it is the cornerstone of the WPS runtime, we will discuss it throughout the book. A BPEL process can consume SCA services, or it can be consumed by other SCA services.

In WebSphere Process Server, a BPEL process is one of the core SCA components (implementation type). Given that a process is an SCA component, it can make use of all the powerful features that SCA has to offer. This includes being exported as one of the different SCA binding types so that clients can communicate with the process using different protocols. Additionally, this also means that a process can invoke external services using a variety of protocols.

Closing the Link

Business integration does not always involve business processes, but in many cases, business processes form the centerpiece of integration. This chapter looked at BPEL as a language for expressing business processes. You saw how BPEL helps orchestrate the instantiations of these processes as discrete, reusable components that can be composed into larger business processes or executed outside the context of a larger application. We introduced the core BPEL features as well as the IBM extensions to BPEL.

Subsequent chapters investigate BPEL further. Chapter 4, "WebSphere Integration Developer," highlights the tooling support for BPEL. Chapter 6 demonstrates how to use WID's Process Editor to build BPEL processes using many of the features and concepts that were discussed in this chapter.

The following URL is the entry point for all WebSphere business integration-related product documentation: http://publib.boulder.ibm.com/infocenter/dmndhelp/v6rxmx/index.jsp.

Links to developerWorks

A.3.1   www.alphaworks.ibm.com/tech/bpws4j

A.3.2   www.ibm.com/developerworks/forums/dw_forum.jsp?forum=167&cat=7

A.3.3   www.ibm.com/developerworks/library/specification/ws-bpel/
?S_TACT=105AGX10&S_CMP=ART

A.3.4   www-128.ibm.com/developerworks/websphere/zones/bpm

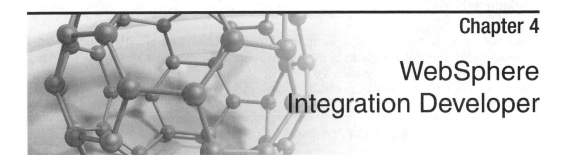

Chapter 4

WebSphere Integration Developer

This chapter examines WebSphere Integration Developer (WID) and its place in developing business integration applications that fit into Service-Oriented Architecture (SOA) solutions. WID is the tool that lets you build composite applications by allowing you to wire components together independent of their implementation and without knowledge of low-level implementation details. These components are actually Service Component Architecture (SCA) components.

SOA then lets you focus on solving your business problems by using and reusing these components rather than diverting your attention to the technology that is implementing the services you use. Developers also can use WID to test the applications before deploying them to the server.

A.4.1

Installing WID

WID is an Integrated Development Environment (IDE) based on the Eclipse 3.0 framework. It is supported on all Windows® operating systems and some Linux® operating systems. Throughout this book, all product installations are described in the appendixes. WID installation is covered in Appendix B, "WebSphere Integration Developer Installation."

Eclipse
You can find information about the Eclipse framework at www.eclipse.org.

At any time after the initial installation of WID, you can add optional features by rerunning *launchpad.exe* and selecting the features you want to add. You must use the same user ID that you used to install the required features.

Working with WID

This book assumes that you will be using the Windows XP version of WID. You start WID by selecting **Start > All Programs > IBM WebSphere > Integration Developer V6.0.2 > WebSphere Integration Developer V6.0.2**. The Workspace Launcher screen appears, as shown in Figure 4.1, asking you to choose a workspace. Enter a workspace name, and click **OK**.

Figure 4.1 WID workspace launcher screen

On a Linux system, you can open a command window, go to your installation directory, and enter the command `./wid.bin`. You can also use the product shortcuts for that particular Linux operating system.

When you start WID, you are asked for a working directory, also called the workspace. We recommend storing WID workspaces in a folder titled WIDworkspace, such as C:\WIDworkspace\booksample.

> **WID Workspace**
>
> Do not check the box that says **Use this as the default and do not ask again**. If you check this box by mistake and need to change the default value, select **Window** > **Preferences** > **Workbench**-> **Startup and Shutdown dialog**, or launch the tool from the command line using the option **-data <work-space path>**.
>
> We recommend keeping the workspace folder separate from the WID installation folder.

By default, the first time you start WID, a dialog box opens with the default workspace directory specified. The welcome screen is displayed; it has links to the samples. Subsequently, the workbench starts with the workspace you specified in the preceding session. It opens in the Business Integration (BI) perspective in a four-pane mode. In this perspective, you assemble your composite applications from SCA components and define related artifacts such as business objects, interfaces, and maps.

If you are new to WID, you will find three useful help options: Tutorials Gallery, Samples Gallery, and Cheat Sheets. You can find them by selecting **Help** > **Cheat Sheets**. The default Business Integration perspective has many editors. The Cheat Sheet collection, for example, enables you to explore seven of the editors found in the Business Integration perspective, as shown in Figure 4.2. We look at some of the editors in this chapter.

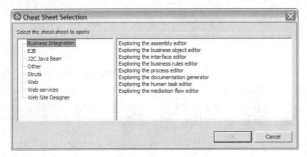

Figure 4.2 Cheat Sheet Selection for Business Integration

Business Integration Solution Building Blocks

When building a business integration solution with WID, you create a module, a mediation module, and/or a library to contain the resources and code. You may also need to declare dependencies for your modules and libraries.

A.4.2

Modules

A *module* is the basic unit of deployment to the WebSphere Process Server (WPS) runtime. It is a Business Integration project that is used for development, version management, and organizing business service resources. It is deployed to WPS. A module consists of an Assembly Diagram, Business Services, Data Types, Interfaces, and Maps. Dependent libraries and Java projects can be added to a module for deployment with the module. When deployed, a module becomes a J2EE enterprise archive (EAR) file.

The Assembly Diagram is the centerpiece of a module. It contains the business services, modeled as SCA components, and the connections, or wires, between them. Any resources, such as business objects or interfaces, contained within a module can be used only by that module. If you want to reuse or share resources, you place them in a library.

Mediation Modules

A *mediation module* is a special type of module that can be deployed to WebSphere Enterprise Service Bus (WESB) or to the WPS runtime. Mediation services consist of flows that intercept and modify messages between services consumers (usually called exports) and services providers (usually called imports). Like other modules, when deployed, a mediation module becomes a J2EE EAR file.

A mediation module is for low-level technical integration. It gives the integration developer access to low-level constructs such as message headers that you cannot access in WPS. Note also that mediation flow components and Java components are all that can be included in a mediation module, and that mediation flow components cannot be included in a module. For more information on WESB, see Chapter 12, "WebSphere Adapters."

Libraries

Often, interfaces, business objects, business object maps, relationships, and Web service ports need to be shared so that resources in other modules can use them. A *library* is the type of Business Integration project that is used to store these kinds of shareable resources. It can contain Data Types, Interfaces, and Maps.

A library cannot be deployed by itself. For a module to use the resources from a library, it has to be added as a dependency to the module. You can also have a library that shares resources with another library. In that case, you have to add the library dependency. Such dependencies are specified and managed via the dependency editor.

Creating Projects and Other Artifacts

A.4.3

You create a new project in the Business Integration perspective of WID. You have two choices: Create a module to contain components that are relevant to a single application, or create a library to contain common components. Most likely, you will define your business objects in a library, because you're most apt to share object definitions across multiple components.

Creating a Library

This section illustrates the steps to create a library project. The library is named *BookSampleLibrary*. It contains the business objects and Web Services Description Language (WSDL) files that are used by components in other modules.

1. Make sure that the WID workbench is open. From WID, select **File** > **New** > **Project** > **Library**. You see the dialog box shown in Figure 4.3.

   Another way to create a library is to expand the Business Integration folder in the wizard selection window and choose Library. A third way is to right-click in the navigation pane, select **New** > **Other**, and choose Library. The intent here is not to confuse you, but to illustrate that WID often has more than one way to do something.

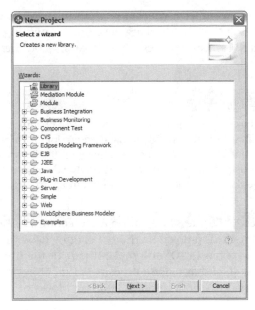

Figure 4.3 Selecting a new library project

2. Click **Next**. The New Library window appears, as shown in Figure 4.4. Enter a Library Name, such as BookSampleLibrary. In most cases, you choose to use the default location. When you click **Finish**, the new library is created and is displayed in the Business Integration navigation tree.

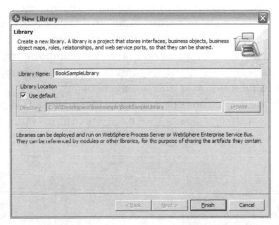

Figure 4.4 Naming the new library

Now that you have a Library project, what do you put in the library? It really depends on the Business Integration solution that is being developed. Anything that is to be shared by other modules (such as interfaces, business objects, and/or business object maps) can be stored in the library.

> **Library Best Practice**
>
> This is from the product's Information Center. Put business objects and interfaces that are used in an assembly diagram into a library so that they can be shared. Then, add a dependency on the library to all the modules that use these common resources. Avoid copying the same business objects and interfaces into different modules to use them.

As mentioned in Chapter 2, "Business Integration Architecture and Patterns," for illustration purposes, we are following the top-down method of coming up with a solution. So, the next step is to create a business object (BO) and make it part of the library. *Business objects* are containers for application data that represent business functions or elements such as a customer or invoice. BOs are one of the primary building blocks of any Business Integration solution.

Creating a Simple Business Object

With the Business Integration perspective open in WID, go to the navigation pane and expand the *BookSampleLibrary* by clicking the plus sign next to it, as shown in Figure 4.5. You see five entities:

- **Dependencies:** If a library, module, or mediation module needs to use resources from another library, you have to specify those dependencies here.
- **Data Types:** These are either business objects (BOs) or business graphs (BGs).
- **Interfaces:** An interface provides the input and output of a component and is created independent of the implementation of the component.
- **Mapping:** Data Maps, Relationships, and Roles make up mapping within a library. Additionally, in modules, you find interface maps.
- **Events:** These are definitions of custom monitoring events that can be produced by modules and captured by the Common Event Infrastructure (CEI) for monitoring purposes.

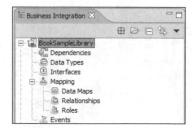

Figure 4.5 *BookSampleLibrary* project structure

We use the Business Object Editor to create a BO. Place the cursor anywhere in the navigation tree, right-click, and choose **New** > **Business Object**. This displays the BO Editor. But if you want the BO to be part of a particular project and use a particular name space, follow these steps:

1. Highlight **Data Types** in *BookSampleLibrary*, right-click, and choose **New** > **Business Object**.

2. In the New Business Object window that opens, enter the Name, such as *OrderLineBO*, and click **Finish**. Accept the default values for all the other fields. The OrderLine Business Object is displayed in the Business Object Editor, as shown in Figure 4.6.

   Currently the BO is empty. A BO contains attributes or fields, each of which has a name, a type (scalar or complex), a default value for scalar types, and cardinality. So, the attributes end up defining the content of the business object. You can add attributes to your *OrderLineBO*, such as Item Number, Item Description, Price, Quantity, and so on, via the BO Editor.

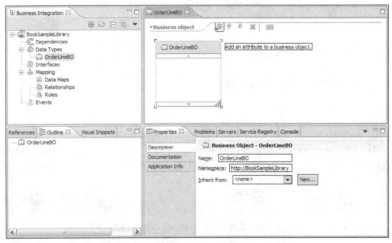

Figure 4.6 WID workspace showing the Business Object Editor

3. Figures 4.6 and 4.7 show the icon (circle with the letter **a** inside it) to click. It adds an attribute to a business object that is being edited. In doing so, *attribute1* of type *string* gets added.

4. You can highlight *attribute1* and change it to a more meaningful name. Similarly, you can click the default type setting of *string* and choose the type from the context menu. In Figure 4.7, the first attribute has been renamed to *orderlineno* of type integer. Attributes can be of the following types:

- boolean
- date
- dateTime
- double
- float
- hexBinary
- int
- string
- time
- Other business objects

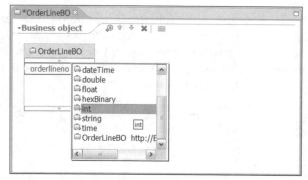

Figure 4.7 Adding attributes to a business object

5. On the Name tab, notice the asterisk to the left of the name. This indicates that something has changed since you last saved. After all the edits are done, press **Ctrl+S** to save. At that point, the asterisk disappears.

WID Editing

To undo saved edit, select **Edit** > **Undo**, or press **Ctrl+Z**.

6. In the properties view below the BO editor, shown in Figure 4.8, you see other constraints that can be specified for each attribute, such as a minimum and maximum value, whether the field is required, and so on. To define an attribute as an array, you have to click the Array checkbox.

Figure 4.8 Specifying constraints for attributes

> **Note**
>
> All the attributes in the properties view of the BO editor are useful as annotation. The WPS runtime does not enforce these constraints. In a mediation module, on the other hand, you can choose to validate the input data on a number of the mediation primitives, which enforces this validation.

Follow the preceding steps to add other attributes based on the purpose of that BO within a business process. Figure 4.9 shows the complete *OrderLine* business object.

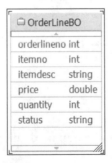

Figure 4.9 The OrderLine business object

In the Business Integration view, if you look under Data Types for the *BookSampleLibrary* project, you should now see OrderLineBO listed.

Creating a Nested Business Object

By dragging and dropping objects onto the canvas in WID, you use the Aggregation pattern to create a complex or nested business object. A complex business object is one that has other business objects as one of its attributes. In our BookSample project, the Order business object is associated with an instance of the OrderLineBO.

The steps to create a complex BO are the same as creating a simple BO; the only difference is the attribute association, as shown in Figure 4.10. It shows another object called *OrderBO,* which contains *OrderLineBO* as an attribute.

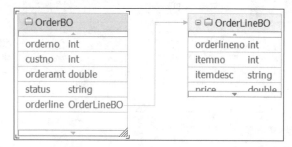

Figure 4.10 The Order business object

You can always use the References view to check out the relationships that exist among the business objects in your project. For example, highlight OrderLineBO in the Business Integration view and click the References tab in the lower-left corner. You can see the relationship between OrderBO and OrderLineBO, as shown in Figure 4.11.

Figure 4.11 The References view

Creating an Interface

If an interface does not exist that can be imported and used, you have to create a new one. Follow these steps:

1. In the Business Integration view of the Business Integration perspective, with the expanded *BookSampleLibrary* project, highlight **Interfaces**, right-click, and choose **New > Interface**.

2. In the New Interface Wizard, shown in Figure 4.12, enter a name for the interface, and click **Finish**. Be sure that the correct module is referenced. In this case, it should point to *BookSampleLibrary*.

Figure 4.12 New Interface Wizard

3. *CreateOrderInterface* gets created and is displayed in the Interface Editor, as shown in Figure 4.12. At this point, you can add a Request-Response operation or a one-way operation by clicking the icons in the palette of the interface editor.

4. Click the icon (⊞) to **Add a Request Response Operation**. By default, you get a table with an operation named *operation1*, with an Input named *input1* and an Output named *output1*, both of type *string*, as shown in Figure 4.13.

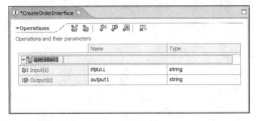

Figure 4.13 Adding a Request-Response operation

5. Follow the same steps of highlighting labels and values and changing them. Highlight *operation1*, and rename it as *create*. Rename *input1* as *order*, and make it of type *OrderBO*.

6. Highlight *output1*, and click the Delete icon on the far right to delete the output variable from the operation. You should be left with just one input. Why didn't we create a one-way operation? We did it this way to illustrate that a two-way Request-Response operation can be turned into a one-way operation, but that you cannot add an output to a one-way operation to convert it to a Request-Response operation.

7. Add a fault to this interface by clicking the Add Fault icon, as shown in Figure 4.14. Before you can add the fault details, you need to create a couple more BOs (see Chapter 6, "Business Processes"). For now, press **Ctrl+S** to save the *CreateOrder* interface, and close the interface editor.

Figure 4.14 Adding a fault

Creating a Module

This section describes the steps to create a module. Most of the resources that this module will contain are explained in detail in Chapter 6.

1. From WID, select **File** > **New** > **Project** > **Module**. The New Module wizard is displayed, as shown in Figure 4.15. Enter a Module Name of OrderModule. At this point, you can click **Finish** to create the module. However, for illustrative purposes, click **Next**.

Figure 4.15 New Module wizard

2. On the next screen, you have the option to select dependency libraries that would be of use to this module. In this case, you select the library *BookSampleLibrary*, and then click **Finish**. Note that all referenced libraries are normally packaged with the module.

3. After the wizard creates the module, you see it listed as a new project in the navigation tree. Figure 4.16 shows the *OrderModule* project structure. It contains seven categories of artifacts:

- **Assembly Diagram** gives you the overall perspective of all the components in the application and how they are wired together.
- **Dependencies**
- **Business Logic**: One or more of the following make up Business Logic: Processes, State Machines, Rule Groups, Rules, Human Tasks, and Selectors.
- **Data Types**
- **Interfaces**
- **Mapping**: This category includes Interface Maps.
- **Events**

Figure 4.16 *OrderModule* project structure

The remaining sections of this chapter discuss the Process Editor, Assembly Editor, and Visual Snippet Editor. The Visual Snippet Editor is actually a view in the Eclipse paradigm.

Dependency

For modules with dependent libraries, you *must* deploy the library with the module (which is the default setting) so that the resources are available during runtime.

Process Editor

The Process Editor, which is sometimes erroneously called the BPEL editor, is used to create business processes. You will also hear the term *orchestration* used to describe the creation of a BPEL-based business process. Although Chapter 6 covers creating a business process in great detail, we want to introduce the editor and its parts in this section. Figure 4.16 showed that after you create a module, you get a folder named Business Logic, which can contain Processes, Business State Machines, Rule Groups, Rules, Human Tasks, and Selectors.

To create a business process, highlight **Processes**, right-click, and choose **New > Business Process**. You enter a process name, choose to generate a new interface or use an existing interface, and then decide whether to disable WPS BPEL Extensions or allow them. After you click **Finish**, you see a skeleton business process within the Process Editor, as shown in Figure 4.17.

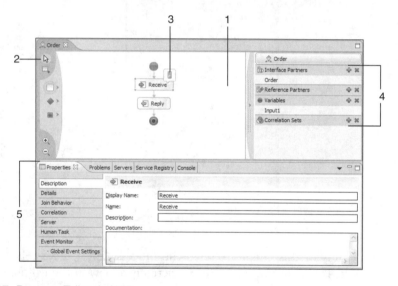

Figure 4.17 Process Editor in WID

The numbered areas in Figure 4.17 are as follows:

1. The *canvas* is the main area where you assemble the activities to compose your business process.

2. The *palette* houses objects that you click and drag onto the canvas. Objects with gray arrows contain submenus. Click the arrow to display the submenu.

3. The *action bar* is a miniature dialog that pops up beside the activity you select on the canvas. It contains one or more icons relevant to that activity.

4. The *tray* on the right displays Partners, Variables, and Correlation Sets associated with your business process. The + and × icons allow you to add and delete these. You can hide the tray by clicking the gray arrow to the left of the tray.

5. The *properties view* displays the configurable properties relevant to the object currently selected on the canvas. You click the tabs to the left to toggle through the pages.

The palette has three sets of submenus—Common Activities, Control Activities, and Error-Handling Activities:

- **Common Activities**, shown in Figure 4.18, are the most common activities in a BPEL process:
  - *Empty Action* serves as a placeholder or what is commonly called a "no-op."
  - *Invoke* is used to call an external service. This activity is probably the most common activity used in a BPEL process.
  - *Receive* exposes an operation that an external caller can use to trigger the process invocation. Short-running processes can have only a single receive activity, whereas long-running processes can have more than one.
  - *Reply* returns information to the external caller and is frequently used in short-running processes in which the process synchronously waits for a response. In long-running processes, it is conceivable that the process asynchronously waits for a response.
  - *Assign* lets you move information from one process variable to another.
  - *Human Task*, also known as a staff activity, represents the involvement of a person in a business process.
  - *Snippet* represents a fragment of Java code that is to be executed.

Figure 4.18 The most common BPEL activities

- **Control Activities**, shown in Figure 4.19, are the common control structures used in a BPEL process:
  - *Choice* is equivalent to the "if-then-else" in programming languages. It enables you to have conditional branches.

- *Receive Choice* is similar to the Receive activity except that it waits for external stimuli while the process is paused.
- *While Loop* enables blocks of activities to be repeated while a certain condition is met. Unlike workflow, you cannot go back in the BPEL process flows.
- *Wait Activity* is really a timer, which enables the process to pause until a specific date and time or for some duration of time.
- *Sequence* specifies a set of activities that need to occur in a certain order. This is commonly seen in standard BPEL processes.
- *Scope* is used to group a set of activities. It is used when dealing with fault handlers, event handlers, and compensation handlers.
- *Parallel Activities* can run independently and in parallel.

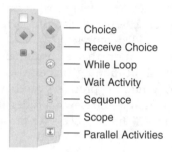

Figure 4.19 Control activities

The Difference Between Receive and Receive Choice

The difference between a plain Receive activity and a Receive Choice activity is that, with a Receive Choice activity, any number of operations can be received. The first operation that the business process receives is taken, and the business process follows its path.

- **Error-Handling Activities**, shown in Figure 4.20, are similar to programming constructs. These are the error-handling activities used in a BPEL process:
  - *Terminate* is used to stop immediately a process instance. As soon as a Terminate acivity is reached, all branches of the instance stop, and the instance itself is ended.
  - *Throw* is used to throw a fault, which is the equivalent of throwing a fault or raising an exception in programmatic terms. The corresponding fault handlers have to be defined to intelligently handle the fault.
  - *Re-throw* enables the BPEL process that has caught a fault to re-throw it.
  - *Compensate* could be considered the equivalent of a rollback. The difference is that, in long-running BPEL processes, if a failure occurs, the transactions that were already committed cannot be rolled back. They can be undone only by way of compensation.

Figure 4.20 Error-handling activities

Assembly Editor

The Assembly Diagram Editor or the Assembly Editor enables you to visually assemble composite applications by adding SCA components and wiring them together. When you double-click Assembly Diagram, the assembly diagram for your module is opened in the Assembly Editor. Like the Process Editor, it has a canvas, palette, and properties view, as shown in Figure 4.21.

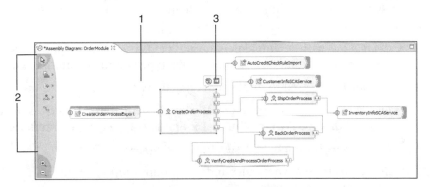

Figure 4.21 Assembly Editor in WID

The important areas are as follows:

1. The canvas is the area where you assemble your components and wire them together to build your assembly diagram.

2. The palette houses objects that you click and drag onto the canvas. Objects with gray arrows contain submenus. Click the arrow to expose the submenu.

3. The action bar is a miniature dialog that pops up beside the component you select on the canvas. It contains one or more icons relevant to that component.

   The properties view, although not shown in Figure 4.21, is similar to what we discussed for the Process Editor. It displays properties that are relevant to the component that is currently selected on the canvas. You click the tabs to the left to toggle through the pages.

The palette has three sets of submenus: business service components; import, export, and stand-alone references; and interface map and selector. A wire icon also appears. You use the Wire element, shown in Figure 4.22, when you want to connect a source component to a target component in the assembly diagram.

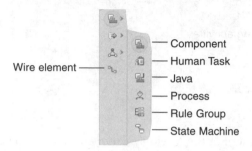

Figure 4.22 Business service components

1. Business service components, shown in Figure 4.22, have implementations to provide the business logic operating on data:

   • *Component* (with no implementation type) is used when you want to create a new component but do not know which type of implementation will be used.

   • *Human Task* is used to implement an activity that will involve humans.

   • *Java* is used when the component is implemented as a Java class. It supports both WSDL-type (W-type) interfaces and Java-type (J-type) interfaces.

   • *Process* is used for a BPEL-based business process.

   • *Rule Group* is used when rules and rule group components are part of the business process solution.

   • *State Machine*, which is meant for event-driven solutions, signifies the business state machine.

2. Import, Export, and Stand-alone References, shown in Figure 4.23, provide access to services that do not have any implementation:

   • *Import* identifies services outside of a module that can be called from within the module.

   • *Export* enables components that are part of the assembly diagram to provide their services to be invoked by external clients.

   • *Stand-alone References* make components in the assembly diagram available so that they can be invoked by J2EE artifacts, such as servlets, within the same J2EE EAR.

Figure 4.23 Components for invocation

3. Interface Map and Selector, shown in Figure 4.24, are special components that do not have business logic implementation:

   • *Interface Map* contains "mapping" logic for interface operations.

   • *Selector* provides the "routing" logic to invoke required services.

Figure 4.24 Special components

Binding Information

Binding information is required of all import and export components. It is a way of specifying the means of transporting the data to and from the module. Whenever you drag an interface from the Navigation pane to the canvas, you are asked for the binding type, as shown in Figure 4.25.

Figure 4.25 Specifying a component's binding type

You can select "no implementation," and at a later date, come back and choose the proper binding. The default binding type is SCA binding. The binding choices are as follows:

- SCA Binding
- Web Services Binding
- EIS Binding
- Stateless Session Bean Binding
- Message Binding
- JMS Binding
- MQ Binding
- MQ JMS Binding

The WID product documentation offers the following when deciding what type of binding to use:

Consider an *SCA* binding when these factors are applicable:

- All services are contained in WID modules; that is, no external services are available. Consider this binding when you are connecting to an internal service hosted on WPS/WESB.
- Performance is important.
- The modules are tightly coupled.

Consider a *Web Services* binding when these factors are applicable:

- You need to access an external Web service or provide a Web service over the Internet.
- The services are loosely coupled.
- The protocol of an external service you are accessing or a service you want to provide is SOAP/HTTP or JMS/HTTP.

Consider an *EIS* binding when these factors are applicable:

- You need to access a service on an EIS system using a resource adapter (for instance, SAP).
- Performance is more important than reliability; that is, synchronous data transmission is preferred over asynchronous.

Consider a *JMS* binding when these factors are applicable:

- You need to access a messaging system.
- The services are loosely coupled.
- Reliability is more important than performance; that is, asynchronous data transmission is preferred over synchronous.

Consider a *Stateless Session EJB* binding when these factors are applicable:

- The binding is for an imported service that is itself a stateless session bean.
- The imported service is loosely coupled.

> **Binding**
>
> The Assembly Editor lists the bindings supported and simplifies their creation when you want to create an import or export. The properties view displays the binding information of any import or export.

Visual Snippet Editor

You can edit Java snippets either visually using the Visual Snippet Editor or via the Java Editor. The Visual Snippet Editor, sometimes called the Visual Editor, enables you to create and manipulate Java code graphically. Visual snippets are organized in groups in which one or more items are linked.

Unlike with the Process Editor or Assembly Editor, you cannot get to the Visual Snippet Editor from the module level. You have to be editing a business process in the Process Editor. When you place a snippet component on its canvas, and then go to the details section of the properties pane, you see the Visual Editor in action. So, it is in some respects a sub-editor of the Process Editor. In other words, it is actually a view. Like the Process Editor, it has a canvas, a palette, and a tray, as shown in Figure 4.26. The two areas that are not seen in other editors are the expression builder and the visual snippets view. You can also use the Visual Snippet Editor to implement a custom mediation.

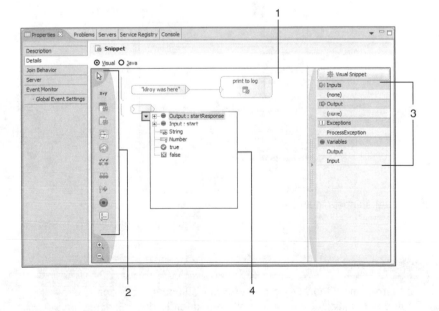

Figure 4.26 Visual Snippet Editor in WID

Snippet Reminder

The Process Editor palette shows you the snippet option only if you enable WPS BPEL Extensions in your business process.

Here are the important areas to note:

1. The canvas is the main area in the middle of the editor. You use it to assemble the activities to compose your visual snippet. When you drag an item onto the canvas, it automatically starts a group until you link to it from another group.

2. The palette houses objects that you click and drag onto the canvas.

3. The tray displays Inputs, Outputs, and Exceptions associated with your snippet, including the variables from the business process. You can hide the tray by clicking the gray arrow.

4. The expression builder is a miniature dialog box that pops up when you click an expression. It provides prompts that you use to graphically compose your expression.

Visual snippets view, shown in Figure 4.27, is the area normally to the left of the properties area. It shows a categorized view of all the existing snippets available to you. Remember to expand the categories to see all the available ones, including those in the product's standard library and any existing user-defined snippets.

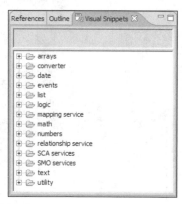

Figure 4.27 Visual snippets view

Visual Expression

If there is more than one group of visual snippets, each one is executed sequentially from top to bottom and left to right. Execution finishes at the end of the last snippet or when a return node is reached.

As shown in Figure 4.28, the palette has ten items that can be used as programming constructs to build your snippet:

- *Expressions* are used to carry user-defined values and pass them to the snippet.
- *Standard* visual snippet is used to add a predefined snippet to the canvas. It displays all the items available in the Standard Visual Snippet Library, such as logic and math functions.
- *Java* visual snippet is used to embed a call to an arbitrary Java method or constructor or to access a field within the context of the visual snippet.
- *Choice*, such as the one in the Process Editor, enables you to have conditional branches. The difference is that it uses a Boolean value to branch.
- *While* control structure is used to repeat the execution of the same code as long as the input value is True.
- *For Each* control structure is used to repeat the execution of the same code for all the items in a list.
- *Repeat* is a similar control structure that is used to iterate the execution of the same code a number of times.
- *Throw* node is used to throw an exception.
- *Return* node is used when you want to return a result from the snippet.
- *Comment* node enables you to put comments or include a note of some kind in the snippet's structure.

Figure 4.28 Visual Snippet Editor palette

The link in a visual snippet represents the flow of data and directs the sequence in which the execution of the node occurs. Thus, the Visual Snippet Editor can be used as a custom control inside the properties view in the editors for business processes, business state machines, business object mapping, and so on. It generates directly executable Java code, which is serialized within the artifacts of the model editor. It provides support for simple conversions between XSD, boxed Java types, and simple Java types (for example, *Integer* to *int*, *Double* to *float*, XSD *int* to *int*, and so on). You also can create your own visual snippets using the custom Visual Snippet Editor.

The other snippet editor—the Java Snippet Editor—is like a blank programming canvas in which you enter Java code that is immediately validated. If you are comfortable coding Java, sometimes you will find that entering simple code into the Java Snippet Editor is easier and probably faster. So, the choice comes down to one of personal preference and skill level.

Exporting Modules

In WID, you can package the Business Integration modules and deploy them to a server. That server can be the integrated test environment (ITE), or you can deploy them to stand-alone WPS. The same principles apply for deploying to WESB. Before you can deploy, you have to export all the application's artifacts.

As far as deployment is concerned, you have three export options:

- Export modules as Enterprise Archive (EAR) files for server deployment
- Export modules as serviceDeploy files for command-line server deployment
- Export modules as project interchange files for project sharing in a development environment

Exporting Modules as EAR Files

A module can be exported as an EAR file and deployed to WPS using its administrative console or command-line tools. As we continue working with our sample, be sure you are in the Business Integration perspective in the WID workbench. Before packaging the application, you should do a clean build of the project to satisfy all dependencies.

Select **File > Export**. In the Select window, choose **Integration module**, and click **Next**. The Integration Module Export window appears, as shown in Figure 4.29. Select the module to be exported, and ensure that the **EAR files for server deployment** radio button is selected. Click **Next**.

In the Export for Server Deployment window, specify a Target directory. You have the option to change the name of the EAR file or accept the default name. Click **Finish**. The selected module or modules are exported as EAR files for server deployment.

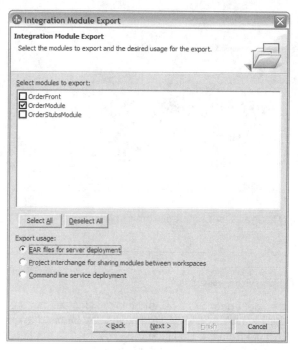

Figure 4.29 Integration Module Export selection screen

Exporting Modules as serviceDeploy Files

WID enables you to export a module as a zip file. It can subsequently be built and deployed as an EAR file using the serviceDeploy command in WPS. You can accomplish that by following the same steps as just described. When you get to the screen shown in Figure 4.29, choose the radio button for **Command line service deployment**.

In the Export for Command Line Deployment screen, shown in Figure 4.30, select a Target filename and location, and then click **Finish**.

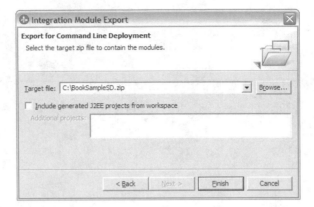

Figure 4.30 Exporting a zip file for command-line deployment

---

serviceDeploy Packaging

By default, all dependencies are automatically included in the serviceDeploy zip file. These dependencies are required to successfully build an EAR file from the zip file and deploy it using the serviceDeploy command-line tool. To better identify a serviceDeploy zip file, we recommend naming it *PROJECT_NAME*SD.zip.

The serviceDeploy utility is found in the *WPS_HOME*/bin folder and in the *WPS_HOME*/profiles/*PROFILE_NAME*/bin folder. The command syntax is

```
serviceDeploy inputArchive [options]
```

Chapter 6 covers the serviceDeploy utility in more depth.

Exporting Modules as Project Interchange Files

You can export a module as a project interchange (PI) file. PI files are not used for deployment. They are a rather convenient way for developers to share modules and their projects with other developers. Before exporting any module as a PI file, you should do a clean build of the project to satisfy all dependencies.

The initial steps are the same as just discussed. When you get to the screen shown in Figure 4.29, choose the radio button for **Project interchange for sharing modules between workspaces**.

In the Export for Project Sharing screen, shown in Figure 4.31, enter the name and location of the Target file, and then click **Finish**. It is a good idea to include dependent projects from the workspace. When we did that, *BookSampleLibrary* got included.

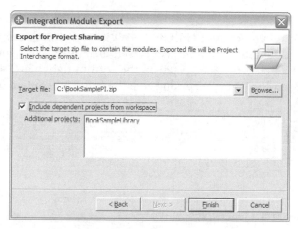

Figure 4.31 Exporting a module as a Project Interchange file

Project Interchange Packaging

To better identify a project interchange zip file, we recommend naming it *PROJECT_NAME*PI.zip.

Testing Modules and Components

You can use the integration test client in WID to test your modules and components. One of the best features of this integration test client is that not all of your modules in a project need to be completed before you test. Any unimplemented component or unwired reference can be emulated by the integration test client.

Module and Component Testing

When you test modules or components, the testing is performed on a component's interface operations. This enables you to determine whether the component is correctly implemented and whether the references are correctly wired. The integrated test client has a user interface that enables you to manage and control the tests. In most cases, the default test configuration is sufficient for you to test your modules and components.

You can use the integration test client to test the following:

- An individual module
- A set of interacting modules
- An individual component
- A set of interacting components

Test Servers

When installing WID, if you chose to install the WPS and WESB test environment profiles, as we suggested, the default test environment servers are already configured. In the Business Integration perspective, click the Servers tab on the bottom-right view (see Figure 4.32). You should see two test servers: WebSphere ESB Server v6.0 and WebSphere Process Server v6.0.

Properties	Problems	Servers	Console			
Server			Host name	Status	State	
WebSphere ESB Server v6.0			localhost	Stopped	Synchronized	
WebSphere Process Server v6.0			localhost	Stopped	Synchronized	

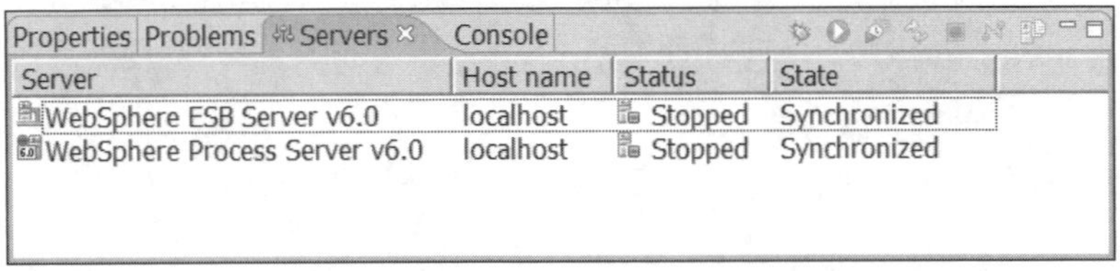

Figure 4.32 The two default test servers in WID

Highlight one of the servers, and click the Start icon (the arrow in a green circle) to start the server, or right-click and choose **Start**. The WID installer is smart enough to configure different ports for the two servers, so you may choose to start both servers at the same time. Before starting a server, check the server configuration by double-clicking the highlighted server. The Server Overview window is displayed. You can choose to use RMI or SOAP as the server's connection type, among other things. You can even enable security in the server if you so choose. Figure 4.32 shows the various options we use when running our test servers.

> **Server Configuration**
>
> Always choose to **Terminate server on workbench shutdown**, as shown in Figure 4.33. That way, when you exit WID, an active server is automatically stopped.

If you change any of the server settings, remember to save the changes by pressing **Ctrl+S** before attempting to start the server. Also, close the Server Overview window, shown in Figure 4.33, before starting a server. If you highlight WebSphere Process Server v6.0 and click the green arrow icon to start it, the Status says *Starting*. Eventually, the status says *Started*, and the state is *Synchronized*.

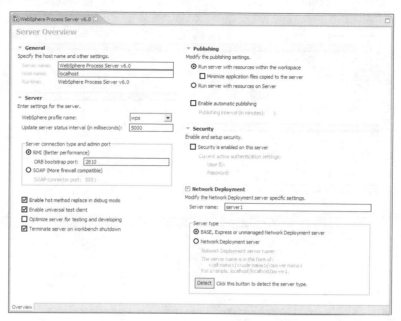

Figure 4.33 Server Overview screen

After the server is in the *Started* state, you can go back to the Servers tab, highlight the started server, and right-click. The context menu that appears lets you do the following:

- Stop or restart the server
- Add and remove projects
- Create tables and data sources
- Run the administrative console
- Launch the BPC Explorer, CBE Event Manager, Business Rules Manager (BRM), Relationship Manager, and so on
- Run or restart the universal test client
- Import or export the server configuration

Before delving into the universal test client, we quickly want to touch on the administrative console for WPS. Highlight the server, right-click, and select **Run administrative console**.

You are asked to log in to the administrative console. In the Welcome screen, shown in Figure 4.34, you should see the Task filtering selector. It is set to **All** by default. You have the choice to control what is displayed in the administrative console.

Figure 4.34 Admin Console of the test WPS

Get familiar with the various menus and submenus in the Navigation pane. The product information center, commonly known as the InfoCenter, contains much online help and information.

Integration Test Client

The integration test client (or test client) is fully integrated into the workbench and is closely integrated with the Assembly Editor. The test client can be launched from either the Assembly Editor or the Business Integration view, and you can launch multiple instances of it. The test client has two main features: Events page and Configurations page.

When you start a test by invoking an operation, the test client automatically detects the deployment state of the module to be tested and the state of the server. If any module is not yet deployed, the test client gives you the option to do that, and if the test server is not running, it starts the server. Chapter 5, "WebSphere Process Server," discusses module deployment to the WPS runtime.

This section discusses four concepts related to the integration test client:

- Test configurations
- Emulators
- Monitors
- Events

A *test configuration* specifies one or more modules to test, each of which can contain zero or more emulators for components or references in the module and zero or more monitors for the wires in the module.

An *emulator* is used when a component or reference in a module is not yet complete. During a test, when control flows to an emulated component or reference, the test client intercepts the invocation and routes it to the associated emulator. Emulators can be either manual or programmatic. When a manual emulator is encountered during a test, the test pauses to enable you, the tester, to manually specify some output parameter values or throw an exception. When a programmatic emulator is encountered, the output parameter values or exception are automatically provided by a Java program contained in a visual or Java snippet.

Monitors listen for any request or response information that flows over the wires and exports during a test. Whenever the integration test client generates a test configuration, monitors are automatically added for component wires and exports that are found in the modules. If either event is detected, the corresponding data that flows is displayed in the events pane of the Component Test editor.

An *event* is something that takes place during a test. When you run a test by invoking an operation in the integration test client, several types of events are generated over the course of the test. Events are either interactive or informational. Only interactive events require you to manually specify values before the test can continue. Return events are always generated by the test client. Some of the other types of events are Invoke events, Started events, Emulate events, Exception events, Attach events, and Stopped events. More detailed information on events can be found in the product online help.

Logging and Troubleshooting

The WID workspace has a Console view that displays the output from the test servers. The Console displays the contents of the SystemOut.log file, which physically resides in the *WID_HOME*/pf/wps/logs/server1 folder. If you need to look up other logs, you can find them in *WID_HOME*/pf/*PROFILE_NAME*/logs. For example, to view the logs associated with starting the WebSphere ESB Server, look in *WID_HOME*/pf/esb/logs/server1, and you will find startServer.log.

> ### Console Configuration
>
> You can use the Preferences dialog (select **Window > Preferences > Run/Debug > Console**) to limit the number of lines displayed in the console.

There is also a Problems view that shows any or all warnings and errors associated with the project in the current workspace. Errors are indicated with an X inside a red circle, and warnings are shown as an exclamation mark in a yellow triangle.

If you double-click any error or warning in the Problems view, WID displays the area of the problem. Sometimes, you can right-click the problem and choose the **Quick Fix** option.

Eclipse Shell Sharing

WID is based on the Eclipse 3.0 framework. It can be configured such that it coexists with either IBM's Rational® Application Developer (RAD) or Rational Software Architect (RSA) in a concept known as *shell sharing*. RAD is installed first, and then WID is installed in the same directory so that the files and libraries common to both products can be shared. On the Windows platform, you have to install RAD in C:\WID, and then you install WID in the same directory.

This enables developers to assume different roles so that they can create business integration applications and web applications or portlet applications that integrate with business process applications. Actually, WID can shell-share with a number of products, such as the WebSphere Modeler, WebSphere Portlet Factory, and others.

Closing the Link

A.4.4

This chapter has touched on some highlights of the power and versatility of WID as an IDE. From a developer's standpoint, the integrated test client and, specifically, the component test feature in WID are invaluable. You can continue developing and testing your piece without having to wait for the rest of the components in a project to be completed.

WID will be used throughout this book to develop various components and showcase its features. We also explain how to integrate the Eclipse plug-ins for WebSphere Business Modeler, WebSphere Business Monitor, and WebSphere Service Registry and Repository.

Links to developerWorks

A.4.1   www.ibm.com/developerworks/websphere/education/enablement/roadmaps.
        html#integration

A.4.2   www.ibm.com/developerworks/websphere/library/techarticles/0612_wayne/0612_
        wayne.html

A.4.3   www.ibm.com/developerworks/websphere/techjournal/0602_gregory/0602_
        gregory.html

A.4.4   http://www-128.ibm.com/developerworks/websphere/zones/devtools/

Chapter 5

WebSphere Process Server

Now that we have discussed the foundation of the programming model and the tools you can use to create business integration solutions, we want to introduce the WebSphere Process Server (WPS) product from IBM. This is the runtime platform where you deploy those applications. At the heart of business integration is a server that facilitates integration of applications, data, and processes. WPS is a robust application server that can run on a single Windows or UNIX® machine, on a mainframe system, or that can be clustered across several different machines.

Describing the details of an integration server is a vast topic that encompasses numerous aspects, such as selecting a deployment topology, planning for availability and failover, security, physical sizing, disaster recovery, and much more. We could easily spend the rest of this book discussing infrastructure aspects. This chapter is an overview that illustrates the fundamental aspects and facilities of the deployment platform.

The *Deploy* step in the Service-Oriented Architecture (SOA) Lifecycle of Model-Assemble-Deploy-Manage, shown in Figure 5.1, follows the development or *Assemble* step. Chapter 2, "Business Integration Architecture and Patterns," and Chapter 4, "WebSphere Integration Developer," discussed in detail the tools and what it takes to assemble the components. This chapter looks at deployment through the eyes of WPS.

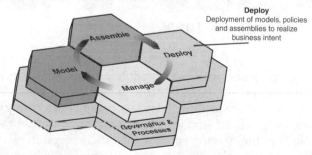

Figure 5.1 Services and components of the SOA Lifecycle

WebSphere Process Server in a Nutshell

A.5.1

WPS can be viewed as an augmentation of the WebSphere Application Server (WAS) product. WAS is IBM's application server for Java enterprise applications and Web services. The primary focus of WAS is providing a robust and scalable deployment platform for standard applications—those that are built around the most popular programming model standards.

WPS and WebSphere Enterprise Service Bus (WESB) are built on top of WebSphere Application Server Network Deployment (WAS ND). WPS provides a runtime for service-oriented architecture built on top of the J2EE runtime provided by WAS. WPS and WESB together provide a runtime environment for an integration developer that hides the complexity of J2EE. WESB is covered in more detail in Chapter 15, "Enterprise Service Bus and Service Registry."

WPS uses the infrastructure and facility provided by WAS and adds significant extensions (based on standards from OASIS and the Open SOA Collaboration) to the base J2EE programming model. The focus of WPS is enabling services-oriented applications. With that said, Figure 5.2 shows the services and components of the Service Component Architecture, which are the services and components available in WPS.

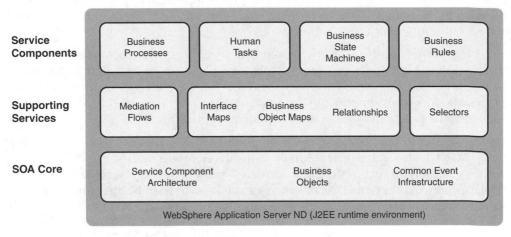

Figure 5.2 Services and components of WPS

The J2EE foundation combined with Service Component Architecture (SCA), Business Objects (BOs), and the Common Event Infrastructure (CEI) forms the SOA Core. The next layer up is Supporting Services, which includes Mediation Flows, Interface Maps, Business Object Maps, Relationships, and Selectors. Mediation Flows are truly a WESB specialty. Rounding it all out are the Service components themselves in BPEL-based Business Processes, Human Tasks, Business State Machines, and Business Rules.

Introduction to WPS Functional Content

Before we discuss how to structure a WPS topology, you need a better understanding of the WPS functional content and the resources needed to support it. Refer to Figure 5.2 to better understand where in the WPS architecture the various functional elements reside.

1. **SCA runtime:** This functional block is responsible for supporting the foundation of the WPS programming model, as discussed in Chapter 2. To properly function, the SCA runtime requires the following:

    - An application server, such as WPS, where the actual SCA runtime code gets executed. SCA is essentially an extension of the base J2EE programming model.
    - A messaging infrastructure. The SCA runtime relies on messaging primarily to implement the asynchronous interaction paradigm. WebSphere Platform Messaging is the current messaging provider used by SCA. Internally, it is called the Service Integration (SI) Bus. The SCA runtime requires two SI Bus instances. The buses are called the SCA Application Bus and the SCA System Bus.
    - A relational database and associated data sources. This database, also called the WPS generic database, stores information about the SCA modules installed on the cell, the failed events that can occur in one-way SCA interactions, and the information about "relationships," as discussed in a moment.

2. **CEI:** The CEI captures events produced by WPS and WESB application components. Those may be "built-in" events, such as the inception of a BPEL process, or the expiration of a Human Task—or custom events—generated by application code that uses the CEI programming interfaces. The CEI can also save the events in a persistent store and distribute them to event consumers for further processing. From an infrastructure perspective, CEI requires the following:

    - An application server to run the CEI Event Server applications. Two applications constitute CEI, and both are based on the J2EE programming model.
    - A messaging infrastructure. Again, you can choose your messaging provider, but we recommend using the SI Bus here, too.
    - A relational database to store the events information and the "event catalog."

3. **Mediation flows support:** Mediation flows can be created as part of the implementation of an ESB. A mediation flow allows a service requester and a service provider to communicate successfully. It also implements the necessary data transformation and endpoint selection logic. These flows are supported by WESB and WPS and are discussed further in Chapter 15. Mediation flows require the following:

    - An application server where they can be installed and run. Mediation flows make use of the SCA programming model.
    - A relational database, where the mediation flows can log the messages they process.

4. **Business Object and Interface Mapping support:** Data transformation is a key requirement of most business integration solutions. WPS supports three types of maps:

- Business Object maps, where you can define the data transformation logic. For example, Application A has a definition of the "Customer" business objects that doesn't exactly match the "Customer" definition in Application B. A BO map can be used to appropriately transform one Customer instance from Application A into a valid Customer instance for Application B.
- Interface maps, where you can define mappings between operations on different interfaces. For example, a component in Application A invokes an operation called *addCustomer* that needs to be reflected in Application B, which defines a similar operation but calls it *createCustomer*. You can create an Interface map to link the two operations, and within the map you can also use a BO map to perform any necessary data transformation.
- Relationship maps are special Interface maps that can ensure that certain instances of BOs are related to each other. For example, the Customer instance with Customer ID equal to "XYZ" in Application A is used to represent the same customer as the Customer instance with Customer Number "0001" in Application B. Relationships can capture this identity and persist it.

All maps are based on the SCA programming model. For the time being, they are supported only in the WPS product. Maps are discussed in Chapter 7, "Business Maps and Business Rules." Maps require the following:

- An application server, such as WPS, where they can be installed and run.
- A relational database, where the relationships can keep their persistent information. As mentioned, this database coincides with the WPS generic database.

5. **Business Rules:** These components allow you to define logic that can be modified using an administrative interface, rather than a development tool. Business rules let you change the behavior of an application solution without needing to redeploy it and enable people who are not members of the development organization to make those changes. The definition of business rules is captured in a persistent store (database). Therefore, Business Rule components require the following:

- An application server, such as WPS, where the Business Rules and the application for their administration can run.
- A relational database to keep the definition of the rules.

6. The **Business Process Choreographer (BPC)** is composed of the Business Process Container and Human Task Container. The BPC is also responsible for running Business State Machines. BPEL processes are discussed in detail in Chapter 6, "Business Processes." Human Tasks and Business State Machines are covered in Chapter 8, "Business State Machines, Human Tasks, and Web Services." BPC requires a set of resources in order to run:

- An application server, such as WPS. Both the BPC and the Human Task Manager (HTM) container take advantage of the server's J2EE programming model.

- A messaging infrastructure. The BPC uses messaging to perform state transitions between the steps of long-running processes. You have a choice of messaging providers, but we recommend that you use WebSphere Default Messaging (SI Bus) for this component as well.
- A relational database and data source. This database stores the "templates" for processes and human tasks and keeps the state of long-running processes.

WPS Infrastructure

Several components make up a typical WPS installation to be completely functional, as shown in Figure 5.3. Later we'll use this figure as a template to help select the optimum topology for our WPS configuration. As mentioned, WPS inherits from WAS and has its own Java Virtual Machine (JVM).

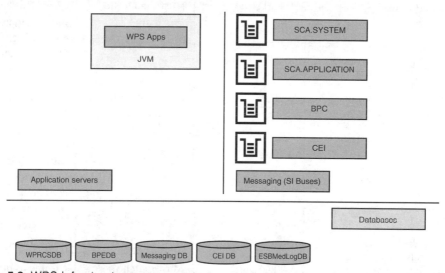

Figure 5.3 WPS infrastructure components

WPS requires a messaging infrastructure for the SCA runtime, the CEI, and the BPC. At present, the only messaging provider that WPS supports for the SCA runtime is WebSphere Default Messaging, internally known as the Service Integration (SI) Bus. We strongly recommend using the SI Bus for the CEI and the BPC. Normally, a WPS installation has four SI Buses:

- Two SI Buses for the SCA runtime (the SCA System Bus and the SCA Application Bus)
- An SI Bus for the CEI
- An SI Bus for the BPC

Finally, WPS uses a number of relational databases to hold, store, and track information. Table 5.1 lists the components of WPS that use databases, along with the default names and schemas.

Table 5.1 Data Abstractions and the Corresponding Implementations

Component	Default Database Name	Default Schema Name	Notes[®]
Business Process Choreographer	BPEDB	None. Must match the username used to connect.	Create this before installing and running any application that uses the BPC. This database *must* be created manually.
Common Event Infrastructure	EVENT	Must match the user name.	Create this before turning on event monitoring. Manual creation is required.
Relationships, Mediation, Recovery, Application Scheduler, Selectors	WPRCSDB	Must match the username.	Create this before starting WPS. This database may be created automatically during installation and configuration, or manually if automatic creation is impractical.
Business Rules	WPRCSDB	Must match the username.	Created as part of the WPS generic database.
SI Bus	None. Determined by the data source used for the connection.	IBMWSSIB	You need to configure either multiple databases (one per SI Bus) or multiple schemas within the same database. These schemas can be created manually, or automatically at server startup.

Component	Default Database Name	Default Schema Name	Notes[®]
Enterprise Service Bus	EsbLogMedDB	ESBLOG (do not modify)	Logger mediation primitive data store. Must be created manually.

As Table 5.1 points out, some database schemas get created automatically, and others have to be created manually. We recommend creating databases manually, because you have better control over the schemas and databases that get created. For the most part, database creation scripts can be found in *WPS_HOME*/dbscripts folder. The ESB Mediation Logger data store creation scripts can be found under *WPS_HOME*/util/EsbLoggerMediation.

> **Database Creation**
>
> The *WPS_HOME*/dbscripts directory has CEI, CommonDB, and ProcessChoreographer subdirectories. The relevant Data Definition Language (DDL) scripts are located in these subdirectories under the specific database type.

Business Process Choreographer (BPC)

The Business Process Choreographer, which is at the heart of WPS, is the J2EE process flow engine that supports BPEL-based business processes and human tasks in WPS. It manages the lifecycle of business processes and human tasks and invokes the appropriate services. Here are some of the functions offered by the BPC:

- It helps expose BPEL processes and human tasks as SCA services.
- It provides Application Programming Interfaces (APIs), which let you develop customized applications that interact with business processes and human tasks.
- It includes the web-based Business Process Choreographer Explorer, which lets you manage and administer the business processes—specifically, human tasks.
- It includes the web-based Business Process Choreographer Observer, which lets you observe the state of running business processes.

The APIs—specifically, the Business Flow Manager (BFM) APIs and the HTM APIs—are explained in Chapter 11, "Business Integration Programming." The related clients—the Business Process Choreographer Explorer and the Business Process Choreographer Observer—are discussed in Chapter 9, "Business Integration Clients."

Terminology and Topology

A.5.2

If you have prior experience with WAS, you will find the following terms and concepts familiar. If you have a basic level of WAS knowledge, it will be easy to understand the concepts and terminology discussed in the following sections. We talk about profiles, nodes, and cells before going into the clustering topologies.

Profiles

Various topologies are made possible by creating one or more profiles. The concept of a profile is also inherited from WAS. With WPS, after you have installed the server, you can create an arbitrary number of profiles. When creating a profile, you can choose from among the following three options:

- The **Stand-alone Profile**, which results in an instance of the Stand-alone configuration (single server). If you want to, you can create multiple Stand-alone profiles on the same physical box and assign different ports to them so that they can run concurrently. However, each configuration has to be administered separately, and you cannot easily balance the application workload across the various instances.
- The **Deployment Manager Profile**, which creates an instance of a Deployment Manager (DM) server. A Deployment Manager alone does not do much in terms of running your applications. Rather, it enables a WPS administrator to control a network of different servers.
- The **Custom Profile**, which represents an empty node, with a Node Agent process definition. After you have successfully created a Custom Profile, you are ready to "federate" the profile with the Deployment Manager. If the DM is running, you have the option to federate the node when you create the Custom Profile. Or you may want to federate later, which you can do via the addNode command.

AddNode Utility

Use the addNode command to federate the node to the Deployment Manager. This command takes two parameters: the hostname of the DM and the port number on which the administrative service listens. Port 8879 is the default port. For example:

```
./addNode.sh adminsystem.mycompany.com 8879
```

If you successfully federate a node, you should see a message that says, "Node has been successfully federated."

Creating a profile is simple. Any time after you install the WPS product, you can open a command prompt and navigate to the *WPS_HOME*/bin/ProfileCreator_wbi directory. There will be an executable prefixed as *pcat* that you can run to kick off the profile creation wizard. The detailed profile creation steps are described in Appendix A, "WebSphere Process Server Installation." Note that if you want to create a base WAS profile, you will find an executable prefixed as *pct* in the *WPS_HOME*/bin/ProfileCreator directory.

> ### Silent Profile Creation
>
> You can even use the "silent" option to create a profile without using the graphical user interface (GUI). However, to do that, you have to supply a response file with all the configuration parameters.

When you create a profile using the profile wizard or use the default profile creation during WPS installation, you have the opportunity to create the WPRCSDB and EVENT databases. By default, they get created as Cloudscape™ databases. These are fine for development and testing, but we do not recommend using Cloudscape in production. If you want to use another database, such as DB2® or Oracle, for your production environment, you have to create a custom profile and run the relevant database creation scripts.

Cells and Nodes

In the Network Deployment configuration, the set of JVM servers controlled by a single Deployment Manager is called a cell. A *cell* is composed of one or more nodes. A *node* is a subset of the servers in a cell, which can be controlled through a special Java process called the Node Agent.

Node Agents are responsible for communicating with the Deployment Manager, which allows centralized administration of a distributed topology. Often, you have a single node per physical system, although it is possible to define multiple nodes on the same physical machine. A node is a logical group of JVM servers that reside on the same physical machine and interact with the Deployment Manager via the same Node Agent.

Figure 5.4 illustrates the concepts described thus far. It shows a cell composed of three systems. System A is dedicated to running the administrative services and hosts the Deployment Manager. System B and System C are nodes within the cell. Each node has its own Node Agent, which enables the Deployment Manager to administer the servers and resources on the nodes. On each node, we have configured two WPS server processes, for a total of four independent processes. Each server can be used to install and run different applications.

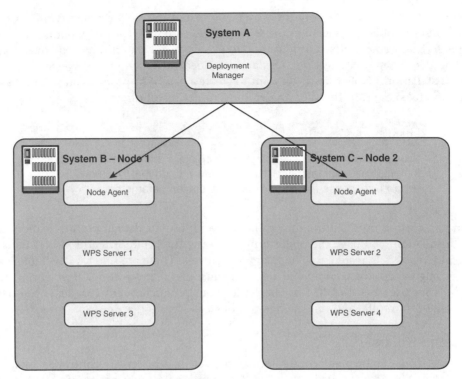

Figure 5.4 WebSphere Process Server cell with two nodes

In WPS, you have the option of creating "plain" WAS profiles. WAS custom profiles can be federated to a WPS Deployment Manager. This means that you can have a "mixed cell" in which WPS nodes and WAS nodes coexist, which is key to large server configurations. Actually, both WPS and WESB support the creation and federation of base WAS ND profiles. Note, you cannot create a WESB profile from WPS.

Here are two common reasons why you might want to create such a mixed cell:

- **Licensing:** WPS licenses have a different cost basis than base WAS licenses. If your applications can run on the base WAS tier, there is no reason to install the tier on a WPS profile, even though you could. It might make more sense to create a base WAS node, for example, to support your web tier, which might not require any of the WPS specific functions.
- **Performance:** Base WAS has a smaller footprint than a WPS server. For applications that do not require any WPS functionality, it makes sense for you to install them on a plain WAS server. WAS servers can also be created out of WPS Custom Profiles. But if you have an entire node dedicated to plain J2EE applications, you will find it advantageous to use a WAS profile.

From a topological perspective, WPS supports two fundamental configurations:

- The **Stand-alone (or single-server) configuration** enables you to run all the WPS components in a single Java process (JVM). This configuration, although supported for production purposes as well, is most suitable for development and testing environments, because it doesn't make any provisions to ensure scalability and failover.
- The **Network Deployment (or cluster) configuration** enables you to run your applications across several different Java processes (or servers). It also supports clustering of servers for scalability and failover. In this configuration, a special process called the Deployment Manager is essentially dedicated to running the administrative facilities.

Installing WPS

WPS can be installed on all the major operating systems. As is done throughout the book, all product installations are described in the appendixes. WPS installation is covered in Appendix A. There is also a section on creating profiles—specifically, a custom profile.

As you see in Appendix A, the WPS installation wizard offers a Client installation choice, which is a partial installation of WPS. It enables you to run client applications, such as WebSphere Portal server, that interact with WPS within the same cell.

> ### Installation Directory
>
> If you are setting up a WebSphere environment, we recommend having a top-level folder of WebSphere and under it have subfolders of AppServer, ProcServer, and so on.

WPS Administration

The WPS administrative console can be accessed at http://*HOST_NAME:PORT*/admin or http://*HOST_NAME:PORT*/ibm/console, where the default port is 9060. The console has been augmented with additional menu items and elements, but the crux of it is still the same administrative console that is used to manage WAS environments. Figure 5.5 shows some of the WPS-specific features in the console. Some of the navigation menus have been expanded to show WPS-unique items, such as the panels for administering SCA Modules under Applications.

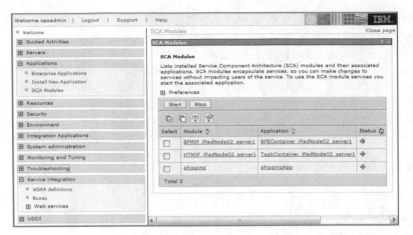

Figure 5.5 Some of the WPS-specific features of the Administrative Console

---

Command-line Utility

The command-line administrative interface, *wsadmin*, is also available in WPS. It can be used to perform administrative tasks, especially when it comes to deleting profiles or doing a non-GUI installation.

Starting and Stopping WPS

You can use the desktop menu to start the process server. For example, on a Windows XP system, you can start the process server by selecting **Start** > **All Programs** > **IBM WebSphere** > **Process Server 6.0** > **Profiles** > *PROFILE_NAME* > **Start the server**. Or you can use the command-line equivalent. For example, on UNIX systems you invoke *WPS_HOME*/profiles/*PRO-FILE_NAME*/startServer.sh. There are corresponding commands to stop the server.

Stopping a Secure Server

If WebSphere Global Security has been enabled and you attempt to stop the process server, you are prompted for the authentication credentials.

Similarly, to start and stop the Deployment Manager, you use the startManager and stopManager scripts found in *WPS_HOME*/profiles/*DMGR_PROFILE*/bin directory. To start and stop the Node Agents, you use the startNode and stopNode scripts that are found in the *WPS_HOME*/profiles/*PROFILE_NAME*/bin directory.

Key Steps in Creating a WPS Cell

You can proceed in many different ways to set up your WPS cell. Here is the high-level sequence of steps to construct a new WPS cell:

1. Install the WPS product binaries on all the physical boxes that the cell is composed of.

2. Create the Deployment Manager profile on the system that you have elected for the administration tasks. During this task, you have the option of creating the database that is needed for WPS. If you prefer, the database can also be created in advance using scripts available in the *WPS_HOME*/dbscripts directory.

3. Create a Custom Profile on the systems that will host the nodes.

4. Start the Deployment Manager process.

5. On each system where you created a Custom profile, federate the node to the Deployment Manager.

6. At this point, you have an "empty cell" where the Deployment Manager and the Node Agents are defined.

However, the cell that is created does not contain any application servers that you can use to deploy and run your applications. You are now ready to configure the logical topology of your WPS cell by creating the servers and clusters you need within the cell. The next few sections discuss the principles you should take into consideration to determine how to structure the cell's logical topology.

WPS Clustered Topologies

If you are new to WPS, you may choose to skip this section. Clustering, failover, scalability, high availability (HA), and workload management are considered to be advanced topics. They are indispensable in a business integration production environment.

A.5.3

Cluster

In WPS, the key technique to allow for scalability and failover is represented by the application server clustering. *Clustering* is made available in the base WAS product, and WPS can also take advantage of its features. A cluster is a set of servers (JVMs) that are logically grouped and that run exactly the same set of applications. Each server that participates in a cluster is called a *cluster member*. When you install an application on a cluster, the application is automatically installed on each cluster member.

After you define a cluster, you have to administer applications at the cluster level. You won't be able to install or make changes on an individual cluster member. This constraint ensures that all the cluster members are functionally equivalent and that application requests can be distributed across the various cluster members. This workload distribution is the key to scalability. Workload can be distributed across cluster members in many different ways:

- HTTP requests can be scattered across the cluster members using a request dis-patcher. An example of such a dispatcher is the Web Server Plug-in, provided by WAS and WPS.
- EJB requests can be distributed across the cluster by the WebSphere Object Request Broker (ORB) itself.
- JMS messages can be consumed by different instances of the same Message-Driven Bean running on different cluster members. A certain message is consumed only on the server cluster member that "grabs" it. However, statistically, you will observe a degree of workload distribution, as the different cluster members "compete" for the messages on the queues or topics.

In terms of failover, the functional equivalence of cluster members ensures that, if a cluster member fails, its workload can fail over to any one of the surviving members. Cluster mem-bers can exist on the same box ("vertical" clustering) or on different systems ("horizontal" clustering).

Vertical clustering is mostly used to ensure failover at the server instance JVM process level: If a JVM experiences a crash, workload can failover on the surviving process (or processes). However, true scalability is ensured only by horizontal clustering, because horizontal topologies are composed of multiple physical systems. Horizontal clustering enables your deployment environment to achieve resilience to hardware failures, because the workload can fail over to a different system if one of the nodes in the configuration becomes unavail-able. Horizontal and vertical clustering can be combined, as shown in Figure 5.6.

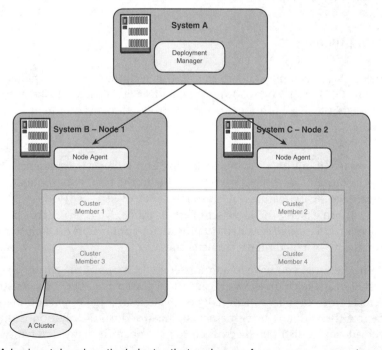

Figure 5.6 A horizontal and vertical cluster that embraces four servers across two nodes

Figure 5.6 depicts a topology similar to what was illustrated in Figure 5.4, but this time, the four servers are not independent; they are part of a single cluster, as shown by the shaded area. This means that we cannot install different applications on each server. Rather, all servers within the cluster run the same applications, which enables workload distribution. If one of these servers (or an entire node) fails, the remaining servers can take care of the workload previously assigned to the failing server or servers. We talk about failover later in this chapter.

Clustering WPS Components

Clustering the SCA Runtime, CEI Event Server, and BPC/HTM Containers relies on the application server's J2EE runtime. To cluster them for failover and availability, all you need to do is configure them in a cluster of WPS servers. When you cluster the J2EE runtime, each of the cluster members can actively process transactions. Each cluster member uses a flat file called the *transaction log* or *tran log*, which permits a two-phase commit transaction recovery.

If a cluster member fails, a component of WAS called the High Availability (IIA) Manager can activate an additional transaction manager on one of the surviving cluster members, and that cluster member can recover the pending transactions. This mechanism is possible only if all the cluster members have access to each others' transaction logs, such as via a shared file system. Figure 5.7 illustrates this mechanism.

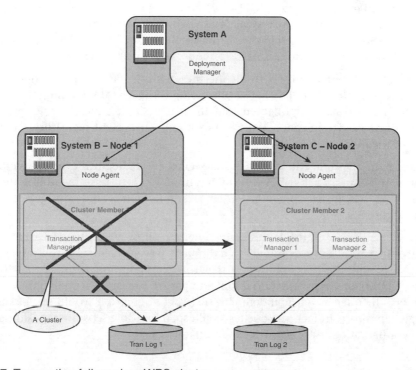

Figure 5.7 Transaction failover in a WPS cluster

Figure 5.7 illustrates how in-flight transactions can be recovered in case of failure of a cluster member. The figure also shows that, when Cluster Member 1 fails, an equivalent transaction manager is automatically activated on the surviving cluster member. The equivalent transaction manager needs access to the transaction log of the failed server (Tran Log 1), which therefore must reside on a highly available and shared file system.

Clustering the SI Bus

An SI Bus is a logical construct that enables you to configure, among other things, messaging destinations such as queues and topics. However, to be of any use, an SI Bus needs a physical infrastructure to run the messaging services. This physical infrastructure is called a *Messaging Engine* (ME).

An ME is created when you add an application server as a *member* of the SI Bus. In fact, not only can you add a server as a member of an SI Bus, you also can add a cluster of servers. By making a cluster a member of an SI Bus, you implicitly cluster the resulting ME.

A clustered ME can take advantage of the failover support provided by the HA Manager in a way that is similar to that described in the previous section for the Transaction Manager. However, from the perspective of workload distribution, clustering an SI Bus is significantly different from clustering transaction managers.

When you add a cluster as a member of an SI Bus, the resulting ME is active on only one of the cluster members, according to a "1-of-*n*" type of HA policy. The reason for this is the nature of the work performed by the ME. The ME may need to ensure that messages from a certain destination are processed in their arrival sequence and are delivered to stateful applications that may be waiting for a specific response on a specific server.

These requirements are common to all the messaging infrastructure products that exist today. The only applicable policy for ME clustering is the 1-of-*n* HA policy, as illustrated in Figure 5.8. Here we have highlighted that there is a single image of the queues in the Messaging database. For instance, there is only a single persistent repository for all the destinations of the ME.

This topology implies that the ME in Cluster Member 2 is idle until Cluster Member 1 fails. If you want to adopt an active/active configuration, you can do so by adding the multiple instances of an ME in the same cluster. For example, you would configure two MEs, as shown in Figure 5.9.

By doing so, you create multiple messaging engines, all of which have an active instance. Each active instance can be "pinned" to a different server, making all the servers "active." However, it is important to understand that this configuration requires that each active instance of an ME use its own database tables to persist messages, as shown in Figure 5.9. In other words, the queues that you define in such a configuration would not be represented by a single repository. In fact, the queues would span multiple separate repositories. We say that this configuration uses "partitioned destinations."

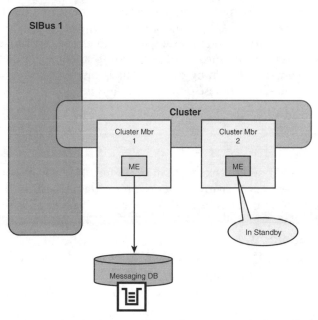

Figure 5.8 A messaging engine is clustered according to an active/standby policy.

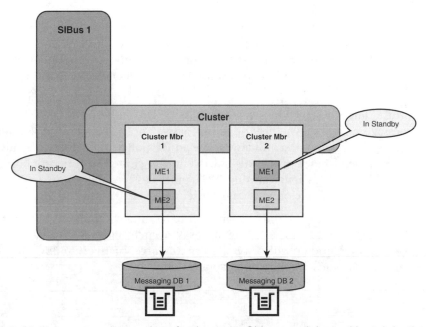

Figure 5.9 Multiple messaging engines for the same SI bus result in partitioned destinations.

Partitioned destinations imply that the messages that are sent to a destination queue can end up in any one of the different physical "bins" where messages are stored. In such a configuration, there is no way to ensure, for example, that messages are processed in sequence, or that a response message is returned to the partition that corresponds to the application that produced the request. Partitioning destinations is discouraged because of the limitations that these configurations impose on the applications.

Topology Choices

Now that you understand how each element can be clustered, let's review some of the common topological options. There can be many variations on a certain topology. This section presents some of the base topologies that can be modified to suit your needs and environment.

Single-Server Topology

In the single-server topology, all the elements of a WPS environment run in the same server. Additionally, the server is not clustered. Such a topology can be obtained either by creating a Stand-alone Profile or by creating a nonclustered server in a Network Deployment cell.

As mentioned, single-server topologies are seldom adopted in production environments because of their lack of support for failover and scalability.

Single-Cluster Topology

The logical next step is to start with a single-server topology and to create a cluster from it. This approach is common in application environments based on WAS, and it is also supported in WPS. However, the presence of the SI Bus in the mix of components required by all WPS applications prompts some important critical considerations regarding this topology.

At present, the SI Bus is designed in a way that Message-Driven Beans (MDBs) always "bind" to a local messaging engine, whether the ME is "active" or in "standby." If you remember from the previous discussion, the MEs always use an HA policy of "1-of-n" in a cluster. This means that only one instance of the ME is active in the cluster. In turn, applications that consume messages—such as long-running BPEL processes or applications with asynchronous SCA calls—also are active on only one cluster member, as shown in Figure 5.10.

In other words, if you configure the MEs and the remaining components within the same cluster and your applications include human tasks, asynchronous SCA calls, or long-running processes, you will end up with a topology that is largely active/standby. This topology allows for failover but not scalability of all applications.

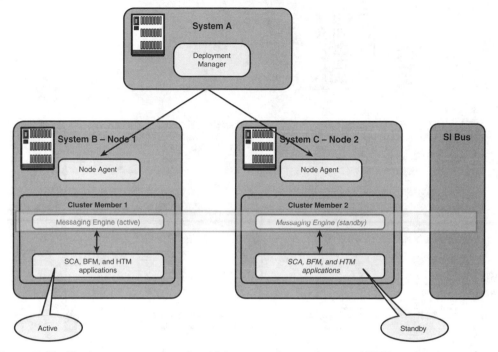

Figure 5.10 Single-server topology in which messaging engines and WPS applications coexist

For this reason, the single-cluster topology is almost never recommended. The only situations in which you can tolerate such a configuration are those in which one of the following conditions is met:

- The active/standby behavior does not impact capacity, and clustering is used only to ensure failover.
- You do not plan to run asynchronous SCA interactions, long-running processes, or human tasks.

Single-Cluster Topology with Partitioned Destinations

Let's see how we can remove some of the limitations of the single-cluster topology. This problem is solved by creating multiple MEs and partitioning the destinations, as shown in Figure 5.11. The figure shows that we have created multiple MEs for the same SI Bus so that there is an active ME on every cluster member.

However, by doing so, we also had to partition the destinations for that bus. This topology has the advantage of being limited to a single cluster, but it introduces additional complexity and new functional limitations because there are partitioned destinations. We suggest that you avoid partitioning your destinations unless you are certain that the ME is becoming the bottleneck for the entire configuration.

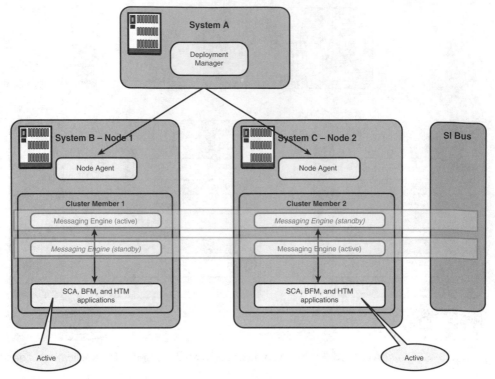

Figure 5.11 Single-cluster topology with partitioned destinations.

Multiple-Cluster Topologies

If you configure the MEs in a separate cluster—different from the cluster where the WPS applications run—the MDBs that use those MEs need to bind to the "remote" MEs. Because there are no local MEs, all MDBs actively consume messages from the remote MEs. In other words, all the members of the cluster where the WPS applications are configured can now actively work.

Figure 5.12 illustrates the first example of a multiple-cluster topology. It illustrates a topology with two separate clusters. The first cluster (composed of cluster members 1 and 2) is used for the messaging engines, and the second cluster (composed of cluster members 3 and 4) is used for the applications. Notice that the ME cluster functions in active/standby, but the application cluster is fully functional (active/active). This is because both cluster members 3 and 4 can "bind" to an active remote ME.

Further, separation can also be achieved by isolating the CEI functionality by way of a cluster of Event Servers, as shown in Figure 5.13. The figure shows three separate clusters, one of which is now dedicated to the CEI Event Server. Such a topology enables you to construct a centralized event server, which can be used to monitor a number of different WPS application clusters.

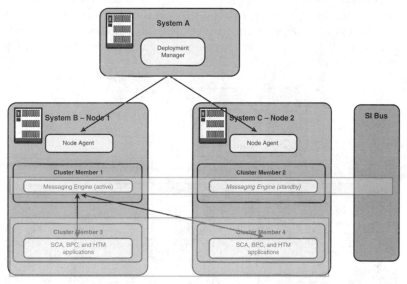

Figure 5.12 Multiple-cluster topology in which the messaging engines run in their own cluster

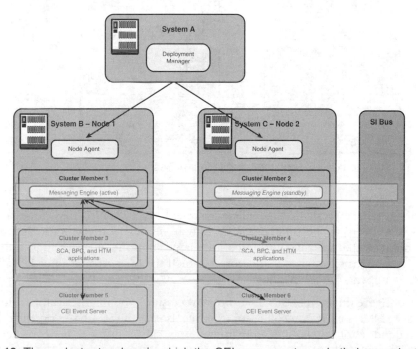

Figure 5.13 Three-cluster topology in which the CEI components run in their own cluster

So far, for the sake of simplicity, we have shown topologies that include only two physical nodes. In larger environments, you might want to configure a larger number of nodes. For example, if four physical systems are available, you can dedicate two of them to running WPS applications, and the remaining two can support the MEs and the CEI Event Server, as illustrated in Figure 5.14. The figure shows a cell with four nodes. Nodes 1 and 2 are dedicated to running the CEI server and the messaging engines. Nodes 3 and 4 are dedicated to running the WPS applications.

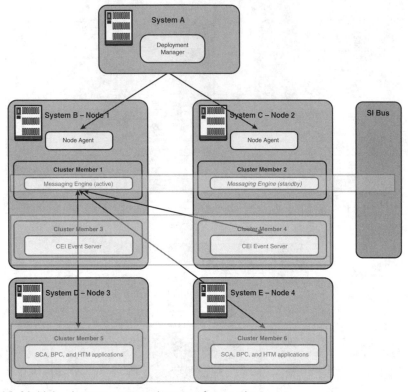

Figure 5.14 Multiple clusters scattered across four nodes

Conceptually, you can scale up such an environment just by adding new nodes and cluster members to the WPS application cluster. Keeping in mind that the MEs run active/standby in the topologies that we have illustrated, in a large environment with high transactional volumes, you might experience a situation in which the MEs become a bottleneck. For the MEs to scale up, you can follow these steps:

1. Configure different SI Buses on different clusters. You might recall that four different SI Buses exist. You could, for example, isolate the SCA buses on their own cluster and set of systems and configure another cluster just for the CEI SI Bus and one for the BPC SI Bus.

2. If that configuration still proves to be insufficient, the next step is to attempt partitioning the destinations. Note that partitioned destinations are incompatible with certain types of asynchronous interactions—for example, when messages need to be processed in a certain order.

3. Application partitioning is sometimes possible and provides a different approach to scalability if the volumes prove to be prohibitively high. You can consider configuring multiple clusters for the BPC and HTM applications.

Closing the Link

The beauty of WPS is that it takes advantage of everything that WAS has to offer plus provides the kind of runtime needed in a business integration solution. We already saw in Chapter 4 that the ITE has a full installation of WPS. Developers can develop and test applications in WebSphere Integration Developer (WID) and be assured that those same applications will work in a WPS production environment.

As we mentioned at the start of this chapter, when it comes to choosing and configuring a WPS topology, numerous options exist. As you complete this chapter, we strongly suggest that you refer to detailed literature on the subject to get a better understanding of what each topological choice implies.

The WPS product documentation covers everything from architecture to installation to administration. It can be accessed (in both HTML and Adobe® Acrobat formats) at http://publib.boulder.ibm.com/infocenter/dmndhelp/v6rxmx/index.jsp.

Additional information on the rather advanced topic of clustered topologies can be found in the following resources:

- The Redbook publication "Production Topologies for WebSphere Process Server and WebSphere ESB V6," SG24-7413, available at www.redbooks.ibm.com/abstracts/sg247413.html?Open
- IBM developerWorks articles:
  "Clustering WebSphere Process Server 6.0.2 (Part 1)," available at www.ibm.com/developerworks/websphere/library/techarticles/0704_chilanti/0704_chilanti.html
  "Clustering WebSphere Process Server 6.0.2 (Part 2)," available at www.ibm.com/developerworks/websphere/library/techarticles/0704_chilanti2/0704_chilanti2.html
  "WebSphere Process Server and WebSphere Enterprise Service Bus Deployment Patterns," available at www.ibm.com/developerworks/websphere/library/techarticles/0610_redlin/0610_redlin.html

Links to developerWorks

A.5.1   www.ibm.com/developerworks/websphere/zones/businessintegration/wps/
         wps.html

A.5.2   www.ibm.com/developerworks/websphere/library/techarticles/0612_wayne/
         0612_wayne.html

A.5.3   www.ibm.com/developerworks/websphere/library/techarticles/0703_redlin/
         0703_redlin.html

Chapter 6

Business Processes

A business process is not to be confused with workflow. We have already mentioned that a business process is a set of interrelated tasks linked to an activity. A workflow, on the other hand, is the way work gets done. It is dependent on the business process underneath it since workflow is driven by the process logic and routing rules.

Chapter 3, "Business Orchestration," showed you how Business Process Execution Language (BPEL) has emerged as the standard for business processes. Chapter 4, "WebSphere Integration Developer," discussed WID, the tooling used to create process artifacts and applications. Chapter 5, "WebSphere Process Server," provided an overview of business processes from the server's perspective and touched on the Business Process Choreographer, popularly called the Choreographer. This chapter takes an in-depth look at creating a sample process application. In the process, no pun intended, we describe how to create and use simple and advanced BPEL features.

A.6.1

Sample Application

This chapter explains WebSphere Process Server's support for BPEL in great detail using an order processing system that is illustrated by the WID assembly diagram shown in Figure 6.1. The assembly diagram gives the overall perspective of all the components in the application and how they are wired together.

The main business process is *CreateOrderProcess*, and users create new orders by invoking it. This process needs to be fast, because its caller is a user sitting at a browser. In *CreateOrderProcess*, if everything goes well, it gets credit information about the customer using *CustomerService*. Then it automatically validates the customer's credit using *AutomaticCreditCheckService* before initiating a shipment of the order using *ShipOrderProcess*.

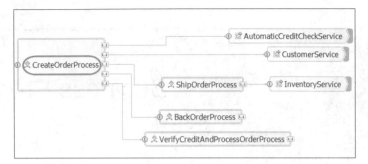

Figure 6.1 Assembly diagram of the sample application

However, several things can go wrong along the way. For example, perhaps the customer's credit cannot be automatically ascertained, or there might be insufficient stock to fulfill the order. In these cases, we still want to accept the order, but we need to free up the customer by letting him know that his order will be processed soon. To fulfill these requirements, we build the business process as a set of processes that interact with other services to complete the order.

Figure 6.2 provides a high-level view of the processes and how they interact with each other.

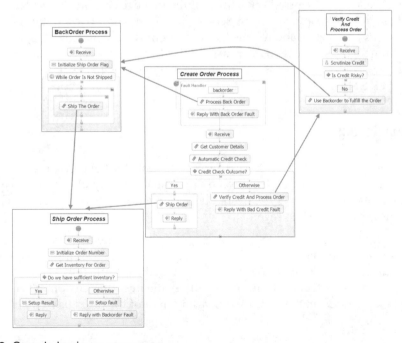

Figure 6.2 Sample business processes

- **CreateOrderProcess** is the main process. Because it needs to be executed quickly, we will make it short-running. This process accepts the order, verifies that the customer's credit is good, and calls *ShipOrderProcess* to ship the order so that we can reply to the customer with that result.

  If the *ShipOrderProcess* determines that there is insufficient stock, it throws a *BackOrderFault*. The main process, *CreateOrderProcess*, then calls the one-way process, *BackOrderProcess*, to fulfill the order and replies to the customer with a *BackOrderFault* informing him that the item he ordered is on back order.

  If the automatic verification of the customer's credit does not establish that the customer has good credit, we won't want to automatically fulfill the order. However, to still try to process the order, we call the one-way process, *VerifyCreditAndProcess OrderProcess*, to manually verify the customer's credit along with any subsequent fulfillment of that order. We then inform the customer that we've received the order and are processing it.

  > **One-Way Operation**
  >
  > Operations can be defined as one-way or two-way operations. One-way operations do not have a return value and do not declare any faults. When a client invokes a one-way process, it does not have to wait for that process to complete. This works well when one of the requirements is for the client process to respond quickly.

- **ShipOrderProcess** is a short-running subprocess that checks the inventory of the ordered item and ships it. If sufficient inventory is not available, this subprocess throws a *BackOrderFault* to let the caller know that it needs to retry shipping the order at a future date.

- **VerifyCreditAndProcessOrderProcess** is a long-running process that involves manual intervention to verify a customer's credit. If you remember from the *CreateOrderProcess* paragraphs, the main process automatically verifies the customer's credit, possibly using some rules. If the automatic rules cannot determine that the credit is good, we don't necessarily want to reject the order. We might want an approver to look at the customer's credit and determine if the credit is acceptable.

  VerifyCreditAndProcessOrderProcess uses IBM BPEL's human task activities to enable a human to verify the credit and then fulfill the order if the approver deems the customer credit acceptable.

- **BackOrderProcess** is a long-running process that is used to fulfill the order if we had insufficient inventory at the time the order was booked. The main task of this process is to wake up periodically to check the inventory and to try to ship the order. As you'll see later in this chapter, this process also provides a mechanism to let an administrator or supervisor request that an attempt to ship the order be made before the process has finished waiting for the next try.

Working with a Short-Running Business Process

 A short-running business process, also known as a microflow, is described as a business
process that runs within a single transaction. We show you how to create one using IBM's
A.6.2 WID as we continue to build our *BookSample* project. All this is done in the Business
Integration perspective in WID.

Creating a Short-Running Process

The name of our short-running process is *CreateOrderProcess*.

1. Select **File** > **New** > **Business Process** to bring up the New Business Process wizard,
   as shown in Figure 6.3.

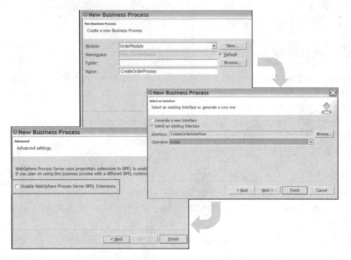

Figure 6.3 Adding a new business process

2. On the main page of the wizard, select **OrderModule** from the drop-down list and
   enter *CreateOrderProcess* as the name of the process. Click **Next**.

3. On the Select an Interface page, click the **Browse** button to bring up a dialog with
   a list of all interfaces that can be used by this module. Select the *CreateOrderInterface*
   for this process, and click **OK**.

4. Back on the Select an Interface page, click **Next** to go to the Advanced Settings page.
   You have the option of disabling IBM BPEL Extensions. Because we want to make
   this a short-running process, uncheck the **Disable WebSphere Process Server BPEL
   Extensions** checkbox.

5. Click **Finish** on the Advanced Settings page to finish creating the *CreateOrderProcess*
   business process.

Adding Reference Partners

A big part of a typical business process is that it invokes a number of services to implement the business logic. The services that the process interacts with are called partners. Each partner that is invoked by the business process needs to be added to the process in the Process Editor as a *Reference Partner*.

As shown in Figure 6.1, *CreateOrderProcess* interacts with a number of services. Some of these services, such as *ShipOrderProcess*, are BPEL processes. Others, such as *CustomerService*, are not. To add *CustomerService* as a Reference Partner, as shown in Figure 6.4, do the following in the Business Process Editor:

1. From the tray on the right side, click the + button next to Reference Partners to add a new partner. This adds a new Reference Partner with a default name of "Partner." You can rename it something meaningful, such as *CustomerInformationPartner*, by typing over the default name.

2. Next, you assign an interface to the partner. With *CustomerInformationPartner* selected in the tray, click the **Details** tab in the Properties view below the Process Editor. In the Details tab, click the **Browse** button to bring up the Interface Selection wizard, where you can select *CustomerInfoInterface* as the partner's interface. Click **OK**.

For each of the other services that are used by *CreateOrderProcess*, you need to add Reference Partners as just shown.

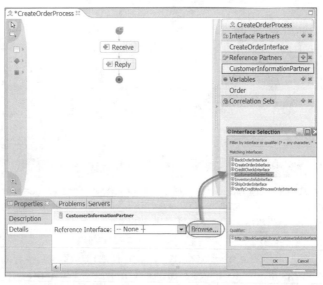

Figure 6.4 Adding a Reference Partner

Invoking a Partner Operation

Now that the partner is added, you can invoke operations on it. To add an Invoke activity, as shown in Figure 6.5, do the following:

1. Click the **Activity** icon in the palette. Move the mouse cursor over the canvas to the area between the Receive and the Reply Activities. Click to add Invoke.

   The activity has a default name of "Invoke." Rename it to something more meaningful, such as *Get Customer Details*.

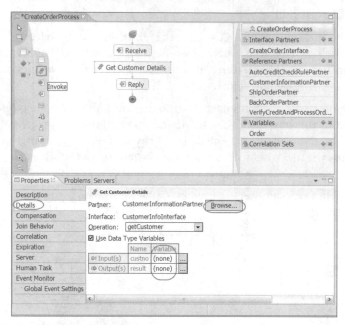

Figure 6.5 Adding an Invoke activity

> **Cursor**
>
> Note that the icon next to the cursor indicates whether you can add the Invoke activity. If the icon is a plus symbol, you can click to add the activity. Otherwise, it is a crossed-out circle.

2. After you've added the Invoke activity, you need to associate it with a partner and choose the operation to invoke on that partner. With the *Get Customer Details* Invoke activity selected in the canvas, click the **Details** tab in the Properties area to edit details about this Invoke. In the Details pane, do the following:

   Click the **Browse** button next to the partner to bring up the Partner Selection wizard. Select *CustomerInformationPartner*, and click **OK**. The *Partner*, *Interface*, and

Operation fields, along with Input and Output field names for the Invoke, get automatically populated.

Assign variables to the activity's Input and Output parameters.

Click the **...** button next to the *custno* input to bring up the Variable Selection dialog. Because a variable corresponding to the *custno* input doesn't exist, click the **New** button in the Variable Selection dialog to create a new variable. Enter *CustomerNumber* in the New Variable dialog, and click **OK**. Click **OK** in the Variable Selection dialog to assign the newly created variable to the Invoke's input.

Do the same for the operation's output, "result," creating a new variable named *Result*.

Using an Assign Activity

In the preceding section, you added an *Invoke* activity to the business process and created the input and output variables for it. To initialize the input variable (*CustomerNumber*) that is passed into the service, we make use of an *Assign* activity.

To add an *Assign* activity, do the following:

1. Click the *Assign* activity in the palette, and move the mouse cursor between the *Receive* and *Get Customer Details* Invoke activities, and click to add the *Assign* activity. Rename the *Assign* to *Init Customer Number*.

2. Making sure that *Init Customer Number* is selected, click the **Details** tab in the Properties view to initialize the *CustomerNumber* variable, as shown in Figure 6.6.

   In the From: section on the left, select **Variable** from the drop-down list. In the variable tree, expand the *Order* variable, and select **custno**. In the To: section, select **Variable** from the drop-down list, and select the **CustomerNumber** variable.

> **Multiple Assignments**
>
> If you want to initialize more than one variable, you can add a new part to this Assign activity by clicking the **New** button.

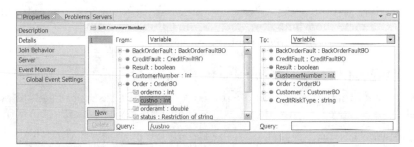

Figure 6.6 Initializing variables using an Assign

Using a Choice Activity

The *CreateOrderProcess* performs a credit check on the customer to determine if it can fulfill the order. Depending on the outcome of the credit check, the process ships the order. We use the *Choice* activity to perform different activities based on the outcome of the *Automatic Credit Check* activity. To add a *Choice*, do the following:

1. Click the **Choice** activity in the Process Editor palette. Move the mouse cursor between the *Automatic Credit Check* activity and the *Reply*, and click (see Figure 6.7). This adds a Choice with one case. Rename the Choice *Credit Check Outcome?* by typing over the highlighted text.

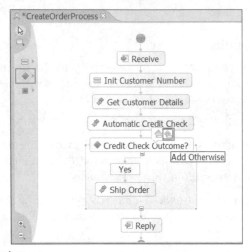

Figure 6.7 Adding a Choice

2. To rename the *Case*, select it in the canvas, and then click the **Description** tab in the Properties view. In the Display Name field, enter the value **Yes**.

3. To add an Otherwise branch, click the **Choice** activity. From the Choice's Action Bar, select the **Add Otherwise** icon. This adds an Otherwise branch to the Choice.

At this point, the short-running business process is mostly done. A few more things need to be added to complete the whole flow, such as the Otherwise branch in the *Choice* activity and throwing faults in case of an error in the process flow.

Using the Visual Snippet Editor for the Choice Branch

The *Choice* activity that was added in the preceding step has a case that needs to evaluate to true or false. To achieve this, we add an expression to the *Yes* case by following these steps:

1. With the **Yes** case selected, click the **Details** tab in the Properties view.

2. For the expression language, select **Same as Process (Java)**, and for the Expression, select the **Visual** radio button.

3. In the Visual Editor canvas, click **true** and replace it with *CreditRiskType.equalsIgnoreCase("LOW")*. This should still be wired to the *Return*.

> **Expression Language**
>
> In addition to XPath as an expression language in the BPEL editor, IBM provides rich support for the use of Java as an expression language.

Defining a Fault

The *CreditOrderInterface* defines a *CreditFaultBO* fault that can be thrown by the BPEL in case a customer's credit is bad. To reply with a fault from the *CreateOrderProcess*, follow these steps:

A.6.3

1. Select the **Reply** Activity in the palette, and add it to the *Otherwise* branch of the choice. Rename the *Reply* to *Reply With Bad Credit Fault* by overwriting the selected text.

2. With **Reply With Bad Credit Fault** selected, click the **Details** tab in the Properties view to edit the *Reply* properties and make it return a fault, as shown in Figure 6.8.

   Click the *Partner* **Browse** button and select *CreateOrderInterface* from the Interface Selection dialog. This populates the other fields in the Details tab.

   Click the **Fault** radio button to indicate that the response is a fault, and then select **badcredit** from the drop-down list of faults.

   Click the ... button next to the *create_badcredit* fault to create a new Bad Credit Fault variable. Name the fault *CreditFault*.

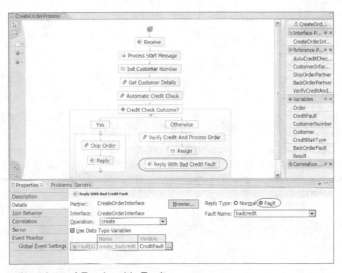

Figure 6.8 Properties view of Reply with Fault

The later section, "Fault Handlers," describes the addition of a fault handler. Make sure you save your edits by pressing **Ctrl+S**.

Working with a Long-Running Business Process

A long-running business process, also known as a macroflow, can span multiple transactions and can be active anywhere from an hour to years. Typically, business processes that contain human tasks or that need to wait for external events to resume execution after they are started are long-running processes.

Creating a Long-Running Process

Just like we did while creating the *CreateOrderProcess* process, launch the process creation wizard and create a process named *VerifyCreditAndProcessOrderProcess* that implements the *VerifyCreditAndProcessOrderInterface* interface. To make this process long-running, follow these steps:

1. Click anywhere in the empty area of the Process Editor canvas to select the process, and then click the **Details** tab in the Properties view.

2. Select the **Process is long-running** checkbox, as shown in Figure 6.9. This makes *VerifyCreditAndProcessOrderProcess* a long-running process.

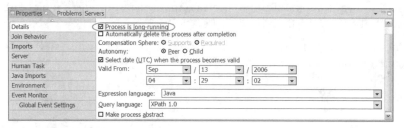

Figure 6.9 Making a long-running process

BPEL Versioning

The Details tab in the Properties view of the business process contains an attribute named **Valid From**. This is important for versioning BPEL processes, as discussed in Chapter 10, "Business Integration Services Management."

Empty Action

The *Empty Action* feature in BPEL enables you to build the process flow without having to worry about wiring all the partners or defining and assigning variables. After you've gotten the flow fleshed out, you can go back and replace the *Empty Action* by changing it to what you really need the process to perform. Figure 6.10 shows an example of the *VerifyCreditAndProcessOrderProcess*, whose flow has been built using *Empty Actions*. The following steps show how to add and subsequently replace an *Empty Action*:

1. To add an *Empty Action*, click the **Empty Action** icon in the Process Editor palette, and then move the mouse cursor to the area in the canvas where you want to add it. Change the name to something meaningful by overwriting the selected text for the *Empty Action*.

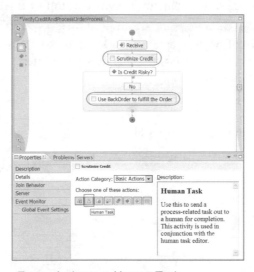

Figure 6.10 Switching an *Empty Action* to a Human Task

2. To replace an *Empty Action,* select it and click the **Details** tab in the Property view. In the Details tab, click the icon of the activity you want to switch the *Empty Action* to. For example, *Scrutinize Credit* requires a person to examine the customer's credit, so click the **Staff Action** icon to make the *Empty Action* a Human Task. Likewise, *Use BackOrder to fulfill Order* is a call to a service, so click the **Invoke** icon after selecting this *Empty Action* to make the change.

Using a Human Task

The *VerifyCreditAndProcessOrderProcess* requires a human to check the customer's credit and then determine the risk. You just modified the *Scrutinize Credit* Activity to be a *Human Task*.

Human Task

WPS supports inline human tasks in a BPEL process and stand-alone human tasks. We modeled an inline task in this example. If we were to use a stand-alone human task, we would have added a partner reference, just as we would have for any other service, and then would have used the Invoke activity to call it. Details about Human Tasks are covered in Chapter 8, "Business State Machines, Human Tasks, and Web Services."

After the *Human Task* activity is added to the process, we need to create a *Human Task* to support it. To create the *Human Task*, select the **Scrutinize Credit** node, and click the **Details** tab in the Properties view. On the Details tab, follow these steps to create a new human task:

1. Click the **New** button to create a new *Human Task*. This brings up the Interface Selection dialog. Select *CreditCheckInterface* as the interface to use for this *Human Task*, and then click **OK**.

2. In the Select Operation dialog, select the **checkCredit** operation, and click **OK** to create the new *Human Task*. The newly created *Human Task* is opened in the Human Task Editor, as shown in Figure 6.11.

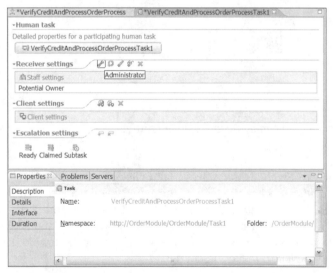

Figure 6.11 Human Task Editor

The Human Task Editor lets you set a variety of properties, such as who can work on or be the administrator of the task and what the escalation policies are for this task.

1. To initialize who can work on the task, select the **Potential Owner** in the **Receiver settings** section of the Human Task Editor canvas. The Properties view changes to display the *Staff Group* properties for this task, as shown in Figure 6.12. Select the verb **Group Members** from the **Staff Group (Verb)** drop-down list.

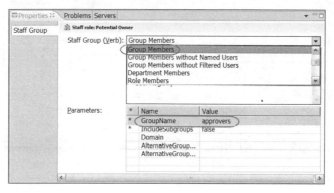

Figure 6.12 *Staff Group* properties

2. The list of parameters that can be set for this verb changes to match the selected verb.

Using the *While Loop*

The *While Loop* is a BPEL activity that provides looping capabilities in a business process. It enables a block of activities to be executed repeatedly while a certain condition holds true. The *BackOrderProcess* process in our sample application uses a *While Loop* to ensure that an Order is shipped. It invokes *ShipOrderProcess* repeatedly in a *While Loop* until the *ShipOrderProcess* service returns a status stating that the Order has been shipped. This process is illustrated in Figure 6.13.

To add a *While Loop*, click the **While Loop** icon (the yellow circular icon) in the palette, and drag the mouse cursor to the area on the canvas where you want to add it. You can then add activities that you want to execute repeatedly inside the *While Loop* block. In our example, we call *ShipOrder* inside the *While Loop*. Just like for the *Case* statement in the *Choice* activity, we need to define a boolean expression for the *While Loop* so that it can exit the loop when the expression returns a false value.

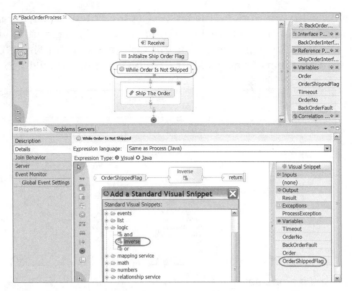

Figure 6.13 *While Loop*

In the *BackOrderProcess*, we initialize the *OrderShipFlag* to false before entering the *While Loop*. The return value of *ShipOrderProcess* sets this flag to true when it successfully ships the product. So, to keep executing the code in the *While Loop* block repeatedly until the order is shipped, the expression of the *While Loop* needs to return the inverse of *OrderShipFlag*.

To create the expression, select **While Order Is Not Shipped** in the canvas, and click **Details** in the Properties view. For the expression language, ensure that either **Java** or **Same as Process (Java)** and the radio button for the *Expression Type* of **Visual** are selected. To build the expression as shown in Figure 6.14, do the following:

1. To begin, the canvas has a node with a constant value of *True* that is wired to the *Return*. Delete the node with the constant *True*.

2. Drag the existing variable *OrderShippedFlag* from the tray onto the canvas.

3. Right-click in the empty area of the canvas and select **Add** > **Standard**. This opens the Add A Standard Visual Snippet dialog.

4. In the dialog's navigation tree, select **logic** > **inverse**, and click **OK** to add the *Inverse* logic node to the canvas. Wire the output of *OrderShippedFlag* to the input of *Inverse*, and then wire the output of *Inverse* to the *Return* to complete the expression.

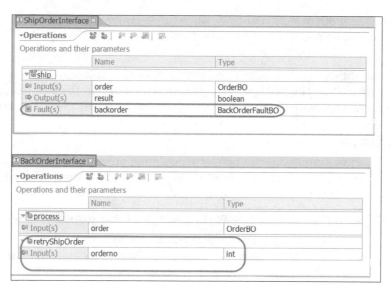

Figure 6.14 ShipOrderInterface and BackOrderInterface

Advanced BPEL Features

Thus far, we have discussed the creation of long-running and short-running processes, along with some of the basic BPEL constructs that can be used to create fully functional business processes. Many more features in BPEL enable you to build more-complex business processes. This section takes another look at the *BackOrderProcess* business process to introduce some advanced BPEL features such as

- Scopes
- Fault handlers
- Correlation sets
- Event handlers

The preceding section showed the *BackOrderProcess* using a *While Loop* to repeatedly call *ShipOrderProcess* until it successfully ships the Order. If the inventory for that item is not available, we would have *BackOrderProcess* running in a tight loop and consuming CPU cycles and other resources. The BPEL Specification recognizes that business processes can run for a long time. Therefore, there is a need to be able to pause and resume business processes such that these could survive server restarts and not consume resources while suspended.

Let's start by looking at the interfaces of *ShipOrderProcess* and *BackOrderProcess*. Notice in Figure 6.14 that, in addition to a normal output, the *ShipOrderProcess* interface declares a fault, *BackOrderFaultBO*, which it throws when it determines that the order cannot be shipped. The caller of this process, *BackOrderProcess* in this case, is expected to catch this fault and initiate processing to retry shipping the order at a later time.

Figure 6.14 also shows the *BackOrderProcess* interface. Unlike other interfaces we've seen, it contains two operations. The first operation, *process*, is used to start the business process. The second operation, *retryShipOrder*, is used to resume the business process if it is suspended.

Adding a Scope

Scopes in BPEL let you group one or more activities in the process. By default, each business process is contained in a default scope called the global scope. Any scope you add to the business process is nested within this global scope.

Apart from the grouping of activities, scopes provide the following capabilities:

- Variables declared within a scope are visible only within that scope.
- You can define fault handlers for your scope. Just like variables, fault handlers that are declared for a scope are visible and active only when the BPEL container executes activities within the scope.
- Likewise, you can define event handlers for your scope.
- You can even define compensation handlers for each scope.

Figure 6.15 shows an example of the *BackOrderProcess* with a *Scope* added inside its *While Loop*. To add a *Scope*, select the **Scope** icon in the Process Editor palette, move the mouse cursor inside the *While Loop* block, and click.

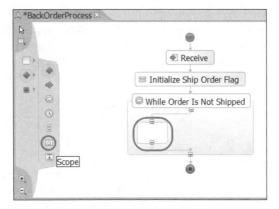

Figure 6.15 Scopes

Fault Handlers

Faults are exceptional conditions that can occur during the execution of a flow. BPEL provides the ability to handle faults by enabling the developer to define *Fault Handlers*. *Fault Handlers* can be added to any scope or alternatively can be added directly on any Invoke activity. As you saw a moment ago, *ShipOrderProcess* throws a *BackOrderFaultBO* if it cannot successfully ship an order. Figure 6.16 shows the use of a *Fault Handler* in *BackOrderProcess* to catch this fault so that it can retry shipping the order. To add a *Fault Handler*, do the following:

1. Click the **Scope** that you added inside the *While Loop*. From its Action Bar (or from its context menu), select the icon to **Add Fault Handler**.

   This creates a new Catch block that shows up beside the scope. Additionally, the scope is annotated with the *Fault Handler* icon.

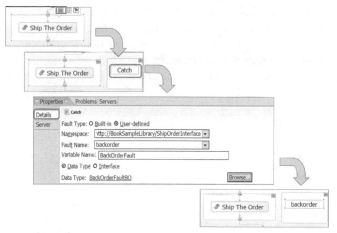

Figure 6.16 Adding a *Fault Handler*

2. Fill out details about the Catch by selecting the Catch in the *Fault Handler* and then clicking the **Details** tab in its Properties view. Do the following in the Details tab:
   - Select the **User-defined** radio button for *Fault Type*.
   - From the **Namespace** drop-down list, select **http://BookSampleLibrary/ShipOrderInterface**.
   - From the **Fault Name** drop-down list, select backorder.
   - In the **Variable Name**, enter *BackOrderFault*.
   - Make sure that the radio button for **Data Type** is selected, and then click the **Browse** button to set the type for *BackOrderFault*.
   - From the Data Type Selection dialog, select **BackOrderFaultBO**, and click **OK**.

BackOrderProcess is now ready to catch the *BackOrderFault* that might be thrown by *ShipOrderProcess*. The code to deal with *BackOrderFault* can be added below the *backorder* Catch block. When execution completes in the Catch block, normal execution of the BPEL flow resumes below the scope block.

Receive Choice

The *Receive Choice* (or Pick) activity is similar to the Receive activity, except that it allows the process to pause and wait for one of several possible external events. For example, *BackOrderProcess* might wait for an administrator to tell it to retry shipping the order, and if the administrator doesn't do so in a specified period of time, it expires, and the process continues and retries anyway. The *Receive Choice* control allows the process to accept calls on one or more operations. It also allows the process to establish a timeout after which the activity expires, and the process continues.

Figure 6.17 shows the use of the *Receive Choice* control to make the *BackOrderProcess* wait before retrying to ship the order. The process waits on the *Receive Choice* until it gets a *retryShipOrder* message with the same order number that started the process and then resumes processing by executing the *Retry Snippet* activity before going back to the top of the *While Loop*. If it doesn't receive this message in a predefined timeout period, the timeout branch fires, and the process executes the *Timeout Snippet* before going back to the top of the *While Loop*.

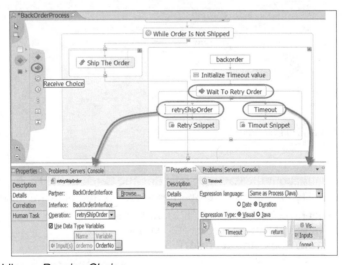

Figure 6.17 Adding a *Receive Choice*

To add a *Receive Choice*, as shown in Figure 6.17, do the following:

1. Select the **Receive Choice** icon from the Process Editor palette. Move the mouse cursor to the location where you want to add it, and click. Rename the *Receive Choice* activity to *Wait To Retry Order* by typing over the selected text.

2. Click the **Receive** branch under the *Receive Choice*, and do the following to initialize it:

   Select the **Description** tab under the Properties view, and enter *retryShipOrder* in the **Display Name** text box.

   Click the **Details** tab in the Properties view, and set up the operation and variables for the *retryShipOrder* message, as shown in Figure 6.17.

3. Add a *Timeout* to this *Receive Choice* activity so that the process automatically resumes and tries to ship the order in case it doesn't receive a *retryShipOrder* message in a reasonable amount of time. To add the *timeout*, select the **Wait To Retry Order** *Receive Choice* control. From its Action Bar, select the **Timeout** icon. This adds a *Timeout* branch to the *Receive Choice*.

4. To initialize the *Timeout*, select it and then click **Details** in the Properties view and do the following:

   Set the Expression Language to **Java**.

   Select the **Duration** radio button.

   Select the **Visual** radio button for the *Expression Type*.

   In the canvas for the Visual Expression, you should see a node with the constant 0 wired to a *Return*. Click the 0, and from the drop-down list, select the *Timeout* variable that contains the timeout value.

Functionally, this process is almost complete. However, when you save the process, it will have errors. This is because the process has multiple entry points, and we have not specified a way to match the *retryShipOrder* message to its corresponding process instance. The way to fix this is by using *Correlation Sets*, as discussed in the next section.

Correlation Sets

You just saw *BackOrderProcess* pause while it waited for a message to resume. However, this is not enough. The container still needs a mechanism to match a *retryShipOrder* message it receives to the correct instance of *BackOrderProcess*. For the container to find the right instance of the *BackOrderProcess* when it receives the *retryShipOrder* message, it needs some sort of correlating mechanism.

Correlation Sets are the BPEL mechanism by which an incoming message sent to a business process can be associated (or correlated) with an already-running process instance. *Correlation Sets* let us define unique parts in the received message that enable us to find a particular process instance. To use correlation sets, we need to do the following:

- Define one or more correlation sets that define properties of messages that will uniquely identify the process instance.
- Associate these correlation sets with each of the entry points into the business process.

Creating a Correlation Set

To create a *Correlation Set*, do the following:

1. From the tray on the right side of the BPEL editor, click the + button next to Correlation Sets to create a new *Correlation Set*. Rename the correlation set to *OrderNumber* by typing over the selected text.

2. With the *OrderNumber Correlation Set* selected, click the **Details** tab in the Properties view.

3. To add a new property named *orderno*, click the **Add** button in the **Details** tab to bring up the Select a Property dialog to create it. As shown in Figure 6.18, do the following to create the *orderno* property:

   Click the **New** button to bring up the Create Property dialog. In this dialog, set the Name to *orderno*. Click the **Browse** button and select **int** as the type for this property.

   In the same Create Property dialog, click **New** to add a new property alias. Property aliases identify parts of messages that uniquely identify the process instance. This brings up the Create Property Alias dialog. The property alias we create here corresponds to the input message that starts the *BackOrderProcess* on the *process* message. In this dialog, do the following:

   Select **BackOrderInterface** from the **Interface** drop-down list.

   Select **process** from the **Operation** drop-down list.

   Select the **Input** radio button for the direction.

   From the *OrderBO*, select the **orderno** property as the property that uniquely identifies the process instance.

   Click **OK** to finish creating this property alias.

   This takes you back to the Create Property dialog. Click **New** again to create another property alias. This one corresponds to the *retryShipOrder* message. In the Create Property Alias dialog, do the following:

   Select **BackOrderInterface** for the interface.

   Select **retryShipOrder** for the operation.

   Set the **direction** to be **Input**.

   From the *retryShipOrder* parameter, select **orderno** as the property of the message that uniquely identifies the process instance.

   Click **OK** to complete the creation of this property alias.

   Click **OK** to complete the creation of the *orderno* property.

Figure 6.18 Creating a Correlation Set property

4. Click **OK** to complete the Select a Property dialog.

Associating Correlation Sets to Process Activities

Now that we have created the correlation set, we need to associate it with all the entry points into the process. We do that by associating the correlation set with the Receive activity that starts the process and with the *Receive Choice* of *retryShipOrder*, which can be used to resume a suspended process instance.

As shown in Figure 6.19, to associate the *OrderNumber* correlation set with the corresponding entry points into the process, do the following:

1. With the **Receive** that starts the process selected, click the **Correlation** tab in the Properties view. In the **Correlation** tab, do the following:

   Click **Add** to add the *Correlation Set* to the Receive. A new row is added for the *Correlation Set*.

   Ensure that the **Direction** of the message is **Receive**. This tells the system that the inbound message to the process contains the correlating information.

   Ensure that **Initiation** is set to **Yes**. This tells the system that this Receive event creates the *Correlation Set*.

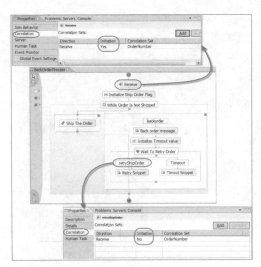

Figure 6.19 Setting Correlation Sets on entry points

2. Repeat these steps for the *retryShipOrder* Receive Choice node in the process. Only this time, the **Initiation** should be set to **No**, because this entry point should not start the business process.

Events

An event is a message that can be sent to an existing business process instance. The *Receive Choice* example you saw earlier is an example of an event that is received synchronously by the process instance (that is, the process blocks waiting for that event.) BPEL also supports asynchronous events, where it can receive and process an event in a separate thread while the main thread carries on with processing the normal flow. As shown in Figure 6.20, we demonstrate the use of events in BPEL by extending *BackOrderProcess* to support a user sending it a message that requests an approximate ship date:

1. We start by creating a new interface, *BackOrderQueryInterface*. It has one operation, *estimateShipDate*, which takes the order number as input and returns the order's estimated ship date.

2. Open the *BackOrderProcess* in the BPEL Editor and do the following:

   In the tray on the right side of the editor, click the + sign next to **Interface Partners** to add a new interface partner. Type over the selected text to set the name of the new interface partner to *BackOrderQueryInterface*.

   With the *BackOrderQueryInterface* partner selected in the tray, click the **Details** tab in the Properties view. In the Details tab, click **Browse** to bring up the Interface Selection dialog. Select the *BackOrderQueryInterface* interface, and click **OK**.

3. Add a new scope that surrounds the existing scope with the *Fault Handler* around the *Ship The Order* activity.

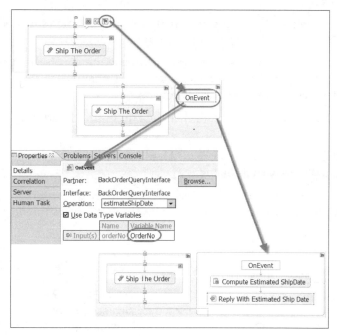

Figure 6.20 Adding an *Event Handler*

Nesting Scope

To add an enclosing scope, add the new scope above the existing scope, and then drag the existing scope into it. This moves the existing scope and all its contents into the new scope.

---

4. With the newly added scope selected, click the **Add Event Handler** icon in the action bar to add a new *Event Handler* to the scope.

5. With the *OnEvent* node selected in the newly created *Event Handler*, click the **Details** tab in the Properties view. Do the following in the **Details** tab:

Click the **Browse** button for the Partner. In the Select a Partner dialog, select *BackOrderQueryInterface*, and click **OK**. The Interface and operation in the Details tab are appropriately initialized.

Enter *OrderNo* as the name of the input variable.

6. With the **OnEvent** node still selected, click the **Correlation** tab in the Properties view. In the Correlation tab, click the **Add** button to add the *OrderNo Correlation Set* to this event.

7. Complete the flow by adding an activity to compute the estimated ship date, and then add an activity to reply with the estimated ship date.

8. Finally, we need to fix the *Correlation Set* to add an alias for this new event. With the **OrderNumber** *Correlation Set* selected in the tray, click the **Details** tab in the Properties view, and then do the following:

   Select the **orderno** property, and click the **Edit** button to bring up the Edit Property dialog.

   In the Edit Property dialog, click the **New** button to add a new Alias. This brings up the Create Property Alias dialog.

   In this dialog, select *BackOrderQueryInterface* from the **Interface** drop-down list. Expand the parts tree, select *OrderNo*, and click **OK** to add the new alias.

   Click **OK** in the Edit Property dialog.

Scope and Handler

You might have noticed that we created a new enclosing scope to hold the *Event Handler* instead of using the existing scope that already had the *Fault Handler* defined on it. We did this because an *Event Handler* is deactivated as soon as the *Fault Handler* at its scope is activated. Because the process uses this *Fault Handler* to do the bulk of back-order processing, the corresponding *Event Handler* at its scope would have been inactive and useless when we needed it most.

Closing the Link

This chapter has shown you how to use the Process Editor in WID to build business processes. We started by building short- and long-running business processes, and then we added control features such as *While Loop* and *Choice*. You also saw how to use *Faults* and *Fault Handlers* and more advanced features such as *Correlation Sets* and *Event Handlers*.

A.6.4

Business integration does not always involve business processes, but in a lot of cases, BPEL business processes form the centerpiece of integration. An example of a business integration solution where a BPEL business process is not involved is when components are created, assembled, and deployed to the Enterprise Service Bus.

Now that we have created a business process with the simple elements, you will see the use of Business Rules, Maps, and the other, more exciting service components in Chapter 7, "Business Maps and Business Rules," and Chapter 8.

Links to developerWorks

A.6.1   www.ibm.com/developerworks/webservices/library/ws-work.html

A.6.2   www.ibm.com/developerworks/edu/wes-dw-wes-hellowid62.html

A.6.3   www.ibm.com/developerworks/websphere/library/techarticles/0704_desai/
0704_desai.html

A.6.4   www.ibm.com/developerworks/websphere/zones/bpm

Chapter 7

Business Maps and Business Rules

The foundation has been laid, the runtime has been introduced, the tooling has been discussed, and we have presented some of the basic components. Chapter 6, "Business Processes," positioned the business process as the central component around which most other services and components revolve. This chapter discusses all the services and some of the remaining service components.

While describing these components, we cover some of the important concepts in business integration, such as mapping and relationships. We also discuss the rules and decision points that drive these business processes, especially business rules (BRs).

Supporting Services

As mentioned in Chapter 5, "WebSphere Process Server," WPS provides the infrastructure, services, and components for the enablement of services-oriented applications. With that said, we want you to visualize the architecture model of WPS that shows the supporting services and service components. This chapter discusses the supporting services, including business object (BO) maps, interface maps, relationships, selectors, and mediation flows. We specifically focus on BO maps, also known as data maps, and interface maps. We touch on relationships, selectors, and mediation flows. Mediation flows are covered in more detail in Chapter 15, "Enterprise Service Bus and Service Registry." Relationships are contrasted with maps. Selectors are contrasted with business rules because sometimes their usage scenarios are not clear.

That leads us to a detailed discussion of business rules, even though they are really a service component. This helps us spread some of the material into different chapters. The remaining two service components, human tasks and business state machines, are covered in the next chapter.

Maps

When Web services, or interfaces from other sources, are used in a business integration solution, often you have to relate those interfaces and data objects to those within your application. You do this by mapping the source data or interface to your target data or interface. Thus, you have data mapping and interface mapping. In WID, data mapping is also called business object mapping.

Relationships

Business applications have certain groups of people, or roles, who perform one or more tasks. For example, in our *BookSample* application, we can identify the roles of customer, credit bureau, and shipper. Roles have relationships. Relationships are useful in business over applications, because they show how specific roles are related through similar data structures and data types. Creating a relationship involves defining a generic role, such as a customer, and then some specific roles, such as a preferred customer or bank customer. These specific roles are tied via a key attribute, such as a customer ID.

Selectors

When you want to route an operation from a client application to one of several possible components in a business application, you can use a selector. A selector decides to select one route over another based on a runtime criterion. It can only be deployed to WPS.

Mediation Flows

A mediation flow implements a mediation, which is a way of dynamically intervening between service requestors and service providers. You could have one service requestor that has to use a service that is a composite of three service providers. In such a case, you use a mediation flow to mediate the information flow. A mediation flow is contained in a mediation module, which can be deployed to either WebSphere Process Server (WPS) or WebSphere Enterprise Service Bus (WESB).

Mapping

Although it is common to use the term *maps,* the more appropriate term is *mapping* or *transformation*. In the Business Integration perspective in WID, if you expand any module, you see a folder called Mapping, which consists of data maps, interface maps, relationships, and roles. In the case of a library, the Mapping folder contains only data maps, relationships, and roles. This section discusses the various maps.

From a business integration solution perspective, data or interfaces available to us in a back-end system do not match our data or the interfaces in our application. That is why mapping or transformation has to be done. It can be as simple as mapping surname to lastname or mapping firstname and surname to customerName by way of a join operation or complex custom mapping, in which a list attribute in input data is mapped to the number of items in output data. The reality is that most business integration solutions use mapping.

Data Maps

Often, when you want to use a Web service, the objects that describe the Web service cannot be used directly in a BPEL business process because the attributes or fields do not match properly. That is when a data map, also known as a business object map, comes in handy. Business object maps are used to transform data between source and target business objects.

BO maps support one-to-many, many-to-one, and many-to-many mappings among business objects. They can be used only in modules for business services, not for mediation services.

Interface Maps

Sometimes, two interacting components might not have matching interfaces. A business integration solution has a fundamental requirement to enable various pieces to fit together despite disparities in the respective interfaces. You can reconcile the differences between such interfaces by creating an interface map. For example, you could have similar interfaces with different method names, such as *CheckCredit* and *GetCreditRating*, and these interfaces need to be wired together. Because the method names are different, you would need some kind of mediator between them. Such a mediator would be an interface map that maps the operations and possibly even the parameters of the source and target interfaces.

There are two levels of interface mapping:

- With operation mapping, an operation in the source interface is mapped or bound to an operation of the target interface.
- Parameter mapping is a level deeper than operation mapping. In this case, the calling or source operation might have different parameters than the receiving or target operation. Therefore, you need an interface map to reconcile the parameters.

Relationships

A relationship establishes an association between data from two or more data sources. More precisely, a relationship correlates two or more semantically equivalent business objects that are represented in different physical formats. Each BO is called a participant in the relationship.

The two different types of relationships are identity and nonidentity relationships. An identity relationship, which is more commonly used, is a one-to-one relationship. A nonidentity relationship, on the other hand, is a one-to-many or many-to-many relationship. If one application uses two-letter state codes such as "CA," and in another application the state code is spelled out as "California," you have to create a relationship between these two pieces of data indicating that they are equivalent. Such a relationship is a static one, or the nonidentity case. In such relationships, the participant data does not change frequently. All these are based on roles—roles that describe how entities can participate in a given relationship. Role definitions are used to capture structure and constraint requirements on participating entities and their mode of participation. You can have broad-based roles such as generic roles, external roles, or internal roles, or you can make them application-specific in name.

Relationships

Relationships cannot be included in mediation modules. Mediation modules are described toward the end of this chapter and in detail in Chapter 15.

At a high level, we present to you the various mapping or transformation components so that you can see what kind of transformation takes place at each level. Figure 7.1 shows a sample mapping between a BO in WPS and a corresponding BO in a SAP system. The interface map maps the interfaces between the WPS system and the SAP system. At the data level, the data map maps the Order object in WPS with the SAPOrder object in the SAP system. Finally, there is the relationship that relates the OrderID in WPS with the SAPID in the SAP system.

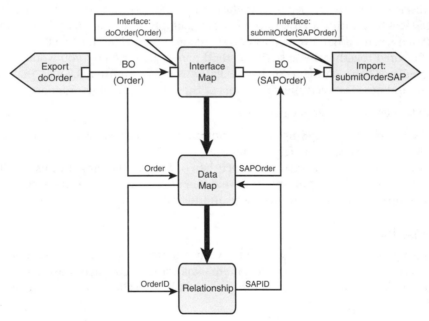

Figure 7.1 Mapping components

Mapping in a Mediation Module

Mediation modules let you perform mapping/transformation involving header information through the use of the XSLT mediation primitive. (XSLT stands for Extensible Stylesheet Language Transformation. You can find more information at www.w3.org/TR/xslt.)

A Mapping Scenario

As we mentioned, one of the most common business integration requirements involves synchronizing two different application subsystems. One significant challenge arises due to the fact that different applications tend to call semantically equivalent functions and data with different names. In fact, different applications may even use different representations of semantically equivalent information. When that happens, you have to map one representation to the other.

At a high level, the steps required to create the map can be summarized as follows:

1. Identify the interfaces to be mapped by determining the source interface and the target interface.

2. Identify the operations that are semantically equivalent.

3. Identify and understand any data-mapping requirement, such as the semantic equivalence of the data elements involved.

4. If needed, create the necessary data maps before you start creating the interface map.

5. Create the interface map, and associate the equivalent operations.

6. Within the interface map, use the data maps you created, or define additional data mapping as required to map the parameters.

The CreateOrderProcess in our *BookSample* project, for example, requires a credit rating service to establish the degree of risk associated with accepting an order for a certain customer. The order process uses an interface called *CreditCheckInterface* to invoke the service that performs the credit verification and that establishes a risk. From WID's standpoint, this interface is used in an Import component within the assembly diagram of the *OrderModule* project, as shown in Figure 7.2.

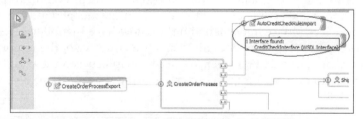

Figure 7.2 CreateOrderProcess invoking a service through *CreditCheckInterface*

Figure 7.3 shows the details of the *CreditCheckInterface*. It has an operation called *checkCredit* that takes two inputs: *OrderBO* and *CustomerBO*. It returns a string output called *riskType*.

Figure 7.3 *CreditCheckInterface* definition

Let's now assume that the credit checking service that was selected to evaluate the risk requires a different interface. The interface exposed by the service is shown in Figure 7.4 and is called *CreditCheckServiceInterface*.

Figure 7.4 *CreditCheckServiceInterface* definition

Notice that the *CreditCheckServiceInterface* definition uses a different name for the operation—*retrieveCreditRating* instead of *checkCredit*—and it takes a different type of input parameter—*CreditCheckingServiceInputBO*.

This scenario is common because a business integration solution typically involves piecing together different services, developed by various people (perhaps even third-party vendors) on different platforms and at different points in time. In the model that we have created for the actual credit check service implementation, we now have the following situation: The interface of the export component does not match the interface of the import component. Therefore, they cannot be wired together. We need a map between the two. The remainder of this section describes how you go about creating the *CreditCheckingMap*, shown in the center of Figure 7.5.

Figure 7.5 The mapping

In WebSphere business integration parlance, establishing equivalence between different operations is called *interface mapping*. It entails mapping the interface operations and signatures of one interface with the operations and signatures of another interface. Developers have to create an interface map component to define the mapping between equivalent operations in different interfaces. In this particular case, we need an interface map to associate the *checkCredit* operation on the *CreditCheckInterface* to the *retrieveCreditRating* operation of the *CreditCheckServiceInterface*. Interface mapping is only part of the overall mapping effort. That is usually the first step.

Often, interfaces expose complex objects, and it might happen that different interfaces expose different representations of the same object. The next step is to map the data between the interface operations. As we pointed out in our example, *CreditCheckInterface* uses two business objects as the input data (*OrderBO* and *CustomerBO*), whereas *CreditCheckServiceInterface* uses a single object (*CreditCheckingServiceInputBO*). Figure 7.6 shows the business objects involved.

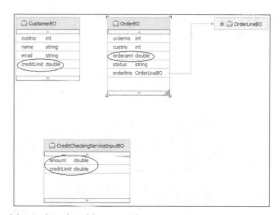

Figure 7.6 Business objects involved in mapping

You will notice that *CustomerBO* and *OrderBO* contain information that is known to be equivalent to the information encapsulated by *CreditCheckingServiceInputBO*:

- The *creditLimit* part of *CustomerBO* maps to the *creditLimit* part of *CreditChecking-ServiceInputBO*.
- The *orderamt* part of *OrderBO* maps to the *amount* part of *CreditCheckingServiceInput-BO*.

The process of transforming a set of business objects into a different set of business objects is called *data mapping*. Within an interface map, a developer can use a data map to define the logical mapping and the transformation rules between data elements in the different interface signatures.

Of the six steps that were identified, we just completed the first three identification steps. The next section describes the steps to implement this simple mapping scenario example, which really breaks down into data mapping and interface mapping.

Implementing Maps

We start by creating a new module called *CreditChecking*. The reason is to isolate the business module so that it does not need to know about the actual credit check service protocol or data format. We then create the data map (business object map) and the interface map.

Creating the Data Map

We start by creating the data map that we need for our scenario. We will create the maps within the same project that uses them. In some cases, when maps are reusable and serve more generic purposes, they can be located in libraries and shared.

1. In the Business Integration perspective in WID, go to the *CreditChecking* Module. Select **Mapping > Data Maps**. Right-click **Data Maps**, and select **New > Business Object Map**.

2. In the ensuing dialog, shown in Figure 7.7, specify the folder to be *com.ibm.test*, and name the map *CreditCheckingDataMap*. Click **Next**.

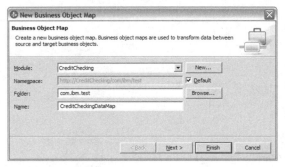

Figure 7.7 Specify a folder and a name for the business object map.

3. Select the BOs that were identified as input and output business objects for the BO Map. Figure 7.8 shows that we selected *CustomerBO* and *OrderBO* as inputs and *CreditCheckingServiceInputBO* as output.

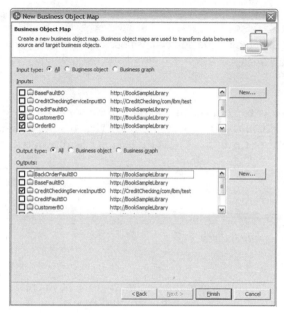

Figure 7.8 Selecting the input and output business objects

4. Click **Finish**. The Business Object Map Editor appears, as shown in Figure 7.9, with the two source BOs on the left and the target BO on the right.

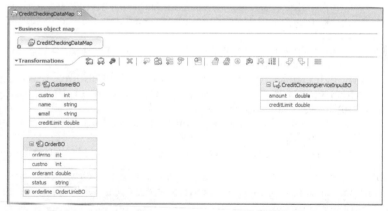

Figure 7.9 Business Object Map Editor

Mapping in WID

When the attributes in the source business object are properly mapped to the target business object and saved, the red X on the map name disappears.

5. The next step is to connect the parts that are semantically equivalent. Let's start with the *creditLimit* part of *CustomerBO*. Click it and drag a connection to the *creditLimit* part of *CreditCheckingServiceInputBO*, as illustrated in Figure 7.10.

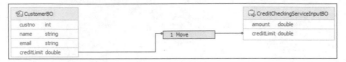

Figure 7.10 Creating a mapping link

6. Notice that by default, the mapping link that we have created includes a box indicating a Move operation. This is the simplest type of mapping. However, this is not the only type of mapping that is supported. If you click the **Move** box, you can see all the options:
   - Move lets you move (copy) information from one part to another without changing anything.
   - Assign lets you set the target data to an arbitrary value.
   - Custom lets you plug in a Java snippet to implement the mapping.
   - Custom Callout is used when you want to invoke an action during the mapping process so that some additional logic can be executed during the mapping.
   - Custom Assign lets you formulate the value to assign to the target data in a Java snippet as opposed to using a constant.
   - Although you might not see it in the drop-down options, this example has an Extract option that enables you to select a portion of the string based on delimiters of your choice.
   - Join is the opposite of Extract. You also have a Join option that lets you concatenate multiple strings into one.
7. Our example requires only a Move, because the data needs to be copied as it is.

   Similarly, repeat the steps for the *orderamt* part of the *OrderBO*. Connect it to the *amount* part of the target BO. Press **Ctrl+S** to save your work. Figure 7.11 shows you the completed business object map.

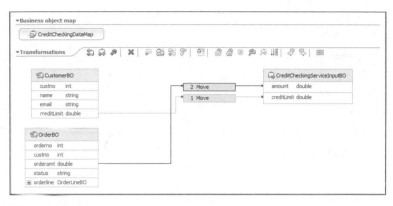

Figure 7.11 Completed BO map

Creating the Interface Map

Now, we can create the interface map.

8. Continuing in the Business Integration perspective in WID, select **Mapping > Interface Maps**. Right-click **Interface Maps**, and select **New > Interface Map**.

9. In the ensuing dialog, again specify the folder as *com.ibm.test*, and name the map *CreditCheckingMap*. Click **Next**.

10. In the following dialog, select the source interface *CreditCheckInterface* and the target interface *CreditCheckServiceInterface*, as shown in Figure 7.12.

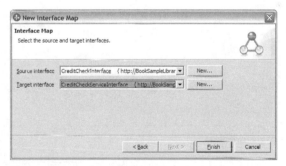

Figure 7.12 Selecting the source and target interfaces to map

11. Click **Finish**. The Interface Map Editor appears, as shown in Figure 7.13, with the source interface on the left and the target interface on the right.

Figure 7.13 Interface Map Editor

12. The next step is to connect the operations. Click in the *checkCredit* cell on the left, and drag a connection from *checkCredit* to *retrieveCreditRating* on the right. Now that we have established this link, every time someone invokes the *checkCredit* operation in the map, the map transforms that invocation into a call to *retrieveCreditRating*.

13. Click the arrow you just created to map the parameters. When you click the operation mapping arrow, you see that the signatures of the two operations become available for mapping.

14. We map the input parameters first by wiring a connection between *order* on the left and *creditRatingInput* on the right. That gives us a Move operation by default, as shown in Figure 7.14.

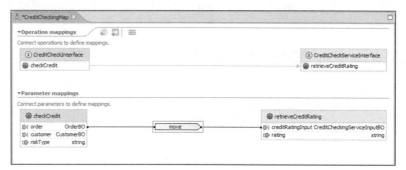

Figure 7.14 Mapping of parameters

15. We need to change the default so that we can use the data map we created in the preceding section. Click the **move** arrow, and go to the Properties view to switch the type from **move** to **map**. You can see that four options appear: map, extract, move, and java. Select **map**.

16. While in the Properties view, click the **Details** tab, shown in Figure 7.15, to select the data map we created.

Figure 7.15 Details of parameter mapping

17. In the Interface Map Editor, you notice that, at this point, both the input parameters of the source operation have been mapped through the newly created connection using the data map.

18. Finally, we need to map the output. This is a bit different from input mapping, because we connect the *rating* parameter on the right to the *riskType* parameter on the left. In this simple example, we assume that the string values returned by the credit rating service are perfectly compatible with the values expected by the calling process, so we need only a Move. The completed *CreditCheckingMap* is shown in Figure 7.16.

Figure 7.16 Completed interface map

19. Save all your work. The interface map can now be dropped on the assembly diagram and wired, as shown in Figure 7.17.

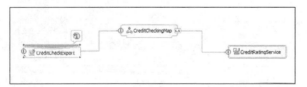

Figure 7.17 Assembly diagram with the interface map

Notice that we have connected the Export component to the Map and the Map to the actual service. By doing so, we have ensured that when the business process invokes the credit checking service, the map will

- Translate the invocation to the appropriate call on the actual service
- Transform the input data provided by the process to the format required by the actual service

Relationships

Relationships are created by defining model data. WID has a Relationship Editor that uses two different data models: relationship model and relationship instance model.

- The relationship model covers the relationship and the roles that are used for the respective definitions. These are stored in .rel and .role files.
- When static instance data is defined in the Relationship Editor, the relationship instance model is used for lookup relationships. They are stored in .ri files, which are visible only in the Physical Resources view.

To create a relationship in WID, you must use the Relationship wizard. You can have static relationships in which the data does not change frequently. These are further divided into identity relationships and nonidentity relationships.

A Relationship Scenario

Let's create a relationship in WID, named *state,* which associates the two-letter state codes with the full state name:

1. Create a new module, or you can use the *Shipping* module. In the navigation tree of the Business Integration perspective, expand the module and select **Mapping** > **Relationships**. Right-click it, and select **New** > **Relationship**. In the window that appears, enter a name (*state*), as shown in Figure 7.18. Click **Next**.

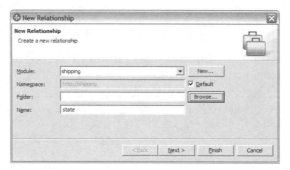

Figure 7.18 Naming a new relationship

2. You then specify the type of relationship, as shown in Figure 7.19. For the example of mapping two-letter state codes to the state name, you choose the identity relationship and check the box to indicate that it is a static mapping. Then click **Finish**.

> ### Specifying the Relationship Type
>
> Based on the earlier definitions, the first radio button in Figure 7.19 is an identity relationship, and the second radio button indicates a non-identity relationship. If the checkbox is checked, it is a lookup relationship, which means that the instance data values for the runtime can be set in the Relationship Editor. Those values are static and will not change during runtime.

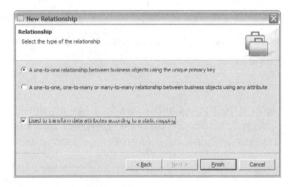

Figure 7.19 Selecting the type of relationship

3. The new relationship is created and is displayed in the Relationship Editor, which has a Relationship section and a Roles section.

Relationship Editor

The Relationship Editor lets you build and edit relationships and their attributes.

4. Initially, it shows the Relationship section with the *state* relationship and the Roles section. Do not worry about the red X. You also see the Properties pane.

5. In the Roles section, click the icon with the + symbol to add a role. The BO you choose to add (*Address*) is displayed with the name *RELATION_NAME_BO_NAME*, as shown in Figure 7.20. Note that if you double-click the BO type (*Address*), the BO Editor is displayed.

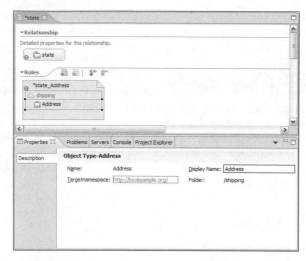

Figure 7.20 Partially completed relationship

6. Click the key icon with the + symbol to add a key attribute. From the list of attributes for the *Address* BO, choose *State*. The Properties view displays the KeyAttribute role. The *KeyAttribute of Role-state_Address* can be seen in Figure 7.21.

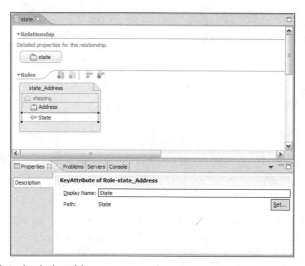

Figure 7.21 Completed relationship

7. Because we specified static mapping, you see in the Properties view of the relationship the Instance Data tab. Click that tab, and in the Name/Value table, enter a value for the KeyAttribute Name, *State*.

8. If you press **Ctrl+S** to save your edits, you will notice that all the red Xs disappear, as shown in Figure 7.21.

You then add the second role—Business Object—and map the corresponding state attribute. Completing this simple relationship is left as an exercise for you.

After you are done creating the entire relationship, save your edits and make sure that no errors exist. Then you can use the relationship as a component in your assembly diagram. When you have successfully built the application, you can deploy it to the WPS test server. You can administer relationships using the Relationship Manager.

Relationship Manager

In WID, you can use the Relationship Manager to create, manipulate, and view relationship instances in the runtime environment. This is available in WID's Servers view. Make sure that the test server is running, and then right-click the server and select **Launch > Relationship Manager** to view it.

In the WPS runtime, you can bring up the Relationship Manager via the WebSphere Administrative Console. Select **Integration Applications > Relationship Manager** to view the initial screen, which is shown in Figure 7.22. In the top-right box, the green arrow indicates that the relationship services are enabled and running. It also tells you how many relationships were found. You can click the **Relationships** link as indicated by the arrow to get details of all the deployed relationships.

Figure 7.22 Initial screen of the Relationship Manager

Figure 7.23 shows the result of clicking the Relationships link. You see the relationship named *state* that was deployed in the preceding section. The Relationship Manager indicates that it is a static relationship of the Identity type. You can further drill down on the name of the relationship to get more details, such as role schema, object name, and so on.

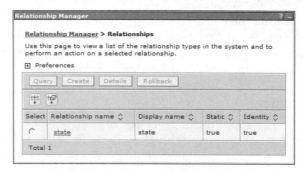

Figure 7.23 List of relationships in the Relationship Manager

Business Rules

In the vocabulary of business rules, an "externalized" rule is one that contains modifiable business logic. In other words, an application administrator or even a member of a line-of-business staff can manipulate this logic, which otherwise would be hard-coded or embedded in the application. Externalized rules are an appealing option for processes in which the business logic may change frequently. Examples are situations that require determining a customer's status, calculating discounts, assessing risks, evaluating compliance with company policy, and so forth.

Using the business rules feature in WID, a developer can isolate a critical area of a business integration solution and enable others to modify the related logic using an administrative interface, such as the Business Rules Manager, rather than a development tool, as follows:

- **At development time:** The application or integration developer identifies sections of the business integration solution that are subject to frequent modification. Using a development tool such as WID, the developer formulates those sections in terms of business rules.
- **At runtime:** After the application has been deployed and is running, application administrators or business analysts can use an intuitive interface, such as the Business Rules Manager, to modify the logical behavior of the sections the integration developer identified.

T.7.1

BPEL allows you to integrate two kinds of business rules: decision tables and rulesets, as shown in Figure 7.24. Both are supported by WPS and can be constructed in WID. Both kinds of business rules are contained in *business rule groups*. Wherever there is logic that might need to change abruptly, you have a good candidate for a business rule group (BRG). One of the main features of the BRG is that rule destinations (rulesets or decision tables) can be scheduled to execute over certain date and time ranges. The BRG is packaged as an SCA component and can be used in the assembly editor to form part of the overall integration solution. Business rules are nonprocedural, and the rules can be changed independently of an application.

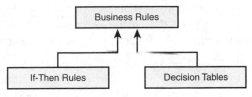

Figure 7.24 Business rules inheritance diagram

Decision Tables

Decision tables are, in essence, balanced decision trees. Although they do not have any explicitly coded logic, decision tables provide functionality that is similar to the logic implemented in a Java `switch` statement. For example, when an application needs to determine the premium for a life insurance policy, it can use a decision tree that starts by discerning the driver's sex (male or female). The application can then distinguish between smokers and nonsmokers. It can then have a subsequent dimension based on the age of the insured person (20 and under, 21 to 30, 31 to 40, and so on).

Rulesets

Rulesets implement logic that is executed in sequence, in a way that is similar to a series of `if-then` code fragments. You can define and use variables within the ruleset. More important, you can use templates to define rules. Actually, even decision tables can have templates. A template provides another way of defining rules where the values are exposed as parameters in the Business Rules Manager, allowing an administrator to make changes to the rules logic or data without redeploying the applications.

A Decision Table Scenario

We can look at the Order application and see how decision tables can be utilized. The section "Maps" introduced a module that was dedicated to determining a customer's credit rating to assess the risk associated with approving an order. Such a service is a good candidate for an implementation that uses business rules, because the line of business might want to change the guidelines that apply to assessing the risk factor over time.

Let's start by creating a decision table for our credit check rule implementation. Whether you create a ruleset or a decision table, you first need to create a business rules group to contain it. A BRG can hold a number of rulesets and decision table. Each ruleset or decision table can be made effective at different points in time. For example, if you want to enact special discounts for a holiday season, you can do so by making sure that a certain ruleset or decision table is effective during the desired period of time. But note that only one rule per operation in a BRG can be active at any given time.

As we said, our ordering application includes a good candidate for business rules—the credit checking service. You might remember that the business process determines the risk involved in accepting the order from the customer, based on a formula that ties the order amount and the customer's credit limit. A decision table can encapsulate such a formula.

Our rule group exposes the *CreditCheckServiceInterface*, as described in the "Maps" section. Figure 7.25 shows the interface definition. The *retrieveCreditRating* operation takes an instance of *CreditCheckingServiceInputBO*, which is a simple business object made of two parts—*amount* and *creditLimit*, both of type *double*. The operation returns a *string* representing the credit rating.

Figure 7.25 CreditCheckServiceInterface

Creating a Rule Group

Let's walk through the steps of creating the rule group and decision table. All this is developed in the Business Integration perspective in WID.

1. In the navigation tree of the *CreditChecking* module, select **Business Logic** > **Rule Groups.** Right-click **Rule Groups,** and select **New** > **Rule Group**.

2. In the ensuing New Rule Group dialog, shown in Figure 7.26, enter *CreditCheckRG* as the rule group name, and assign it to a folder of your choice. Click **Next**.

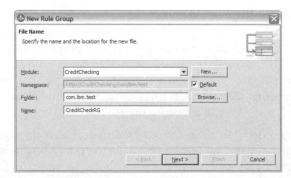

Figure 7.26 Naming a rule group

3. In the subsequent dialog, select *CreditCheckServiceInterface* as the interface for which business rules will be created.

4. Click **Finish**. The Rule Group editor appears, as shown in Figure 7.27, with the source interface on the left. The newly created rule group needs at least one destination for each operation in the interface. A destination can be either a ruleset or a decision table.

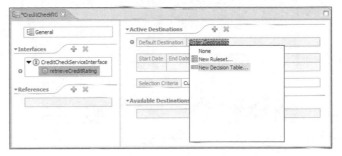

Figure 7.27 Creating the default destination for the rule group

5. Do not worry about the red X. Highlight the operation, click the Enter Destination link, and choose **New Decision Table**.

6. In the New Decision Table window that appears, you are prompted to specify the folder and name of the decision table. We named it *CreditRatingDT*. Click **Next**.

7. You are prompted to select the decision table layout. Our simple table has only two dimensions: the total amount and the customer credit limit.

   Therefore, we need only one row condition and one column condition in a **Row and Column** layout, as shown in Figure 7.28. The tool accommodates more than two dimensions, but beware that you can end up with tables that are much more complex and difficult to manipulate.

   The **Number of actions** value essentially represents the number of result values you expect to get back when the rule is invoked. Because the table only needs to return a string, the default value of 1 is adequate.

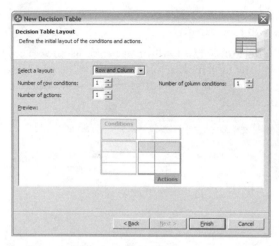

Figure 7.28 Selecting the layout of the decision table

8. Click **Finish**. The Decision Table Editor appears, as shown in Figure 7.29, with many more red Xs.

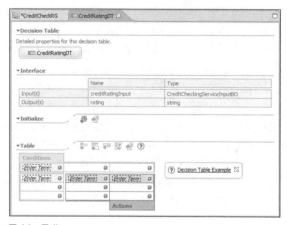

Figure 7.29 Decision Table Editor

9. Under **Conditions**, you must define which parts of the input message you want to use to define the dimensions of this matrix. You can click **Enter Term** to define the dimensions of the rows and columns. Figure 7.30 shows that we defined the *amount* as the condition for the columns, and we were about to select the *creditLimit* as the row condition.

Figure 7.30 Defining the dimensions of the matrix

10. Now you can complete the table by adding values for the necessary columns and rows. Figure 7.31 shows how we filled out the initial cells in the table. Note that after all the cells in the table are filled out and saved, the red Xs disappear.

Figure 7.31 Filling the decision table with values

11. As it is configured now, the table is static, which means that a user cannot modify the values at runtime after the application is deployed. If you want to enable an administrator or another user to make changes to the values in the table at runtime, you must convert some or all of its values to template values. Highlight a cell, right-click, and select **Convert to template**. Of course, you can select multiple cells at once and convert them all to a template.

Expanding the Decision Table

What if more conditions are needed? You can highlight a cell in any of the conditions in the decision table, right-click, and choose **Add Condition Value**. Depending on where you click, you can add a row of cells or a column of cells. The other options are Add Initialization Rule, Add Condition, and Add Condition Otherwise.

---

12. To demonstrate a realistic decision table, we expanded it and filled in values, as shown in Figure 7.32. Given the current set of values, if a customer with a credit limit of $15,000 places an order for $35,000, the table would return a risk rating of "HIGH."

▾Table					
Conditions					
creditRatingInput.amount	<5000.00	>=5000.00 and <=10000.00	>10000.00 and <=25000.00	>25000.00 and <=50000.00	>50000.00
creditRatingInput.creditLimit	rating	rating	rating	rating	rating
<10000.00	"LOW"	"MEDIUM"	"HIGH"	"VERY HIGH"	"VERY HIGH"
>=10000.00 and <=20000.00	"VERY LOW"	"LOW"	"MEDIUM"	"HIGH"	"VERY HIGH"
>20000.00 and <=30000.00	"VERY LOW"	"VERY LOW"	"LOW"	"MEDIUM"	"HIGH"
>30000.00	"VERY LOW"	"VERY LOW"	"VERY LOW"	"LOW"	"MEDIUM"
					Actions

Figure 7.32 Decision table with an initial set of values

13. Figure 7.33 shows the entire table converted into a template. Notice that the values in the matrix are now shown within modifiable text fields. Those fields will be exposed as parameters that can be adjusted using the Business Rules Manager.

Figure 7.33 The entire decision table converted into a template

14. You can have multiple rulesets or decision tables in the same rule group. For instance, if the company needs to establish different risk rating criteria by the beginning of 2008, you can add a new decision table and set the validity start date to January 1, 2008, as shown in Figure 7.34.

▾Active Destinations	✚ ✖	
Default Destination	CreditRatingDT	
Start Date	End Date	Destination
🗓 Jan 1, 2008 12:00 AM	🗓	CreditRatingDT2008

Figure 7.34 A rule group with two destinations

15. We have completed the development tasks related to creating a decision table. Save the decision table and rule group, and add the rule group to the assembly diagram of the *CreditChecking* module, as shown in Figure 7.35.

Figure 7.35 The rule group in the assembly diagram

We can now deploy the *CreditChecking* module to WPS and make changes to the table using an administrative interface—the Business Rules Manager.

A.7.2

Administering Business Rules

In the WID test environment, you can use the Business Rules Manager (BRM) to manipulate and view business rules in the runtime environment. In WID's Servers view, make sure that the test server is running, and then right-click the server and select **Launch > Business Rules Manager** to view it.

From a runtime perspective, the BRM gets installed when you configure your stand-alone WPS server or cluster. It can also be separately installed later. (For example, you can use the wizard that is accessible via the **Business Integration Configuration** link in the WebSphere Administrative Console under the server or cluster properties.)

Bringing up the Business Rules Manager

You can bring up the BRM via the URL http://HOST_NAME:9080/br/webclient. The default port is 9080.

Here we assume that the BRM application has been installed and that the *CreditChecking* module has been deployed successfully to WPS. Let's take a look at using the Business Rules Management application.

1. Bring up BRM in a separate browser, because that is the recommended way of administering BRs. In Figure 7.36, you can see on the left side a **Rule Books** view—a navigator that enables you to view and access the rule groups you have installed on your server.

Figure 7.36 Business Rules Manager

2. In Figure 7.36, you can see that we expanded the CreditCheckRG rule group. The operation and the decision table are also visible. Click **CreditRatingDT** to display the table shown in Figure 7.37.

CreditRatingDT - Decision Table						
Back Edit Copy						
General Information						
Last Published	Feb 15, 2007 17:06 (Local Time)				Status	Original
Description						
Decision Table						
creditRatingInput.amount		< 5000.00	>= 5000.00 and <= 10000.00	> 10000.00 and <= 25000.00	> 25000.00 and <= 50000.00	> 50000.00
creditRatingInput.creditLimit		rating ⬇	rating ⬇	rating ⬇	rating ⬇	rating ⬇
< 10000.00		LOW	MEDIUM	HIGH	VERY HIGH	VERY HIGH
>= 10000.00 and <= 20000.00		VERY LOW	LOW	MEDIUM	HIGH	VERY HIGH
> 20000.00 and <= 30000.00		VERY LOW	VERY LOW	LOW	MEDIUM	HIGH
> 30000.00		VERY LOW	VERY LOW	VERY LOW	LOW	MEDIUM

Figure 7.37 The decision table shown in the BRM

3. Notice that three buttons exist:

   - **Edit** enables you to make changes to the table.
   - **Copy** enables you to create a completely new decision table from the current table.
   - **Back** takes you back to the previous view.

4. Click **Edit**. This is where you can manipulate the content of the decision table. In edit mode, you can make changes to any of the values that we turned into a template at development time. You can also modify the table's structure. For example, let's insert a new column. Click the icon (▤) by the value **10,000.00** on one of the columns. Then select the action **Add to the right**, as shown in Figure 7.38.

Figure 7.38 Adding a new conditional column in the decision table

5. After we change the ranges and insert the new column, we can start filling in the new values for the new range, as shown in Figure 7.39.

>= 5000.00 and <= 10000.00 ▤	> 10000.00 and <= 17500.00 ▤	> 17500.00 and <= 25000.00 ▤
rating ⬇	rating ⬇	rating ⬇
MEDIUM	HIGH	HIGH
LOW		MEDIUM
VERY LOW		LOW
VERY LOW		VERY LOW

Figure 7.39 Entering the new set of values

6. After the changes are completed, the administrator can save the table. The BRM indicates that the table has been changed, and the changes can be published if necessary. Note that these changes are only saved in the current session. They are not published to the server until an explicit publish command is executed. This allows for multiple BRGs to be changed and then published.

7. On the main navigation menu of the BRM, we can select **Publish and Revert**, as shown in Figure 7.40. This link appears only when there are changes.

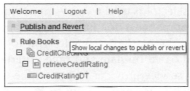

Figure 7.40 The Publish and Revert link appears only when there are changes.

8. On the Publish and Revert screen, you can click **Publish** to make the changes immediately active or **Revert** to go back to the original version of the table.

Exporting the Rules

Now that we have made changes to the rule and published it, you might wonder how we can get those changes back to the development platform or how we can save the new definitions. To do that, we need to use the Administrative Console.

1. In the WebSphere Administrative Console, select **Servers** > **Application Servers**. Assuming that server1 is where you have installed the business rules, click **server1**.

2. In the Business Integration properties, you see a folder called **Business Rules**. Expand it.

3. Click the **Business Rules** link. You should see a screen similar to the one shown in Figure 7.41.

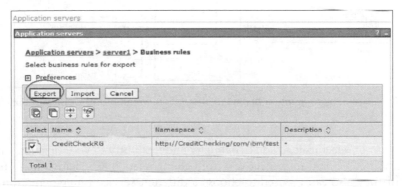

Figure 7.41 Exporting and importing rule definitions from a server

4. Select the rule group, and click the **Export** button to export the selected rule group into a zip file. This can then be imported on a different server, or within the WebSphere Integration Developer environment.

Selectors

A.7.3

In a BPEL business process, a selector is used to route an operation from a client application to one of several possible components for implementation. Note that selectors do not require a BPEL process to operate. A selector enables you to indicate which service implementation should be invoked based on date and time criteria. For instance, a bank might want to switch to a different service provider for its online trading clearinghouse services after a certain date. Or a retail business might want to use different algorithms for discount calculations depending on the time of year.

Business rules have additional logic in them, but selectors do not. But selectors are similar to business rules in WID, particularly in two respects:

- **At development time:** Developers can identify the sections of the process or service whose implementation is dependent on date and time rules.
- **At runtime:** Application administrators can modify the date and time range for selectors and add, remove, or change implementations through the WebSphere Administrative Console.

Figure 7.42, taken from the WPS product InfoCenter, shows how selectors fit into a business integration solution and work with business rules.

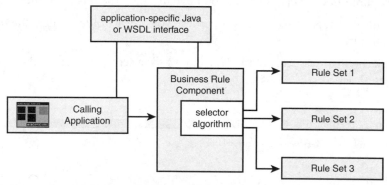

Figure 7.42 How selectors fit into a business integration solution and work with business rules

The main point of selectors is to add dynamicity and flexibility to your business integration. Not only can they be used to protect you from changes (such as placing one in front of an import), but they also can be used to choose a different service implementation based on time and date. Finally, selectors can be invoked by any other SCA component, not just by BPEL.

Mediation

Mediation is a way of dynamically intervening between two services that do not exactly match in terms of their inputs and outputs. A mediation component operates independently of the services it connects to. For example, you can use mediation when you need to transform data from one service into an acceptable format for a subsequent service.

From WID's perspective, mediation in the assembly editor appears as a mediation flow component between exports and imports. Figure 7.43 shows how three service requestors, or exports, send their output data to the interface of the mediation flow component. The mediation flow component then routes the appropriate data to two service providers or imports.

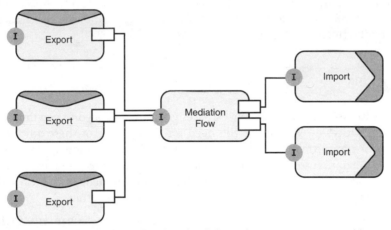

Figure 7.43 Sample mediation flow showing the linkage between exports and imports

Mediations are contained in a mediation module. This is primarily a WESB functionality and is explained in Chapter 15. However, mediation modules can also be deployed and run on WPS. They contain mediation flows, which link operations for modifying and routing messages between service consumers and service providers. They exist as a special kind of module in WID. Figure 7.44 shows the folder structure of a mediation module, which is similar to that of a process module. However, instead of having Business Logic with business processes, the mediation module has Mediation Logic with mediation flows.

Figure 7.44 Sample mediation flow module folder in WID

When you work on a mediation flow in WID, you do so in the Mediation Flow Editor, wherein an operation from one service, the service requestor or export, is mapped to the operation of another service, the service provider, or import. In addition, you use functions called mediation primitives to complete the wiring within these flows.

There are two key reasons for using mediation modules:

- To manipulate the headers of service request or responses
- To implement routing and connectivity logic between service requesters and service endpoints. This logic can be made more dynamic by using a Service Registry (such as the WebSphere Service Registry and Repository) to allow mediations modules to dynamically select the endpoints at runtime.

The common pattern of using a mediation module is to hide the Application-Specific Business Object (ASBO) and protocol information from the business module. These concepts and more are described in Chapter 15.

Closing the Link

This chapter discussed supporting services. After you progress beyond creating simple BPEL-based business processes, you realize the need for using some of these advanced services, such as maps or transformations. Anytime an enterprise information system (EIS) back end is part of the integration solution, you invariably find yourself using maps—either interface maps or data maps or both. Actually, BPEL by itself is not enough to create a business integration solution; you need these extra services to glue it all together.

We went into some detail on relationships, which is another "advanced" topic. Business rules are commonplace in business applications. Hence, we described in great detail business rule groups—specifically, decision tables. It is only fair to point out that WPS can integrate with other rules engines such as ILOG's JRules, which is a Java-based rules engine.

Finally, we touched on selectors and mediation. We have noticed that as integration scenarios become more complex, more of these service components come into play.

Links to developerWorks

A.7.1   www.ibm.com/developerworks/websphere/techjournal/0609_gregory/0609_gregory.html

T.7.1   www.ibm.com/developerworks/edu/wes-dw-wes-hellowid62.html

A.7.2   www.ibm.com/developerworks/websphere/library/tutorials/0610_kolban/0610_kolban.html

A.7.3   www.ibm.com/developerworks/library/ar-cbspov3/index.html

Chapter 8

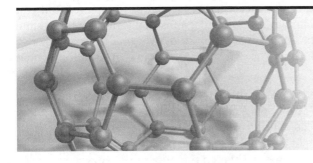

Business State Machines, Human Tasks, and Web Services

Of the four service components depicted in the WebSphere Process Server Architecture, business processes, the core component, was covered in Chapter 6, "Business Processes," and business rules were discussed in Chapter 7, "Business Maps and Business Rules." The other two—business state machines and human tasks—are covered in this chapter.

How can anyone forget the state machine? Every computer science student, at some point, learns about a state machine. In business integration today, we have business state machines (BSMs), which are driven by business events. This chapter shows you the use of a BSM as a Service Component Architecture (SCA) component. The latter part of the chapter elaborates on human tasks in business processes and details the use of Web Services because these are the two common entities that come into play in business integration solutions. We also show you how you can import a Web Service into a business process application.

This promises to be an exciting chapter because of the divergent, yet important, topics that are covered. But we leave the question of which is better, a Business Process Execution Language (BPEL) business process or a business state machine, unanswered, because both have their place in a business integration solution.

Business State Machines

A BSM is an event-driven business application in which external events trigger changes in the state. Certain business processes are heavily event-driven and may require the invocation of only a limited number of external services. Such processes may also require the ability to repeat sequences of steps multiple times and can be described with graphs where loops are frequently used.

A.8.1

These processes are well represented, conceptually, using state transition diagrams. You can implement these processes using the BPEL constructs that we have already explored, but you would find it awkward to create and maintain the BPEL diagrams that represent these state machines. For example, the BPEL editor doesn't allow you to draw a link from an activity "backwards" to a prior state. You would need to use a loop construct in that situation, which diminishes legibility.

For this purpose, WebSphere Process Server (WPS) supports a BSM, a special type of process. A BSM is, essentially, the implementation of a state transition diagram. WebSphere Integration Developer (WID) has a special editor to support the creation of BSMs. The next section walks through a simple example of a BSM. Because you are already familiar with the Order process from our *BookSample* project, we will sketch out an alternative way to implement that same process as a state machine.

State Transition Diagram of the Order Process

This section looks at the overall Order process from the perspective of the *states* in which an order may find itself during its lifetime. This section also looks at the events that can trigger transitions between states. A good way to represent state diagrams is by means of a Unified Modeling Language (UML) statechart diagram. (IBM Rational Software Architect supports the creation of such UML diagrams.) Here, we do not intend to elaborate on the nuances of UML; we use UML to provide a standard representation of the state transition diagram. Take a close look at Figure 8.1. We will traverse through the diagram and clarify its meaning.

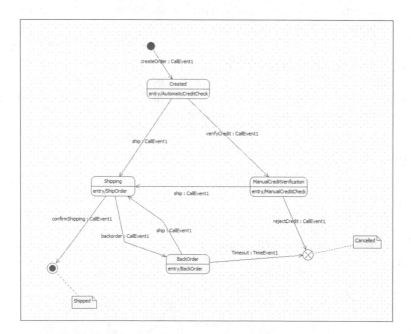

Figure 8.1   A state diagram representing the Order process

The diagram represents the lifecycle of an incoming order. We can walk through each stage:

1. The diagram has an initial state at the top, which represents the state of an order instance before inception.

2. The order gets created (transitioning to the *Created* state) when the *createOrder* operation is invoked on the state machine. A client application is responsible for calling the *createOrder* operation.

3. Upon entering the *Created* state, the state diagram performs an "entry action," invoking the *AutomaticCreditCheck* action (or process). Typically, this invocation is a one-way invocation. The state machine "sits" in the *Created* state until some external stimulus causes a state transition. In this case, the state machine expects some external agent to invoke either the *ship* or *verifyCredit* operation. In our example, it would be up to the credit checking process to invoke either operation, depending on the results of the credit checking.

Business State Machine

It is not mandatory to design the state machine this way. We could also have invoked an action using a request/response operation and checked the outcome. But it makes a lot more sense to use a totally asynchronous model. By doing so, we fully decouple the state machine from the services or actions that it invokes.

---

4. If the automatic credit checking service invokes the *ship* operation, the state machine transitions to the *Shipping* state.

5. Otherwise, if the *verifyCredit* operation is invoked, the state machine enters the *ManualCreditVerification* step. Upon entering that state, the state machine starts the corresponding process, which includes the human task. That process, instead of replying to the state machine, calls the appropriate operation. If the human decides to deny credit, the *rejectCredit* operation is called, and the process is terminated. Otherwise, the *ship* operation is called, and the state machine goes to the *Shipping* state through this route.

6. When entering the *Shipping* state, the state machine invokes the corresponding process. This process may realize that the inventory for shipping is unavailable and calls the backorder process. Notice that between the *Shipping* state and *Backorder* state is some sort of loop.

7. Upon entering the *Backorder* state, the state machine activates the *BackOrder* process. This process waits until there are goods that allow the company to fulfill the order and ship it. Otherwise, a timeout occurs, which causes the order to be canceled.

As you can tell, this description is very close to the overall flow illustrated when discussing the sample application in Chapter 6. We have extracted from that flow the key states to which an order can transition. We also have created a small state machine that controls those transitions and the invocation of the relevant subprocesses.

The main difference between this approach and the BPEL implementation that we described in Chapter 6 is that the state machine has no notion of *why* a certain transition occurs, because the business logic is external to the state machine. BPEL processes tend to be driven by the business logic they implement, rather than by external stimuli. Another aspect of the state machine is that the graph contains "loops" and backward links, which are not possible in BPEL. Nevertheless, the state machine gives you a clear, high-level representation of the macroscopic stages of the entity's lifecycle—in this case, the Order process.

Implementing the Order Business State Machine

WID gives you a specialized editor for creating business state machines. If you're familiar with UML, using the editor will be natural and simple, because it adopts some of the same constructs and terminology. However, in general, creating a BSM is a simpler task than developing a BPEL process that implements the same functionality. One of the advantages of using a BSM is that it can be assembled relatively quickly.

The Order Business State Machine Interface

Just like any other SCA component, a BSM needs an interface. The interface must expose all the operations that are available as "stimuli" that can trigger state transitions. Figure 8.2 shows the interface we designed for our Order state machine.

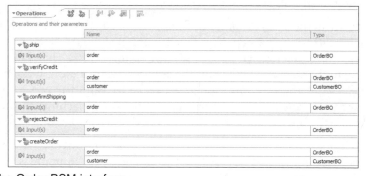

Figure 8.2 The Order BSM interface

We call this interface *OrderBSMIntf*. Notice that it exposes an operation for each of the "call events" shown in Figure 8.2. Now we need to create the BSM that implements this interface. For this purpose, we have created a separate module called *OrderBSM*.

Creating the Order BSM

1. In the Business Integration perspective, expand the *OrderBSM* module. Navigate to **Business Logic**, and right-click **State Machines**. Select **New** > **Business State Machine** to initiate the creation of a BSM.

2. Name the BSM *OrderBSM*, and specify a folder, as shown in Figure 8.3. Click **Next**.

Figure 8.3 Naming the BSM

3. On the screen to Select an Interface, shown in Figure 8.4, choose *OrderBSMIntf*. Select the *createOrder* operation as the operation that allows the creation of the state machine.

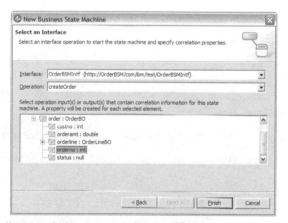

Figure 8.4 Selecting the correlation property for the BSM

4. You will notice a red X with a message that says, "A correlation property must be of a simple type." State machines need a piece of information that can act as a correlation identifier. That way, when an external system wants to cause a state transition, that correlation can be used to interact with the correct instance of the BSM.

5. In our case, a suitable correlation property is the order number, because it is unique, and it uniquely identifies an instance. Expand the *order* part of *OrderBO* and select *orderno*. The red X should disappear. Click **Finish** to complete the creation of the component.

6. Upon creation of the business state machine, the BSM editor is displayed. It shows the initial skeleton of the BSM, as shown in Figure 8.5. It shows InitialState1, FinalState1, the *createOrder* operation, and a simple State1.

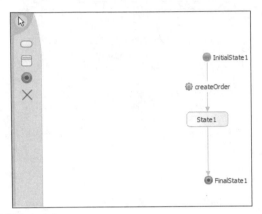

Figure 8.5 The initial BSM skeleton

7. Notice the palette on the left of the BSM editor. It offers the following choices (see Figure 8.6):

   • State (or Simple State) is used to represent the stages at which the state machine can pause.

   • Composite State is essentially a combination of states, thus implementing a smaller state machine.

   • Final State indicates normal completion of the state machine.

   • Terminate State indicates abnormal or premature completion.

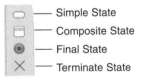

Figure 8.6 The BSM editor palette

8. On the initial BSM skeleton, click the State1 label and change it to *Created*, as shown in Figure 8.7. Then highlight the state. You should see two icons in the Action menu—*Add an Entry* and *Add an Exit*. These let you add Entry and Exit actions to the state.

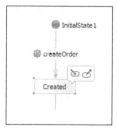

Figure 8.7 The BSM editor showing the Entry and Exit icons

9. We need an Entry action, as indicated by our UML model. But before we do that, we need to define the Partner Reference that we can use to invoke the action.

10. Consistent with the functionality of the BPEL editor, on the right side of the BSM editor is a tray that allows us to define Interfaces, References, Variables, and Correlation Properties. Click the + by the References. Define the *CreditCheckInterfacePartner* by selecting the *CreditCheckInterface* from the list, as shown in Figure 8.8. Click **OK**.

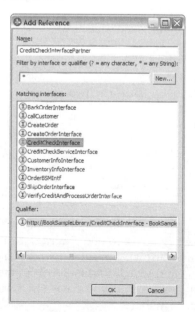

Figure 8.8 Adding a reference

11. Expand *CreditCheckInterfacePartner* and click the *checkCredit* operation. In the Properties view you see the parameters required by that operation. In this case *checkCredit* takes *order* and *customer* as input and returns *riskType*.

But you will notice that the operation requires an instance of *OrderBO* and an instance of *CustomerBO*. To call it successfully, the BSM needs to have variables of those types, and the variables need to be initialized. Go back to the palette and click the + by **Variables** to create the two variables *orderVar* (of type *OrderBO*) and *customerVar* (of type *CustomerBO*).

12. These variables need to be initialized. This can occur at the time the BSM instance is created. To do so, go back to the BSM graph, as shown in Figure 8.9, and click the first transition arrow. Select the **Add an Action** icon.

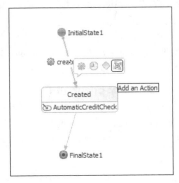

Figure 8.9 Adding an action to initialize the variables

13. In the Properties view for the action, select **Java** for its implementation. Write a simple Java snippet to initialize the two variables we just created, as shown in Listing 8.1.

Listing 8.1 Java Snippet to Initialize the Variables

```
orderVar = createOrder_Input_order;
customerVar = createOrder_Input_customer;
```

14. Notice how the snippet has visibility of the input parameters of the *createOrder* operation. Now we can go back to our *Created* state and select the **Entry** icon (the one with the inbound arrow). An entry named Entry1 gets created. Rename it *AutomaticCreditCheck*, and switch to the Properties tab. In the Details view, shown in Figure 8.10, you can see that you have three ways to implement this entry action—Visual, Java, or Invoke.

Figure 8.10 Completing the invoke definition

15. We choose **Invoke** because we want the automatic credit check to be performed by our credit check service. We then select the *CreditCheckInterfacePartner* as a reference for the invocation. We also set the variables *orderVar* and *customerVar* to the input parameters *order* and *customer*, respectively.

16. That state is now complete. We have added the remaining states and transitions and completed the BSM. The complete business state machine is shown in Figure 8.11.

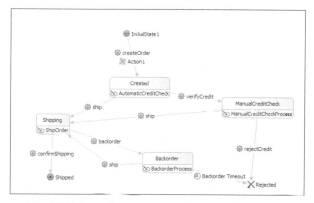

Figure 8.11 The completed BSM graph

17. You may recall that, right after choosing the interface for our BSM, we had to define a "correlation property" and that we chose the order number. This implies that every operation exposed by the BSM needs to have that order number information. You need to associate the correlation property to the appropriate information for every operation in the BSM. This is done by selecting the correlation property (Property1) in the BSM editor.

18. We need to switch to the Properties view and update the definition for each operation. Because all our operations take an instance of *OrderBO*, we just need to point to the *orderno* part in that instance, as shown in Figure 8.12.

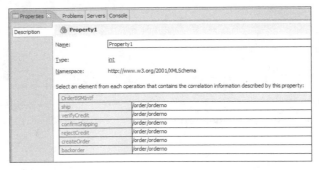

Figure 8.12 The correlation property is bound to the order number

Completing the Assembly Diagram

Now we are ready to create the assembly diagram for the BSM. Figure 8.13 shows how we assembled the BSM. Notice that we had to resolve the references and that we used imports to indicate that the BSM will invoke the relevant BPEL processes.

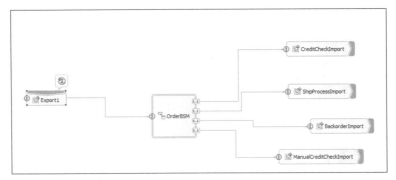

Figure 8.13 The complete assembly diagram

It is important to keep in mind that this BSM requires that the BPEL processes "call back" the BSM to cause the appropriate state transition. The processes we have illustrated so far do not do that. We would need to modify them so that they can interact with the state machine.

Figure 8.14 shows an example of how this should be done. It shows the modified shipping process that invokes the BSM state transitions. Notice that the two circled additional Invoke operations for "call back" have been added, with a corresponding partner reference pointing to the BSM.

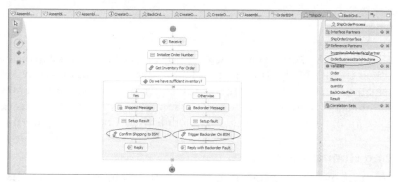

Figure 8.14 The shipping process "calling back" to the BSM

Deploying and Running the BSM

A business state machine is just another SCA component. Therefore, all you need to do to deploy it is generate the deployment code in WID, export the EAR file, and install it on WPS. It is interesting to mention, however, that BSMs are "converted" under the covers into long-running BPEL processes. As such, they are subject to the same rules that apply to installing, uninstalling, and versioning interruptible BPEL processes.

Additionally, instances of a BSM can be started and administered using the Business Process Choreographer Explorer, which also allows you to manipulate "regular" BPEL processes. The Business Process Choreographer Explorer is a browser-based client that you can use to administer and test your process instances. It is covered in detail in Chapter 9, "Business Integration Clients." Figure 8.15 shows how the BPC Explorer shows the BSM template among the list of long-running process templates.

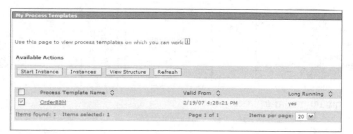

Figure 8.15 BSM template shown in the BPC Explorer

You can start an instance and work on a task using the BPC Explorer just like you would any other long-running BPEL business process. That is the beauty of business state machines.

Human Tasks

A.8.2

Chapter 6 described the process of creating a Human Task activity in a BPEL business process and showed you the use of the Human Task Editor. BPEL describes three types of human tasks—participating human tasks, originating human tasks, and pure human tasks. Usage of these human interaction patterns is based on the scenario within the BPEL business process. A human task cannot be used in a mediation module. It can only be deployed to WPS.

Participating Human Task

A participating task (p-Task) is a human interaction that is invoked from a service component such as a BPEL business process. As shown in Figure 8.16, the computer originates the call to the human.

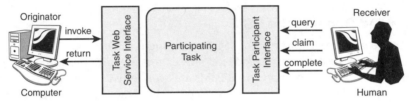

Figure 8.16 Participating human task

Originating Human Task

An originating task (o-Task), shown in Figure 8.17, is one in which a human invokes a service component such as a BPEL business process. It is used to initiate a business process.

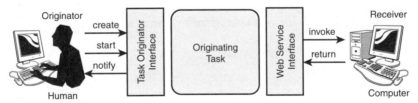

Figure 8.17 Originating human task

Pure Human Task

A pure human task (h-Task) is a service component that is originated by and received by a human. Figure 8.18 shows that the originator and receiver of the task is a human. This task creates work items based on the specified template.

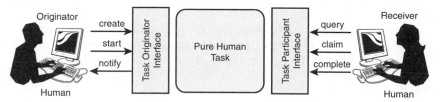

Figure 8.18 Pure human task

Administrative Human Task

An administrative task (a-Task) grants a human administrative powers such as the ability to suspend, terminate, restart, or force-complete a business process. Administrative tasks can be set up either on an Invoke activity or on the process as a whole. This type of task is available only with inline human tasks. So what are inline human tasks?

From an IBM WebSphere architecture perspective, there is another way of looking at these tasks, depending on whether they are used in the BPEL flow or in the assembly diagram. These tasks can be inline human tasks or stand-alone human tasks.

Stand-alone Human Task

When you define a Human Task SCA component in the assembly diagram in WID and then call it via an Invoke activity, that human task is known as a stand-alone task. A stand-alone human task, like all stand-alone tasks, is wired in the context of an assembly diagram and can be reused elsewhere.

Inline Human Task

If you use a Human Task activity (the one with a human icon) directly in a BPEL flow, this is commonly called an inline human task. An inline human task is useful if you want to use any dynamic feature based on process variables. A BPEL flow can use any number and combination of inline and stand-alone human tasks.

Ad Hoc Task

The tasks we have described thus far are predefined human tasks that are created in the tooling, such as WID, and are deployed as part of an SCA module using the normal deployment mechanism. Ad hoc tasks, on the other hand, are defined at runtime using the ad hoc task creation API of the Human Task Manager component in SCA and are created programmatically. There are no originating ad hoc tasks. Ad hoc tasks can be either participating human tasks or pure human tasks. Ad hoc tasks allow for a couple of scenarios that are more common in workflows—subtasks and follow-on tasks.

Subtask

With subtasks, you can dynamically create one or more tasks that can be assigned or delegated to another human to finish. The parent task is considered incomplete until all the subtasks are done. The owner of the parent task is responsible for completing all the subtasks.

Follow-on Task

A follow-on task is created when the parent human task wants another human to do the remaining work. So, the parent task delegates or forwards the task to another person or group to complete. Thus, the owner of the follow-on task is responsible for completing the task. Follow-on tasks are pure human tasks.

User Interface

A.8.3

Human tasks require that we humans have a user interface (UI) to interact with the service component, such as the BPEL business process. The business user really does not care if the UI is a simple Java Server Page (JSP), a Java Server Face (JSF) page, or a sophisticated portlet, as long as there is a screen to enter input values and get the required output from the business process.

User Interface Generator in WID

As mentioned earlier, one of the options is to use process portlets to interact with business processes. The other option is to use the User Interface Generation option in WID. This is available in the Business Integration perspective at the module level. The shipping module shown in Figure 8.19 has four human tasks:

- fonHT is the follow-on human task.
- HT is the participating human task.
- phoneShipperHT is the pure human task.
- startshipHT is the originating human task that starts the shipping process.

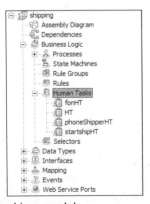

Figure 8.19 Human tasks contained in a module

> ## User Interface Generation
>
> To be able to use the User Interface Generator, the human task nodes should be part of the assembly diagram and should be wired.

Select the human task you want to generate a user interface for, right-click, and select **Generate User Interfaces**. You can choose more than one human task component by pressing the **Ctrl** key and highlighting the next human task component. To illustrate this, highlight the human task named *HT*, right-click, and choose **Generate User Interfaces**.

Figure 8.20 shows that you can choose all the human tasks that have been assembled on the assembly diagram. Also notice that only the participating (HT), pure (phoneShipperHT), and originating (startshipHT) human tasks are listed. Ad hoc tasks are not listed, which include follow-on tasks and subtasks.

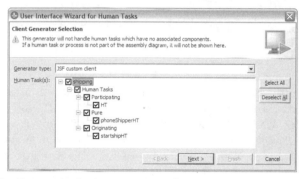

Figure 8.20 Selecting human tasks to generate a client

Do the following in the JSF client configuration screen shown in Figure 8.21:

- Give the dynamic web project a name (shipHT).
- Optionally, specify a gif or jpg file for the company logo.
- Choose the default local client location.
- Select a style—either IBM Style or Cool Blue™ Style.

Click **Finish** to begin the client generation.

> ## Client Styles
>
> If you want more style choices, you have to create a new Cascading Style Sheet (CSS) or change the existing one. The CSS file is located in the generated web project in WebContent\theme\styles.css.

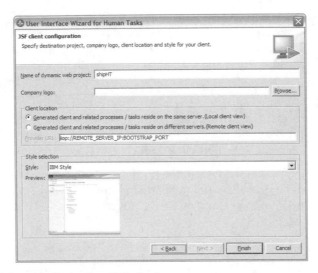

Figure 8.21 Providing details for the JSF client

The wizard generates the web project called *shipHT* and displays a message window indicating what to do next. If you go to the Web perspective in WID, you see a Dynamic Web Project named *shipHT*. You need to deploy the project EAR file to WPS and then access it via http://*HOST_NAME:PORT*/shipHT. The default port is 9080. If you enable WebSphere global security, you will be able to view, claim, and work on tasks based on your role and access settings using this generated JSF client.

Figure 8.22 shows the generated user interface with the New Business Case view. Notice that the two tasks that can be originated by humans are visible—*startshipHT* and *phoneShipperHT*. The participating human task (HT) would come into play in the My ToDo's section when an instance of the task is created.

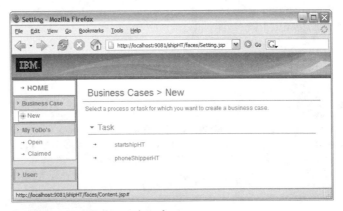

Figure 8.22 Viewing the generated user interface

Web Services

The Web services technology enables you to invoke service applications using Internet protocols such as HTTP. They are self-contained, self-describing, language-independent, and loosely coupled. Yet they are modular in nature and can be published, located, and invoked across the World Wide Web. The following core technologies are used by Web services:

- **Extensible Markup Language (XML)** is used to describe any kind of content in a structured way without any knowledge of the presentation platform.
- **SOAP** is a network, transport, and programming language protocol that is platform-neutral, allowing a client to call a remote service.
- **Web Services Description Language (WSDL)** is an XML-based interface and implementation description language. When dealing with Web services, you must be familiar with WSDL. It contains the operations that a Web service provides and the parameters and data types of these operations, along with the service access information.
- **Web services Inspection Language (WSIL)** is an XML-based specification on how to locate Web services without the need for UDDI.
- The **Universal Description, Discovery, and Integration (UDDI)** server is used to store and retrieve information on service providers and Web services.

There are many standards in Web services. In the business integration space, you should be primarily concerned about BPEL4WS and the corresponding WSDL documents. These documents are commonly called WSDLs. Based on XML, WSDLs provide the schema description of the Web service:

- Name and address information
- Protocol and encoding style to be used when accessing the public operations
- Type information, including operations, parameters, and data types of the interface

> **WSDL**
>
> A WSDL document can be created in one or more physical files. If there are multiple files, you have to connect these files using an Import element. For more information on WSDL, refer to www.w3.org/TR/wsdl.

The main elements of a WSDL document are as follows:

- **Schema:** The data type definitions or schema
- **Port:** A single endpoint that is an aggregation of a binding and a network address
- **Port type:** An abstract set of operations supported by one or more ports
- **Binding:** The concrete protocol and data format specification for a particular port type
- **Service:** A collection of related ports
- **Message:** An abstract, typed definition of the data being passed around

Working with Web Services in WID

WSDL defines four types of port types or operations that a port can support. It is important to know them, because they tell you what sort of input and outputs to expect from the Web service:

- **One-way:** The port receives an input message.
- **Request-response:** The port receives an input message and sends back a related output message.
- **Solicit-response:** The port sends a message and receives a related response.
- **Notification:** In a publish/subscribe scenario, the port sends an output message.

A.8.4

Quite often, you will be asked to invoke a Web service from your business process application. For example, a loan processing application or an order fulfillment application could have a task to check the customer's credit before approving the loan or fulfilling the order. Let's see how that is accomplished. A common practice is to be handed a WSDL file or the URL to the WSDL. To illustrate this scenario, we have a URL that points to a WSDL file that describes the shipping component. As you know, if you open that URL in a web browser, you can view the contents of the WSDL file.

> **WID Capabilities**
>
> To work with Web Services and J2EE applications, you have to enable Advanced J2EE and Web Service Developer in WID's workbench capabilities.

Importing the WSDL file

There are two ways you can get the WSDL into your WID project. In the first option, you can point to the WSDL URL within WID. In the second option, you can save the WSDL file on your local drive before importing it into WID.

1. Point to the WSDL file in a web browser, and import it as an HTTP resource.

   In the Business Integration perspective, select **File** > **Import**. In the Import dialog box, shown in Figure 8.23, choose **HTTP** as the resource to import from a Web server.

   Browse for and choose the folder you want the WSDL file to be imported into, and specify the URL. In most cases, you will use the default option of **No limit** because you want to grab all the information about the Web Service. Click **Next**.

   You can set a timeout connection option on the ensuing screen, which has a default of 10,000 milliseconds. Accept all the other default settings. Click **Finish** to import the WSDL file into the project.

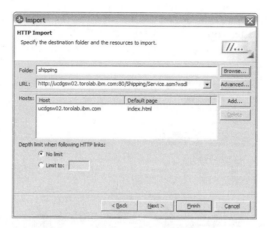

Figure 8.23 Importing a WSDL file as an HTTP resource

2. The other option is to point to the resource in a web browser and save it on your local drive as a WSDL file by giving it a .wsdl file extension. Then import that file into the project.

Open a web browser and point to the WSDL resource. Save a local copy of the file with a .wsdl extension. Even if it is a .NET resource (.asmx), you should save it as a .wsdl file.

In the Business Integration perspective, select **File > Import**. In the Import dialog box, shown in Figure 8.24, choose **WSDL/Interface** to import the WSDL file.

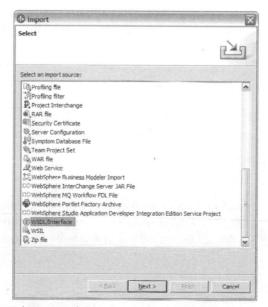

Figure 8.24 Choosing an import option

Specify the source folder to import from and the target module to import into. Select the .wsdl file, and click **Finish**. Figure 8.25 shows *service.wsdl* being imported into the *shipping* module.

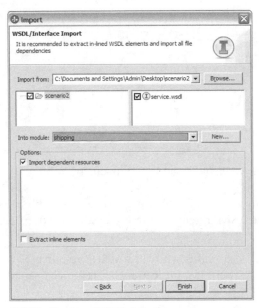

Figure 8.25 Importing a WSDL file as a WSDL/Interface resource

The physical WSDL file is visible in the Physical Resources view. If you look in the WSDL source or look at the expanded view of the *service.wsdl* file, as shown in Figure 8.26, you see the defined types, bindings, and interfaces.

Figure 8.26 Expanded file listing of the imported WSDL

It's worth pointing out the **Extract inline elements** option, which we encourage you to use. A good reason for doing this is to enable reuse of business object and interface definitions elsewhere in a module. Inline elements have a triangle in the top-right corner, and the extracted ones don't.

As a result of importing the WSDL file, you should see the following:

- In the Business Integration perspective, under Interfaces, the new interface, *ServiceSoap*, with a marking indicating that it was a Web service import.
- Under Web service Ports, the bindings described in the WSDL. This particular WSDL contains *ServiceSoap* and *ServiceSoap12*.
- New Data Types added. In this case, *Address*, *ArrayOfItem*, and *Item* should be added.

Testing and Using the WSDL File

Before using the file, you can validate the WSDL using the WSDL validation function in WID:

1. In the Physical Resources view, highlight the WSDL file (*service.wsdl*), right-click, and choose **Validate WSDL file**. Look for the message, "The WSDL file is valid."

2. Again highlight the WSDL file, right-click, and choose **Web services > Generate Java Bean skeleton**. As shown in Figure 8.27, do the following:

   - Make sure the Web service type is **Skeleton Java bean Web service**.

   - Check the **Generate a proxy** option, and choose a Java client proxy.

   - Optionally, you may want to test the Web service.

   Click **Next**.

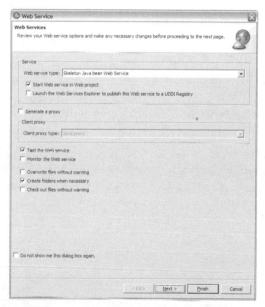

Figure 8.27 Specifying the Web service type

3. Verify that you are using the correct Web service, and click **Next**.

4. On the Service Deployment Configuration screen, click the **Edit** button.
   - Choose WebSphere Process Server v6.0 from the Existing Servers list.
   - Choose IBM WebSphere from the Web service runtime.
   - Choose J2EE version 1.4.

   Click **OK**. The choices should be displayed, as shown in Figure 8.28. Click **Next**.

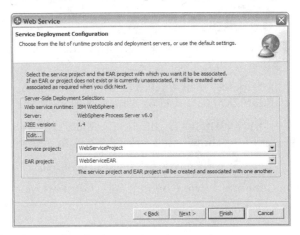

Figure 8.28 Selecting the service deployment environment

5. On the next screen, you may specify security options. For illustration purposes, we chose **No Security**. Click **Next**.

6. If you choose to test the Web service, you get the option to launch the test facility, which by default is the Web Services Explorer. You can launch it now to test the service via the Web Services Explorer, or click **Finish**. The other path is to click **Next** if you want to publish this Web service.

7. The Web Services Explorer is displayed. Any bindings that are described in the Web service are shown in the WSDL Service Details screen. For example, *service.wsdl* has two bindings, *ServiceSoap12* and *ServiceSoap*. Click *ServiceSoap*. You are taken to the Operations and Endpoints screen, as shown in Figure 8.29.

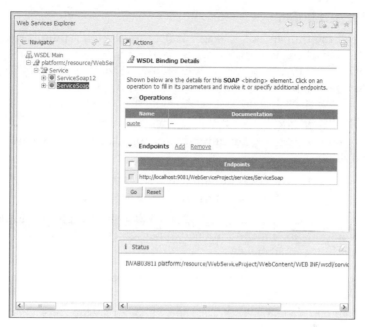

Figure 8.29 Web Services Explorer showing the operations and endpoints

8. You can test any method or operation in the Web service via the Web Services Explorer.

9. Going back to the BPEL Editor, you can add an Invoke activity to the BPEL flow and specify the SoapService interface from the imported WSDL file, just as you would with any other interface.

Importing Inline WSDL Files

A large part of the apparent complexity of WSDL has nothing to do with WSDL itself; it is usually caused by the inline inclusion of XSDs. So, if you have to use such a WSDL file in your business integration solution, the process to import that file is similar to what was explained in the preceding section. The default selection is to leave the inline elements inline. However, you also have the option to separate the inline elements by choosing the option **Extract inline elements** (refer to Figure 8.25).

One of the reasons we encourage people to use the extract inline option is to enable reuse of the business object and interface definitions elsewhere in a module. You will notice, in the navigation tree, that the inline elements have a decorator icon in the top-right corner, whereas the extracted ones do not. Note that the inline elements of dependent WSDLs also are extracted.

Publishing WSDL Files

What if you need the Human Task Manager WSDLs to develop a third-party client to communicate with WebSphere Process Server via Web services? You can use the WebSphere Administrative Console to publish the corresponding WSDL files. These WSDL files contain detailed descriptions of all the operations available with the Web Services API. For example, if you want to work with a .NET client, you must first publish these WSDL files. Then, copy them to your development environment, where they can be used to generate a proxy .NET client:

1. Bring up the WebSphere Administrative console, and log in as a user with administrative rights.

2. Select **Applications** > **SCA Modules**. You should see two container applications—BPEContainer and TaskContainer.

3. Click the *TaskContainer_NODE_NAME_SERVER* application link. In the Configuration tab, under Additional Properties, click the option to **Publish WSDL files**, as shown in Figure 8.7.

> **WSDL Publishing**
>
> Before publishing the WSDL files, be sure to specify the correct Web services endpoint address. This is the URL that your client application uses to access the Web Services APIs.

Figure 8.30 Additional properties of the TaskContainer application showing the publish WSDL option

4. You are asked to click the zip file that contains the application's published WSDL files and save it to a local folder. The file is named *TaskContainer_NODE_NAME_ SERVER_WSDLFiles.zip*, and it contains the HTM WSDLs.

5. You can similarly publish the BPEContainer zip file, which will contain the Business Flow Manager (BFM) WSDLs.

Closing the Link

This chapter covered business state machines, human tasks, and Web services—some of the key components of BPEL and any business integration solution. We also touched on the user interface generation feature, which is extremely useful, because hardly any programming is involved.

A.8.5

BSMs provide a powerful way to quickly assemble event-driven processes, where transitions between states are caused by external stimuli. These processes may be represented by transition graphs that include loops and backward branches, which are hard to implement directly in BPEL. The key difference between a BSM and a BPEL process is that the BSM rarely includes decision logic—its flow is determined by the stimuli coming from outside. Nevertheless, BSMs are translated into BPEL processes before deployment. You can take advantage of the same administrative tools and facilities to manipulate instances of BSMs as if they were regular BPEL processes.

Both BSMs and BPEL processes can have human tasks. A human task lets you intervene and override a business rule, or it could be a simple approval step in a business process. In the runtime environment, an instance of a human task is identified by a name, namespace, and valid-from date. A portal, eForm, JSP, and JSF are some of the user interface options you can create for use with human tasks.

Links to developerWorks

A.8.1   www.ibm.com/developerworks/websphere/library/techarticles/0607_beers/ 0607_beers.html

A.8.2   www.ibm.com/developerworks/websphere/library/techarticles/0607_roach/ 0607_roach.html

A.8.3   www.ibm.com/developerworks/websphere/library/techarticles/0703_shankar/ 0703_shankar.html

A.8.4   www.ibm.com/developerworks/websphere/library/techarticles/0703_xu/ 0703_xu.html

A.8.5   www.ibm.com/developerworks/websphere/techjournal/0602_gregory/ 0602_gregory.html

Business Integration Clients

This chapter discusses client applications within the context of a business integration solution. We specifically discuss the Business Process Choreographer Explorer and the Business Process Choreographer Observer (BPCO). These WebSphere Process Server (WPS)-related client applications use published application programming interfaces (APIs). Users can use these same APIs to create custom clients if they so choose.

After a brief introduction to the Business Process Choreographer, we take a detailed look at the workings of the two web-based clients that come with WPS. Because the Observer provides a sort of monitoring function, it could have been part of Chapter 14, "Business Monitoring." But we decided to discuss it in this chapter because it is really a client application of WPS. Chapter 14 concentrates on WebSphere Business Monitor, which is a separate product that offers a lot more functionality.

A.9.1

Business Process Choreographer (BPC)

As mentioned in Chapter 5, "WebSphere Process Server," BPC is the J2EE process flow engine that supports BPEL-based business processes and human tasks in WPS. It manages the lifecycle of business processes and human tasks and invokes the appropriate services. BPC provides the following facilities:

- It helps expose both BPEL-based business processes and Task Execution Language (TEL)-based human tasks as services in a Service-Oriented Architecture (SOA) and Service Component Architecture (SCA).
- APIs for developing customized applications that interact with business processes and human tasks
- Web-based Business Process Choreographer Explorer, which lets you manage and administer the business processes—specifically, human tasks

- Web-based Business Process Choreographer Observer, which lets you observe the states of running business processes

The APIs—specifically, the Business Flow Manager (BFM) APIs and the Human Task Manager (HTM) APIs—are explained in Chapter 11, "Business Integration Programming." Figure 9.1 shows the set of configurable Java Server Faces (JSF) components and the client model objects that are used to communicate with the process engine.

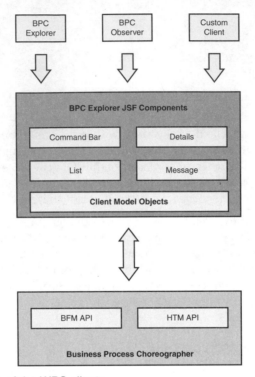

Figure 9.1 Architecture of the WPS clients

Business Process Choreographer Explorer

Business Process Choreographer Explorer, or BPC Explorer, is a web-based application in WPS that implements a generic web user interface for interacting with business processes, especially the human tasks in a business process. The BPC Explorer is installed during the profile creation if you choose to install the sample Business Process Choreographer configuration in either a stand-alone WPS environment or a WPS cluster. It is usually installed on the application server or cluster where the business process container and human task container are installed.

BPC Explorer is used to view information about process and task templates, process
instances, task instances, and their associated objects. You can also start new process
instances, create and start tasks, restart failed activities, manage work items, and delete completed process and task instances. But you need administrator privileges to perform these
tasks. Figure 9.2 shows how the BPC Explorer relates to WPS.

A.9.2

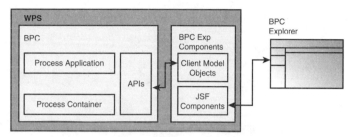

Figure 9.2 Business Process Choreographer Explorer application architecture

The BPC Explorer components are a set of configurable, reusable elements that are based on
JSF technology. The components consist of a set of JSF components and a set of client model
objects. These elements can be embedded in web applications, which can then access
installed business processes and human task applications.

- **JSF components** can be embedded in your Java Server Pages (JSPs) files when build-
  ing your web applications. The following components are supplied:
  - The List component displays a list of application objects in a table. It comes
    with an associated list handler.
  - The Details component displays properties of tasks, work items, activities,
    process instances, and process templates. It has an associated details handler.
  - The CommandBar component displays a bar with buttons representing com-
    mands that operate on the object in a details view or on the selected objects in
    a list.
  - The Message component displays a message list that can contain either a
    Service Data Object (SDO) or a simple type.
- **Client model components** are used with the JSF components. The objects imple-
  ment some of the interfaces of the underlying BPC API while wrapping the original
  object. They provide national language support (NLS) for labels and other text.

Working with the BPC Explorer

The BPC Explorer is available in a stand-alone WPS environment and in the test environment in WID. From the test environment in WID, you can go to the Servers view and make
sure that the test WPS v6.0 is running. Right-click and choose **Launch** > **Business Process
Choreographer Explorer**. You see the screen shown in Figure 9.3.

Figure 9.3 Launching the Business Process Choreographer Explorer

Remember, you can use this client application to view information about process and task templates, process instances, task instances, and their associated objects. If you, as a user, have the authority, you can also act on these objects. For example, you can start new process instances, create and start tasks, repair and restart failed activities, manage work items, work on tasks, and even delete completed process and task instances.

BPC Explorer Installation

If you ever have to install the BPC Explorer manually, you will find the JACL script, named *clientconfig.jacl*, in *WPS_HOME\ProcessChoreographer*. Go to that folder and enter the `wsadmin` command, specifying the JACL script as input:

```
WPS_HOME/bin/wsadmin -f clientconfig.jacl
   ( [-username
username] [-password password] | [-conntype NONE] )
```

From a runtime perspective, you can go to the WebSphere Administrative Console. Among the list of enterprise applications that are installed, you will find an application named BPCExplorer_*NODE_NAME_SERVER_NAME*; it should be running. (This is shown in Figure 9.10 later in this chapter.) The BPC Explorer can then be launched from a stand-alone or clustered WPS server via http://*HOST_NAME*:9080/bpc. The default port is 9080; it could be different in your environment. The initial screen should look like Figure 9.4. If WebSphere Security is enabled, you are prompted for the user credentials.

Figure 9.4 The initial screen of the Business Process Choreographer Explorer

The navigation pane on the left has four menu groups—Process Templates, Process Instances, Task Templates, and Task Instances. Initially, the main screen on the right displays details of My Tasks. Assuming that the *BookSample* project has been deployed, you can click **My Process Templates** to view the various process instances. You should see something similar to what is shown in Figure 9.5. We continue to use our *BookSample* process and show you how, as a user, you can start a process instance, claim and work on a task, and view the various business processes.

Figure 9.5 Starting a new process instance

Starting a Process Instance

In the BPC Explorer, select **My Process Templates**. That should display all the process templates that have been deployed.

1. Select the checkbox for **CreateOrderProcess**, and click the **Start Instance** button (see Figure 9.5).

2. You are taken to the page where you can enter data for the order. Enter the order information, and click the **Submit** button to complete the creation of an instance of *CreateOrderProcess*.

Claiming and Working on a Task

In the BPC Explorer, click **My Tasks** to view the tasks that you can work on. Do the following to claim and complete the *ScrutinizeCredit* task:

1. Click the checkbox next to that task, and click the **Work On** button. This action causes the task to be claimed by you. You are taken to the Task Message Page, shown in Figure 9.6.

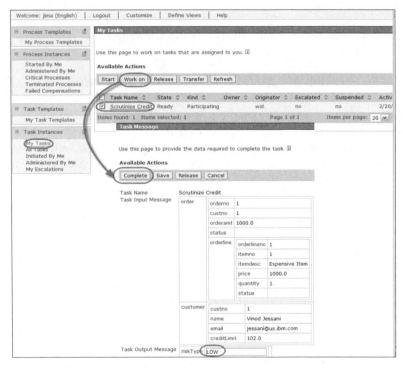

Figure 9.6 Work on a task by entering the input values.

2. On the Task Message page, enter LOW in the **riskType** field, and click the **Complete** button. This completes the task.

So what does completing a task mean? What happens next? Completing a task does not mean that the process is done. This one task among many within a business process, which required human intervention, has been completed. Control is now given back to the business process. The business process goes on to the next task.

Viewing the Business Process

In the BPC Explorer, select **My Process Templates**. Select one of the Process Templates, and click **View Structure**. This facility is used to view the graphical image of the process template. Figure 9.7 shows the *CreateOrderProcess* structure.

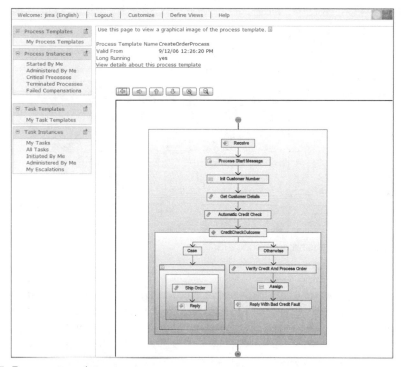

Figure 9.7 Process template structure

Hovering the mouse pointer over any of the activities displays a callout with details about that activity. Clicking an activity takes you to a page with further details about that activity. Additionally, this page has a link to view the details about the process template. Clicking the **View details about the process template** link takes you to a page that displays tabular information about the template in greater detail.

In addition to showing the structure of a process template, the BPC Explorer graphically displays information about a running or finished process instance. Figure 9.8 shows an instance of *BackOrderProcess* that is waiting to retry the order.

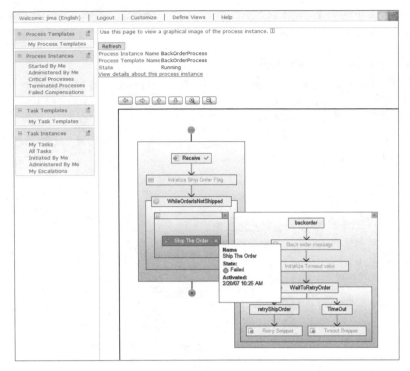

Figure 9.8 Structure of a running process instance

An examination of that structure shows that the receive completed successfully (indicated by a green checkmark in the node) and that the *Ship The Order* Invoke activity raised a fault (indicated by a red X in the node). Clicking the *Ship The Order* activity takes you to a page that has further details about this particular call. You can see the input to that call as well as the fault it received from the service it called.

Many more tasks can be performed in the BPC Explorer. It also can be extended using the BPC APIs. You can use the generic BPC APIs, which the BPC Explorer uses, to customize the user interface. You can do the following:

- Change the appearance of the default web application by modifying the JSP and JSF files.
- Customize the interface for different groups and roles.
- Personalize the interface by modifying the predefined views.
- Customize the input and output forms.

The main package is *com.ibm.bpc.clientcore*. These APIs can be viewed at http://publib.boulder.ibm.com/infocenter/dmndhelp/v6rxmx/index.jsp?topic=/com.ibm.wsps.javadoc.doc/doc/com/ibm/bpc/clientcore/package-summary.html. Developers should look at the following packages:

- com.ibm.bpc.clientcore
- com.ibm.bpc.clientcore.converter
- com.ibm.bpc.clientcore.exception
- com.ibm.bpe.clientmodel
- com.ibm.bpe.clientmodel.bean
- com.ibm.bpe.jsf.component.taglib
- com.ibm.task.clientmodel
- com.ibm.task.clientmodel.bean

Observing Versus Monitoring

There are levels of observation. An enterprise might want to observe or keep an eye on things at the IT infrastructure level—the hardware components and software components such as services. The IT department might want to observe things at the component level, so that they can identify and track various objects as they are deployed. At the application or business level, companies want to interpret the data contained in the objects and monitor the information flow. Products can be used at each level, such as Tivoli® Monitoring products, Business Process Choreographer Observer, and WebSphere Business Monitor.

We will mainly discuss event and audit logging as it pertains to WPS. The logging architecture is shown in Figure 9.9. Audit data is stored in Audit database tables, which are actually part of BPEDB. All other event data is stored in the Common Event Infrastructure (CEI) data store. State Observer Plug-ins (SOPs) need to be installed before they can observe the state of WPS and store the data in repositories. Both the SOPs—CEI SOP and Audit SOP—need to be installed.

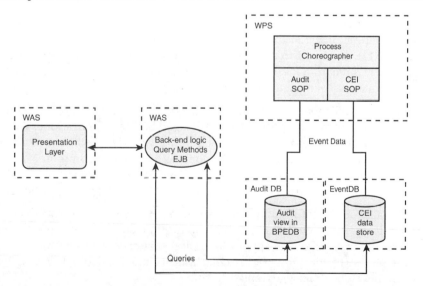

Figure 9.9 Logging architecture of WPS

The next section looks at CEI, followed by a discussion of the BPCO, commonly called the Observer.

Common Event Infrastructure (CEI)

The CEI is part of the core SOA infrastructure and serves as the foundation for monitoring applications. Actually, CEI is a core technology of the IBM Autonomic Computing initiative. This provides basic event management services, including consolidating and persisting raw events from multiple heterogeneous sources and distributing those events to event consumers.

Common Base Event (CBE)

A.9.3

IBM uses the CEI throughout its product portfolio, the event definition of which is based on the Common Base Event (CBE). Before we get into CBE, let's look at this from an application perspective. An application creates an event object whenever something happens that either needs to be recorded for later analysis or that might require the trigger of additional work. An event is a structured notification that reports information that is related to a situation. An event reports three kinds of information:

- The situation (what happened)
- The identity of the affected component, such as the particular server that shut down
- The identity of the component reporting the situation, which might be the same as the affected component

The application that creates the event object is called the *Event Source*. Event sources can use a common structure for the event. The CBE is the accepted standard for such a structure. The CBE is an XML document that is defined as part of the autonomic computing initiative. The CBE defines common fields, the values they can take, and the exact meanings of these values. The format has been standardized by OASIS.

More precisely, the CBE model is a standard that defines a common representation of events that is intended for use by enterprise management and business applications. This standard, which is developed by the IBM Autonomic Computing Architecture Board, supports encoding of logging, tracing, management, and business events using a common XML-based format. This format makes it possible to correlate different types of events that originate from different applications. CEI currently supports version 1.0.1 of the CBE specification.

The CBE contains all the information that is needed by the consumers to understand the event. This information includes data about the runtime environment, the business environment, and the instance of the application object that created the event. More information about CBE can be found in the specification document at ftp://www6.software.ibm.com/software/developer/library/ac-toolkitdg.pdf.

One of the Integration Applications in the WebSphere Administrative Console is called the CBE Browser. It lets you view details of CBEs from the Common Events Infrastructure. You can get to the CBE Browser either from the WebSphere Administrative Console or by entering http://*HOST_NAME:PORT*/ibm/console/cbebrowser in a web browser. The default port is 9060. WPS uses the same WebSphere CEI to log and access logged events.

Enabling CEI in WebSphere

During the WPS installation process, you are required to configure CEI-related EJBs, Queue Manager, and the database. All the common database products are supported. For performance reasons, the CEI database should be configured on a remote database server.

> **CEI Database Configuration**
>
> When installing WPS, the recommendation is to name the CEI database CEIEVENT rather than use the default name of EVENT.

Also during WPS installation process, the EventServer and EventServerMdb applications get deployed, along with the associated JMS configurations. You can verify this by bringing up the WebSphere Administrative Console and selecting **Applications** > **Enterprise Applications**. You should see the *EventServer* and *EventServerMdb* applications listed and started, as shown in Figure 9.10.

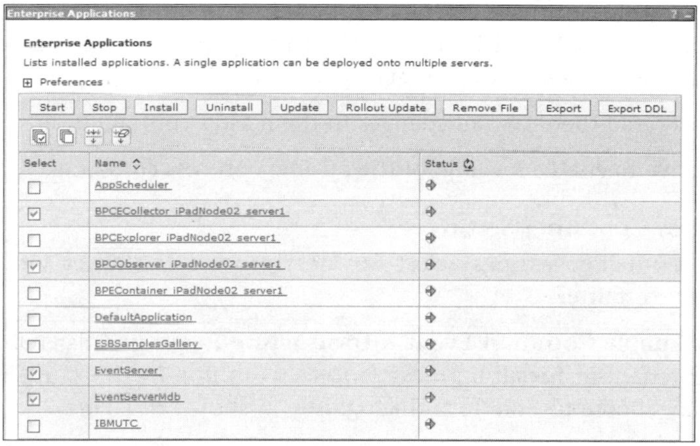

Figure 9.10 The Observer and CEI applications shown in WebSphere Administrative Console

If you do not see these applications, you can manually install them using the *wsadmin* utility. The event application and event message application enterprise archive (EAR) files, along with the relevant JACL scripts, can be found in the *WPS_HOME*\profiles*PROFILE_NAME*\event\application directory. We show the sample commands here, but for more details, refer to the product InfoCenter.

Use the following to install the event application:

```
wsadmin -profile event-profile.jacl -f event-application.jacl
-action install -earfile event-application.ear -backendid
DATABASE_TYPE -node NODE_NAME -server server1
```

Use the following to install the event messaging application:

```
wsadmin -profile event-profile.jacl -f default-event-message.jacl
-action install -earfile event-message.ear -node NODE_NAME
-server server1
```

CEI Monitoring

If you want to monitor or observe CEI events, you have to enable CEI logging in WPS. You can do that via the WebSphere Administrative Console. That setting has to be activated in both the Human Task Container and the Business Process Container.

Bring up the Administrative Console in a web browser, and select **Servers** > **Application servers** > **server1** or the name of your WPS.

Human Task Container Setting

1. Under Container Settings, select **Human task container settings** > **Human task container**.

2. Check **Enable Common Event Infrastructure logging**. This enables the CEI logging mechanism for all human tasks running in this container. Optionally, you may choose to **Enable audit logging**.

3. Click **OK**, and then save all changes to the master configuration.

Similarly, you have to enable logging for the business process container.

Business Process Container Setting

1. Under Container Settings, select **Business process container settings** > **Business process container**.

2. Check **Enable Common Event Infrastructure logging**. This enables the CEI logging mechanism for all business processes running in this container. Optionally, you may choose to **Enable audit logging**, as shown in Figure 9.11.

3. Click **OK**, and then save all changes to the master configuration.

After you configure these settings, you must restart the server for the changes to take effect. You then can use the BPC Observer, as discussed next.

Figure 9.11 Enabling CEI logging in the Administrative Console

Business Process Choreographer Event Collector

From an implementation perspective, the Business Process Choreographer Event Collector, commonly called the Event Collector, is a J2EE application that collects all the CEI events and stores them in a database. By default, it uses the BPEDB. The Business Process Choreographer Observer in turn is configured to monitor that database. The Collector is installed during profile creation if you choose to install the sample BPC configuration. Among the Enterprise Applications listed in the WebSphere Administrative Console, you will notice an application named BPCECollector_*NODE_NAME_SERVER_NAME* (refer to Figure 9.10). Even though we mention the Event Collector here, users normally do not have to concern themselves with this Event Collector application.

Business Process Choreographer Observer (BPCO)

Business Process Choreographer Observer, also called the Observer, is a utility that lets you visualize either audit trail data that has been generated with the BPC components or event data generated with the CEI component.

The Observer, like the Collector, is installed during profile creation if you choose to install the sample BPC configuration. The corresponding log files—setupEventCollector.log and

A.9.4

setupObserver.log—can be found in the *WPS_HOME*\profiles*PROFILE_NAME*\logs folder. If you bring up the WebSphere Administrative Console and select **Applications > Enterprise Applications**, you see an enterprise application named BPCObserver_*NODE_NAME_ SERVER_NAME* (refer to Figure 9.10). In WID, you can go to the Servers view and make sure that the test WPS server is running. Right-click and choose **Launch > Business Process Choreographer Observer**.

The Collector and the Observer work together to show you the states of running business processes and human tasks. They are called raw process reporting tools. If you want to use the Observer with events generated by CEI, the CEI Consumer should be installed. You cannot drill down and find processes by a policy ID or find out how long it took to work on a human task. For that you need a business monitoring and business reporting tool, such as the WebSphere Business Monitor.

Installing BPCO

In a clustered environment, there might be a need to install the Observer manually. A *setupObserver* script can be used in that situation. BPCO is based on two J2EE enterprise applications:

- Business Process Choreographer Event Collector
- Business Process Choreographer Observer

These applications use the same database. The Event Collector reads event information from the CEI bus and stores it in the Observer database. Periodically, the raw event data is transformed into a format suitable for queries from the Observer.

> **BPCO Installation**
>
> If you ever have to install the Observer manually, you will find the setup script, called *setupObserver*, in *WPS_HOME*\ProcessChoreographer\ config.

If you invoke the *setupObserver* script, you can follow the screen prompts, which are self-explanatory. The initial screen is shown in Figure 9.12. Follow the prompts for the remainder of the script. Note that if WebSphere Security is enabled, you are prompted to supply the security credentials.

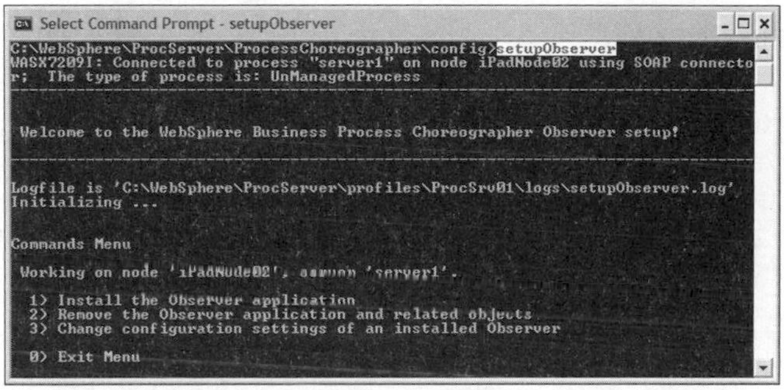

Figure 9.12 Observer setup menu

After installing the BPCO, we recommend stopping and restarting the application server. Table 9.1 shows some of the values that we used with the *setupObserver* script. Note that a related *setupConsumer* script can be found in *WPS_HOME*\sample\observer.

Table 9.1 Values Used to Install the BPC Observer Application

Input Field	Value Used
Application name	BPC_Observer
JNDI name of the database	jdbc/BPEDB
Database schema	BPCOschema

Enabling Logging for the BPCO

To enable logging for the business process container, follow these steps:

1. In the WebSphere Administrative Console, select **Servers** > **Application servers**. Click the server where the business process container is configured.

2. Under Container Settings, choose **Business process container settings** > **Business process container**.

3. In the **General properties**, enable one or both of the following options:
   - Enable Common Event Infrastructure logging
   - Enable audit logging

4. Click **Apply**, and save the configuration.

We recommend restarting WPS.

Working with the Observer

As soon as the BPC Observer is running, you can use its web-based interface to work with it. In a web browser, enter http://*HOST_NAME:PORT*/bpcobserver, where the default port number is 9080. If you are working in WID, you can launch the BPC Observer from the Servers view. In Figure 9.3, you can see the option to Launch the Business Process Choreographer Observer. Note that if WebSphere Security is enabled, you are prompted for the user credentials. Figure 9.13 shows the initial screen of the BPC Observer.

Figure 9.13 Initial screen of BPC Observer

The navigation pane on the left has five menu groups—Overview, Lists, Charts, Process Reports, and Activity Reports. The Overview is just that. It gives you an overview of what the Observer can currently see, as shown in Figure 9.13. The main screen on the right displays the current overall statistics:

- Time stamps of the oldest record and the most recent record
- Total number of events
- Total number of process templates
- Total number of activity templates
- Total number of users

You can use the predefined reports or create your own Process reports and Activity Reports by clicking the icons shown in Figure 9.13. Peering into our test system, where we deployed our *BookSample* application, we can observe processes, activities, or users over a period of time. Or you may even display the information in the form of charts—line chart (which is the default), bar chart, or pie chart. Figure 9.14 shows a Process Instance Snapshot. Notice the ten predefined states shown in the legend on the right and along the x-axis.

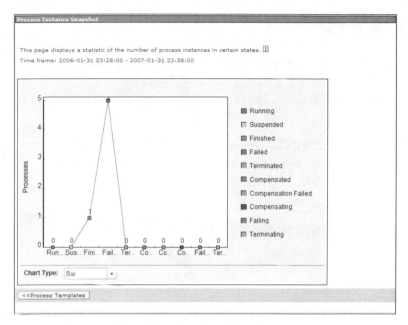

Figure 9.14 Process Instance Snapshot showing a line chart

Further exploration of the Business Process Choreographer Observer is left to you. There is also quite a bit of information in the WPS Product InfoCenter.

Closing the Link

In the Servers View in WID, if you highlight the WPS Test Server and right-click, you have an option to launch applications, as shown in Figure 9.15. The BPC Explorer is a true WPS Client. And to some extent, so is the BPC Observer. The rest of them, except for the WPS Samples Gallery, can be classified as administrative clients.

Figure 9.15 Launch application screen in WID

From a monitoring perspective, only Business Process Choreographer Observer was discussed in this chapter. As mentioned, WebSphere Business Monitor is covered in Chapter 14.

Links to developerWorks

A.9.1   www.ibm.com/developerworks/websphere/library/techarticles/0612_wayne/
0612_wayne.html

A.9.2   www.ibm.com/developerworks/websphere/library/techarticles/0702_shankar/
0702_shankar.html

A.9.3   www.ibm.com/developerworks/webservices/library/ws-odbp7/

A.9.4   http://www-1.ibm.com/support/docview.wss?uid=swg27008553

Chapter 10

Business Integration Services Management

A n Important aspect of the Service-Oriented Architecture (SOA) is the Information Technology (IT) Service Management, which includes managing, securing, and monitoring services, applications, and resources. These aspects are normally part of the underlying foundation. So, be it a small environment or a large multinode environment, these are relevant to all architectures.

This chapter discusses enabling security, collecting audit logs, and setting up tracing within the context of a business integration solution. We touched on event logging and the Common Event Infrastructure when we discussed the Business Process Choreographer Observer in Chapter 9, "Business Integration Clients." WebSphere Business Monitor is covered in Chapter 14, "Business Monitoring."

This chapter also discusses versioning of business processes. What would seem like an innocuous thing actually presents a unique aspect of managing long-running business processes in BPEL.

Security

Security is always to be addressed at the enterprise level. Security in a SOA is applicable at all layers. You have operating system security, application security, network security, and various other forms of security. This section talks about enabling security at the application server level. Then we look at how it affects the WPS components.

Whether it is securing data at an enterprise level, certain applications at the department level, or individual user accounts at the main level, security has the following facets:

- **Authentication:** Credentials of the user or a process are validated.
- **Authorization:** Does the authenticated user have permission to perform a certain task?

- **Integrity and privacy:** Ensuring that the data sent over the network is not modified and cannot be viewed by unauthorized parties.
- **Identity propagation with single sign-on (SSO):** The client should be asked to authenticate once, and the context should be propagated to multiple systems.

WebSphere Security

A.10.1

WebSphere security addresses the core security provisions of any enterprise system. In particular, we focus on two aspects of security for business integration:

- Enabling authentication and authorization mechanisms for incoming requests by enabling Global Security at the application server level. This operation accomplishes two objectives:
  - Turning on administrative security so that only authorized users can operate on the WPS administrative console or use scripts to administer WPS resources.
  - Activating the standard J2EE security interceptors for authentication and authorization so that client applications can access protected resources (such as web pages, EJBs, or SCA components) only after they have been successfully authenticated, and if they are authorized to do so.

> **Note**
>
> WebSphere administrative security and J2EE (application) security will be enabled in future releases. However, the remainder of this chapter assumes that enabling Global Security also enables application security.

- WPS components need to invoke other services and require the support of a database and messaging infrastructure. For example, the SCA runtime uses a database and relies on the SI Bus for messaging. Similarly, the Business Process Choreographer uses a relational database and messaging support. CEI also requires messaging and a relational database. In a secure environment, these WPS components need to be able to forward security credentials (user ID and password) to those services. We will briefly discuss the mechanisms that allow WPS to do so.

Enabling WebSphere Global Security

As mentioned, WebSphere Process Server security relies on the WebSphere Application Server security infrastructure for authentication and authorization of client requests. Three areas require security credentials when installing WPS. If you do not provide the usernames and passwords during the installation process, you can always enter the information using the WebSphere administrative console. Those three components are the Service Component Architecture runtime, Business Process Choreographer container, and Common Event Infrastructure.

Figure 10.1 is a block diagram showing the WebSphere security stack, which is what WPS uses. It illustrates that all incoming requests, whether they are processed by the web container or the SCA runtime, are filtered by the WebSphere Application Server security interceptors, if they are enabled. To activate those interceptors, you need to enable WebSphere Global Security.

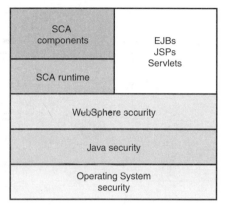

Figure 10.1 WPS security stack

> **WPS Security Tip**
>
> When you create a WPS profile, you are prompted for a username and password at various steps. The credentials you supply are required after you enable Global Security and must correspond to identities in the user registry chosen for the profile.

In a stand-alone server configuration, you can enable Global Security at any time using the administrative console after the server is started. In a WebSphere Network Deployment cell, it is recommended that you enable security after you have federated the nodes to the cell and you have successfully started the Deployment Manager process and all the Node Agents. After you have enabled Global Security, you need to restart your server, or all the servers in the cell, for the security changes to take effect.

Steps to Enable Global Security in WebSphere

The first step in securing your WPS environment and the applications is to enable Global Security. This must be done for each profile. Assuming that WPS is installed and the server has been started, follow these steps:

1. Bring up the WebSphere administrative console via http://*HOST_NAME*:9060/admin. Note that 9060 is the default port.

2. Because security is not yet enabled, you can log in with any username.

3. In the navigation pane, select **Security** > **Global security**. Check the **Enable global security** box, as shown in Figure 10.2. Then uncheck **Enforce Java 2 security** unless you are very sure that your applications require and are configured for this type of security.

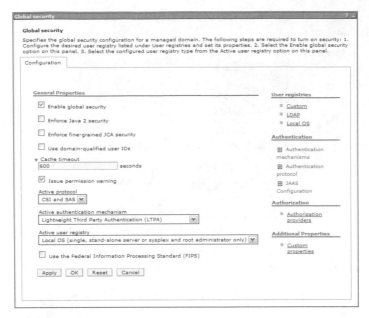

Figure 10.2 Enabling WebSphere Global Security

4. We also made a couple of subtle changes:
    - In the **Active authentication mechanism** setting, we chose **Lightweight Third Party Authentication (LTPA)**. That is because WPS does not support Simple WebSphere Authentication Mechanism (SWAM).
    - For the **Active user registry** setting, **Local OS** was chosen. This setting implies that incoming requests will be authenticated against the user registry provided by the operating system; therefore, users and passwords must match those defined at the OS level. Note that Local OS can be used for only single stand-alone configurations. In a Network Deployment cell or a production environment, you will use a Lightweight Directory Authentication Protocol (LDAP) server. However, this setting determines which user registry WPS uses to authenticate incoming requests.

5. Click the **Apply** button, and then save the changes to the master configuration.

> ## J2EE Security
>
> If you enable Java 2 security, any application that requires more Java 2 security permissions than are granted in the default policy might fail to run properly.

Configuring Security Using an LDAP Server

WebSphere Application Server (and therefore WPS) supports three user registries, shown on the top right of Figure 10.2: Custom, LDAP, and Local OS. We mentioned that the Local OS registry requires that users and passwords be defined at the OS level. You would choose the Custom user registry if you intend to use or develop your own repository of users and passwords, such as a database. You need to implement certain interfaces to configure the custom user registry (CUR).

Assuming that you have the IBM Tivoli Directory Server, which is an LDAP server, accessible by the WPS node, we can proceed to use it as the user registry rather than the Local OS. The main steps are as follows:

1. In the WebSphere Administrative Console, on the Global security page, under User registries, click the **LDAP** link. Enter the LDAP server information:

   Give the LDAP Server user ID, password, and hostname.

   Click **OK**, and save the changes.

2. Back on the Global security page, select **Authentication > Authentication mechanisms**. Click the only choice that is available—**LTPA**.

   Enter a password and confirm it.

   Click **OK**, and save the changes.

3. Back on the Global security page, do the following:

   Check the **Enable global security** box. Then uncheck **Enforce Java 2 security**.

   In the Active authentication mechanism field, choose **Lightweight Third Party Authentication (LTPA)**.

   For the Active user registry setting, choose **Lightweight Directory Access Protocol (LDAP) user registry**.

   Click the **OK** button. If the connection to LDAP works and the users are validated, you have an opportunity to save the configuration.

   Save the changes to the master configuration.

Note that WPS must be restarted for the security changes to take effect. After a restart, when you bring up the WebSphere Administrative Console, you are challenged. Enter the user ID and password you used during configuration to log in, as shown in Figure 10.3.

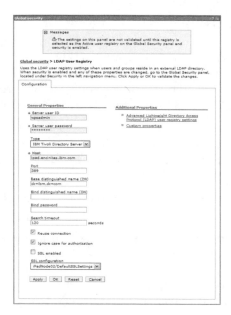

Figure 10.3 LDAP server settings when enabling WebSphere Global Security

Initially, only the user you specified when configuring security is allowed to use the WebSphere Administrative console. What if you want other users to be able to use the console? Before we explain how that can be done, you need to know that you can assign four administrative roles to different users or groups:

- The **Administrator** role has full access to all the administrative activities.
- The **Operator** role can modify the status of existing configuration objects. For example, an Operator can stop and start applications. An Operator is not allowed to make changes to the configuration objects or create new ones.
- The **Configurator** role can create new configuration objects, such as data sources or Java Messaging Service (JMS) destinations. However, in the Configurator role, one cannot act on the status of resources.
- The **Monitor** role is assigned to people who can only inspect the configuration and the status of resources. They are not granted the authority to make any changes.

Now that you know about the roles, we can show you how easy it is to allow users to access the console:

1. After logging onto the console, select **System administration** > **Console settings**, and click **Console Users**, as shown in Figure 10.4. Note that if you wanted to authorize a group of users, you would click **Console Groups**.

Figure 10.4 Choosing the console settings

2. On the main console panel, click **Add**, and then enter the user ID of the user you want to add, as shown in Figure 10.5. Select a role from the list of four roles.

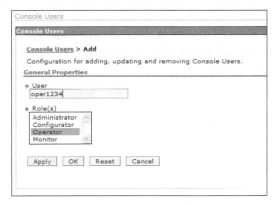

Figure 10.5 Adding a console user and selecting the role

3. Click **OK**, and save your changes.

As we mentioned, protecting the administrative facilities from unauthorized access is one of the effects of enabling Global Security. The other major consequence of enabling Global Security is that all the interceptors for J2EE authentication and authorization become active. These interceptors provide an access control mechanism for J2EE resources that are protected by an authentication or authorization scheme.

The J2EE security model is role-based, along the lines of what we saw for the security settings for the administrative console:

- Users need to establish an identity by authenticating to the server, either by providing user ID and password or using certificates.
- After a valid identity is established, the server can associate the user with one or more J2EE roles, which application developers have previously defined. The association between these roles and the actual users or groups occurs at application deployment time and can be modified administratively. For example, an application may define a *Manager* role. At deployment time, you can associate the *Management* LDAP group to the *Manager* role. When a member of that group performs authentication, the server can establish that the user is in the *Manager* role.

- At application execution time, the server also can verify whether the user can perform certain protected actions, such as hitting a certain protected JSP or calling an EJB. Again, the application developers must have defined an authorization scheme for their application components by specifying which roles are authorized to access the various resources. For instance, if a user who is not assigned the *Manager* role attempts to access a web page that is visible only to users in the *Manager* role, the server throws an authorization exception. No authorization checking is performed unless the resource is explicitly protected and assigned to a role.

The J2EE programming model also includes APIs for the programmatic enforcement of authorization schemes. If you want to protect only a section of a method in an EJB, or if you want an EJB to perform different actions depending on the role of the current user, you can utilize the *isUserInRole* API in your code and make the appropriate decision. That API will work as expected only if Global Security is active. It is outside the scope of this book to provide a description of the many aspects of J2EE security. We suggest you refer to the ample literature that is available on this subject.

Mapping Security Roles for the BPC Applications

The Business Process Choreographer, which comprises Business Process and Human Tasks support, relies on J2EE applications and on the J2EE authentication and authorization mechanisms we explained earlier in this chapter. You may need to customize the security role mappings of the enterprise applications that are related to the Business Process Choreographer.

Modifying these mappings is no different from mapping users to roles for any J2EE application installed on the system. As an example, here we show you how to access and change the role mappings for the Business Process Engine application:

1. Access the administrative console, and navigate to **Applications** > **Enterprise Applications**.

2. Click the application called **BPEContainer_*node_name_server_name***. For instance, if you are working with the WID test server, the application name will be **BPEContainer_widnode_server1**.

3. Click **Map security roles to users/groups**, the first of the two links highlighted in Figure 10.6.

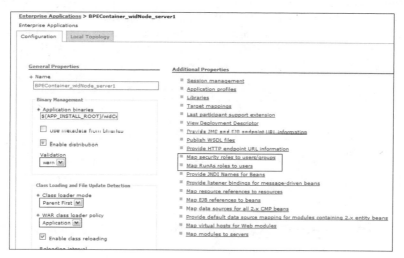

Figure 10.6 Assigning security roles to the BPC Application

4. You see that four roles have been defined for this application, as shown in Figure 10.7. Select the **BPESystemAdministrator** role, and click **Look up users** to map to an individual user. You can also map the role to an entire group by clicking **Look up groups**.

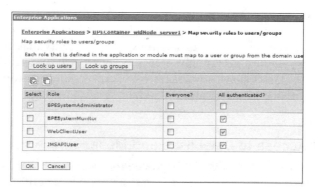

Figure 10.7 Mapping security roles to users or groups

5. On the subsequent dialog, you can run a query against the user registry to extract valid users from the registry and then select them for mapping. In Figure 10.8, we chose user **T60MC\Administrator** and then clicked the >> button to associate it with the role.

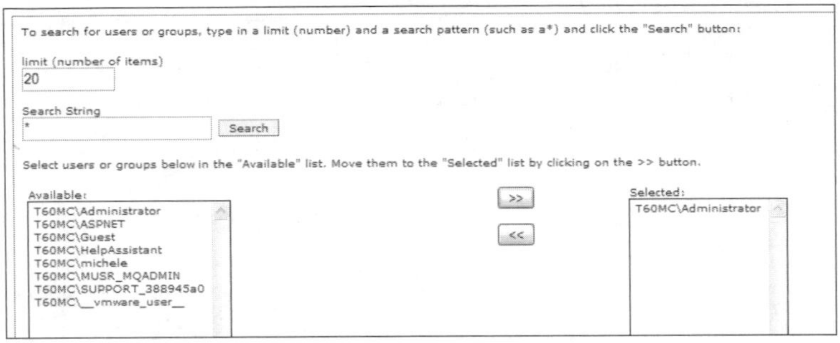

Figure 10.8 Picking a user for the role

6. Click **OK**, and save your changes. Now the *BPESystemAdministrator* role is assigned to the *T60MCAdministrator* user.

7. Similarly, you may want to click **Map RunAs roles to users** (the second link highlighted in Figure 10.6) and assign the user identity for the message-driven beans that are part of the BPEContainer application.

This security role mapping operation may also be necessary for other applications such as the Human Task Container, the Business Process Choreographer Observer, and so on. Even after changing the J2C authentication data entries for the various aliases, these system-supplied SCA enterprise applications might not run when WebSphere Global Security is enabled. Go to the WebSphere Administrative Console and examine the Enterprise Applications. If you notice any applications that have a red X for status, indicating that they have not started, you need to map the security roles.

Securing WPS Access to Databases and Messaging

You may remember from Chapter 5, "WebSphere Process Server," that WPS requires access to relational databases and to a messaging infrastructure. By default, the messaging infrastructure of choice is the WebSphere SI Bus. Both databases and the SI Bus require security credentials to grant access to their resources.

Relational databases may require users to provide a valid username and password when a connection is first established from WPS, whether or not WPS Global Security is enabled. The user registry utilized by the relational database you have selected for your installation most often will not coincide with the user registry used for WPS Global Security. Make sure you ask your database administrator and obtain a valid set of users and passwords for database authentication.

As far as messaging is concerned, the SI Bus is a component of WPS. Therefore, it requires authentication only if Global Security is enabled. The user registry used by the Messaging Engines for authentication is the same as the registry used by WPS for Global Security.

These are important considerations, because not only do users and passwords need to be provided at WPS install time, but if those users and passwords change after installation, you need to know what has to be modified in the WebSphere administrative configuration.

WPS relies on standard J2EE mechanisms to propagate credentials to databases and messaging infrastructures. Namely, it uses the Java Connection Architecture (JCA and J2C are both acronyms to designate this standard). Database data sources and messaging connection factories both rely on the J2C standard to communicate with their respective back ends. In J2C connections, you can specify a so-called *J2C authentication alias*, which contains the security credentials necessary to authenticate to the back end. The authentication alias can be created using the WebSphere Administrative Console.

During WPS installation, a few authentication aliases are created for the runtime to use to authenticate the runtime code for access to databases and the messaging engine. The installation wizard collects the usernames and passwords and creates these aliases. These can be reached from the same Global security screen shown in Figure 10.2 by going to the Authentication area and selecting **JAAS Configuration** > **J2C Authentication data**.

Figure 10.9 shows the J2C authentication aliases created after a typical installation of WPS and the corresponding User IDs. Notice that *wasadmin* was given as the user ID during the WPS installation process. If you want to change it to any other user ID to match your security setup, click the link in the alias list, and you will be given a screen to change the user ID and password.

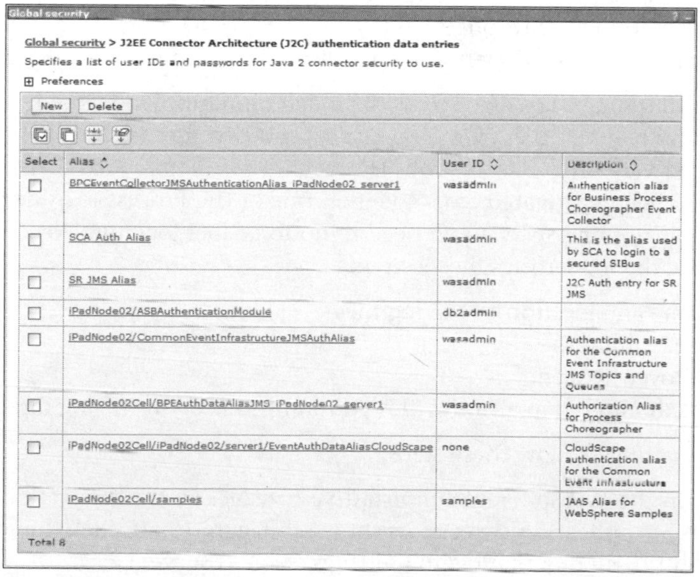

Figure 10.9 J2C authentication aliases

> **Global Security Tip**
>
> If you initially set up things in a nonsecure environment and then you enabled WebSphere Global Security, some of the WPS applications might not start. Remember to change the user ID and password for the various WPS-related aliases to match the security settings. Save the configuration, and restart the server.

Logging and Tracing

To comply with various regulations, such as the Sarbanes-Oxley Act (SOX) in the U.S. or MiFID (Markets in Financial Instruments Directive) in the U.K., logging, especially audit logging, has taken on a whole new meaning. Enterprises are forced to keep track of events from inception to completion. This section shows you that WPS adopts and expands the logging and tracing approach of the underlying WebSphere Application Server platform.

At runtime, relevant logging information is logged in four key files which, by default, are located in the *WPS_HOME*\profiles*PROFILE_NAME*\logs*SERVER_NAME* folder:

- *SystemOut.log* is home to most of the informational and warning messages and to any output directed by applications and components to the Java System.out output stream.
- *SystemErr.log* is home to any output directed by any application or component to the Java System.err output stream.
- *native_stdout.log* hosts the standard output of native components—that is, using native platform code through JNI (DLLs, .EXEs, UNIX libraries, and other modules).
- *native stderr.log* hosts the error output of native components.

By far, the most important log files for problem determination and troubleshooting are the first two files, also referred to as *JVM logs*. The second two files (also called the *Process logs*) generally contain very little information. However, information such as the output of *verbose garbage collection*, if activated, goes to either one of the Process logs, depending on the platform. There is nothing special you need to do to enable logging. However, WPS allows you to customize the log settings by specifying

- The name and location of the log files
- Their maximum size
- The rollover frequency
- The maximum number of log files you want to keep in the log directory

To access these settings, follow these steps:

1. Bring up the WebSphere Administrative console. In the navigation pane, expand **Servers > Application servers**. As shown in Figure 10.10, click the server for which you want to modify the logging settings, such as **server1**.

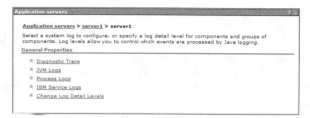

Figure 10.10 Application server system logs in WebSphere Administrative Console

2. Under Troubleshooting, click **Logging and Tracing**.

3. Click **JVM logs** to change the settings for the JVM logs.

The panel shown in Figure 10.11 also allows you to turn on the diagnostic trace of WPS. At a fine granular level, you can select the WPS component you want to trace. For example:

1. Click **Change Log Detail Levels** on the panel shown in Figure 10.11.

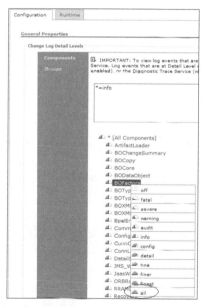

Figure 10.11 Turning on tracing for a component

2. On the dialog that appears, click the component you want to trace, and select the level of detail for the trace. We selected the *BOFactory* component and are about to turn on the *all* details for that component. The other options are fatal, severe, warning, audit, info, config, detail, fine, finer, and finest. And, of course, you can turn it off.

> **Trace Settings**
>
> In Figure 10.11, notice that the dialog has two tabs—**Configuration**
> and **Runtime**. If you define your trace settings on the **Configuration**
> tab and save them, you need to restart the server for the settings to
> take effect. If you set the trace level on the **Runtime** tab, the effect is
> immediate.

Note that defining the trace setting at the configuration level allows you to trace the server startup. Also, keep in mind that tracing generally is invasive from a performance standpoint. You may want to use tracing only in case of real necessity, or when instructed by product support.

Tracing User Applications

The tracing facility we just illustrated can also be used to perform some basic tracing on user-written applications installed on WPS. All SCA components expose three events for which trace can be turned on—Entry, Exit, and Error. In other words, the path taken by user requests during execution of your WPS SCA modules can easily be traced using the same facility we just discussed.

Figure 10.12 shows that under the *WBILocationMonitor.LOG* entry, you can select user-defined components and activate tracing for them. The *bpe* namespace suggests that the selected component is a Business Process.

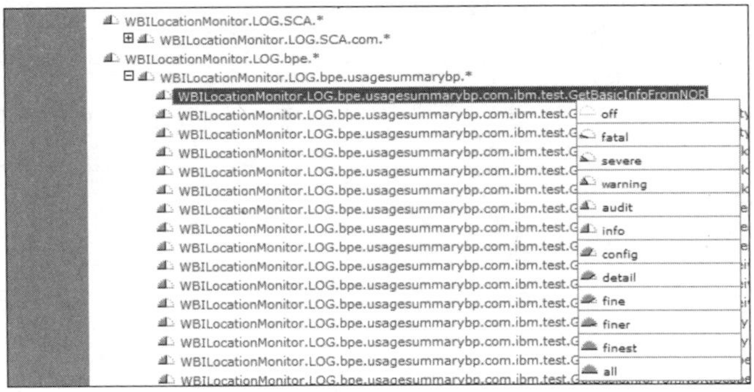

Figure 10.12 Tracing user-written SCA components

This feature is extremely powerful, because it allows you to dynamically turn on tracing for your own SCA components at runtime. The trace, at its finest level, also shows the payload of the requests and responses occurring between those SCA components. Keep in mind that this tracing facility is only built into SCA components. Standard J2EE components you may include in your applications (such as EJBs) or standard plain Java classes are not automatically visible through this interface. However, programmers can use the *java.util.logging* APIs to hook their own logging and tracing into the WPS logging and tracing facilities.

Details on how to configure and code loggers using *java.util.logging* are available in the WebSphere Application Server V6.x Information Center.

Installation Log Files

Various log files are created during the installation of WebSphere Process Server and during profile creation and augmentation. Table 10.1 shows the log filenames, content, and status indicators. Similarly, log files are created during the unaugmentation and deletion of profiles.

Table 10.1 WPS Installation and Profile Creation Log Files

Log File	Content	Status Indicator
WPS_HOME\logs\wbi\log.txt	WPS installation events	INSTCONFFAILED INSTCONFSUCCESS INSTCONFPARTIALSUCCESS
WPS_HOME\logs\wbi\ instconfig.log	Configuration actions at the end of the installation process	
WPS_HOME\logs\pcatLog*TIME_ STAMP*.txt	Default profile creation log during a complete installation	INSTCONFFAILED INSTCONFSUCCESS INSTCONFPARTIALSUCCESS
WPS_HOME\logs\wasprofile\ wasprofile_create_*PROFILE_ NAME*.log	Named profile creation log	INSTCONFFAILED INSTCONFSUCCESS INSTCONFPARTIALSUCCESS
WPS_HOME\logs\wasprofile\ wasprofile_augment_*PROFILE_ NAME*.log	Named profile augmentation log	INSTCONFFAILED INSTCONFSUCCESS INSTCONFPARTIALSUCCESS

Message Logger

A Message Logger mediation primitive can be used to store messages in a database during a mediation flow. It uses an IBM-defined database schema and does not write to other storage media such as flat files. And it logs an XML-transcoded copy of the Service Message Object (SMO).

Although the default behavior is to log just the message payload, the mediation primitive can be configured to log the complete SMO, or a part of the SMO defined by an XPath expression. More importantly, along with the message contents, the mediation primitive also logs a timestamp, the message identifier, the primitive instance name, the mediation module instance name, and the SMO version number.

The Message Logger mediation primitive has one input terminal that accepts a message and two output terminals—one for successful output and one for failure output—that propagate a message. The input message triggers logging to a database. If the logging is successful, the successful output terminal propagates the original message. If an exception occurs, the fail terminal propagates the original message along with any exception information.

Message Logger Usage

You can use the Message Logger mediation primitive to store messages that you process later. Logging the data as XML means that it can be processed by any XML-aware application. The logged messages can be used for data mining or auditing.

Long-running processes are composed of multiple separate transactions. Their duration may last an extended period of time, which ranges from a few minutes to days or even months. This extended duration is caused by the nature of the processes. Long-running processes are structured to wait for events such as human intervention, or for a timed event, or for inbound calls coming from external systems. For this reason, the Business Process Choreographer keeps the state of long-running processes in its relational database (its default name is BPEDB). You may have a number of instances of long-running processes awaiting an event or a human act. All such instances are represented by a set of rows in the BPE database.

The stateful nature of long-running processes has a couple consequences for maintaining applications that contain such process templates:

- Before you can remove (uninstall) an application that contains long-running BPEL process templates, WPS requires that all the process instances for those templates be complete (either successfully or terminated) and that those instances be removed from the BPE database. You cannot remove an application that has process instances that are in the BPE database, even if those processes are idle.
- If you want to install a new version of a business process template, you need to take into account that there may be a number of active process instances that were started with an older version of the template. Those instances need to complete using the template that was used at their inception or be terminated.

You can certainly install a new version of the process template while the older instances are driven to completion—but only newer instances of the process use the latest version. The older instances will keep following the old template. Also, the older enterprise application, which contains the older template, cannot be uninstalled until all those instances are done.

Steps to Versioning a Process in WID

A.10.2

Let us take one of the processes, *VerifyCreditAndProcessOrderProcess*, from our *BookSample* module and walk through the steps to version it. The BPEL process is shown in Figure 10.13.

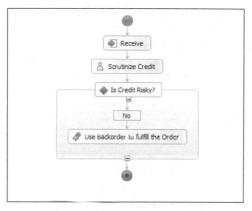

Figure 10.13 Original version of *VerifyCreditAndProcessOrderProcess*

This process is obviously long-running, because it includes a human task, *Scrutinize Credit*. After this process has been taken to production, numerous instances may be waiting for the human task *Scrutinize Credit* to be completed. Assume that there was a business need to add a step in this process after the human task. A practical example would be a notification step, as shown in Figure 10.14.

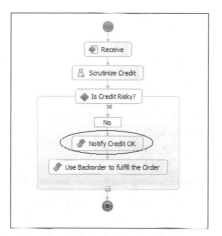

Figure 10.14 New version of *VerifyCreditAndProcessOrderProcess*

You can use the Process Editor in WID and make the change to add the new invoke step named *Notify Credit OK*. Finish configuring the other details for that step, save your edits, and make sure that there are no errors.

The new version can be installed on the same server where the original version is running. However, all the instances that are waiting on the human task do *not* see the new step. They keep following the original template, which does not include the *Notify Credit OK* activity. Also, you cannot uninstall the old application until all the existing instances have completed, which may add some intricacy to the administration of your WPS environment. However, new instances of this process will pick up the latest template, which includes the new step.

To be able to install the application with the newer template, follow these additional steps in WID:

1. Display the properties of the BPEL process. In the Details tab, set the template's Valid From date to a value that is later than the Valid From date of the original template that is already deployed. The original Valid From date for our process was June 12, 2007. As shown in Figure 10.15, we set the new date to July 27, 2007.

Figure 10.15 Setting the new Valid From date

2. Make sure you save your changes.

3. The last step is to change the module name of the WID project that contains the process. Then you have to refactor the project. WPS does not support two applications that contain exactly the same module name. Therefore, when you install the Enterprise Application on WPS, you need to give it a name that is different from any previous version of the same application that already may be installed.

Recommendations for Versioning BPEL Processes

A.10.3

The following are recommendations for versioning BPEL processes that have been successfully implemented:

• **Keep the number of long-running process templates in an EAR file to a minimum.** If you need to version a single process template, you will have to version all the process templates that coexist in the same EAR file.

• **Do not package additional code within the process EAR files** other than the code that is strictly necessary to run the processes. In other words, if your process calls an EJB service, do not package that EJB within the process EAR file, or you will have a hard time making changes to that EJB logic.

• **Minimize the number of Java snippets in your business process.** Making changes to Java snippets implies versioning the process.

- **Keep in mind that the only API that supports versioning is the native Business Process Choreographer API (through the Business Flow Manager or Human Task Manager).** In other words, if you invoke a business process through an SCA binding (whether it is a Web services binding, a JMS binding, or a native SCA binding), you will not experience the versioning support just described. The SCA binding will always invoke the version of the process that it was wired to, even if a more recent version is made available. However, instead of invoking the process directly through the SCA binding, you could wire the SCA binding to a micro-flow that acts as a façade. The micro-flow can then use a "late binding" invocation technique and will invoke the latest version of your process.
- **Break up your long-running processes into subprocesses when possible.** Do not plan for long-running processes that last for many months or years, or you will be exposed to the inconveniences of versioning. Break those processes into phases, or sections, and package each phase as a separate template.

Closing the Link

Security, logging, versioning procedures—each one is a major topic in itself. We hope we have provided enough information to get you started with them so that you can expand on them within your own WebSphere Process Server environment.

In business integration, solutions security is absolutely essential. With the use of Web Services becoming more prevalent, in addition to system and application security, SOA architects have to address Web Services Security (WS-Security). Actually, OASIS has a WS-Security specification.

And with business integration dealing with a lot of mission-critical back-end systems, logging and tracing are essential. These are not exciting topics, nor are they easy to design. Nevertheless, enterprises are legally required to have such systems in place.

The last topic of BPEL versioning makes changing BPEL processes very interesting. Although it is an advanced topic, change is inevitable. Therefore, we provided a glimpse of what you have to be aware of when deploying new versions of a business process.

Links to developerWorks

A.10.1   www.ibm.com/developerworks/websphere/library/techarticles/0602_khangaonkar/0602_khangaonkar.html

A.10.2   www.ibm.com/developerworks/websphere/library/techarticles/0602_brown/0602_brown.html

A.10.3   www.ibm.com/developerworks/websphere/library/techarticles/0705_narayan/0705_narayan.html

Chapter 11

Business Integration
Programming

This chapter covers the programming aspects of a business integration solution. As you know, Java is the language of choice in the WebSphere platform. It is only fair to point out that you will also encounter XPath (XML Path Language) when working with WebSphere Integration Developer (WID). XPath is an expression language that allows the processing of values in the data model. Many of the editors in WID use XPath.

This chapter starts with the Service Component Architecture (SCA) programming model. Then it describes qualifiers. A fair amount of Java code is presented. Some of those lines of code come by way of business graphs, which, as you know, are part of the Business Object Framework. Visual programming by way of Visual snippets in WID makes up a section of this chapter. Here, the lines of code are actually represented by graphical entities. This chapter also explains the Application Programming Interfaces (APIs)—specifically, the Business Flow Manager (BFM) APIs and the Human Task Manager (HTM) APIs.

SCA Programming Model

Chapter 2, "Business Integration Architecture and Patterns," introduced the Service Component Architecture (SCA) programming model as the foundation on which WebSphere Process Server (WPS) and WebSphere Enterprise Service Bus (WESB) components can interoperate. In that chapter, you saw that SCA provides a generic service invocation mechanism that relies on the Business Object Framework to represent and exchange information between components. There, we also introduced the various invocation styles supported by SCA:

A.11.1

- Synchronous invocation
- Asynchronous invocation
- Asynchronous invocation with callback

This section digs a bit deeper into these concepts by providing some coding examples. You'll see how to use the SCA programming model in your Java-based components. However, you may have gathered from the previous chapters that very frequently you do not need to write Java code to perform service invocations. For example, you may use a BPEL process or a WESB mediation flow to call other services or components.

SCA has a rich set of declarative qualifiers that allow you to tweak the behavior of SCA invocations even if you do not have full programmatic control over the formulation of such calls. For example, you can instruct the SCA runtime to prefer asynchronous invocations when necessary, by specifying a declarative qualifier on the appropriate SCA reference in the assembly diagram.

Programmatic Use of SCA: Java References

As mentioned in Chapter 2, the SCA programming model includes a *ServiceManager* class. It can be used to obtain a reference to a service so that you can subsequently invoke it. How can you use the SCA programming model to invoke a simple service, such as the *Credit Check Rule Group* we described in Chapter 7, "Business Maps and Business Rules"? Let's start by creating a simple Java component with the intent to test the Business Rule Group (also called the "rule group"):

1. As shown in Figure 11.1, drop a Java component on the assembly diagram canvas, name it *CreditCheckTest*, and give it the *CreditCheckInterface*, which you may recall from Figure 7.3 in Chapter 7. This interface takes an order business object and a customer business object and returns a risk type (a string).

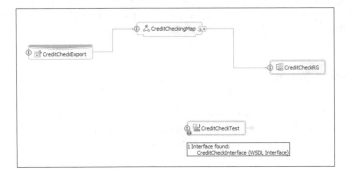

Figure 11.1　*CreditCheckTest* Java component

2. Wire the *CreditCheckTest* component to the *CreditCheckRG* rule group component. Chapter 7 discussed how this component exposes the *CreditCheckServiceInterface*, which you can review in Figure 11.2. This interface takes a wrapper object that encompasses the order amount and the customer credit limit.

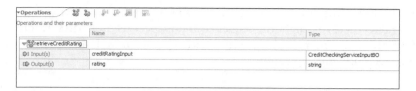

Figure 11.2 Rule group interface

3. Click **OK** on the dialog that asks you whether a matching reference should be created.

4. As shown in Figure 11.3, WID asks whether you want to use a Java invocation style by letting the tool generate a Java interface for you, or whether you want to use the WSDL interface when performing the invocation.

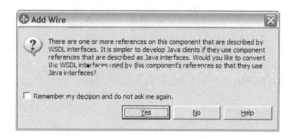

Figure 11.3 Choosing the reference interface

5. Click **Yes**, but do not check the box to remember your decision. WID generates a Java interface that corresponds to *CreditCheckServiceInterface*. The wired diagram is shown in Figure 11.4.

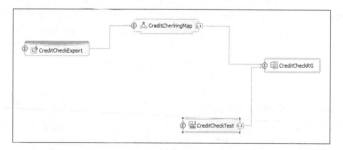

Figure 11.4 The test Java component is wired.

6. If you hover the cursor over the reference we just created, you will see that it is a Java reference. Highlight the reference and inspect its properties. Figure 11.5 shows the reference name (*CreditCheckServiceInterfacePartner*) and its wiring to the *retrieveCreditRating* operation.

Figure 11.5 Properties of the reference

7. Double-click the Java component. You are asked if you want WID to generate an implementation. Click **Yes**, and select a package for the implementation. The Java editor opens, showing the implementation skeleton.

Let's focus on some of the generated Java methods to better understand how to use the SCA programming model. One of the generated methods allows you to obtain a service reference to the rule group service to which we have wired the Java component. This method is shown in Listing 11.1.

Listing 11.1 Generated Service Locator

```
public CreditCheckServiceInterface locateService_CreditCheckServiceInterfacePartner()
{
     return (CreditCheckServiceInterface) ServiceManager.INSTANCE
               .locateService("CreditCheckServiceInterfacePartner");
}
```

Notice that this code uses the *ServiceManager* singleton to acquire a reference to the component that implements the *CreditCheckServiceInterface*. The name of the reference specified in the call to the ServiceManager is *CreditCheckServiceInterfacePartner*. That name matches what was automatically assigned to the reference that was created in step 6. WID also generates an empty skeleton for the method exposed by the rule group, as shown in Listing 11.2.

Listing 11.2 Generated Method Skeleton

```
public String checkCredit(DataObject order, DataObject customer) {
    //TODO Needs to be implemented.
    return "Result from calling the checkCredit(DataObject order, DataObject
    customer) method.";
}
```

In that method (*checkCredit*), you are supposed to formulate the call to the *retrieveCreditRating*. Writing such an implementation is pretty simple, now that you understand how to use the Business Object Framework and now that we have a helper method that allows us to acquire a reference to the target service. Listing 11.3 is an example of such an implementation.

Listing 11.3 Implementing a Service Invocation in SCA

```
public String checkCredit(DataObject order, DataObject customer) {
    BOFactory factory = (BOFactory)
ServiceManager.INSTANCE.locateService("com/ibm/websphere/bo/BOFactory");
    DataObject creditCheckRGInput =
        factory.create("http://CreditChecking/com/ibm/test",
"CreditCheckingServiceInputBO");
            //create an instance of the BO for the rule group

    creditCheckRGInput.setDouble("amount", order.getDouble("orderamt")); //sets the
        order amount
    creditCheckRGInput.setDouble("creditLimit", customer.getDouble("creditLimit"));
        //sets the credit limit

    CreditCheckServiceInterface creditCheckRG =
    locateService_CreditCheckServiceInterfacePartner();
        //obtains a reference to the rule

    String creditRating = creditCheckRG.retrieveCreditRating(creditCheckRGInput);
        //calls the rule using the Java reference

    return creditRating;

}
```

Notice that we use the generated locator to get a reference to the rule and then use the Java interface to make a call as if the target SCA service were in fact a Java object.

Programmatic Use of SCA: WSDL References

The technique discussed in the preceding section is powerful and simple, but it forces you to hard-code the name of the operation you want to call. In addition, this technique does not give you full control over whether you want to use a synchronous or asynchronous invocation style. A.11.2

Let's now explore a more generic way to invoke SCA components from the same Java implementation. To do that, we have to return to step 5 in the preceding section.

1. In the dialog shown in Figure 11.3, instead of choosing to generate a Java reference, let's click **No** and keep the WSDL invocation style.

2. If you hover the cursor over the reference, you will see that it is of type *WSDL*, as shown in Figure 11.6.

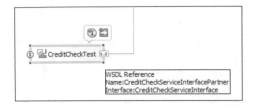

Figure 11.6   The WSDL reference

The name of the reference is *CreditCheckServiceInterfacePartner*, just like in the previous case. However, after you generate the implementation of *CreditCheckTest*, you will observe the generation of the service locator shown in Listing 11.4.

Listing 11.4   Generated Service Locator for Generic Service Invocation

```
public Service locateService_CreditCheckServiceInterfacePartner() {
    return (Service) ServiceManager.INSTANCE
        .locateService("CreditCheckServiceInterfacePartner");
}
```

Also notice that this method returns an instance of *Service*, which generically represents an SCA service. It doesn't return a Java type, because we chose to use the generic WSDL-based invocation mechanism.

In the generated implementation, shown in Listing 11.5, you see the skeleton of the invocation of the service, which is identical to what you saw in the previous section.

Listing 11.5   Using the Generic SCA Service Invocation API

```
public String checkCredit(DataObject order, DataObject customer) {
    //TODO Needs to be implemented.
    return "Result from calling the checkCredit(DataObject order,
    DataObject customer) method.";
}
```

However, you would implement this method differently. For example, you would use the following implementation approach:

```
public String checkCredit(DataObject order, DataObject customer) {
    BOFactory factory = (BOFactory)
      ServiceManager.INSTANCE.locateService("com/ibm/websphere/bo/BOFactory");
    DataObject creditCheckRGInput =
        factory.create("http://CreditChecking/com/ibm/test",
          "CreditCheckingServiceInputBO");
        //create an instance of the BO for the rule group
```

```
creditCheckRGInput.setDouble("amount", order.getDouble("orderamt")); //sets the
    order amount
creditCheckRGInput.setDouble("creditLimit", customer.getDouble("creditLimit"));
    //sets the credit limit

Service creditCheckRuleService =
    locateService_CreditCheckServiceInterfacePartner();
        //obtains a reference to the rule service in a generic way

String creditRating = (String)
creditCheckRuleService.invoke("creditCheckRGInput", creditCheckRGInput);
        //calls the rule using the generic SCA invocation style
    return creditRating;
}
```

If you closely compare this code fragment with the implementation of the same method in the previous section, you will see that the code just shown is completely generic. It doesn't have any hard-coded reference to Java data types or method names. The data types, operation names, and parameters are strings, which can be dynamically set.

WID also generates the skeleton for another method, as shown in Listing 11.6. This method is meant to be called by the service invoked by this component when the invocation style is "asynchronous with callback."

Listing 11.6   Generated Method for Callback

```
public void onRetrieveCreditRatingResponse(Ticket __ticket,
        String returnValue, Exception exception) {
    //TODO Needs to be implemented.
}
```

You can take advantage of this mechanism using the generic SCA invocation API *invokeAsyncWithCallback*, exposed by the *Service* interface. Because it is beyond the scope of this book to provide you with all the details of this rather advanced usage of SCA, we provide you with pseudocode for that invocation technique.

For example, you would add a method to your implementation to support asynchronous invocation, as shown in Listing 11.7.

Listing 11.7   Implementing an Asynchronous Service Invocation

```
public void checkCreditAsync(DataObject order, DataObject customer) {
    BOFactory factory = (BOFactory)
      ServiceManager.INSTANCE.locateService("com/ibm/websphere/bo/BOFactory");
    DataObject creditCheckRGInput =
        factory.create("http://CreditChecking/com/ibm/test",
          "CreditCheckingServiceInputBO");
        //create an instance of the BO for the rule group
```

```
creditCheckRGInput.setDouble("amount", order.getDouble("orderamt")); //sets the
    order amount
creditCheckRGInput.setDouble("creditLimit", customer.getDouble("creditLimit"));
    //sets the credit limit

Service creditCheckRuleService =
    locateService_CreditCheckServiceInterfacePartner();
        //obtains a reference to the rule service in a generic way

Ticket creditRatingTicket =
    creditCheckRuleService.invokeAsyncWithCallback("creditCheckRGInput",
    creditCheckRGInput);
        //calls the rule using the asynch SCA invocation style

saveTicket(creditRatingTicket, customer);
        //Save the ticket and the customer in the persistent store

}
```

Notice that this method doesn't return the credit rating to the caller, because it is meant to be invoked in an asynchronous way. In fact, it uses the *invokeAsyncWithCallback* API to invoke the credit rating.

That API returns a "ticket," which is an object that can be used later to associate the response with the request that produced it. The ticket needs to be saved somewhere. (We call it the *saveTicket* method, which you should implement. That method could use a relational database, for instance, to store the ticket and the customer who issued the request.)

When the credit rating service produces the response, the SCA runtime invokes the *onRetrieveCreditRatingResponse* method on the Java component. This invocation may occur long after the request was issued—even after the WPS server may have restarted a few times. For that reason, the SCA runtime provides the ticket to the callback method so that you can use it to retrieve the context information and notify the correct requester. Listing 11.8 is an example of such an implementation.

Listing 11.8   Implementing the Callback Method

```
public void onRetrieveCreditRatingResponse(Ticket __ticket,
        String returnValue, Exception exception) {
    DataObject customer = retrieveCustomer(__ticket);
        //Using the ticket, get the customer to be notified

    notifyCustomer(returnValue);
        //Notify the customer
}
```

Here we use the ticket to go back to the persistent store and retrieve the customer we associated with it. Using this information, we can notify the customer, such as by sending an e-mail, or by using some other asynchronous mechanism.

Declarative Use of SCA: Qualifiers

The first part of this chapter explored some of the programmatic aspects of SCA. Very often, however, you will not need to use the SCA programming model by writing Java code. As you may have gathered by reading the previous chapters, most of the time, the invocation of SCA services is formulated implicitly for you by components such as BPEL processes or WESB mediation flows.

You can still influence some key aspects of such invocations—such as security and transactional characteristics—by specifying some declarative qualifiers on the wirings among components at assembly time. WID allows you to define the qualifiers on the assembly diagram by tailoring the properties of the interfaces and references exposed by the various components.

Next, we'll look at the qualifiers you can define on the *CreditCheckTest* component we created earlier in this chapter:

1. In the assembly diagram, click the *CreditCheckTest* component, and view its properties.

2. In the properties, expand Interfaces, and select *CreditCheckInterface*. Click the Qualifiers tab, as shown in Figure 11.7.

Figure 11.7   Interface qualifiers

3. Notice that the list of Quality of Service (QOS) Qualifiers is empty. Click **Add**. You have a choice of which qualifier to add, as shown in Figure 11.8:

The qualifier **Join activity session** can be set to either true or false. This determines whether the component joins an existing Activity Session context. An Activity Session is an extension of the concept of transaction, in that the Activity Session attempts to coordinate multiple single-phase commit resources into a single unit of work.

The value of the **Join transaction** qualifier determines whether the component joins a distributed transaction context (a two-phase commit transaction).

The **Security permission** qualifier allows you to restrict the execution of the component to only certain roles, along the lines of the J2EE authorization scheme.

A.11.3

Figure 11.8   Available qualifiers for the interface

4. Click **Cancel**, and go back to the Properties tab. Expand References and click *CreditCheckServiceReferencePartner*. Select the Qualifiers tab.

5. Click **Add**. You see a different set of applicable qualifiers, as shown in Figure 11.9:

   Asynchronous invocation suggests to the SCA runtime that the preferred way of performing a certain service invocation is the asynchronous mechanism. However, keep in mind that this qualifier represents just a hint to the runtime, which may decide that the only available invocation mechanism is synchronous.

   Reliability can be set to either Best effort or Assured. With Assured, the SCA runtime ensures that if a service is unavailable at the time the call is formulated, the call is asynchronously delivered to the service at a later time.

   Request expiration allows you to set the maximum amount of time your component will wait for a request to be successfully accepted by the counterpart.

   Similarly, **Response expiration** allows you to set a timeout for the response to be produced.

   Suspend activity session keeps your component from propagating any activity session context to the callee.

   Similarly, **Suspend transaction** avoids propagating the transactional context.

This section has discussed how SCA allows you to declaratively influence how components invoke each other using the concept of qualifiers. The next section discusses a special type of qualifier that allows you to force related events to be processed in sequence.

Figure 11.9 Available qualifiers for the reference

Event Sequencing in WPS

You have seen what events are—a request or a response sent from one component to another, encapsulating data and invocation metadata. Some implementations require the target component to process events in the same order as they were sent by the source application, because if they are processed out of order, this causes an error or exception condition. For example, an object has to be created before it can be updated; therefore, the create event must be processed before the update event. That is where event sequencing comes into play. Event sequencing guarantees that WPS components process events from asynchronous invocations in the order in which they were delivered.

Certain order management applications offer a classic scenario in which event sequencing is a requirement. An order may be subject to a number of events that need to be processed in the same sequence as they were produced. For example, if you want to add an order line to the order, and later you want to change the ordered quantity on that order line, WPS needs to make sure that the event that corresponds to the creation of the order line gets processed before the update event.

Event sequencing is supported only for asynchronous invocation requests. As such, in an asynchronous invocation, events are stored in destinations on a service integration bus (SIB) and can be handled by multiple instances of Message-Driven Beans (MDBs). The non-sequential processing of events can cause problems for certain application designs—hence, the need for event sequencing. Before we get into its usage, we have to quickly talk about qualifiers.

Adding Event Sequencing Qualifier

Chapter 2 mentioned that event sequencing can be applied only to interface operations. This is done by enabling event sequencing qualifiers during the process development phase in WID. These qualifiers must be set on each method that requires event sequencing, because that is how the runtime knows that the invocation of these methods needs to be sequenced. You specify a group of one or more operations and a key. When two or more events are received that invoke any of those operations that have the same key, the event sequencing qualifier ensures that they are processed in the order in which they are received.

The qualifiers normally are added to components in the Assembly Editor. Make sure that the *BookSample* project is open in the Business Integration perspective in WID.

1. Open the assembly diagram, and highlight *CreditCheckInterface*.

2. In the Properties view, click the **Details** tab to view the details of the component, as shown in Figure 11.10. Expand the **Interfaces** tree, and highlight one of the methods in the interface.

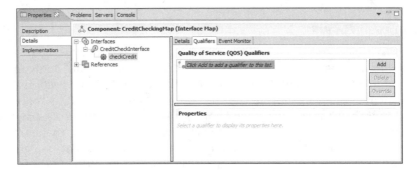

Figure 11.10   Initial qualifier screen for an interface

3. Click the Qualifiers tab to view the QoS Qualifiers.

> **Setting the Event Sequencing Qualifier**
>
> The component must have a WSDL interface; you cannot set event sequencing qualifiers on a component with a Java interface.

A qualifier might already be defined. Click the **Add** button on the right. A window appears, showing the qualifiers that can be added, as shown in Figure 11.11. Select **Event sequencing**, and click **OK**.

Figure 11.11   Adding the event sequencing qualifier

You see Event sequencing added to the Quality of Service (QOS) Qualifiers list, as shown in Figure 11.12. Highlight it to see its properties in the subordinate view. You can accept the default group name or create your own group, like we did. We clicked the **Add** button at the top right and created a group named *CallGroup*. Events for all the operations in the same group are considered together for sequencing. Events in the same group that have the same key value are guaranteed to be delivered in the order in which they arrive.

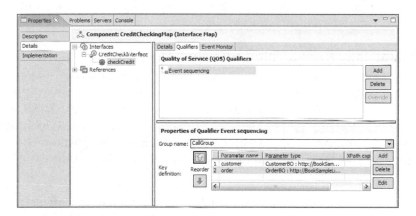

Figure 11.12   Details of an event sequencing qualifier

You may add parameters by clicking the lower **Add** button. If there are two or more parameters, you can specify their order by clicking the up or down **Reorder** arrows. After you are done, press **Ctrl+S** to save the changes. Figure 11.12 shows all the details.

That's it. During runtime, when that particular interface is invoked, the events are executed in the specified sequence. However, make sure you check the product documentation in order to understand the limitations imposed by event sequencing on your clustering options.

Business Graphs and Programmatic Manipulation of Business Objects

Thus far, we have only created definitions of business objects. We can create instances of these objects and manipulate their content in other ways. To recap, business objects are the primary mechanisms for representing business entities, or documenting literal message definitions, enabling everything from a simple, basic object with scalar properties to a large, complex hierarchy or graph of objects. In WPS, the business object framework (BOF) is made up of these elements:

- Business object definition
- Business graph definition
- Business object metadata definition
- Business object services or the service APIs

This section shows you how business integration components can exchange data as business objects or business graphs in their interfaces. Specifically, you will see how business objects can be manipulated programmatically from within Java-based components. Business Graph (BG) is another construct that you can create in WID. Business graphs are wrappers that are added around business objects or a hierarchy of business objects to provide additional capabilities such as carrying change summary.

Programmatically Manipulating Business Objects

Listing 11.9 is code to create an instance of an order object (the *OrderBO*) and print it to the system output stream. Notice that this method uses two of the Java services in the BOF—*BOFactory* and *BOXMLSerializer*. From the SCA runtime, the ServiceManager singleton is used to acquire a reference to those services. The service is then looked up using the fully qualified service name, which includes the service namespace designation. The namespace matches the Java package name, but it has slash separators instead of the dot notation.

Listing 11.9   Code to Create an Instance of a Business Object Named *OrderBO*

```
public void createOrder(Integer orderno, Integer custno) {
    //Get Service Manager singleton
    ServiceManager mgr = ServiceManager.INSTANCE;
    //Access BO Factory service
    BOFactory boFactory =(BOFactory)
mgr.locateService("com/ibm/websphere/bo/BOFactory");
    //Create the object
    DataObject order = boFactory.create("http://BookSampleLibrary", "OrderBO");
    //Populate the object
```

```
order.setInt("orderno", orderno.intValue());
order.setInt("custno", custno.intValue());

//Creating an Order Line
DataObject orderLine1 = boFactory.create("http://BookSampleLibrary",
  "OrderLineBO");
orderLine1.setInt("orderlineno", 1);
orderLine1.setInt("itemno", 1234);

//Creating another Order Line
DataObject orderLine2 = boFactory.create("http://BookSampleLibrary",
  "OrderLineBO");
orderLine2.setInt("orderlineno", 2);
orderLine2.setInt("itemno", 4567);

//Set other order properties here - for ex. a List of order lines
ArrayList orderLines = new ArrayList();
orderLines.add(orderLine1);
orderLines.add(orderLine2);
order.setList("orderlines", orderLines);

BOXMLSerializer xmlSerializer = (BOXMLSerializer)
  mgr.locateService("com/ibm/websphere/bo/BOXMLSerializer");
try {
    xmlSerializer.writeDataObject(order,"http://BookSampleLibrary", "OrderBO",
      System.out );
} catch (IOException e) {
    //handle IO exception
}

}
```

Executing the code shown in Listing 11.9 produces the output shown in Listing 11.10. Notice the Java method created the business object based on the top element name (*OrderBO*) and the namespace URL (http://BookSampleLibrary).

Listing 11.10 XML Listing of the *OrderBO* Object

```
<?xml version="1.0" encoding="UTF-8"?>
<_:OrderBO xsi:type="book:OrderBO" xmlns:xsi="http://www.w3.org/2001/
  XMLSchema-instance" xmlns:book="http://BookSampleLibrary" xmlns:_="http://
  BookSampleLibrary">
  <orderno>1</orderno>
  <custno>2</custno>
  <orderlines>
    <orderlineno>1</orderlineno>
    <itemno>1234</itemno>
  </orderlines>
  <orderlines>
    <orderlineno>2</orderlineno>
    <itemno>4567</itemno>
  </orderlines>
</_:OrderBO>
```

Listing 11.11 is an example of how to create the business graph, *OrderBG*, which we associated to the business object, *OrderBO*. The programming model for creating a business graph is similar to that of creating a business object.

Listing 11.11   Code to Create an Instance of the Business Graph

```
public void createOrderBG(Integer orderno, Integer custno) {
    //Get Service Manager singleton
    ServiceManager mgr = ServiceManager.INSTANCE;
    //Access BO Factory service
    BOFactory boFactory =(BOFactory)
      mgr.locateService("com/ibm/websphere/bo/BOFactory");
    //Create the object
    DataObject orderbg = boFactory.create("http://BookSampleLibrary", "OrderBOBG");
    //Another way to create a contained data object
    DataObject order = orderbg.createDataObject("OrderBO");

    //Populate the object
    order.setInt("orderno", orderno.intValue());
    order.setInt("custno", custno.intValue());

    //Creating an Order Line
    DataObject orderLine1 = boFactory.create("http://BookSampleLibrary",
      "OrderLineBO");
    orderLine1.setInt("orderlineno", 1);
    orderLine1.setInt("itemno", 1234);

    //Creating another Order Line
    DataObject orderLine2 = boFactory.create("http://BookSampleLibrary",
       "OrderLineBO");
    orderLine2.setInt("orderlineno", 2);
    orderLine2.setInt("itemno", 4567);

    //Set other order properties here - for ex. a List of order lines
    ArrayList orderLines = new ArrayList();
    orderLines.add(orderLine1);
    orderLines.add(orderLine2);
    order.setList("orderlines", orderLines);
    System.out.println("Print out the business graph before manipulation...");
    try {
        BOXMLSerializer xmlSerializer = (BOXMLSerializer)
          mgr.locateService("com/ibm/websphere/bo/BOXMLSerializer");
        //Prints out the "before image"
        xmlSerializer.writeDataObject(orderbg,"http://BookSampleLibrary",
          "OrderBOBG", System.out );
    } catch (IOException e) {
        e.printStackTrace();
    }
    manipulateOrderBG((BusinessGraph) orderbg);

}
```

The code in Listing 11.12 shows how you would manipulate objects within a business graph and record your changes.

Listing 11.12 Code to Manipulate the Objects in a Business Graph

```
public void manipulateOrderBG(BusinessGraph orderBG) {
    //Get the change summary
    ChangeSummary cs = orderBG.getChangeSummary(true);
    //Start recording
    cs.beginLogging();
    DataObject orderBO = (DataObject) orderBG.get("OrderBO");
    //Make the change
    orderBO.setDouble("orderamt", 1000.00);
    List orderLines = orderBO.getList("orderlines");
    //Delete an order line
    orderLines.remove(1);
    //Stop recording
    cs.endLogging();
    //Call a method that consumes the BG
    printOrderBG(orderBG);

}
```

Listing 11.13 shows how to print the contents of the *orderBG* business graph. This example shows the implementation of the *printOrderBG* method, which inspects the *orderBG* business graph object. This method retrieves the change summary that is created by the *manipulateOrderBG* method, shown in Listing 11.12. The *printOrderBG* method then prints the business graph's "after image," which lists the objects that were changed by *manipulateOrderBG*. An "after image" contains all of an updated object's data, not just the primary key and updated data. Notice the line in bold, which shows how to get each object's type and then, from the type, get the namespace URL and name to print.

Listing 11.13 The *printOrderBG* Method Inspects the *orderBG* Business Graph Object

```
private void printOrderBG(BusinessGraph orderBG) {
    //Get Service Manager singleton
    ServiceManager mgr = ServiceManager.INSTANCE;

    BOXMLSerializer xmlSerializer = (BOXMLSerializer)
      mgr.locateService("com/ibm/websphere/bo/BOXMLSerializer");

    //Access BO Factory service
    DataObject orderBO = orderBG.getDataObject("OrderBO");
    try {
        System.out.println("Print out the business contained object after
          manipulation...");
        //Prints out the "after image"
        xmlSerializer.writeDataObject(orderBO,"http://BookSampleLibrary",
          "OrderBO", System.out );
    } catch (IOException e) {
```

```
            e.printStackTrace();
    }

    ChangeSummary cs = orderBG.getChangeSummary(false);
    //Gets a list to iterate over
    List changedObjs = cs.getChangedDataObjects();
    Iterator it = changedObjs.iterator();
    while (it.hasNext()) {
        DataObject obj = (DataObject)it.next();
        try {
            xmlSerializer.writeDataObject(obj,obj.getType().getURI(),
                obj.getType().getName(), System.out);
        } catch (IOException e) {
            e.printStackTrace();
        }
    }

}
```

If you were to run the *createOrderBG* sample method shown in Listing 11.11, you should get the output shown in Listing 11.14, which is a set of objects. The listing has four groups of output text lines. Each group lists the contents of a particular business object:

- The first object (*OrderBOBG*) is the "before image"—the business graph right after creation. Notice that there are two order lines (*orderlineno* 1 and 2).
- The second object is the contained *OrderBO* "after image"—the order after *manipulateOrderBG* has been run. Notice that we have removed an order line and that we have set a dollar amount (*orderamt*) for the order itself.
- The third and fourth objects are the objects that were changed since we turned on the recording of the changes (the order line that was deleted, and the order itself). This information is kept in the Change Summary, as shown near the end of Listing 11.13.

Listing 11.14 Contents of the "Changed Objects" in the Business Graph

```
[1/12/07 0:06:06:812 CST] 00000053 SystemOut   O Print out the business graph before
                                                 manipulation...
[1/12/07 0:06:06:812 CST] 00000053 SystemOut   O <?xml version="1.0" encoding=
                                                 "UTF-8"?>
<book:OrderBOBG xsi:type="book:OrderBOBG"
  xmlns:xsi="http://www.w3.org/2001/XMLSchema-instance"
xmlns:book="http://BookSampleLibrary">
  <OrderBO>
    <orderno>1</orderno>
    <custno>2</custno>
    <orderlines>
      <orderlineno>1</orderlineno>
      <itemno>1234</itemno>
    </orderlines>
    <orderlines>
      <orderlineno>2</orderlineno>
      <itemno>4567</itemno>
    </orderlines>
  </OrderBO>
```

```
</book:OrderBOBG>
[1/12/07 0:06:06:812 CST] 00000053 SystemOut    O Print out the business contained
                                                  object after manipulation...
[1/12/07 0:06:06:812 CST] 00000053 SystemOut    O <?xml version="1.0" encoding=
                                                  "UTF-8"?>
<book:OrderBO xsi:type="book:OrderBO" xmlns:xsi="http://www.w3.org/2001/
  XMLSchema-instance" xmlns:book="http://BookSampleLibrary">
  <orderno>1</orderno>
  <custno>2</custno>
  <orderamt>1000.0</orderamt>
  <orderlines>
    <orderlineno>1</orderlineno>
    <itemno>1234</itemno>
  </orderlines>
</book:OrderBO>
[1/12/07 0:06:06:812 CST] 00000053 SystemOut    O <?xml version="1.0"
                                                  encoding="UTF-8"?>
<book:OrderLineBO xsi:type="book:OrderLineBO"
  xmlns:xsi="http://www.w3.org/2001/XMLSchema-instance"
xmlns:book="http://BookSampleLibrary">
  <orderlineno>2</orderlineno>
  <itemno>4567</itemno>
</book:OrderLineBO>
[1/12/07 0:06:06:812 CST] 00000053 SystemOut    O <?xml version="1.0"
                                                  encoding="UTF-8"?>
<book:OrderBO xsi:type="book:OrderBO" xmlns:xsi="http://www.w3.org/2001/
  XMLSchema-instance" xmlns:book="http://BookSampleLibrary">
  <orderno>1</orderno>
  <custno>2</custno>
  <orderamt>1000.0</orderamt>
  <orderlines>
    <orderlineno>1</orderlineno>
    <itemno>1234</itemno>
  </orderlines>
</book:OrderBO>
```

Business graphs offer a powerful way to record and track the manipulation that occurs on business object instances. The Change Summary provides a sort of "journal" of all the changes that were applied to the object during the period of recording.

This information is extremely useful when those changes need to be reflected to the persistent store, or onto other back ends, such as an ERP. This is why business graphs are a key ingredient of the WebSphere Adapters technology.

APIs or SPIs

When we talk about SCA APIs, we are really referring to the Java APIs that accompany WebSphere Process Server for the most part, and to some extent, those that are used in WESB. APIs are meant to be used by application developers in constructing an application.

With the advent of business objects and services, a new kind of interface called the Service Provider Interface (SPI) became popular. SPI is software that supports replaceable components. With an SPI, the organization effectively delegates or outsources some type of processing to an external service, usually provided by a vendor such as IBM. For example, the actual SCA SPIs are not published and are meant for internal use only. This external service returns data that can then be used by the organization. With that said, WPS APIs and SPIs are broken into the following subtopics:

- Business Flow Manager (BFM) APIs
- Business object package APIs
- Business Process Choreographer Explorer APIs
- Human Task Manager (HTM) APIs
- Mediation Context Store SPIs
- Mediation Engine SPIs
- Mediation Flow Action SPIs
- Service Message Object (SMO) APIs
- Services addressing APIs
- Services interfaces APIs
- Services package APIs

We take a detailed look at the BFM APIs and the HTM APIs because they are used when you want to interact with business processes or handle human tasks in a business process from an external client such as a portal server. If you have installed the WebSphere Process Server documentation along with your runtime, you can access the APIs locally at http://*LOCAL_HOST*/web/apidocs/index.html. The same documentation can also be accessed in the development environment in WID at http://*WID_HOME*/runtimes/bi_v6/web/apidocs/index.html.

Business Flow Manager APIs

The main package in the BFM APIs is *com.ibm.bpe.api*. These APIs can be viewed at http://publib.boulder.ibm.com/infocenter/dmndhelp/v6rxmx/index.jsp?topic=/com.ibm.wsps.javadoc.doc/doc/com/ibm/bpe/api/package-summary.html. The BFM APIs are used to manage process-related objects in the Business Process Choreographer. You can create applications that use the APIs to manage runtime information related to business processes such as the following:

- Query process instances, deployed process templates, and their properties
- Send messages to a process instance, such as starting it
- Claim activities and return results of a user operation
- Operation of work lists
- Query activities assigned to the calling user
- Issue administrative commands, such as terminating a process instance

The BFM API contains a stateless session bean BusinessFlowManager for local and remote access. A BusinessFlowManagerService interface describes the functions that can be called locally and remotely. It exposes the functions that can be called by an application but requires a reference in the application's deployment descriptor. Table 11.1 shows where the descriptor is to be added, depending on the type of application.

Table 11.1 Adding References to the Application Deployment Descriptor

Type of Client Application	Deployment Descriptor File
J2EE client application	application-client.xml
Web application	web.xml
EJB application	ejb-jar.xml

APIs Used to Initiate a Business Process

Code snippets are presented here that collectively can be used to initiate a business process. The code snippet shown in Listing 11.15 shows the reference to the remote interface.

Listing 11.15 Reference to the Remote Interface

```
<ejb-ref>
    <ejb-ref-name>ejb/BusinessFlowManagerHome</ejb-ref-name>
    <ejb-ref-type>Session<ejb-ref-type>
    <home>com.ibm.bpe.api.BusinessFlowManagerHome</home>
    <remote>com.ibm.bpe.api.BusinessFlowManager</remote>
</ejb-ref>
```

Listing 11.16 shows the reference to the local interface.

Listing 11.16 Reference to the Local Interface

```
<ejb-local-ref>
    <ejb-ref-name>ejb/LocalBusinessFlowManagerHome</ejb-ref-name>
    <ejb-ref-type>Session<ejb-ref-type>
    <local-home>com.ibm.bpe.api.LocalBusinessFlowManagerHome</local-home>
    <local>com.ibm.bpe.api.LocalBusinessFlowManager</local>
</ejb-local-ref>
```

Getting to the BusinessFlowManager EJB

The process container makes the BFM home interface available to the client. If the client is a portlet, the portlet can communicate with the process engine using the home interface of the BFM stateless session bean running on the process server. To get access to this EJB, the code does a Java Naming and Directory Interface (JNDI) lookup for *com/ibm/bpe/api/ BusinessFlowManagerHome* on the process server machine to get the home object. The code uses this to create a business process EJB object, as shown in Listing 11.17.

Listing 11.17 Accessing the Remote Interface

```
//Obtain the initial JNDI context
Context ctx = new InitialContext(env);

env.put(Context.PROVIDER_URL, "corbaloc:iiop:localhost:2815");
ctx = new InitialContext(env);

//Lookup the remote home interface of the BFM bean
Object obj = ctx.lookup("com/ibm/bpe/api/BusinessFlowManagerHome");

//Convert lookup object to the proper type
BusinessFlowManagerHome bpHome = (BusinessFlowManagerHome)
PortableRemoteObject.narrow(obj,com.ibm.bpe.api.BusinessFlowManagerHome.class);

if (bpHome != null)
this.businessFlowManager = bpHome.create();
```

Querying the ProcessTemplateData Object

A process template is a versioned, deployed, and installed process model that contains the specification of a business process. You can query the data within the process template by getting the ProcessTemplateData object, which returns information pertaining to things such as

- Whether the process is long-running
- The list of input messages it takes
- The list of output messages

Listing 11.18 shows you how you can get access to the ProcessTemplateData object and query the type of input message it is expecting.

Listing 11.18 Acquiring the Input Message Type of a Business Process

```
//Get ProcessTemplate
ProcessTemplateData templateData
  BusinessFlowManager.getProcessTemplate(templateName);

String inputTypeName = templateData.getInputMessageTypeName();
```

Starting a Business Process with an Input Message

You use the *ClientObjectWrapper* (*com.ibm.task.api.ClientObjectWrapper*) to wrap messages and variables passed between the caller application and the business process. When the process engine is accessed through its EJB interface:

- Invocation parameters are automatically deserialized by the application server.
- Messages and variables are deserialized before the process engine sets the appropriate class loader.

The *ClientObjectWrapper* class (COW) defers deserialization until the wrapped message or variable is accessed. This allows the process engine to set the appropriate class loader. If the process is successfully initiated, it returns the process instance ID (PIID) of the business process. Listing 11.19 shows the call to *process.initiate*.

Listing 11.19   Initiating a Process

```
//Create the Client Object Wrapper (COW)
ClientObjectWrapper input = process.createMessage (templateData.getID(),
  templateData.getInputMessageTypeName());

DataObject myMessage = null;
if ( input.getObject() != null && input.getObject() instanceof DataObject )
{
     myMessage = (DataObject)input.getObject();
//set the values in the message, like a customer name
     myMessage.setString("CustomerName", "Smith");
}
//Start the process
PIID piid = process.initiate(template.getName(), "BackOrder", input);
```

> **Short-Running Process Initiation**
>
> If you are starting a short-running process, you have to use the call()
> method instead of the initiate() method. When invoking the call()
> method, the response of the business process is returned inside a
> COW object.

Packaging the Client Application

If you are using the remote interface, as is typically the case when creating portlets that interact with business processes, the generated API stubs must be packaged with the client application. Keep the following in mind:

- Package the files contained in *WPS_HOME*\ProcessChoreographer\client\ bpe137650.jar with the client application EAR file.
- Set the *classpath* parameter in the manifest file of the client application that includes the bpe137650.jar file.
- You also have to package the JAR file containing the WSDLs and the business objects.

Human Task Manager APIs

The Human Task Manager (HTM) APIs are very similar to the BFM APIs. They can be viewed at http://publib.boulder.ibm.com/infocenter/dmndhelp/v6rxmx/index.jsp?topic=/com.ibm.wsps.javadoc.doc/doc/com/ibm/task/api/package-summary.html. These APIs are used to manage task-related objects in the Human Task Manager. The two main packages are

- *com.ibm.task.api*
- *com.ibm.wbi.tel*

You can create applications that use the APIs to manage information related to tasks such as

- Query tasks assigned to the calling user
- Claim tasks and return the result of the operation
- Issue administrative commands, such as transferring a work item to another user

The HTM API contains a stateless session bean, HumanTaskManager, for local and remote access. A HumanTaskManagerService interface describes the functions that can be called locally and remotely. It exposes the functions that can be called by an application but requires a reference in the application's deployment descriptor, as was described in the section, "Business Flow Manager APIs." The packaging is a bit different, because instead of *bpc137650.jar*, you package the client application with *WPS_HOME*\ProcessChoreographer\client\task137650.jar.

One thing to know about HTM APIs is that the calls are executed as transactions. A transaction is either established and ended explicitly by the client application, or it is established by the container when the client application calls the Task Manager and is ended by the container when the client application receives the result (the deployment descriptor specifies TX_REQUIRED).

Listing 11.20 shows the reference to the local interface.

Listing 11.20   Reference to the Local Interface

```
<ejb-local-ref>
    <ejb-ref-name>ejb/LocalHumanTaskManagerHome</ejb-ref-name>
    <ejb-ref-type>Session<ejb-ref-type>
    <local-home>com.ibm.task.api.LocalHumanTaskManagerHome</local-home>
    <local>com.ibm.task.api.LocalHumanTaskManager</local>
</ejb-local-ref>
```

Visual Programming

We talked about Visual Snippets and Java Snippets when we introduced the Visual Snippet Editor in Chapter 4, "WebSphere Integration Developer." Although the Visual Editor palette has many items to choose from, one primitive that we find useful is a snippet to print a BO or SMO. This section describes how you can create that snippet. This forces us to illustrate a fairly complex visual snippet. Actually, you will learn how to create a custom visual snippet.

The Setup

Start WID, and use the same *BookSample* workspace. In the Business Integration perspective, you may edit any BPEL process, but using what we have created thus far, we chose to edit the *ShipOrderProcess*. There should be an *OrderVar* of type *OrderBO*. Add a snippet anywhere in the process, preferably toward the end of the flow. That should open the Visual Snippet Editor.

Creating the Custom Visual Snippet

The rest of the work will be done in the Visual Snippet Editor, also known as the Visual Editor. This is also the Visual Programming aspect.

1. Drag the *OrderVar* variable onto the Visual Editor canvas, which should look like Figure 11.13.

Figure 11.13   Visual Snippet Editor canvas with *OrderVar*

2. Right-click in the editor's canvas, and select **Convert to custom snippet**.

3. Name it *PrintBO*, and put it in the *utility* category, as shown in Figure 11.14. Click **Finish**.

4. You are returned to the original snippet, with a new activity named *PrintBO* that is wired to *ObjectVar*.

5. Highlight *PrintBO*, and double-click it. This displays the editor for the custom snippet.

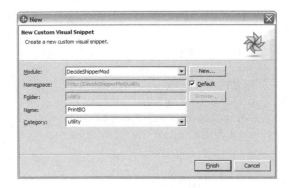

Figure 11.14   Naming the custom visual snippet

6. From the palette select the **Standard** icon. Under SCA services, choose *get BOXMLSerializer Service*, as shown in Figure 11.15 . Click **OK**.

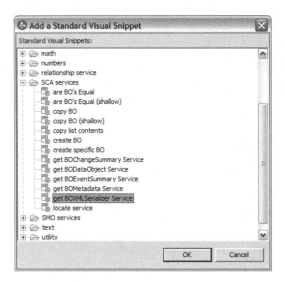

Figure 11.15   Selecting *get BOXMLSerializer Service* from the SCA services

7. Click anywhere on the canvas to add the selected snippet.

8. From the palette, select the **Java** icon. In the selection pop-up, enter *BOXMLSerializer* for the type, and choose the visual snippet method named *writeDataObject*, as shown in Figure 11.16.

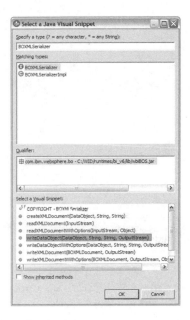

Figure 11.16 Choosing the Java method

Java Types

From the Visual Editor palette, use Java snippets and not expressions to call the methods. For example, to add the *printStackTrace* method to the Exception Handler, remember to specify the Java type and check the box to **Show inherited methods** for the *java.io.IOException* type.

---

9. Click **OK**, and then click the triangle of the *get BOXMLSerializer Service* snippet. You will notice that it gets wired as the first input to *writeDataObject*.

10. Wire the *ObjectVar* variable to the second input of *writeDataObject* by dragging the yellow connector from *ObjectVar* to *writeDataObject*. Your canvas should look like Figure 11.17.

11. From the right side of the Visual Editor, drag *OrderVar* onto the canvas.

12. From the palette, select the **Java** icon. In the selection pop-up, enter *DataObject* for the type, and choose the visual snippet method named *getType*.

13. Click **OK**, and then click the triangle of *OrderVar*. You will notice that it gets wired as the input to *getType*.

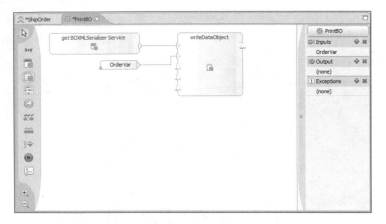

Figure 11.17   Partially finished custom visual snippet

14. Right-click the output triangle of the *getType* snippet, and select **Add** > **Java**. Select the *getURI* method, as shown in Figure 11.18.

Figure 11.18   Choosing the *getURI* method from the commonj.sdo package

15. Click **OK**, and then click the cursor on the triangle of *getType*. You will notice that it gets wired as the input to *getURI*.

16. Repeat steps 14 and 15 to add *getName* to an output branch of *getType*.

17. Wire *getURI* and *getName* to the remaining two inputs of *writeDataObject*, as shown in Figure 11.19.

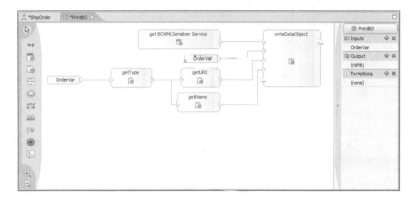

Figure 11.19 Output from business object methods are typed and wired.

18. If you hover the cursor over the fifth triangle on the left of the *writeDataObject* snippet, you will notice that it is of type *OutputStream*. Right-click that triangle, and select **Add > Java**.

19. In the Type field of the selection pop-up, enter **System**. Select the **System class** from Matching types, and choose **System.out** (out - System) as the visual snippet.

20. Click **OK**, and then click the fifth triangle of *writeDataObject*. You will notice that *System.out* gets wired to *writeDataObject*.

21. There is one block arrow on the top right of *writeDataObject*, which is the Exception Handler. Right-click that arrow, and select the only option available: **Exception Handler**. The Visual Editor automatically wires a *Handle ex* snippet.

22. If you hover the cursor over the output triangle (on the right) of the *ex* snippet, you will notice that it is of type *java.io.IOException*. Right-click that triangle, and select **Add > Java**.

23. In the selection pop-up, you will notice there are only three methods to choose from. Check the box at the bottom to **Show inherited methods**, as shown in Figure 11.20.

24. Select the *printStackTrace* method, and click **OK**.

25. Click the output triangle of *ex*. You will notice that *printStackTrace* gets wired to it.

26. The completed visual snippet is shown in Figure 11.21. Press **Ctrl+S** to save the custom snippet. Notice that the yellow warning triangles from *OrderVar* and *ex* disappear.

Figure 11.20   Selecting one of the inherited methods from java.io.IOException

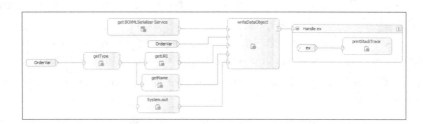

Figure 11.21   The completed *PrintBO* visual snippet

Where is the custom visual snippet? Back on the original Visual Snippet Editor, delete the *PrintBO* snippet from the canvas. From the palette, select **Standard**. If you look under **utility**, you will see the custom snippet that we created, named *PrintBO*. Select it, and re-add it to the canvas by clicking the output triangle of *OrderVar*. You have to delete and re-add the *PrintBO* snippet because we changed its method signature.

When the process is deployed and tested, the contents of the *ObjectBO* are written to SystemOut. With this simple example, we illustrated the visual programming capability in WID. This custom snippet can be reused in this and any other BPEL flow in the module. Needless to say, you can create rather complex visual snippets using the editor and all the snippet primitives available in the palette. And if you ever want to see all the generated code, you can always click the Java radio button on the Snippet Editor. Beware that results are not guaranteed if you revert to Visual mode.

Closing the Link

This chapter was definitely geared toward developers. With code samples and visual snippets, we covered the SCA programming model, business graphs, APIs available in WPS, and even visual programming by way of visual snippets. As noted, a lot of the code is generated for you by the tooling.

Build-time qualifiers in WID were discussed, and we pointed out the importance of event sequencing, a special type of qualifier.

Java purists might not like the notion of visual programming. But the beauty of visual snippets is that you really do not have to write any code. This shows the versatility of WID, where, if need be, you can easily fall back to writing Java code or use XPath expressions. We hope visual snippets are somehow made more intuitive and that there will be a much larger selection of primitives.

 ## Links to developerWorks

A.11.1 http://www-128.ibm.com/developerworks/webservices/library/specification/ws-sca/

A.11.2 www.ibm.com/developerworks/websphere/techjournal/0510_brent/0509_brent.html

A.11.3 www.ibm.com/developerworks/websphere/library/techarticles/0602_charpentier/0602_charpentier.html

Chapter 12

WebSphere Adapters

Business integration involves integrating other external, third-party, or legacy applications. After all, this is the promise of Service-Oriented Architecture (SOA). Enterprise application integration (EAI) was supposed to achieve this goal, and to some extent it did through creating and using proprietary resource adapter interfaces. However, it required a resource adapter to be developed for each EAI vendor and Enterprise Information System (EIS) combination. Therein lay the need for a common connector architecture, and hence the emergence of JCA[1] or J2EE Connector Architecture. The JCA standard provides a mechanism to store and retrieve enterprise data in J2EE (Java 2 Platform, Enterprise Edition). JCA is to EIS connectivity what JDBC is to database connectivity.

This chapter discusses application adapters and technology adapters. Most of the focus is on the JCA adapters. We address how and where adapters fit within SOA—specifically, in the service component architecture (SCA). We also discuss WebSphere JCA Adapters and touch on the WebSphere Adapter Toolkit, which is primarily used to create custom adapters. Finally, we give you an overview of the two commonly used application adapters: SAP adapter and Siebel adapter.

---

[1] The JSR 112 committee, which works on the J2EE Connector Architecture specification, has not sanctioned any abbreviation for this specification. This chapter uses J2C or JCA to mean the J2EE Connector Architecture specification.

Adapters

Adapters as a software component follow the adapter software design pattern. Before JCA adapters, there were WebSphere Business Integration Adapters (WBIA), which were also popularly known as legacy adapters. They are called legacy adapters because they connect to legacy or mainframe applications, many of which are old mission-critical applications. In fact, there are more than a hundred such adapters, but they are not JCA-compliant. JCA and WBIA adapters fall into two classifications: application adapters or technology adapters:

- *Application adapters* are designed to integrate with popular industry applications that can be easily reused. These are adapters for SAP, PeopleSoft, Clarify, and so on.
- *Technology adapters* are meant to allow integration with standard types of technology. They are useful when there are applications to be integrated that do not have a published API. Examples of such technology adapters are JDBC, JText, JMS, WebSphere MQ Workflow, and Web services.

  Quite often, these technology adapters support a transport or invocation method in which you have to deal with a particular data format. Examples are XML, EDI, and HTTP adapters.

A.12.1

In the service-oriented approach, JCA adapters are meant to provide a common mechanism for integrating existing applications with process applications. Adapters abstract the low-level functions or events in the form of business objects (BOs). This enables service components running WebSphere Process Server (WPS) to interact with EIS applications by passing BOs. WID comes with the following JCA adapters that you can work with. Below is a list of supported application adapters. From a WPS perspective, certain application adapters require other vendor licenses.

- Email
- Flat File
- FTP
- JDBC
- JD Edwards Enterprise One
- Oracle E-Business Suite
- PeopleSoft Enterprise
- SAP
- Siebel Business Applications

> ### WebSphere Adapters
>
> Information about the various WebSphere adapters can be found at http://www-1.ibm.com/support/docview.wss?uid=swg21252626.
>
> The JCA specification can be downloaded from http://java.sun.com/ j2ee/connector/download.html.

When it comes to integration, there is inbound integration and outbound integration. *Inbound integration* is when a change in an outside system initiates data requests to the WPS system. *Outbound integration* means the WPS system initiates data requests to other systems. JCA's main components are the resource adapter, system contracts, and the Common Client Interface (CCI), which together give JCA the power to access data in enterprise systems. Thus, the term resource adapter comes from JCA.

The resource adapter plays a central role in the integration and connectivity between an EIS and WPS. It serves as the point of contact in JCA. The resource adapter, along with the other components, communicate with one another on well-defined contracts, as shown in Figure 12.1. The system contracts handle functions such as connection management, transaction management, and security.

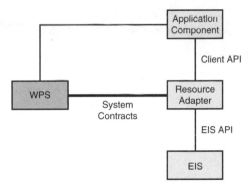

Figure 12.1   Connector architecture

These resource adapters enable managed, bidirectional connectivity and data exchange between EIS resources and J2EE components inside WPS. It would not be inaccurate to say that adapters fall into the supporting services category among WPS components. The modified WPS architecture diagram is shown in Figure 12.2. It is worth noting that the JD Edwards (JDE) JCA Adapter currently provides only outbound functionality.

We have discussed how WPS uses Service Data Objects (SDOs) to exchange data between service components. Adapters, on the other hand, use a special kind of BOs called business graphs (BGs). The WebSphere resource business object model extends SDO. It is this extension that enables data communication between WPS and the adapter. Each adapter consists of the following:

- Foundation classes are used to implement a generic set of contracts that define the Service Provider Interface (SPI) that WPS uses to manage the interactions.
- EIS-specific subclasses of the foundation classes provide additional support and typically are used when developing custom resource adapters.
- The Enterprise Metadata Discovery component complies with the metadata discovery framework.

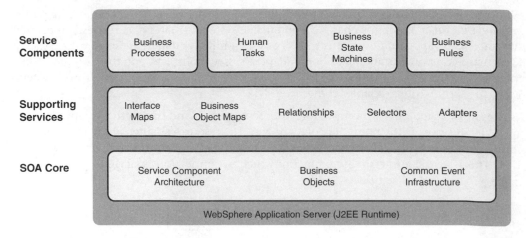

Figure 12.2   Modified WPS architecture

Adapter Architecture

Now that you know how adapters help encapsulate EIS business functions and events in the form of business objects, let's take a look at the architecture. Figure 12.3 shows the relationship of adapters and WPS or WebSphere Enterprise Service Bus (WESB).

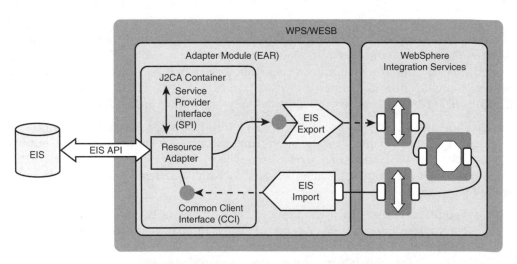

Figure 12.3   Adapters within WebSphere Process Server

Common Client Interface

The Common Client Interface (CCI) is a standard Java API that helps application components and Enterprise Application Integration (EAI) frameworks interact with the resource adapter. Applications can use it to invoke functions on an EIS and get the returned results.

Service Provider Interface

Resource adapters communicate with their hosting application server through the Service Provider Interface (SPI). This common infrastructure programming model enables adapters to have a standard view of the environment in which they operate.

> **Adapter Interfaces**
>
> With JCA adapters, the interface between the adapter and the service is JCA CCI. In the case of WBIA, the interface is either MQ or JMS.

Outbound Processing

An application in WPS or WESB might be interested in invoking an operation on the EIS (for instance, SAP), such as writing to a database. That is an example of outbound processing, in which the application component sends request data to the adapter that connects to the EIS using native APIs. If a response is expected, the EIS sends the retrieved data back to the application via the adapter. Figure 12.4 shows the outbound interaction. In SCA terms, the SCA component connects to EIS through an EIS import to the adapter.

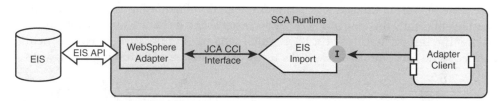

Figure 12.4 Outbound processing flow

An adapter is used to provide a standard interface on one end while it connects to an EIS-specific interface on the other end. This enables application components to interact with various EIS resources using a standard application programming model through resource adapters.

The EIS Import shown in Figure 12.4 makes EIS service accessible as a service to clients inside the SCA module. It defines the binding of the service to the external EIS service.

Inbound Processing

The J2EE component, also known as the endpoint application, might be interested in events that occurred on the EIS, such as when something was added or a database record was created, updated, or deleted. That is an example of inbound processing that can be either synchronous or asynchronous. In an asynchronous mode, the adapter polls the EIS, whereas in a synchronous mode, the EIS pushes the event onto the adapter.

The EIS Export shown in Figure 12.5 subscribes to a service that listens to external EIS requests. It defines the binding of the EIS service to the SCA service.

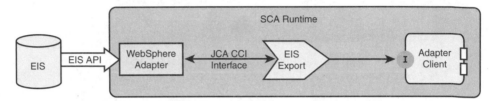

Figure 12.5   Inbound processing flow

Enterprise Discovery

You will often see the terms Enterprise Metadata Discovery (EMD) and Enterprise Service Discovery (ESD) being used when people talk about resource adapters. EMD and ESD have to do with metadata. To connect to an EIS, integration developers need to know what services are exposed and generate the business graph (BG) to represent data and metadata in EIS. If you remember from Chapter 11, "Business Integration Programming," business graphs are a special kind of BO that contain another BO, a verb, and a change summary. Manually discovering the information inside a BG is rather tedious, so this is where EMD is helpful. It defines a standard contract between the resource adapter and EAI tooling frameworks.

> **EMD**
>
> The EMD specification published by IBM and BEA is available at
> www.ibm.com/developerworks/library/specification/j-emd.

Enterprise Service Discovery (ESD) encompasses two components: the metadata in the EIS and the EMD implementation in the adapter. The user can use ESD to automatically generate the SCA artifacts and BOs needed for an integration solution that runs on WPS.

> **ESD Wizard in WID**
>
> The ESD wizard uses the resource adapter you specify to query the
> metadata on an EIS system and uses the information it finds to create
> imports and exports for your service.

Resource Adapter Archive Files

All adapters require a Resource Adapter Archive (RAR) file. A RAR file that has a .rar extension is a Java archive (JAR) file used to package a resource adapter for the Java 2 Connector (J2C) Architecture for WebSphere application servers. It can contain EIS supplied resource adapter implementation code in the form of JAR files or other executable components, utility classes, and static documents such as HTML and image files. Table 12.1 lists the resource archive files that are shipped with WID.

Table 12.1 Technology and Application Adapters and Their Corresponding RAR Files

Adapter	WebSphere Resource Archive File
CICS®	CICSECI5101.rar
CICS15	CICSECI602.rar
Email	CWYEM_Email.rar
Flat File	CWYFF_FlatFile.rar
FTP	CWYFT_FTPFile.rar
IMS™	IMSICO91013a.rar
IMS15	IMSICO91022a.rar
JDBC	CWYBC_JDBC.rar
JDE	CWYED_JDE.rar
OracleEBS	CWYBC_JDBC.rar
PeopleSoft	CWYES_PeopleSoft.rar
SAP	CWYAP_SAPAdapter.rar, CWYAP_SAPAdapter_Tx.rar
Siebel	CWYEB_SiebelAdapter.rar

To facilitate the development of projects containing adapters in WID, the RAR files are provided. All adapter libraries and files can be found under *WID_HOME*\Resource Adapters, as shown in Figure 12.6. Within those named adapter folders, you will find the resource archive (.rar) files. Note that the WebSphere JCA adapter resource files are prefixed with *CWY*.

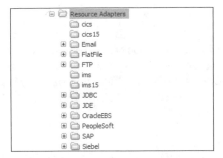

Figure 12.6   Resource adapter folders in WID

Working with an Adapter

This section shows you how to configure, deploy, and test an outbound JDBC Adapter application. We chose the JDBC adapter because it is one of the most common adapters. The development work is done in WebSphere Integration Developer, and we will deploy the adapter application to WebSphere Process Server.

> **Development Terminology**
>
> We are not developing the adapter here; we are merely creating an adapter application or component. To develop an adapter, you would need the WebSphere Adapter Toolkit (WAT).

Depending on the kind of adapter you will work with, you must complete some preparatory work before beginning to develop the adapter application. For example, with the JDBC Adapter, after deciding which database system you will use, you have to make sure the requisite tables exist. Furthermore, you need to have defined the JDBC provider and the data source on the server where you will be deploying the adapter application. In addition, you must obtain a JDBC driver for your target database from either the database vendor or a third-party Independent Software Vendor (ISV).

We will use DB2 as the database and the SAMPLE database that comes with it. Specifically, we plan to use the EMPLOYEE table that exists in the SAMPLE database, so make sure the SAMPLE database has been created in the DB2 server. Last, you need to know the user ID and password that can access the database.

Create the JDBC Outbound Adapter Component

An outbound JDBC adapter component takes information from the server to the SCA application. In this case, the JDBC Adapter accesses a DB2 database. Before you can work on any adapter project, the relevant RAR file needs to be imported into the project. This is to be done only once within a project.

1. As we continue working with the *BookSample* project, make sure you are in the Business Integration perspective. You first import the JDBC Adapter RAR file by selecting **File > Import**. On the selection screen, choose **RAR file**, and then click **Next**.

2. In the Connector Import window, shown in Figure 12.7, browse for the JDBC RAR file under *WID_HOME*\Resource Adapters\JDBC\deploy, and choose **CWYBC_ JDBC.rar**. Make sure you choose the right target server. You can choose either WebSphere ESB Server or WebSphere Process Server. We chose WPS. You may change the values for the Connector project and EAR project or accept the defaults shown in Figure 12.7, but ensure that the **Add module to an EAR project** check- box is not checked.

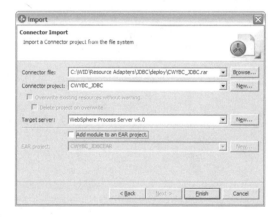

Figure 12.7 Details about the RAR file being imported

3. When you click **Next**, you might get a perspective switch confirmation window. Click **Yes** to switch to the J2EE Perspective.

4. In the Project Explorer, if you expand the Connector Projects folder, you will notice the newly created project, CWYBC_JDBC.

Project Explorer View

To open the Project Explorer View, in WID select **Window > Open Perspective > Other**. Then select the J2EE perspective, which has the Project Explorer View.

---

5. Add any external dependencies the adapter has. In this case, the dependencies might be on the JDBC applications. You do need to add *db2java.zip*, which has the JDBC driver classes for DB2, to the build path of the connector project. You do that by right-clicking the CWYBC_JDBC project and selecting **Properties**.

From the properties list on the left, choose Java Build Path, as shown in Figure 12.8.

Click the Libraries tab, and click **Add External JARs**.

In the *DB2_HOME*\java folder, browse for *db2java.zip*. Select it, and click **Open**.

The list of JARs and class folders will now contain db2java.zip. Click **OK**.

The dependent file (db2java.zip) shows up in the CWYBC_JDBC connector project.

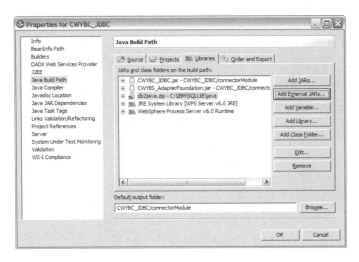

Figure 12.8 Java Build Path Settings

6. Because we will use the WPS test server in WID to deploy and test the adapter component, the dependent files should also be available to the test server. Therefore, you should copy the *db2java.zip* file to the *WID_HOME*\runtimes\bi_v6\lib folder.

7. Switch to the Business Integration perspective, and run the Enterprise Service Discovery wizard to create an SCA component for the adapter. From WID, select **File > New > Enterprise Service Discovery**.

8. In the Enterprise Service Discovery window, shown in Figure 12.9, highlight the JDBC EMD Adapter, and click **Next**.

ESD Best Practice

Use Enterprise Service Discovery to import the resource adapter (RAR) file at this point rather than doing it up front as we did.

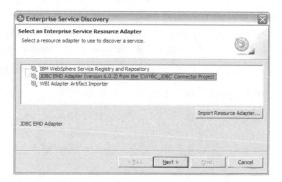

Figure 12.9 Selecting an enterprise service resource adapter

9. Configure the settings for the discovery agent so that the wizard can connect to the back end, which is the DB2 database in this case. For illustration purposes, we will connect to the SAMPLE database in DB2. Enter the following values in the Discovery Agent Settings screen, as shown in Figure 12.10, and click **Next**:

- Leave the Prefix field blank.
- Enter the Username and Password to connect to the DB2 system.
- Database URL should be *jdbc:db2:sample*.
- Jdbc Driver Class should be *COM.ibm.db2.jdbc.app.DB2Driver*.

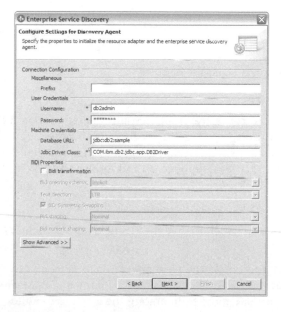

Figure 12.10 Settings for the discovery agent

10. Click **Execute Query** on the Find and Discover Enterprise Services panel, shown in Figure 12.11. A connection is made to the SAMPLE database, and the metadata objects existing in that database are presented in a tree-like structure.

Expand the ADMIN schema, expand Tables, and highlight EMPLOYEE.

Click the **Add to import list** button.

EMPLOYEE gets added to the list of objects to be imported. Click **Next**.

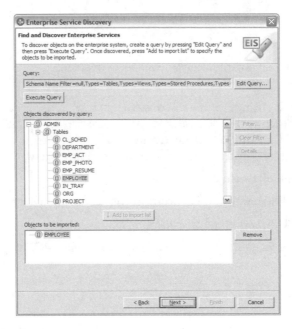

Figure 12.11   Choosing the objects to discover

11. The next step is to specify properties and operations for the objects that will be imported by the discovery agent. For Inbound processing, you can Create, Update, or Delete operations. For Outbound processing, you have more options: Create, Update, Delete, Retrieve, RetrieveAll, and ApplyChanges (see Figure 12.12). Choose **Outbound** as the Service Type.

Leave the NameSpace and MaxRecords as they are.

Enter a location in which to save the business object, such as *booksample/data*. Click **Next**.

12. The first thing to do on the Generate Artifacts screen is to create a new module. Click the **New** button, and create a module named *JDBCModule*. You can give it any name you want or choose from among the existing modules.

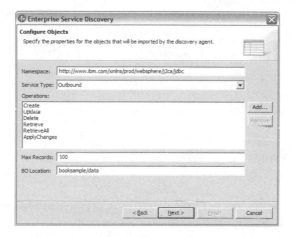

Figure 12.12   Property settings for the discovered objects

13. There are many fields to fill out in the Generate Artifacts screen. The ones you need to fill out are listed here:

    Module: JDBCModule

    Use default namespace should be checked

    Folder: booksample/data

    Name: JDBCOutboundInterface

    Deploy connector with module must be checked

    Use discovered connection properties must be selected

    J2C Authentication Data Entry: widNode/jdbc/booksampleAlias

    Enter Username and Password

    Database URL: jdbc:db2:sample

    Jdbc Driver Class: COM.ibm.db2.jdbc.app.DB2Driver

    Adapter ID: ResourceAdapter

    Database Vendor: DB2

    The alias (widNode/jdbc/booksampleAlias) will have to be created in WebSphere Process Server during deployment of the application.

14. When you click **Finish**, the wizard creates artifacts in the newly created *JDBCModule* project in WID. Specifically, it creates the JDBCOutboundInterface that is shown as an SCA import with an EIS binding in the assembly diagram and data types pertaining to the EMPLOYEE table from the SAMPLE database. The tree structure shown in Figure 12.13 is visible in the business integration view.

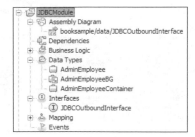

Figure 12.13   Adapter module tree structure

15. If you double-click booksample/data/JDBCOutboundInterface under the assembly diagram, the assembly editor displays the one new element in the diagram, with the single interface—JDBCOutboundInterface—with an EIS binding (see Figure 12.14).

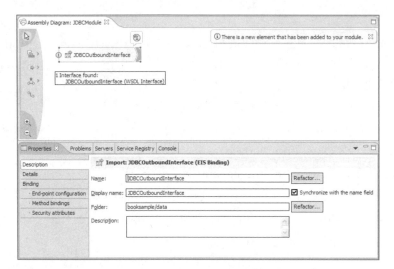

Figure 12.14   Assembly diagram showing JDBCOutboundInterface

Test the Adapter

To test the JDBC adapter we just configured to see if it works correctly, we will use the Test Component feature of WID:

1. Make sure the assembly diagram editor is displaying our JDBCModule, as shown in Figure 12.14. Select the JDBCOutboundInterface import component in the assembly editor. Right-click, and choose **Test Component**.

2. In the Events screen under Detailed Properties, shown in Figure 12.15, use the following values:

Operation: create

In the Initial request parameters table:

verb: create

Enter values for empno, firstnme, lastname, workdept, and sex.

Click the **Continue** button.

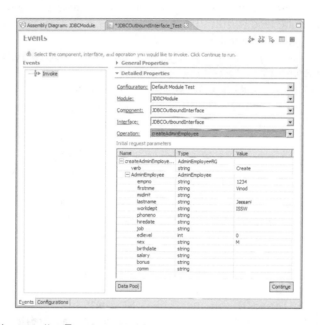

Figure 12.15 Values on the Events screen

3. In the Deployment Location selection window, choose **WebSphere Process Server v6.0**. The mode should be set to **Run**. Then click **Finish**.

The integration test client and server are started. If all goes well, you should see a return in the Events pane without any errors.

FTP, Flat File, and Email Adapters

The three other WebSphere technology adapters are FTP, Flat File, and Email. They work like the JDBC adapter.

- The FTP adapter allows the exchange of business data between remote file systems and J2EE applications by connecting to an FTP server for retrieving and writing to the files. Both inbound and outbound processing are supported.
- WebSphere Adapter for Flat Files lets you exchange business data in the form of delimited records in the event file between file systems and J2EE applications. The adapter is embedded within the application server runtime and maintains an event store. It supports inbound and outbound operations.
- The adapter for Email helps integrate Enterprise Information Systems (EISs) by facilitating the sending and receiving of e-mails to and from different mail servers using SMTP, IMAP, and POP3 e-mail protocols. The adapter is equipped to handle both inbound and outbound communication with an application server. The interactions are handled by the JavaMail API.

SAP Adapter

A.12.2

The WebSphere Adapter for SAP enables J2EE clients to send requests to a SAP server and to receive events from a SAP server. You need to know a few SAP-related terms and components when working with the SAP adapter, such as BAPI, IDoc, and so on. The adapter provides three interfaces that you use to interact with SAP:

- **BAPI:** The Business Applications Programming Interface (BAPI) is a SAP-standardized application programming interface that allows third-party systems to interact with the SAP server. The adapter models SAP BAPI function calls to create, update, and retrieve data as business objects. The BAPI interface is used for outbound processing only.
- **ALE:** IDocs are SAP Intermediate Document structures that are used for data exchange. Application Link Enabling (ALE) integrates processes between SAP systems and external applications as well as between SAP systems. ALE uses IDocs and can be configured for both outbound and inbound processing.
- **SQI:** The SAP Query Interface (SQI) retrieves data from SAP application tables. These tables are modeled as hierarchical business objects that get generated during the enterprise service discovery process. SQI is used for outbound processing only.

No matter which interface you decide to configure, you can use the Enterprise Service Discovery wizard to find the right set of elements.

SAP Adapter Installation

The SAP adapter is installed using the same basic installation instructions common to all adapters. There are a couple of unique preparatory steps:

- Copying sapjco.jar to the lib subdirectory of WebSphere Process Server
- Copying the SAP JCo Windows DLLs or UNIX runtime libraries into the *WPS_HOME*\bin subdirectory
- Knowing the following information about the SAP application:
    SAP username
    SAP password
    SAP hostname (or IP address)
    SAP system number (usually 00)
    SAP client number (usually 100)
- Making the appropriate connector file part of your WID application. Two RAR files are actually associated with SAP:
    CWYAP_SAPAdapter.rar
    CWYAP_SAPAdapter_Tx.rar[2]

Siebel Adapter

The WebSphere Adapter for Siebel facilitates the exchange of business objects between J2EE clients and Siebel Business Applications. It supports both outbound and inbound operations. Siebel business applications allow data exchange and business process execution using services, components, and objects that are part of the business object layer in the Siebel application architecture. The Siebel system does this via its Siebel Data Bean. The Siebel Java Data Bean interacts with the following types of application objects:

- Siebel business objects and business components
- Siebel business services with Siebel integration objects and components

The Siebel Data Bean exposes the Siebel entities, thus enabling the adapter to use these interfaces to communicate with the Siebel Object Manager for data exchange. The Siebel BOs and components are objects typically tied to specific data and tables in the Siebel data model, whereas the Siebel business services are not. The Adapter itself is metadata-driven and supports hierarchical BOs. It supports the following operations:

- ApplyChanges
- Create
- Delete
- Exists

- Retrieve
- RetrieveAll
- Update

---

[2] Use this file if you want the container (WPS) to control local transaction support for BAPI processing. In this case, the adapter participates in the local transaction started by the WebSphere application container.

Siebel Adapter Installation

The Siebel adapter is installed using the same basic installation instructions common to all adapters. There are a couple of unique preparatory steps:

- Installing either the Siebel Industry or Enterprise Applications. This consists of
    Siebel Gateway Server
    Siebel Application Server
    Database Server
    Web server and the Siebel Web Server Extension (SWSE)
    RDBMS, including database configurations
- Having the Enterprise Application Integration (EAI) object manager online (within the Siebel Server)
- Copying Siebel.jar and the SiebelJI_enu.jar to the lib subdirectory of WebSphere Process Server
- Making the appropriate connector file part of your WID application CWYEB_SiebelAdapter.rar

Custom Adapters

If you want to develop custom adapters, you have to use the WebSphere Adapter Toolkit (WAT), which is an Eclipse plug-in that gets configured in the WebSphere Integration Developer (WID). Note that WAT requires that WID be installed on top of Rational Application Developer. The installation and verification of WAT are covered in Appendix F, "WebSphere Adapter Toolkit Installation."

We do not get into the details of how to create a custom adapter in this book. We consider this to be an advanced topic. This section provides the high-level steps of developing a custom resource adapter and gets you going with the creation of the adapter project in WID. It is left to you to complete the details.

At a high level, these are the steps of developing a custom adapter:

1. Identify and establish the resource adapter configuration properties.

    Identify properties for connecting to the EIS instance for outbound processing, such as hostname and port.

    Identify properties usable by a client for a specific outbound connection instance, such as username, password, and language.

    Identify properties for inbound event processing similar to what you did for outbound.

    Establish a list of general configuration properties not related to outbound or inbound properties.

2. Provide implementation for the outbound classes and command patterns.

3. Provide implementation for the inbound classes.

4. Provide implementation for the Enterprise Metadata Discovery (EMD) classes.

> **WAT**
>
> There is a WebSphere Business Integration Adapter Development Kit and a WebSphere Adapter Toolkit (WAT). Make sure you are using WAT to develop JCA adapters.

Starting the Adapter Project in WID

In WID, select **File > New > Project**. In the New Project window, shown in Figure 12.16, expand Adapter Toolkit, and choose **J2C Resource Adapter Project**. Click **Next**.

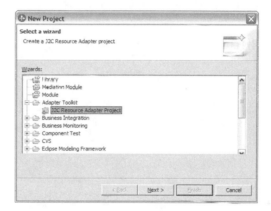

Figure 12.16 Starting a new adapter project

Name the adapter project, also known as the connector project, as shown in Figure 12.17. If you show the advanced settings, you will notice that the J2C Version is 1.5. Make sure the Target server is **WebSphere Process Server v6.0**. Click **Next**.

Name the adapter, as shown in Figure 12.18. Specify a package name. The class prefix is usually the project name. Click **Next**.

Finally, you can specify which specific options to generate. Because we are creating an outbound adapter, select the option **Generate Outbound Adapter classes**, as shown in Figure 12.19. Under Adapter Specification, you have two options: IBM WebSphere Resource Adapter and J2EE J2C Resource Adapter. Choose **IBM WebSphere Resource Adapter**, and click **Finish**.

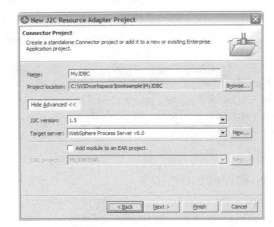

Figure 12.17   Adapter project properties

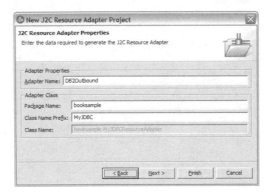

Figure 12.18   Specifying the adapter properties

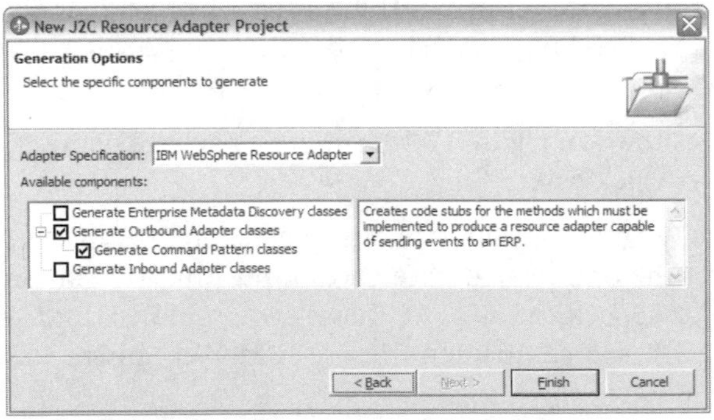

Figure 12.19   Specifying the components to generate

You will see the newly created project listed under Connector Projects in the J2EE perspective with the Overview page showing in the main pane. If you expand the project folder, you will see a whole bunch of generated files by the WebSphere Adapter Toolkit. The next step is to provide implementations for all the required classes. This is left as an exercise for you to do.

Closing the Link

Whether you call them connectors or resource adapters, the area of business integration adapters is vast and, in our opinion, rather specialized. From legacy WBIA adapters to JCA adapters, from application adapters to technology adapters, you could write a whole book on this topic. We have been rather focused in this chapter on the JCA adapters that are hosted on WPS, and we explained all the concepts by way of the JDBC adapter.

The technology adapters are easier to grasp if you are familiar with the underlying technology, such as JDBC, FTP, Email, and so on. Application adapters, on the other hand, are a bit more challenging, because you must thoroughly understand how that application software, such as SAP or Siebel or PeopleSoft, works.

WebSphere Adapter Resource Archive (RAR) files cannot be installed and administered via the WebSphere Administrative Console. Enterprise applications that contain WebSphere adapter components must contain the requisite RAR files.

Nevertheless, adapters play an important role in a business integration solution, because often you have to integrate with an existing third-party back-end system.

 Links to developerWorks

A.12.1   www.ibm.com/developerworks/websphere/techjournal/0704_gregory1/
0704_gregory1.html

A.12.2   www.ibm.com/developerworks/websphere/library/techarticles/0706_jin/
0706_jin.html

Chapter 13

Business Modeling

Thus far in the Service-Oriented Architecture (SOA) lifecycle, we have covered the Assemble and Deploy steps. This chapter concentrates on the Model step—also known as business modeling or business process modeling. Before business objects and service components exist, the business analyst (BA) comes up with a business process model. It is driven by a business need and is truly a business process. It could affect everybody in the enterprise, or it could be critical only on the shop floor. Nevertheless, the business analyst creates this business process model, and he or she typically uses a software tool to do so.

The word model can be a person, a concept, or a structure representation. Even within the context of the business model you will discover various subtypes. These will be explained as we discuss business modeling concepts. Even though some people consider business modeling and business monitoring bookends in an end-to-end business integration scenario, everything has to start somewhere. In this case, we start with the business model. Figure 13.1 shows the SOA Lifecycle of Model, Assemble, Deploy, and Manage, in which modeling, in most cases, starts the lifecycle. We will use the Eclipse-based WebSphere Business Modeler to explain the modeling concepts.

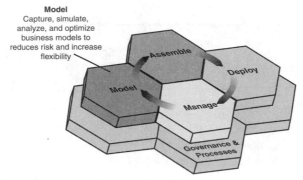

Figure 13.1 SOA Lifecycle showing the modeling step

Enterprises used to employ static drawing tools to depict a business flow, but now business modeling software is more than just a drawing tool. In addition to modeling, you can annotate, simulate, define business measures, and analyze the model as you create it. Although such software is presented as tools that bridge the gap between business and information technology (IT), the main idea concerns what it will do for the business. Creating a good business model and then implementing it eventually benefits the customer and, hence, the business enterprise.

Installing WebSphere Business Modeler

WebSphere Business Modeler is meant to be used by nontechnical as well as technical people. As such, it can be installed as a stand-alone software tool or installed as part of an Eclipse-based Integrated Development Environment (IDE) such as WebSphere Integration Developer (WID). So, before starting the installation, you have to decide if you will use the Modeler in a stand-alone environment or if you will use it as a plug-in within WID as part of an existing development environment. Either way, the installation process is simple, as shown in Appendix C, "WebSphere Business Modeler Installation."

Mimicking the role of a business analyst, we will work with the stand-alone version of WebSphere Business Modeler, because it can do simulation and dynamic analysis. We will look at the genesis of the sample we have been working with thus far within Business Modeler.

Business Modeling Terms and Concepts

Many of the concepts and terminology in business process modeling or simply business modeling come from Unified Modeling Language (UML). In business modeling terms, a business process contains a number of activities performed in a certain order with a defined goal. It has specific inputs and outputs, uses resources, and may affect one or more organizational units in an enterprise. The key difference between business system modeling in UML and business process modeling is the emphasis on how the work is done within an organization, rather than what work is done.

Business process modeling is the discipline of defining and outlining business practices, processes, information flows, data stores, and systems. Process design, process execution, and process monitoring are its three main categories of activities. From a modeling perspective, business process modeling often involves using a notation such as UML to capture graphical representations of the major processes, flows, and stores. One of the first aspects of business modeling is understanding the business drivers, which can be any of the following:

- **Modeling for execution:** Future state business processes are associated with run-time characteristics for the purpose of business process development. Enterprises like to be able to change the business process in response to changes in the market.
- **Modeling for what-if analysis:** The ability to do simulation and to perform a what-if type of analysis, combined with real-time monitoring, can provide feedback on process improvements.
- **Modeling for compliance:** Enterprises meet requirements for compliance regulations (Sarbanes-Oxley or Basel II).
- **Modeling for documentation:** Enterprises like to capture and document their current business processes to better understand them and facilitate their maintenance.
- **Modeling for redesign:** Helps enterprises discover potential areas for process improvement and latent value in the business processes.
- **Modeling for optimization:** Compares the current state and future state of business processes to determine return on investment (ROI). You can also establish and track measurable process metrics for performance.

After the need for a business model has been established, the business analyst (BA) first documents and sketches the business process flow. Then he or she lists the details that make up the business process, which fall into three broad categories—resources, business items, and business rules. Resources can be people, material, and equipment. Existing documents, records, and products make up the business items. Business rules are the current decision logic and constraints. The process input and the output at various stages of the process are noted. Finally, the roles of the people involved with the business process are established. With all that information, the business analyst can then create an initial model of the business process. We want to stress the word initial, because inevitably, the model will change due to resource constraints, the timetable, and input from IT. In the end, the business model has to realize the business intent or goal.

A.13.2

The current business model is also known as the as-is model or current-state model. To help you understand the current model, quite often you create a to-be model or a future-state model. You use the to-be model to make improvements and changes in the as-is model. Remember that we mentioned that many subtypes of business process models exist. There are physical models, simulation models, and execution models. One of the most relevant is the Business Measures model. It describes business metrics, their dependencies on incoming events, business conditions warranting business action, and situation events that represent notifications of such conditions. The section "Business Measures" discusses this topic in more detail.

Working with WebSphere Business Modeler

On the Windows platform, bring up the Business Modeler by selecting **Start** > **Programs** > **IBM WebSphere** > **Business Modeler**. Whenever you start the Business Modeler, just like in WID, you are asked for a working directory, also called the workspace. Similar to our recommendation of storing WID workspaces in a folder titled WIDworkspace, we recommend storing Business Modeler workspaces in a folder titled MODworkspace—for example, C:\MODworkspace.

> **Business Modeler Workspace Tip**
>
> Do not check the box that reads **Use this as the default workspace, and do not show this dialog box again**, as shown in Figure 13.2. We recommend keeping the workspace folder separate from the Business Modeler installation folder.

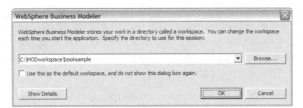

Figure 13.2 Choosing a workspace for Business Modeler

If you cancel the Quickstart wizard window, you see the Welcome Screen, as shown in Figure 13.3. You can hover the cursor on each of the icons on the Welcome Screen to see the choices. The choices from left to right are Overview, What's New, Tutorials, Samples, Migration, Hints and Tips, Troubleshooting and Support, and Web Resources. Because this chapter presents only an overview of Business Modeler, we want to draw particular attention to the prebuilt samples that you can explore.

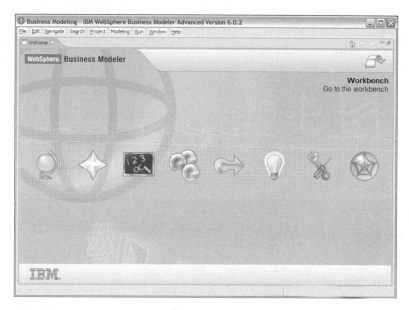

Figure 13.3 WebSphere Business Modeler welcome screen

Click the curved arrow on the top right to open the workbench. You see the welcome screen only when you open a new workspace. After you have opened a workspace and worked with it, you are taken directly to the workbench. If you want to go back to the Welcome screen, select **Help > Welcome**.

WebSphere Business Modeler

To keep the Quickstart wizard from showing up every time WebSphere Business Modeler is started, uncheck the option **Always show this wizard on startup**.

If the workbench does not open in a four-pane mode, click the icon titled **Apply 4-pane layout**. The first thing to do is to create a new project.

1. In the Project Tree pane, right-click, and select **New > Business Modeling Project**.

2. In the window that appears, shown in Figure 13.4, enter a new project name. Leave the Default process catalog name as Processes. Create a process named *CreateOrder*. You could click **Finish** at this point, but for illustrative purposes, click **Next**. You may also choose not to create a process at this time.

Figure 13.4 Creating a new business modeling project

You can choose between the Free-Form Layout and Swimlane Layout, as shown in Figure 13.5. Free-Form Layout, which is the default, places no restrictions on where elements can be placed in the diagram. The Swimlane Layout rearranges the elements in a process diagram into a set of rows called swimlanes (similar to the swimming lanes in a competition swimming pool). The elements are arranged according to one of many definitions—organization unit, location, resource definition, bulk resource definition, role, or classifier value. At the left of each swimlane is an area called the swimlane header, which identifies the element associated with the swimlane. The main purpose of arranging the elements this way is to make unnecessary handoff between elements in different rows easy to identify and to aid in resolving bottlenecks and redundancies.

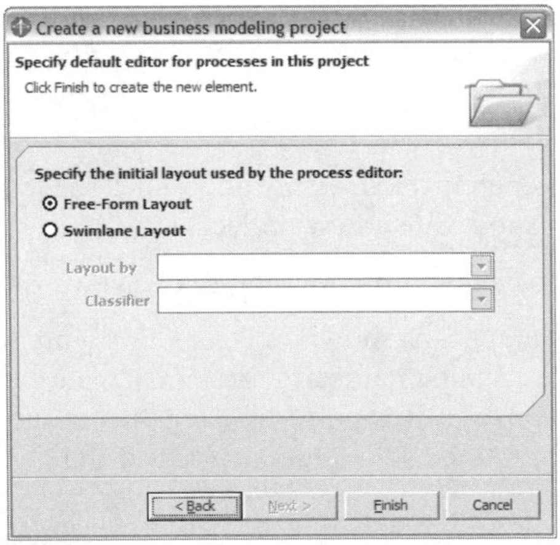

Figure 13.5 Choosing the layout

You can switch from one layout to another by right-clicking in the Process editor canvas and choosing the **Switch to** option. As we continue creating our sample project, accept the **Free-Form Layout**, and click **Finish**.

Project files are created and initialized, and you see a large canvas on the top right of the four-pane layout. It has a *CreateOrder* process diagram containing two elements—a green start node and a blue stop node. In the Project Tree, you will find folders for business items, resources, and business service objects, among other things.

Select **Modeling** > **Mode**. Then choose **WebSphere Process Server**, as shown in Figure 13.6.

Figure 13.6 Setting the modeling mode

The Advanced version of WebSphere Business Modeler offers the following choices:

- **Basic:** This is the default mode. It focuses on creating and displaying sequence flows and does not expose low-level technical details of process and data modeling.
- **Intermediate:** This mode gives the technically focused user the opportunity to specify and view additional details of the process and data models.
- **Advanced:** Meant for the experienced user, this mode helps you create models that will be used as the basis for business applications.

The other three modes are geared toward the targeted IBM software products: WebSphere Business Integration Server Foundation, WebSphere MQ Workflow, and WebSphere Process Server. The tool applies a set of validation rules to the Advanced Business Modeling mode to support exporting models that fit the constraints of the particular product.

We recommend working in Advanced mode. More specifically, because you know that the model you create will eventually be deployed to WebSphere Process Server (WPS), you might as well choose this mode.

> **Views**
>
> When the business process model is opened in the editor, other views are shown by default in the lower half of the main screen—Attributes view, Business Measures view, Errors view, and Technical Attributes view.

Before we add business items and other elements to the process, we will briefly describe the various elements of a process diagram. WebSphere Business Modeler lets you create multiple types of catalogs to organize and store modeling elements. Catalogs are like containers performing the function of folders; they let you group a related set of elements in a project. And catalogs can have subcatalogs. The following types of catalogs are available:

- *Data* catalogs hold business item templates, business items, business item instances, notification templates, and notifications.
- *Process* catalogs hold processes, tasks, repositories, and services.
- *Resource* catalogs hold resource definition templates, resource definitions, resources, roles, and timetables.
- *Organization* catalogs hold the model elements required to represent organizational elements and structures.
- *Classifiers* catalogs hold classifiers. These allow you to categorize and color-code process elements so that elements with a particular set of characteristics are easily recognized.
- *Report* catalogs hold report templates.
- *Queries* catalogs hold query templates.

Along with these catalogs, you should have naming standards in place. You will need guidelines for naming and versioning projects, catalogs, process models, tasks, repositories, and other resources. At a higher level, identifying workspaces and creating backups would also have to be addressed. The whole area of source code or Eclipse project management is relevant but is beyond the scope of this chapter. Our focus is on business processes—specifically, process diagrams.

Business Process Diagrams

The process diagram is a graphical representation of a business process flow, consisting of activities and the connections or data flow between these elements. Each process has an entry point or an input, and an exit point or an output. A process diagram can contain one or more of these elements or even another child process:

- *Annotations* are explanatory notes added to a process diagram or structure diagram.
- *Connections* are links or the data flows between two elements in a business process diagram.
- *Decisions* are similar to a programmatic `if` statement. They route inputs to one of several alternative outgoing paths.
- *Forks* split the process flow into two or more concurrent paths, enabling two or more tasks to be performed in parallel. A fork makes copies of its inputs and forwards them along each path.
- *Inputs* are entry points through which an element (such as a process or task) is notified that it can start. The inputs define the data that the element needs. An element starts after it has received all the required inputs.
- *Loops* are repeating sequences of activities contained within a process, similar to a programmatic `while-do`.
- *Maps* are specialized tasks that transform data from one structure to another.

- *Merges and joins* combine multiple processing paths, recombining alternative flows into a single flow. Joins also synchronize the flows by combining two or more parallel paths that must all complete before they continue along a single path.
- *Notifications* are occurrences within a process that can trigger actions. A process uses a notification to send information to one of its already executing subprocesses. The opposite is also true. A subprocess can use a notification to send information to its parent process.
- *Observers* are specialized tasks that watch a process and its associated repositories and initiate a flow when a certain condition becomes true.
- *Outputs* typically are exit points. The output from a process, task, or other element also defines the data that the element will produce after it has run.
- *Repositories* are storage areas for the information created in a business process. Every repository has a name and an associated type. Usually the name of a repository is the same as the name of the business items it contains.
- *Services* are external processes outside the organization that can be used within the organization's processes. Services have well-defined inputs and outputs and can either provide input or receive output.
- *Tasks* are the basic building blocks representing activities in a process model. Each task performs a certain function. From a visual perspective, a task represents the lowest level of work shown in the process.
- *Timers* typically initiate a flow at a specified point in time.

Business Measures

Companies used to focus on financial measures such as turnover and profit as key indicators of business performance. But increasingly, companies are looking for a wider set of measures, including business measures. Business measures are developed in the business modeler. Although the term is used synonymously, Key Performance Indicators (KPIs) are a subset of business measures. Business measures that support business monitoring requirements should not be generated in the modeler until the execution model is believed to be complete and ready to be deployed to the assembly tool, WID.

The WebSphere Business Modeler product InfoCenter specifies that the Business Measures model can perform the following tasks:

- Gather information from inbound events that are in real time
- Aggregate information to calculate higher-level business metrics or KPIs
- Recognize business situations or conditions
- Emit situation events that may be used to trigger actions
- Based on business needs, be able to represent the calculated values in reports and graphs

Apart from KPIs, there are metrics, stopwatches and counters, triggers, events, and dimensions. Incidentally, these terms are also part of the business monitoring vocabulary, as you will see in the next chapter.

Working with the Business Model

We use the *BookSample* project to illustrate features of the WebSphere Business Modeler. With the skeleton *CreateOrder* process diagram displayed in the Process editor, you will notice a palette on the left. It contains the following elements that you can add to the process diagram:

- Tasks
- Processes
- Notification broadcasters
- Notification receivers
- Loops
- Decisions
- Joins
- Forks
- Merges
- Repositories
- Start, stop, and end nodes
- Connections
- Annotations

Business Items

Anything that is created, assembled, inspected, tested, modified, or worked on can be modeled as a business item. Examples of potential business items are Customer, SalesOrder, Receipt, MaterialRequest, InsurancePolicy, EngineAssembly, StockClerk, and CircuitBoard. A business item instance is based on a business item, which defines its attributes. The business item instance optionally has a specific value for each attribute defined by the business item. Data that the process would need is passed in as one or more business items. In SOA terms, it is a business object (BO). You can either create new business items in the Business Modeler or import existing business objects, represented as XSDs. Business items are put in a data catalog.

With the *BookSample* project open in the WebSphere Business Modeler, go to the Project Tree, highlight Business items, right-click, and select **New** > **Business Item**. As shown in Figure 13.7, enter a name for the business item and an optional description, and then click **Finish**.

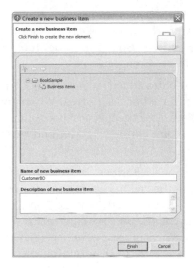

Figure 13.7 Creating a new business item

> **Business Item**
>
> If there is a data catalog, you would find a folder under Business Items.
> The business item name must be unique within the selected catalog.

The business item editor is displayed, as shown in Figure 13.8. You can start adding attributes by clicking the **Add** button. Give each attribute a name, and specify the type. Attribute types can be either Basic or Complex.

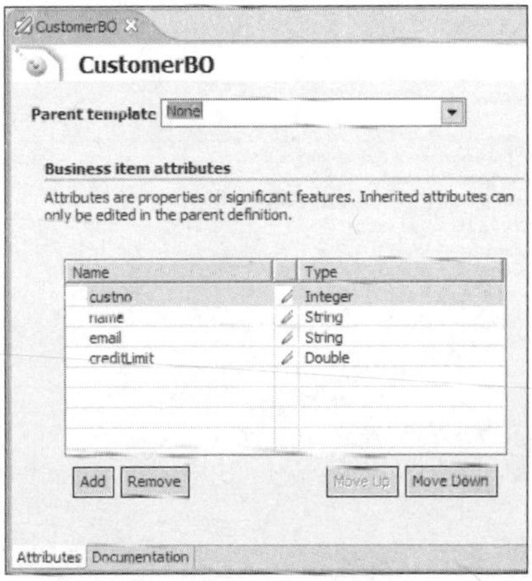

Figure 13.8 Adding business item attributes

The Basic types are Boolean, Byte, Date, DateTime, Double, Duration, Float, Integer, Long, Short, String, and Time. Predefined resources such as Communication Service, Equipment, Facility, General Service, Machine, Person, Staff, and Tool, and Predefined organizations such as Organization, make up the Complex types.

Figure 13.8 shows the four attributes added to *CustomerBO*. An asterisk next to the name in the tab indicates that the edits have not been saved. When you're done, remember to press **Ctrl+S** to save the edits and then close the business item editor. If you close the editor before saving your work, the Save Resource window appears and asks you if the changes need to be saved. At that point, click **Yes**.

The business analyst uses WebSphere Business Modeler to start the business modeling step. Occasionally, we have seen that the creation of BOs is left to the Business Process Execution Language (BPEL) business process designers in WID. These objects are then imported into WebSphere Business Modeler. The reason for doing this is that either there are preexisting BOs in the enterprise, or the business process developers have the expertise to determine the makeup of the various BOs, especially in determining the attribute types. For example, a business analyst might not be comfortable creating objects with Complex Type attributes. He or she might want to import an existing BO.

Importing a Business Item

Among other things, you can import an existing WSDL or XSD. Be aware that the import options you get by selecting **File** > **Import** are different from the import options you get from the context menu in the navigation pane when you right-click.

1. In the navigation pane, right-click, and select **Import**. In the Select type window, shown in Figure 13.9, highlight **Business services and service objects (.wsdl, .xsd)**. Click **Next**.

Figure 13.9 Importing business services and service objects

2. Choose the Source directory, as shown in Figure 13.10. Then pick the artifact you
    want to import. The Target project in this case is *BookSample*. Then click **Finish**.
    Figure 13.10 shows us importing *OrderBO* into the project.

Figure 13.10 Importing *OrderBO*

The next step is to create the business process model.

Business Process Model

A.13.4

As discussed in the previous chapters, business processes are service components that provide the primary means through which enterprise services are integrated. When you break
it down, you see that a business process is actually a series of individual tasks, and each task
is executed in a specific order. WebSphere Business Modeler does not force a particular
methodology. It is a tool that business analysts (BAs) can use in their chosen business
process methodology to store business process data. Using the Free-Form Layout in the
Modeler, we will construct the business process flow by placing elements and denoting tasks
on the canvas and then connecting them.

In the *BookSample* project tree, expand Processes, and double-click *CreateOrder* to open it in
the Process editor. Notice the tabs associated with the Process editor. In the Advanced version of WebSphere Business Modeler, the Process editor has the following tabs: Diagram,
Specification, Visual Attributes, Page Layout, and Technical Specification.

The diagram of every new process model has a *Start* node and a *Stop* node. They are flagged
as errors because there are no connections. You can delete those nodes by highlighting each
one, right-clicking, and choosing **Delete**. If necessary, those nodes can be added later. Now
we show you the steps to create a task and wire it:

1. From the palette on the left, click the brown rectangular icon to **Create local task**, and then click the canvas. A task activity node appears. Change its name to *Get Customer Details* by typing on the highlighted area.

2. Go back to the palette, and click the **Create Connection** arrow. Place the cursor on the canvas, click the left edge of the canvas (which will be the source), and then click the **Get Customer Details** task node (which will be the target). A connection or wire is created.

3. Highlight the connection arrow, right-click, and select **Associate Data**. A Type Selection window appears. You can either choose a Basic type or a Complex type or not associate a type. For our *BookSample*, select *CustomerBO* from among the Complex types, and click **OK**.

4. The process model diagram should look like what is shown in Figure 13.11. Press **Ctrl+S** to save the edits.

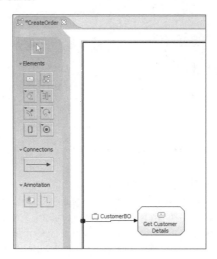

Figure 13.11 Adding and connecting a task element

In the same manner, complete the process diagram, as shown in Figure 13.12. The diamond-shaped element titled *Credit Approved* is a decision node with a *Yes* or *No* output. Be sure to periodically save your work.

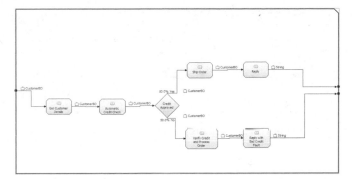

Figure 13.12 CreateOrder process model

You will notice that only one data item, *CustomerBO*, has been used throughout the process model. That is but one pattern. You can definitely use multiple data items as input and output. If the task calls for using one data item as input and another data item as output, you would employ a map node.

Figure 13.13 shows how we made a slight change to the initial part of the process model and introduced a map node. The data item we created, *CustomerBO*, and the BO we imported, *OrderBO*, are both part of the data flow in the process model.

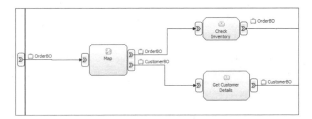

Figure 13.13 Introducing a map node

If you look on the Project menu, you will find that Build Automatically is the default setting. As you keep building the business process model, the tool does a build and flags errors. Check the Errors view to make sure no build errors exist.

Project Clean
Occasionally, after completing a significant amount of work, you should select **Project** > **Clean**. In the message window that appears, shown in Figure 13.14, click **OK** to rebuild from scratch.

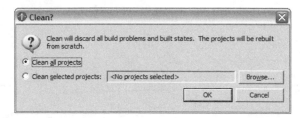

Figure 13.14 Invoking a clean build of all projects

Exporting a Business Item

Let's assume that the BA has built the process model and wants to hand it over to the business process developer. In that case, the project has to be exported. It is important to make sure that the project has no errors.

1. In the navigation pane, right-click, and select **Export**. In the Select type window, shown in Figure 13.15, highlight **WebSphere Process Server**, and click **Next**.

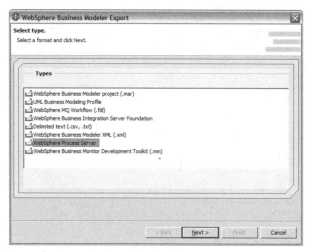

Figure 13.15 Exporting WebSphere Process Server

2. Choose the Target directory, as shown in Figure 13.16. You can export the entire project or specific elements. Choose **Export entire project**.

Figure 13.16 Specifying a destination and source for exporting the artifacts

3. Name the project module, the project library, and the project interchange file. Because this is a project interchange file from the Business Modeler, we like to give it a suffix of *ModPI*. Click **Finish**.

The exported files can be imported into WID to create an implementation for WPS.

Generating a Monitoring File

If you want to generate a monitoring (.mon) file and have the default events enabled, select the **Enable default events** checkbox, as shown in Figure 13.16. If you do not enable the checkbox, WebSphere Business Modeler does not generate the .mon file and does not enable the default events. You can, however, enable the default events in WID after you have completed the import.

You can import the model elements into WID, make the necessary changes, and then prepare to deploy the application on WPS. This is part of the premise of the SOA Lifecycle. The business model is created in the Model step and then is assembled with the business logic in the Assemble step. It is deployed to a runtime in the Deploy step and is monitored in the Manage step. Table 13.1 shows the mapping of some of the common elements in WebSphere Business Modeler to BPEL in WID. You will notice that many elements in business modeling do not appear in the table. The reason is that there are no corresponding BPEL elements.

Table 13.1 Mapping of Elements

WebSphere Business Modeler	BPEL Construct in WID
Connection with associated data	Assigning or retrieving from variables
Connection with no associated data	BPEL link
Decision	Links with transition
	Switch activity
Expression	BPEL Java condition
Input	BPEL variable
Map	Empty Java activity
Output	BPEL variable
Top-level global process	BPEL process with a flow structured activity
Local subprocess	BPEL scope with a flow structured activity
Global process within another process	Invoke
Local repository	BPEL variable
Resource/role requirement	Human task
Local task	Invoke
while loop	BPEL while with a flow structured activity

Business Measures

Now that the business process flow is complete, we can turn our attention to defining business measures. This is dictated by what the enterprise wants to measure and monitor when the business process is deployed and executed. The Business Measures model that is created in the Business Measures view is used to monitor a process instance by defining what should be monitored—process instances, KPIs, metrics, and business situations—and to specify when the situation events are sent to trigger specific actions. This is done in the Business Measures view. Look for the Business Measures tab under the Process editor canvas.

Business measures information that you can specify in WebSphere Business Modeler is separated into two types:

- Information to be used for dashboard display and analysis (specified in the Business Performance Indicators tab).

- Information to collect from running process instances (specified in the Monitored Values tab). You can use this information to improve the accuracy of simulations in WebSphere Business Modeler.

When the Business Measures model is complete, it is exported from the WebSphere Business Modeler, ready to be imported into WebSphere Business Monitor. In Chapter 14, "Business Monitoring," you will learn about a WID plug-in called Monitor Model Editor (MME). When we talk about importing the Business Measures model into WebSphere Business Monitor, this actually means importing it into the development tool, the MME.

In the MME, additional attributes are added to the Business Measures model before it is exported as an EAR file for deployment to the runtime monitor server. The Business Measures model can actually be built in its entirety in the MME. However, using the Business Measures Editor in WebSphere Business Modeler gives the BA an opportunity to describe the things that should be measured in the business process. Only the MME can generate the EAR file that will be required by the monitor server to monitor the process. The WebSphere Business Monitor recognizes the model to be monitored and the measurements to be captured from incoming events.

Business Simulation

Business simulation is also known as process simulation or dynamic analysis. The simulation model allows you to review the results of a process simulation in which the volume of work and the number of available resources over a specific period of time affect the following:

- Cycle times
- Cycle costs
- Utilization
- Resource constraints
- Throughput

A process simulation is a simulated performance of either an existing real-world business process or one that is planned for the future. It enables organizations to observe how a process will perform in response to various inputs to the process. When you simulate a process, the tool adds a simulation snapshot in the project tree view as a child element of the process. You might want to create multiple simulation snapshots of the same process to compare the effects of changes to the input.

> **Simulation Snapshot**
>
> A simulation snapshot is a record of the complete process model at the moment you simulated the process. It also contains a set of snapshot settings of the simulation profile. After you create a simulation snapshot, the copy of the process model it contains is no longer affected by changes to the original model.

To create a Simulation model, right-click the process (CreateOrder) in the Project Tree and select Simulate. After the Simulation model is created, it is displayed in a different canvas with the original process name and the word Simulate (CreateOrder (Simulate)). As noted earlier, the simulation diagrams are read-only in that the elements that make up the diagram cannot be moved or renamed. In the Project Tree, you will see a new simulation snapshot folder under the process, as shown in Figure 13.17. Notice that each simulation snapshot has a date and time stamp.

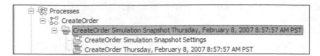

Figure 13.17 Simulation snapshot folder

Figure 13.18 shows a close-up of a simulation diagram. When you run a simulation, you can watch an animated view of the process in operation. You can watch the movement of tokens from the inputs of the process and between activities in the process. A *token* represents a unit of work that is received by a process and transferred between different activities in the process flow. By observing a process during animation, you can see where the process is operating efficiently and where delays are occurring.

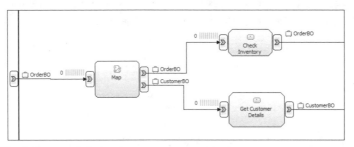

Figure 13.18 Simulation model

When a token is added to a queue on an input, the number that appears next to the queue is incremented by 1, and one of the vertical bars that represent the queue may darken in color. Note that each bar in the queue represents two tokens.

If the simulation model is synced with the runtime Business Measures model, data, such as task duration and decision percentages, can be imported into the model from WebSphere Business Monitor Server. Using real data from the runtime environment to establish task duration and decision percentages can improve simulation accuracy. As mentioned earlier, the Simulation option is available in the Advanced edition of WebSphere Business Modeler.

Closing the Link

This chapter discussed the Business Analyst's tool of choice—the Business Modeler. Enterprises should not only view the business process model as the starting point; it should be viewed as something that is dynamic and conducive to change.

If you're wondering why this chapter was not presented earlier as the first steps in the SOA Lifecycle, it is something we debated. After the three introductory chapters, this chapter could have been presented as the first step in the SOA Lifecycle. It could have illustrated the modeling of the sample process and then delved into the export/import exercise in WID as a starting point for the *BookSample* module and library. However, the thrust of this book is not the SOA Lifecycle; it is business integration. A.13.5

A single chapter on WebSphere Business Modeler is not sufficient to explain the versatility of the tool and to show all its features. We think the simulation feature is invaluable to the business analyst. Finally, we want to reiterate that the SOA Lifecycle is a continuum.

Links to developerWorks

A.13.1 www.ibm.com/developerworks/websphere/techjournal/0702_koehler/0702 koehler.html

A.13.2 www.ibm.com/developerworks/websphere/library/techarticles/0705_ fasbinder/0705_fasbinder.html?S_TACT=105AGX10&S_CMP=LP

A.13.3 www.ibm.com/developerworks/library/ar-model1/?S_TACT=105AGX78&S_ CMP=ART

A.13.4 www.ibm.com/developerworks/websphere/library/techarticles/0706_fasbinder/ 0706_fasbinder.html

A.13.5 www.ibm.com/developerworks/websphere/library/techarticles/0706_perepa/0706_ perepa.html?S_TACT=105AGX10&S_CMP=LP

Chapter 14

Business Monitoring

S o, you've modeled your business process and deployed it to WebSphere Process Server. What is left to be done? We need to monitor the process to understand how it is functioning. But how do we know whether the business process is effective? How do we know the service is performing in compliance with business guidelines and customer expectations? How can business executives know to take corrective actions with changes in the business environment? To find the answers to these questions and more, we have to step into the realm of Business Monitoring, also known as Business Activity Monitoring (BAM). This chapter discusses the architecture of WebSphere Business Monitor and Key Performance Indicators (KPIs), triggers, metrics, measures, and dashboards. The goal is to present a dashboard with graphs and gauges to help business executives understand how business processes are performing.

Business Modeling and Business Monitoring are the bookends in an end-to-end business processing scenario. After the process or service is deployed, the final step in the Service-Oriented Architecture (SOA) is to manage the business process. Actually, we might be remiss in characterizing it as the final step, because as we have mentioned, Model-Assemble-Deploy-Manage is a continuum, as shown in Figure 14.1. Part of managing a SOA is to monitor business processes. BAM is software that helps monitor business processes. Increasingly, BAM is built in as a feature of Business Integration Software and Business Process Management software. WebSphere Business Monitor is an example of such BAM software, which is part of the WebSphere Business Integration Suite.

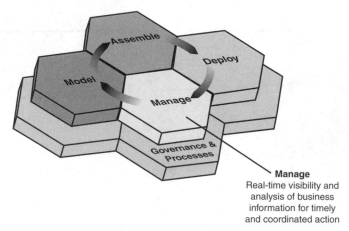

Manage
Real-time visibility and
analysis of business
information for timely
and coordinated action

Figure 14.1   SOA Lifecycle showing the Manage step

Business Activity Monitoring

The term Business Activity Monitoring was originally used by analysts at the Gartner Group. It refers to the aggregation, analysis, and presentation of information about business activities in an enterprise. The information typically is presented in real time via dashboards displayed via computers, or it could be reports about historical data. Three main components of BAM are data, timely collection of that data, and detailed analysis of that data.

A.14.1

The goal of any BAM software is to provide real-time or near-real-time information about the status and results of various activities or operations in business processes. This enables organizations to quickly address problem areas, reallocate resources, or react to a changing business climate. Another facet of BAM software is the ability to do root-cause analysis and alert organizations of impending problems.

IBM WebSphere Business Monitor v6.0.2 is the version on the market (as of this writing) that complements WebSphere Process Server. Support for BAM is provided through an enhanced authoring environment and a BAM software development kit (SDK). In keeping with the three main components of any BAM product, WebSphere Business Monitor has three main software components—the Monitor Server, Dashboard Server, and Databases (Monitor and Datamart)—as shown in Figure 14.2. DB2 Cube Views™ is used to obtain dimensional representation of the data. WebSphere Portal, with the help of DB2 Alphablox, is used to create and display the dashboards.

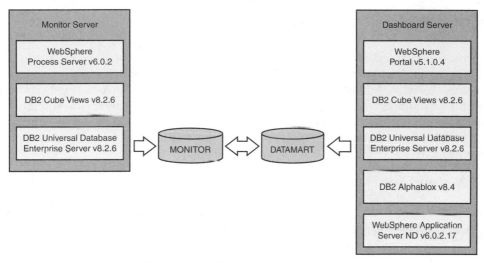

Figure 14.2 Components of WebSphere Business Monitor

There is also the WebSphere Business Monitor Development Toolkit, commonly called the Monitor Development Toolkit; it is targeted toward developers. Monitor Development Toolkit is an Eclipse-based plug-in that installs within WebSphere Integration Developer (WID) and has two main components: Integrated Development Environment (IDE) and Integrated Test Environment (ITE), as shown in Figure 14.3. The toolkit lets you create monitor models without the need for WebSphere Business Modeler. Although the Business Modeler provides significant value for the business analyst in the monitoring lifecycle, you can optionally create instrumented monitor models in WID or in the Business Measures View of Business Modeler and then complete them using the Monitor Toolkit.

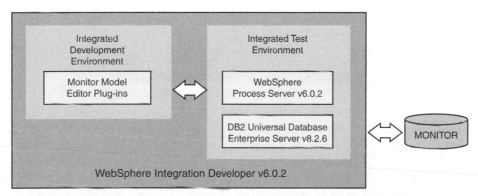

Figure 14.3 Components of WebSphere Business Monitor Development Toolkit

Installing WebSphere Business Monitor

The three installation options are Basic, Advanced, and ITE. In the Basic installation, the Monitor Server, Dashboard Server, and the Monitor Databases are all installed on a single machine. In the Advanced installation, the three components can be on either a single machine or multiple machines. If the databases are on a remote server, you should create those Monitor Databases before installing the Monitor or Dashboard Server. In the ITE installation, the Monitor Server and Databases must be installed on the development machine only.

> ### Business Monitor Installation Scenario
>
> One of the recommended advanced installation scenarios is the three-machine setup. The Monitor Server, Dashboard Server, and Databases are each installed on a separate computer system.

At a high level, the WebSphere Business Monitor installation wizard does the following:

- Installs the database (DB2)
- Augments the DB2 database product with the OLAP Engine—namely, DB2 Cube Views
- Installs WebSphere Application Server Network Deployment
- Installs WebSphere Process Server
- Creates a standalone profile named wbmonitor and use DB2 as the repository
- Installs WebSphere Portal and creates a WebSphere Application Server profile named wp_profile
- Installs DB2 Alphablox and references it to WebSphere Portal
- Installs WebSphere Business Monitor, the Dashboard, and the Databases

The WebSphere Business Monitor Basic installation procedure is described in Appendix D, "WebSphere Business Monitor Installation."

Installing WebSphere Business Monitor Development Toolkit

This Eclipse-based development toolkit enables users to develop and test a monitoring model within the WebSphere Integration Developer (WID) environment. The tooling component for creating monitor models, which is a set of Eclipse plug-ins, is called the Monitor Model Editor (MME). There is also a Monitor Test Server for testing the monitor models. This test server is equivalent to the regular Monitor Server, but without the Adaptive Action Manager and the Replication Manager.

The WebSphere Business Monitor Development Toolkit installation procedure is also described in Appendix D. Before you can work with the Monitor Development Toolkit in WID, make sure you have enabled the Business Monitoring capability in the workbench, and configure a test WebSphere Monitor Server.

Bring up WID, open any workspace, and select **Window** > **Preferences**. Expand **Workbench** and select **Capabilities**, as shown in Figure 14.4. Make sure **Business Monitoring** is checked. Click **Apply**, and then click **OK**.

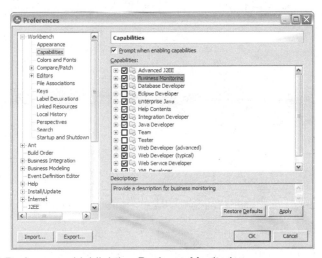

Figure 14.4 WID Preferences highlighting Business Monitoring

From WID, select **Window** > **Open Perspective** > **Other**. In the Select Perspective pop-up window, you should see **Business Monitoring**. Highlight it, and click **OK**. This opens the Business Monitoring perspective.

Go to the **Servers** view, and double-click **WebSphere Business Monitor Server v6.0.2** to view its properties. In the Server Overview window, notice that the WebSphere profile name is *wbmonitor*. Remember to check the box to **Terminate server on workbench shutdown**. Save any edits made to the server properties, and then start the test server.

Launch the Administrative Console. In the navigation pane, select **Applications** > **Enterprise Applications**. Notice the two WebSphere Business Monitor-related applications: *BPCECollector* and *UTEDashboard*, as shown in Figure 14.5. Under Applications you will also notice a new submenu titled **Monitor Models**.

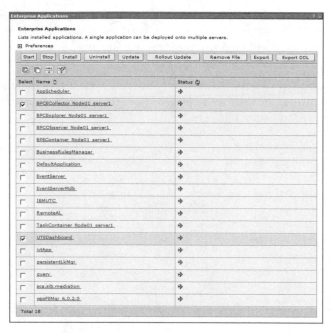

Figure 14.5 Enterprise applications related to WebSphere Business Monitor

In the **Servers** view, highlight the **Test Monitor Server**, right-click, and choose **WBM Web Dashboard**, as shown in Figure 14.6. You see the Unit Test Environment (UTE) Dashboard.

Figure 14.6 Test Monitor Server context menu

This lightweight environment provided in WID avoids the Dashboard Server prerequisites such as WebSphere Portal, DB2 Alphablox, and DB2 Cube Views. The new servlet/JSF-based dashboard offers a quick verification of event processing and the metrics associated with the collected data.

Working with WebSphere Business Monitor

The analogy that befits monitoring is that of a patient going in for a digestive tract checkup. He drinks a radiopaque liquid, such as barium, so that doctors can see what is happening inside his body's digestive system via x-rays. In Business Monitoring terms, this is called instrumentation, and it is used to start at the business modeling step. Now, you can create monitor models using the Monitor Toolkit in WID. Figure 14.7 shows WebSphere Business Monitor's logical architecture. Two abbreviations have not yet been mentioned in this chapter: CEI, which stands for Common Event Infrastructure, and CBE, which stands for Common Base Event. A CBE is an Extensible Markup Language (XML) document holding process event data. CEI is the part of WPS that receives and optionally stores or publishes CBEs to interested consumers, such as WebSphere Business Monitor. Both CEI and CBE are discussed in Chapter 9, "Business Integration Clients," where the Business Process Choreographer Observer is introduced.

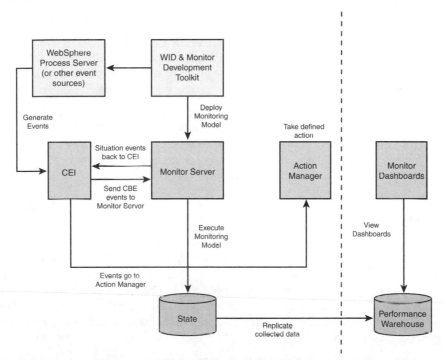

Figure 14.7 Logical architecture of WebSphere Business Monitor

Although business monitoring is more than just KPIs and Dashboards, we felt they warranted their own sections, because they are almost synonymous with business monitoring.

KPIs

We talked about business measures in Chapter 13, "Business Modeling." Key Performance Indicators (KPIs) are a subset of the business measures that can be developed in the Modeler. We find that in the design phase, people describe what they want to monitor in their business processes. Those business measures to support monitoring requirements should not be generated in the Modeler until the execution model is believed to be complete.

In business intelligence parlance, KPIs are used to assess the present state of the business and to prescribe a course of action. From a BAM perspective, it is the act of monitoring these measures in real time. KPIs are used to assess the present state of the business and, if need be, to prescribe a corrective course of action. But it all starts with having a predefined business process. The next step is to have clear goals and performance requirements for those business processes. The organization should have a yardstick—some quantitative and/or qualitative measurements of the goals. Finally, there has to be a way of tweaking those processes or resources to achieve those goals.

> **KPIs in the Test Environment**
>
> In WID, the Integrated Test Environment, which is part of the WebSphere Business Monitor Development Toolkit, does not include the DB2 Cube Views infrastructure. Thus, no KPIs are available in that environment.

KPIs can be defined using a top-down or bottom-up approach. In the top-down approach, the new KPI is defined first and you leave the data source undefined, which initially is flagged as an error. You then fill in the required data definitions for the KPI. In a bottom-up approach, you first create the required lower-level elements, such as triggers, counters, and metrics, and then define the KPI that uses them.

Dashboards

Each dashboard is composed of one or more data snapshots, called *views*. Various views can be combined to create role-based dashboards. For example, you can have high-level views meant for executives in a company, or you could create instance-specific views for customer-facing roles, such as customer service representatives. These dashboards are really portlets that are displayed on portal pages within WebSphere Portal. The following types of dashboard views can be set up:

- **Alerts:** Displays notifications that are sent when a certain business situation occurs.
- **Diagram:** Formerly known as the Process view, this displays diagrams and instance diagrams associated with a particular monitoring context.

- **Dimensional:** Provides a multidimensional view of business performance data by generating reports that analyze different aspects of data retrieved from a multi-dimensional data mart. Charts and grids present data for analysis in different dimensions by pivoting.
- **Export Values:** Enables the user to export data resulting from a specific monitor model to an XML file that can then be imported by WebSphere Business Modeler.
- **Gauges:** Displays an individual KPI value in the form of a gauge, relative to its range or target.
- **Instances:** Displays values of all the business measures defined in the business measures model available in the monitoring context in either individual instances or user-defined groups of context instances. Both active and completed instances are displayed.
- **KPIs:** Displays details of modeled KPIs relative to their acceptable limits and defined ranges.
- **Organizational:** The structure of the organization is displayed in the form of a navigation tree as defined and stored in a user registry such as an LDAP server that WebSphere Portal utilizes.
- **Report:** Displays performance reports relative to a time axis. These reports contain tables and graphs with textual descriptions summarizing the analysis.

Even though the full dashboard functionality is not attainable within the Monitor Model Editor in WID, it helps to know what can be done with the full monitor configuration that includes a portal server. Monitor Models and the Monitor Model Editor are described in the next section.

Monitor Models

The preceding chapter touched on how to create a business model and instrument it for monitoring. This chapter discusses the process of creating a Monitor Model using the Monitor Toolkit in WID, better known as the Monitor Model Editor (MME). A Monitor Model describes business measures (such as metrics and KPIs), their dependencies on incoming events, business situations, and outbound events that report on such conditions and might trigger business actions.

A Monitor Model file is the core artifact that defines what will be monitored, recorded, and reported. The file itself has an .mm extension. It contains the description and five key parts, as shown in Figure 14.8:

A.14.2

- **Monitor Details model:** Definitions of what to record
- **KPI model:** Aggregations and situation definitions
- **Data Mart model:** Structure of the data
- **Visual model:** Pictorial representation of the process to be used in the dashboard to visualize the data
- **Event model:** Definition of the events being processed

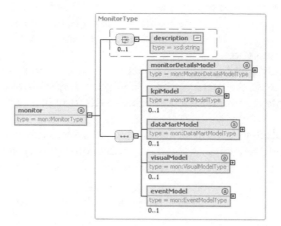

Figure 14.8 Structure of a Monitor Model (.mm) file

Every Monitor Model has a Monitoring Context (MC) that defines a single activity and contains the grouping of data recorded by the monitor. A Monitoring Context can contain other child Monitoring Contexts. The other related artifacts are Inbound and Outbound Events, Triggers, Maps, Metrics, Stop Watches, Counters, and Keys. The end product of a Monitor Model is an Enterprise Archive (EAR) file that can be deployed on to the Monitor Server. And each Monitoring Context results in an Enterprise Java Bean (EJB).

Similarly, every KPI Model has KPI Context, which serves as a container for all the KPI definitions. It contains, among other things, the trigger definitions that can be used to evaluate KPIs. The other related artifacts are the KPIs themselves, KPI Range, and KPI Target.

The Data Mart Model contains a DB2 Cube View (or just "Cube"), which is a dimensional representation of data that is commonly associated with Business Intelligence products. The other related artifacts that really are represented in the Cube are Facts, Measures, and Dimensions.

The MME is used to create all the monitor-related artifacts. The starting point is a BPEL-based business process. The high-level steps for creating a Monitor Model are as follows:

1. Create a BPEL process definition in WID.

2. Enable CBEs for the BPEL process.

3. Use the MME to instrument the model.

4. Deploy the Monitor Model in the Monitor ITE.

5. Bring up the WBM Web Dashboard to view the dashboard.

Working with MME

The Monitor Development Toolkit, which contains the MME, provides the tools for creating Monitor Models that can be transformed into executable code for WebSphere Business Monitor. The MME is a visual editor that is used to create Monitor Models. As discussed earlier, these are really XML documents that specify how values are to be extracted from Common Base Events (CBEs) at runtime and collected, combined, and stored for display in dashboards.

Figure 14.9, from the IBM WebSphere Business Monitor product InfoCenter, illustrates the high-level architecture. It shows how WebSphere Business Monitor Development Toolkit and WebSphere Business Monitor relate to each other, as well as how they interface with external components such as an LDAP Server. Notice also how the various roles come into play wherein the Monitor Dashboard is the single main output to the Line of Business (LOB) Executives.

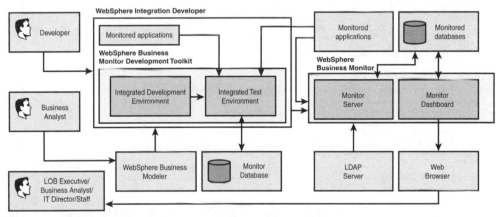

Figure 14.9 High-level architecture of WebSphere Business Monitor

> ### Monitor Model
>
> Before you can create a Monitor Model, the project should be free of any compilation errors. It is recommended that you do a component test of the BPEL process flow.

The Scenario

We take our *BookSample* project, which we know is a clean-running, business integration project in WID. We added a new module to this project called the shipping module, which has a business process named *xpathit*. An input flag (*shiptype*) determines if it is a preferred customer. If it is a preferred customer, the order is shipped overnight via the preferred ship-per, Federal Express. Otherwise, the lowest-priced of the four shippers is used. The shipping prices are supposed to be obtained by comparing the responses from four Web services. The Web services are not functional in this sample module. There are some other minor nuances in the business process that we really do not have to worry about. For illustrating the creation of a Monitor Model, this incomplete yet functional business process should suffice.

The aim here is to create a KPI starting from the bottom up. There are quite a few steps from creating the Triggers to deploying the Monitor Model, and it is easy to lose focus. Figure 14.10 shows the relationship among Triggers, Counters, Metrics, and KPIs. It is also meant to give you a high-level view of what the various steps, discussed in the following sections, are meant to do.

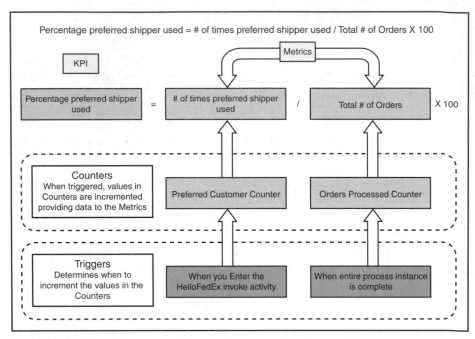

Figure 14.10 Relationship among Triggers, Counters, Metrics, and KPIs

We enable CEI logging on some parts of this newly added *shipping* module rather than the whole project. We use the *HelloFedEx* Invoke activity, shown in Figure 14.11, to illustrate things related to creating the Monitor Model and eventually the dashboard.

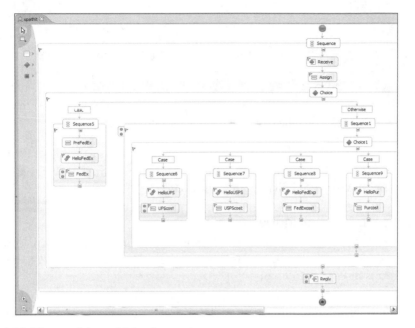

Figure 14.11 The partial *xpathit* business process

Enabling CEI Logging

Notice the triangular flags in the top-left corner of many of the activities in the BPEL process shown in Figure 14.11. They indicate that CEI logging was enabled for that activity. You enable CEI logging as follows:

1. Click the activity or scope in the BPEL editor, and then click the **Properties** view. Figure 14.12 shows the Properties view for the *HelloFedEx* Invoke activity.

2. Click the **Event Monitor** tab, as shown in Figure 14.12.

   - The **Destination** choice is set to **CEI** by default.
   - Under the **Monitor** column, select the **All** radio button, indicating that you want to log all events from Entry to Terminated. The other options are None and Selected.
   - In the **Event Content** column, select **Full** from the drop-down menu. The other options are Digest and Empty.
   - In the **Transaction** column, select **Default** from the drop-down menu. The other options are Existing and New.

Figure 14.12 Event Monitor settings in the test server's properties pane

Similarly, you can enable CEI logging for the other activities in the BPEL process. When done, remember to save your edits by pressing **Ctrl+S**.

Generating the Monitor Model

We did not create this business process in WebSphere Modeler to begin with. Thus, no specific events were defined for our *xpathit* business process. Therefore, we have to generate the event definitions in WID as follows:

1. While still in the Business Integration perspective, select the business process (*xpathit*). Right-click, and select **Monitor Tools** > **Generate Event Definitions**.

2. The pop-up message window lets us know that event definitions (.cbe) have been generated and that these events are visible in the Business Monitoring perspective. Click **OK**.

3. We now need to generate a "seed" Monitor Model for the process. This monitor model will include essential information for matching the events from the business process to the appropriate monitoring context (MC). Back in the Business Integration navigation pane, right-click the *xpathit* business process, and select **Monitor Tools** > **Generate Monitor Model**.

   Because we are creating a new business monitoring project, click the **New project** button, and name the project *shippingMon*. Then click **Finish**.

   Back on the Generate monitor model screen, name the target monitor model *shippingMM*, as shown in Figure 14.13. Then click **Next**.

> **Monitor Model Naming**
>
> For a naming convention, we usually add a suffix of **Mon** (*shippingMon*) to the monitor project and a suffix of **MM** (*shippingMM*) to the target monitor model, even though the file is stored with an extension of .mm.

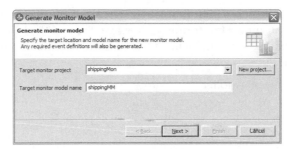

Figure 14.13 Naming the monitor project and the monitor model

4. Now you get to choose the BPEL activities and corresponding events you want emitted. For illustration purposes, you may click the **Select All** button on either side. This is definitely not recommended in a production environment. Figure 14.14 shows the events we chose for the *HelloFedEx* element—ENTRY and EXIT.

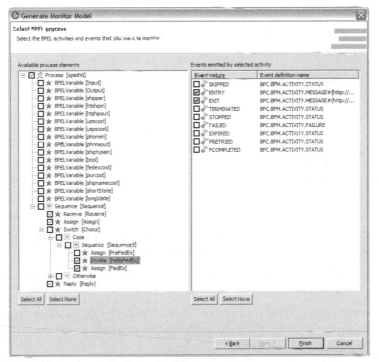

Figure 14.14 BPEL activities and events that can be selected

5. When you have chosen your process elements and the events, click **Finish**. You are taken to the Business Monitoring perspective. Expand the Monitor Model (MM) to see the details, as shown in Figure 14.15. Also notice the six tabs on the main canvas of the MME:

   - Monitor Details Model
   - Data Mart Model
   - KPI Model
   - Visual Model
   - Event Model
   - *MM_APPLICATION_NAME*.mm

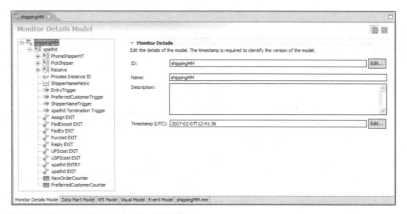

Figure 14.15 Details as viewed in the MME

The rest of the tasks will be done in WID's Business Monitoring perspective in the default **Monitor Details Model** view. We will create triggers, counters, metrics, and KPIs.

Creating a Trigger

Because we are following the bottom-up approach toward creating a KPI, first we have to create the lower-level elements. So we start by creating a Trigger:

1. In the MM details window, highlight the *xpathit* business process. Right-click, and select **New > Trigger**.

2. Name the trigger *PreferredCustomerTrigger*, and click **OK**. It will be triggered whenever the process enters the *HelloFedEx* Invoke activity. So the next step is to create a trigger source.

3. Highlight the newly created *PreferredCustomerTrigger*. Click the **Add** button under the Trigger Sources section.

4. In the Select Trigger Source window, shown in Figure 14.16, expand *HelloFedEx*, and choose HelloFedEx ENTRY. Then click **OK**.

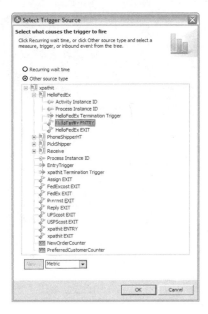

Figure 14.16 Choosing the source of the trigger

5. Back in the MM details page under Trigger Sources, you should see an *Event* entry in the Source Type column and HelloFedEx ENTRY as the source of the trigger. Remember to periodically save your changes by pressing **Ctrl+S**.

Creating a Counter

Now we can create a Counter and use the newly created Trigger to control it. Follow these steps to create the Counter:

1. In the MM details window, highlight the *xpathit* business process. Right-click, and select **New > Counter**.

2. Name the counter *PreferredCustomerCounter*. It will keep count of the number of preferred customers who used the shipping service.

3. We want to increment the counter (*PreferredCustomerCounter*) every time the process goes through the *HelloFedEx* Invoke activity, which is instrumented as HelloFedEx ENTRY.

4. In the Counter Controls section, do the following:

   - Click the **Add** button
   - In the Select Trigger or Inbound Event window, shown in Figure 14.17, you will notice the existence of *PreferredCustomerTrigger*. Select it, and click **OK**.

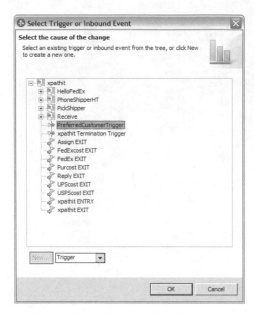

Figure 14.17 Choosing the trigger as the cause of the change

5. Click in the **Resulting Action** cell. From the drop-down list, select **Add One**, as shown in Figure 14.18. The other operations in the Resulting Action column are Subtract One and Reset to Zero.

Make sure you save your edits by pressing **Ctrl+S**.

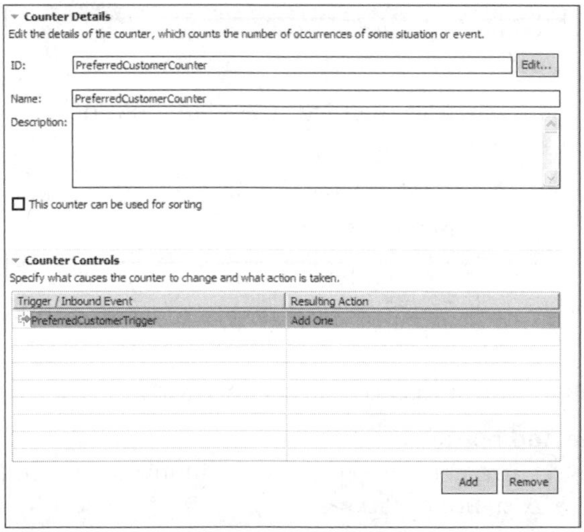

Figure 14.18 Details of a counter that shows the causes for the counter to change

Similarly, create two other triggers and a counter by following these steps:

1. One trigger is called *EntryTrigger* and uses the BPEL flow ENTRY (xpathitENTRY) as the Trigger Source.

2. The counter is named *NewOrderCounter*. Use the *EntryTrigger* as the counter control, and specify *Add One* as the resulting action.

3. The other trigger is called *ShipperNameTrigger*. It uses the business process's *Reply EXIT* as the Trigger Source.

Creating a Metric

Continuing in the Business Monitoring perspective within the default **Monitor Details Model** view, now we can create a Metric based on the Triggers that we already created. Follow these steps to create a Metric:

1. Use the newly created triggers to affect the Metric. In the MM details window, highlight the *xpathit* business process. Right-click, and select **New > Metric**.

2. Name the Metric *ShipperNameMetric*, and click **OK**. We will use it as a way to keep tabs on the different shippers that were used in the business process over a certain period.

3. Under the Metric Value Maps section, click the **Add** button.

4. Click in the Trigger column. A ... button is displayed. Click it.

5. In the Select a Trigger window, shown in Figure 14.19, you will notice the existence of *ShipperNameTrigger*. Select it, and click **OK**.

Figure 14.19 Selecting the trigger that will affect the metric

6. Click in the Expression column. Again, click the ... button. The Expression dialog is displayed.

7. You can enter XPath expressions here. We recommend pressing **Ctrl+Space** to get the context-sensitive help. Enter an expression similar to what is shown in Listing 14.1, and click **OK**.

Listing 14.1   XPath Expression for Getting the Shipper Name

```
if ((Reply_EXIT/extendedData/message/out = 'UPS') or
(Reply_EXIT/extendedData/message/out = 'USPS') or
(Reply_EXIT/extendedData/message/out = 'FedEx') or
(Reply_EXIT/extendedData/message/out = 'Purolator')
then 'valid' else 'unset')
```

> **XPath Expression**
>
> Look for errors in the XPath expression. If there is a problem, you will see it in the Problems view under the MME.

Save all your edits by pressing **Ctrl+S**. Then perform a clean build (select **Project > Clean**) and make sure that there are no errors before performing the next step.

Creating Dimensions and Measures

Now we go to the **Data Mart Model** view in the Business Monitoring perspective to create dimensions and measures. You should see three sections: Dimensions, Facts, and Measures, as shown in Figure 14.20. There are no Dimensions or Measures at this point.

Expand the Facts section, and look at the Cube/Fact Table column. The Business Process Cube (*xpathit* Cube), when expanded, should show the Facts that were created in the previous sections—*PreferredCustomerCounter*, *NewOrderCounter*, *ShipperNameMetric*, and so on.

In our Shipping Scenario, we are not using Dimensions. However, we show you the screen (Figure 14.20) that you would use to create a new Dimension. This is done by clicking the **Add Dimension** button and following the on-screen prompts. Note that while creating Dimensions, you will also create Measures.

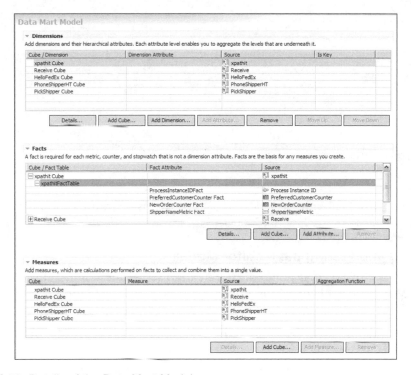

Figure 14.20 Details of the Data Mart Model

Creating a KPI

Next, we go to the **KPI Model** view in the Business Monitoring perspective to create a new KPI. Follow these steps:

1. There may not even be a context in this model. Highlight the *xpathit* MM. Right-click, and select **New** > **KPI Context**. Name it *ShipperKPIContext*.

2. Select the KPI Context. Right-click, and select **New** > **KPI**. Name it *PreferredCustomerTargetKPI*.

3. Select the newly created KPI. On the right of the tree, make it type **Decimal**. Then you can give the KPI a target and a range. These will be used to track the KPI.

4. Enter a target of 1. For the range, enter three ranges—Low, Medium, and High—with the Start and End values shown in Figure 14.21.

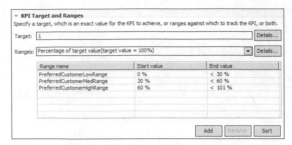

Figure 14.21 The range setting for the KPI

Remember to save your edits. That should be it in terms of creating the various elements that go into the KPI in the Monitor Model.

Deploying and Testing the Monitor Model

A.14.3

Now we can deploy the model onto the test monitor server and test it. But we need to generate the Monitor EAR file first. This is done from the Business Monitoring perspective:

1. In the Project Explorer, expand the Monitor project (*shippingMon*). Under Monitor Models, highlight the Monitor Model file (*shippingMM*). Right-click, and select **Generate Monitor EAR**.

2. In the window that pops up, enter the EJB Project Name (*shippingMMEJB*) and EAR Project Name (*shippingMMEAR*). Giving an MM suffix helps differentiate the process application from the Monitor Model.

3. You then deploy it like you normally would any other application. The difference is that this time you use the Monitor test server as the deployment target. In the Project Explorer of the J2EE perspective, under EJB Projects, highlight the process application EJB (*shippingEJB*), right-click, and select **Deploy**.

4. Go to the **Servers** view, select the WebSphere Business Monitor Server v6.0.2, and start it. After the status shows "started," right-click the server, and choose to **Add and remove projects**. Add both the business process application and the MM application to the server.

5. Go to the WebSphere Administrative Console, and select **Applications > Monitor Models** to make the MM application "startable." You click the version link and use the Setup Wizard to make the application active. In the end, the MM application should be started, as shown in Figure 14.22. It is a series of steps to make these Monitor Model applications active. Please follow the WebSphere Business Monitor product documentation, where it is well explained.

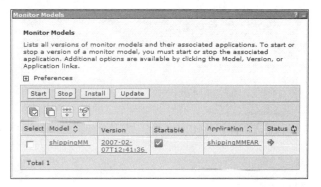

Figure 14.22 Monitor Model started in the WebSphere Administrative Console

6. Before you start testing, make sure you have enabled CEI logging at all levels, and then restart the test Monitor server in WID.

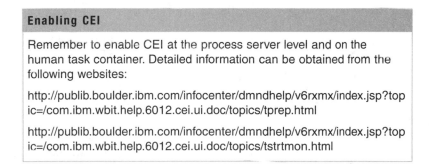

> **Enabling CEI**
>
> Remember to enable CEI at the process server level and on the human task container. Detailed information can be obtained from the following websites:
>
> http://publib.boulder.ibm.com/infocenter/dmndhelp/v6rxmx/index.jsp?topic=/com.ibm.wbit.help.6012.cei.ui.doc/topics/tprep.html
>
> http://publib.boulder.ibm.com/infocenter/dmndhelp/v6rxmx/index.jsp?topic=/com.ibm.wbit.help.6012.cei.ui.doc/topics/tstrtmon.html

7. Now that the applications are deployed and started, we should be able to view the dashboard. Follow these steps:

- Launch the BPC Explorer, and run a few instances of the process. This provides data that is displayed in the dashboard.
- Bring up the WBM Web Dashboard either from within WID (right-click the monitor test server and choose WBM Web Dashboard) or in an external web browser by going to the following URL:
  http://localhost:908x/WBMDashboard/faces/UTE.jsp
- From the Instances View, select the Monitor Model, the Monitoring Context, and one or more Business Measures, as shown in Figure 14.23. Then click the View button to view the dashboard.

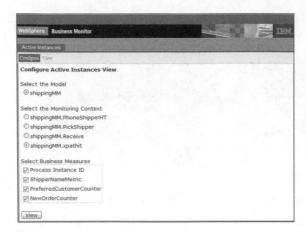

Figure 14.23 Configuration screen of the WebSphere Business Monitor Dashboard in WID

We realize that some details on getting to the monitor dashboard were omitted. The intention was to make you, the developer, aware of the main tasks in creating the Monitor Model using the Monitor Model Editor in WID. You can also deploy this model to a stand-alone WebSphere Business Monitor Server and see the graphical entities in dashboard-like gauges and charts, which allow you to drill down.

Closing the Link

A.14.4

Business Activity Monitoring (BAM) is the use of technology to proactively define and analyze critical opportunities and risks in an enterprise to maximize profitability and optimize efficiency. It can be used to evaluate external as well as internal factors. This chapter gave you an overview of BAM from the perspective of the WebSphere Business Monitor Server. The Monitor Model Editor is a plug-in for the Eclipse-based WID tool.

You do not need a stand-alone WebSphere Business Monitor Server to show monitoring of a BPEL process or part of a BPEL process, as was done in the sample scenario. You can use the Business Monitoring perspective and the Monitor test server in WID to show a stripped-down version of the dashboard, which would suffice in many "proof of concept" engagements. The full dashboard, running in WebSphere Portal server along with required graphics software such as IBM's Alphablox, has a lot more graphical features.

Links to developerWorks

A.14.1   www.ibm.com/developerworks/websphere/library/techarticles/0706_perepa/
0706_perepa.html

A.14.2   www.ibm.com/developerworks/ibm/library/ar-bam1/

A.14.3   www.ibm.com/developerworks/ibm/library/ar-model2/index.html

A.14.4   http://publib.boulder.ibm.com/infocenter/dmndhelp/v6rxmx/index.jsp?topic=/
com.ibm.btools.help.monitor.doc/Doc/concepts/welcome/InfoWelcome.html

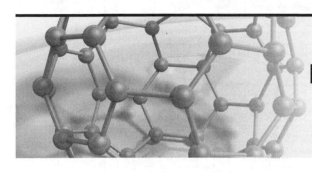

Chapter 15

Enterprise Service Bus and Service Registry

No Service-Oriented Architecture (SOA) discussion is complete without mentioning the Enterprise Service Bus (ESB) and the Service Registry. Publishing and discovery of SOA business services are facilitated by a Service Registry because this encourages reuse across the organization and saves time by allowing for easy searching and browsing of services. All this facilitates SOA governance, which is a key requirement in any SOA solution. Services are enterprise assets that will stay with companies for years to come. They need to be produced while adhering to certain standards and policies and stored in a manner that would make them accessible across the enterprise. This is not to mention the governance processes that have been established, especially the ones that address the management of the services or, more specifically, the metadata management of the services.

The ESB, on the other hand, is a standards-based software architecture that provides foundational services via an event-driven messaging engine. We might be guilty of oversimplifying things, but one of the aims of an ESB is to remove the coupling between the service called and the transport medium. IBM's service-oriented reference architecture depicts the ESB as the "interconnect" between all service components, as shown in Figure 15.1. An ESB is a general architectural pattern that provides the infrastructure needed to integrate service applications in a quick and flexible manner.

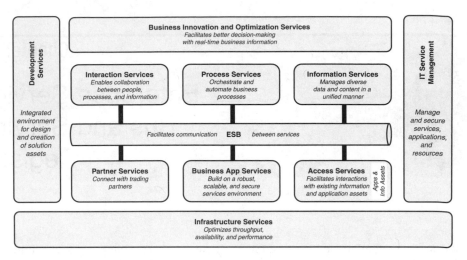

Figure 15.1 IBM's SOA architecture

This chapter presents an overview of IBM's WebSphere Service Registry and Repository (WSRR) and the WebSphere Enterprise Service Bus (WESB). You will see how the service registry and ESB (more precisely, how WSRR and WESB) work together and how they fit into a SOA solution.

WebSphere Service Registry and Repository (WSRR)

A.15.1

The common thinking in enterprises is that if developers cannot readily find and reuse services, they essentially don't exist. Hence, having a standards-based registry that can publish Web services as SOA business services, ready for mapping and interoperability, is essential for enterprises thinking about SOA. WSRR provides such a standards-based means for publishing and discovering reusable business services and SOA artifacts. It is the master metadata repository, if you will, for services (including traditional Web services). It handles the metadata management aspects of operational services and, in doing so, becomes the overall system of record for the entire SOA.

WSRR can be used across all phases of the SOA lifecycle: model, assemble, deploy, and manage. It provides management for service metadata, including WSDL and XML Schema documents, Service Component Architecture (SCA) modules, and policy files. It also helps describe the capabilities, requirements, and semantics of the services in a SOA. IBM's vision is for WSRR to interact and federate with other metadata stores that support specific phases of the SOA lifecycle. As it stands today, WSRR plays a key role in the end-to-end governance underpinnings of the SOA lifecycle.

WSRR supports governance of service metadata throughout the lifecycle of a service from its initial publication in a development space through deployment to service management. The Governance lifecycle has four phases, as shown in Figure 15.2:

- **Plan:** SOA governance needs are defined based on existing realizations in WSRR.
- **Define:** The governance approach is specified.
- **Enable:** The most important phase, where governance policies and processes are actually implemented.
- **Measure:** Governance requirements are monitored and measured using information stored in WSRR.

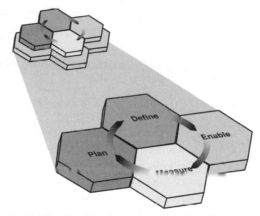

Figure 15.2 SOA lifecycle highlighting the four phases of the Governance lifecycle

WSRR is like "Big Brother." Access to service artifacts is controlled, the various versions are managed, any changes made to the artifacts are analyzed and reported, and usage is monitored. In describing the WSRR content model, it is broadly split into service description entities (SDEs) and service description metadata.

A.15.2

> **WSRR Metadata**
>
> There is metadata that directly relates to the content documents. Then there is service semantic metadata, which is used to decorate the service description entities to explain their semantics.

WSRR supports three types of service semantic metadata, all of which can be used to decorate entities in the physical or logical model and in the concepts:

- **Properties:** Simple name/value pairs that are associated with any of the service description entities
- **Relationships:** Named entities that tie together one source SDE to one or more target SDEs
- **Classifiers:** Encoded documents that are used to apply semantic meaning to SDEs

One other kind of entity in WSRR is called a *Concept*. This is a generic object that can be used to represent anything that does not have a physical document in WSRR such as a portlet in a portlet catalog. A Concept can be used to group physical artifacts for ease of retrieval. It can also be used to represent a business-level view of the SOA metadata managed in WSRR. This could include concepts such as Business Process, Business Service, Business Object, and Business Policy.

Installing WSRR

WSRR can be installed in three different modes: GUI, Console, or Silent. The installer copies all the relevant files to the file system. After that, the deployment scripts are run to create the databases and deploy the applications to the application server. In our sample setup, explained in Appendix E, "WebSphere Service Registry and Repository Installation," we install WSRR on the WebSphere Process Server (WPS).

Assuming that WPS is running, we can look at the user interface. Similar to the WebSphere Administrative Console, WSRR has its own web-based console that is accessed via http://*HOST_NAME*:*PORT*/ServiceRegistry. The default port is 9080. The port number might vary on your system, depending on available ports. Figure 15.3 shows the layout of the console, with the navigation pane on the left and the main console pane on the right. There is also a user perspective option that lets you tailor the user interface (UI) for a specific role. For example, a business analyst might get a different look for existing services, compared to an administrator, who would like to see the operational information about the deployed services.

Figure 15.3 WSRR user interface

When WSRR is installed, a base configuration is loaded that defines two types of users: Administrator and User. This is chosen via the User perspective drop-down menu at the top of the console. In the Administrator perspective, you see the Administration option in the navigation pane, among other things. These are in fact the two J2EE roles for the WSRR application, ServiceRegistry, that need to be mapped to user or group principals, which is done via the WebSphere Administrative Console:

- **Administrator:** The administrator role is used to control access to all administrative functions, including those involving MBean operations.
- **User:** The user role is given permission to perform any nonadministrative operation. Any fine-grained access control is done via the WSRR console. Thus, all users who require access to any function exposed in WSRR must be mapped to this role.

After a set of roles and their mappings have been defined, it is possible to persist the role mappings by generating an Extensible Access Control Markup Language (XACML) file. This is the standard for encoded data exchange. Support for XACML makes the UI customizable, and it can be optimized for each role. More information on XACML can be found at http://xml.coverpages.org/xacml.html.

Governance Lifecycle

Service registries maintain one or more lifecycles, and stored artifacts are transitioned through their various states. During installation, WSRR is loaded with a simple default lifecycle. Although this lifecycle is good for learning and prototyping, we feel that enterprises will configure their own lifecycle to match the governance processes and roles established within their organization.

The default lifecycle is based on IBM's SOA lifecycle, which you know has four stages—model, assemble, deploy, and manage. The *Created* stage begins the lifecycle, and the end is denoted by the *Retired* stage. This lifecycle has seven transition states, as shown in Figure 15.4:

- Plan
- Authorize development
- Certify
- Approve
- Deprecate
- Revoke
- Repair

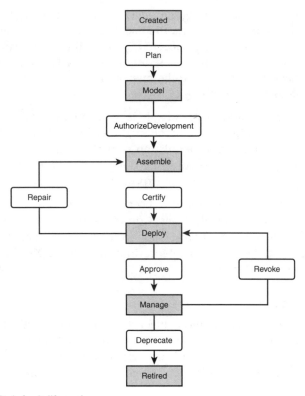

Figure 15.4 WSRR default lifecycle

Working with WSRR

A.15.3
Role-based security policies are an important part of SOA governance because that is how you control who can contribute to the service registry. This is also true of WSRR. The next important aspect is taxonomy and classification. Another common term associated with service registries is ontology, which describes a knowledge domain. This includes describing the entities in the domain and their relationships. The Web Ontology Language (OWL) is a W3C-endorsed format for defining ontology. At a simpler level, OWL can also be used to describe taxonomies. Taxonomy uses a hierarchical system of describing entities. WSRR can load and understand OWL files but does not exploit all its features. It does use the subclasses definition, which means that you can classify your entities using different levels within the classification. Any WSRR artifact can be tagged or "classified." You can use any combination of the classification classes in WSRR to organize and find artifacts in the registry.

> **WSRR Ontology**
>
> A classification system is imported in WSRR as a whole and cannot be modified via WSRR functions. Updates are done by importing a modified version of the ontology.

Loading Documents

We use the artifacts from the *BookSample* project to illustrate some of the WSRR functionality. Bring up the WSRR Console (http://*HOST_NAME*:*PORT*/ServiceRegistry) as explained earlier. In the navigation tree, select **Service Documents** > **XSD Documents**. In the main pane, click **Load document**. You see a screen to load a document, as shown in Figure 15.5. Browse for the *CustomerBO* on the local file system, and click **OK**. Even though entering a document description and version is optional, in production systems, it is essential to have them.

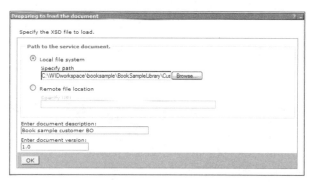

Figure 15.5 Loading a document into WSRR

Before the XSD file is loaded, the schema definition is validated. If the file is loaded successfully, you see the message shown at the top of Figure 15.6, and some details about the file are displayed. The name, namespace, and version are important to note. At this point you may click **OK** to save the file. You see the document (*CustomerBO.xsd*) listed in the collection of XML schema definition documents.

Figure 15.6 General properties of an uploaded XSD file

Document Descriptions in WSRR

When documents such as XSDs are loaded, the tooling picks up the namespace from the XML. But you should provide a description and version to help in classifying the documents.

In the list of XSD documents, if you click the name (*CustomerBO.xsd*), you see the details again. The Content tab shows you the actual XML source. If you look at the source, you will notice that it is of Complex Type with four elements.

There is also a tab for doing Impact Analysis, which requires dependency relationships to be defined first. This analysis is based on the analysis of the artifacts and their metadata stored in WSRR. Among other things, WSRR has a shredding capability. This is where WSRR understands some part of the WSDL or XSD specifications, which allows you to manipulate the logical entities defined in the physical documents, such as a WSDL file. This simplifies the management of the logical parts of those physical documents. For example, you can directly find all the port types that exist in your repository without having to look at all the WSDL files.

The last tab is the Governance tab. We will describe the governance features in detail.

Making a Document Governable

WSRR provides a basic level of support for governance in the form of service lifecycles. WSRR supports a single lifecycle definition that represents a set of states, with transitions denoting possible changes between the states. All actions to make or remove governance of artifacts are protected by the ManageGovernance access control. Only users authorized to do so can perform the governance functions.

If you click the Governance tab, as shown in Figure 15.7, the Governance Status is displayed. Currently, the object or file that we loaded is not governable, as shown in Figure 15.7. Because we do not have any other transition states, we will use the default transition for the initial state transition. Click the **Make Governable** button to see what happens. You should see the Governance state change.

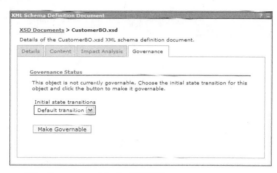

Figure 15.7 Making an artifact governable in WSRR

Notification

We should also point out that to socialize and make sure consumers of services (or the people in roles responsible for them) are aware of changes, WSRR provides notification facilities to alert users or systems about these changes. E-mail notification is a particular use of the notification framework in WSRR. Changes to objects in WSRR invoke a user-extensible set of notifiers, classes that implement the *com.ibm.serviceregistry.ServiceRegistryNotifier* interface. One sample notifier included in the base WSRR publishes JMS messages whenever an object in WSRR is created, modified, or deleted.

> **Governance Lifecycle in WSRR**
>
> The Governance lifecycle can be initiated either through the Web UI or through the WSRR application programming interface (API).

In the following screen (Figure 15.8), the first state of the Governance lifecycle is shown. Notice that the Governance State is set to *Created*. At this point, we will not do anything with the state transition. If you click the Governed objects link on the right, you are shown the collection of objects that are governed by the default common root governance record with the name, description, and object type. The *root governance record* is found when an object is not the root of a governed collection and, when selected, displays the details of the object that is, in fact, the root.

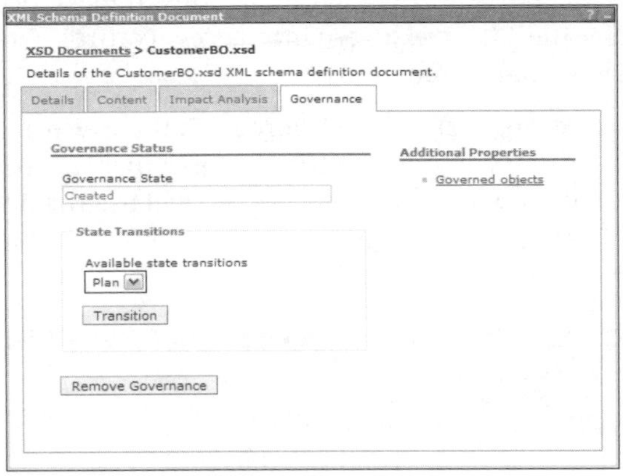

Figure 15.8 Initial governance state of an artifact

Transitioning the State of a Governed Object

On the Governance Status screen, shown in Figure 15.8, you can click the **Transition** button to take the object—in this case, *CustomerBO.xsd*—to the next state in the lifecycle. The state transitions to *AuthorizeDevelopment*, as shown in Figure 15.9. This transition also causes the document to be moved from the Created state to the Model state, as indicated in the Governance State field. This matches the states of the WSRR default lifecycle shown in Figure 15.4.

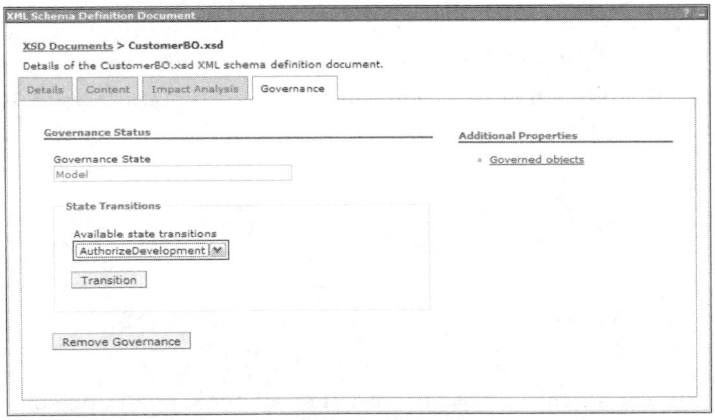

Figure 15.9 Taking the object to the next state in the lifecycle

Searching for Documents

In the navigation pane of the WSRR Console, select **Queries** > **Query wizard**. In the main pane is a drop-down list for selecting the kind of query to run. Select **XSD Documents**, and click **OK**. Most service registries have more than one way to search for artifacts. WSRR offers these other kinds of query options:

- Concepts
- Entities by Classification
- Entities with Custom Relationships
- Policy Documents
- WSDL Documents
- WSDL Ports
- WSDL Port Types
- WSDL Services
- XML Documents

On the details screen, you can enter one or more values to help in the document search. You can choose the AND function or the OR function. If you remember from Figure 15.6, our document was in the namespace—http://BookSampleLibrary. Enter this, as shown in Figure 15.10, and click **Next**.

Figure 15.10 Values sent to the query

You see a Summary screen with all the values that will be used in the search query. Click **Finish**. The resulting screen should display the number of rows the query returned, and the collection details should be listed. Figure 15.11 shows that our *CustomerBO.xsd* was returned.

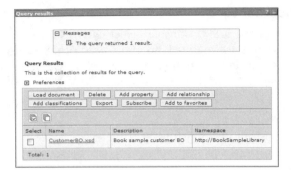

Figure 15.11 Results of the search query

WSRR Querying

You can use the asterisk (*) as a wildcard character in the Name field
of the query wizard to see a list of all the documents of a particular
type.

In the navigation pane, if you select **Service Metadata** > **XML Schema** > **Complex types**,
you should see the *CustomerBO* listed, because as we mentioned before, it is a complex business object.

WSRR and WID

If you followed the directions in Appendix E on how to install the WSRR Eclipse plug-in,
you should have a Service Registry View in WID, and it should be configured to talk to an
instance of WSRR.

Click the Service Registry tab to see the four main items in the registry: Concepts, WSDL
Documents, XML Documents, and XSD Documents. The idea is to retrieve the business
object from WSRR and use it in a Business Integration project in WID.

In the Service Registry pane, right-click, and select **Retrieve XSDs**. We could have chosen
the general *Retrieve* option, but because we knew the kind of file we had stored in WSRR, we
chose to do a focused retrieval. You should see a Retrieved Items window showing the results
of the search and retrieve, as shown in Figure 15.12. It should have one item—
CustomerBO.xsd. Click **OK**.

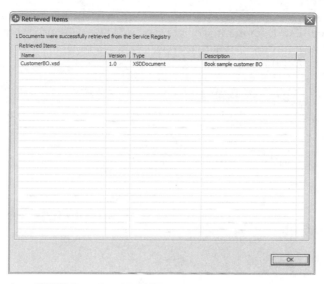

Figure 15.12 Results of WSRR retrieval in WID

The results are also displayed in a hierarchical view in the Service Registry view. Now you can import that file into any project in WID. Highlight *CustomerBO.xsd*, as shown in Figure 15.13, right-click, and select **Import Document**. You will have the choice to import that document into any project.

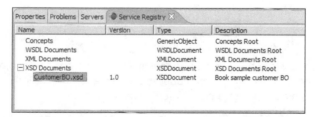

Figure 15.13 Details of WSRR retrieval in WID's Service Registry view

In a similar manner, a developer can easily store an artifact from WID into WSRR. This is done using the Resource perspective. For example, if you store the *CustomerInfoInterface.wsdl* from our *BookSampleLibrary*, these are the steps:

1. Select **Window > Open Perspective > Other**. Choose **Resource**, and click **OK**.

2. In the Navigator pane, open the **BookSampleLibrary** folder. Highlight *CustomerInfoInterface.wsdl*, right-click, and select **Service Registry**.

3. You have two publishing options: Publish as Concept and Publish Document. Choose **Publish Document**. The file type is WSDL. The other types are XSD, POLICY, and XML. In the dialog that appears, shown in Figure 15.14, you may enter a description and then click **Finish**.

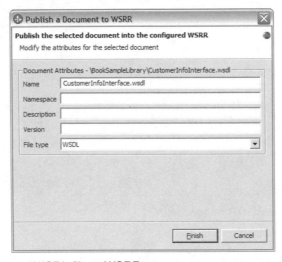

Figure 15.14 Publishing a WSDL file to WSRR

4. The document gets stored in WSRR. You can check this by retrieving all documents using the Service Registry view.

> **WSRR Publishing**
>
> If you try to store the same document in WSRR more than once, you get an error. However, you can publish the same document to WSRR multiple times if you give it a different version number.

A.15.4

You can acquire services from various sources or create your own. Eventually, every enterprise starts accumulating lots of services, and you need a place to store them. Actually, you want the service interface stored, not the implementation. That is what WSRR does. As the integration point for service metadata, WSRR establishes a central point for finding and managing these services, including service application deployments and other service metadata and endpoint registries and repositories, such as UDDI. This is where service metadata that is scattered across an enterprise is brought together to provide a single, comprehensive description of a service.

After that happens, visibility is controlled, versions are managed, proposed changes are ana-lyzed and communicated, usage is monitored, and other parts of a SOA can access them with confidence, because every service goes through the Governance lifecycle.

We have presented an overview of WSRR. The intent was to introduce the concepts of a serv-ice registry in the context of a SOA and discuss its role in business integration. In the process, we demonstrated some of the basic functionalities of WSRR.

Enterprise Service Bus (ESB)

In an ESB, applications that require the services of another application are known as service requesters. Correspondingly, applications that offer services are called service providers. This is shown in Figure 15.15.

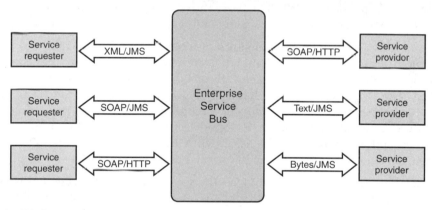

Figure 15.15 Sample message and network protocols handled by ESB

As a service request travels between requesters and providers, logic that controls what hap-pens to it and how the request is routed can be inserted. This is often called the mediating or service interaction logic, and it is performed by mediation modules. The logic performs the following functions:

- Message routing
- Enrichment
- Logging
- Transformation

Mediation modules must be deployed on an ESB-enabled application server such as WESB or WPS. Thus, we have the three main parts of an ESB: service requesters and providers, mediation modules, and the application server.

> ### ESB
>
> If all your applications are new and conform to the Web services standards, you may only need an ESB focused on the integration of these standards-based interfaces. But if you have to integrate legacy applications that do not conform to SOA standards, you will need an ESB that can mediate between the SOA standards and everything else.

WebSphere Enterprise Service Bus

WESB provides the capabilities of a standards-based ESB supporting the integration of service-oriented, message-oriented, and event-driven technologies in its messaging infrastructure. From an SCA perspective, WESB manages the flow of messages between SCA-described interaction endpoints and enables the quality of interaction these components request.

A.15.5 In an SCA-based solution, mediation modules are a type of SCA module that perform a specialized role. Therefore, they have slightly different characteristics than other components that operate at the business level. These mediation components operate on messages exchanged between service endpoints. Rather than performing business functions, they perform routing, transformation, and logging operations on the messages. The concept or pattern is to use a mediation module to encapsulate the binding-specific information and perform the Application-Specific Business Object (ASBO) to Generic Business Object (GBO) conversion, allowing you to have business modules that use only GBOs and SCA bindings.

The IBM SOA programming model introduces the Service Message Object (SMO) as a generic way of representing message data. WESB supports interactions between service endpoints on three levels: broad connectivity, mediation capabilities, and a spectrum of interaction models and qualities of interaction.

WPS is built on WESB, providing it with the mediation functionality of WESB. Because both make use of the WebSphere Application Server (WAS) as the foundation, they take advantage of the quality of service (QoS) that WAS provides, the J2EE runtime environment, and the broad support for open standards and Web services. Figure 15.16 shows an expanded view of an ESB. We mapped it to the WebSphere platform to show how the three products—WESB, WSRR, and WPS—relate. Implicit in this diagram is the underlying WAS foundation.

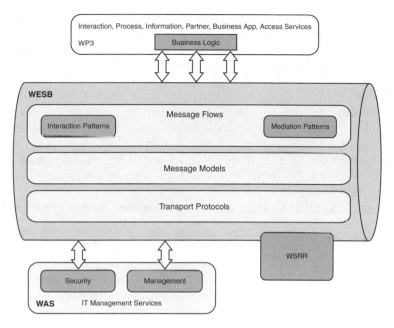

Figure 15.16 WESB in relation to the WebSphere platform

WESB Terminology

ESBs are all about mediation. We briefly describe the various terms in WESB. In fact, some of these are generic ESB terms.

Mediation

The role of an ESB is to intercept the service requests from consumers and initiate mediation tasks to support loose coupling. When the mediation task completes, the relevant service provider or providers should be invoked. WESB supports the following mediation models:

- One-way interactions
- Request-reply
- Publish/subscribe

Mediation Module

The mediation module is the core piece in an ESB wherein the interactions with external service requesters and providers are defined by imports and exports using Web Services Description Language (WSDL). Different kinds of requesters and providers are made available via different *bindings* for the imports and exports. So the other key piece is the binding.

Each binding in the mediation module enables an interaction with a particular kind of service requester or service provider. Binding information determines how a service connects to and interacts with an application. Specifically, bindings are the protocols and transports assigned to imports and exports.

WESB provides for the following:

- **JMS binding:** Support for JMS 1.1 is provided by WebSphere Platform Messaging (sometimes internally known as the Service Integration or SI Bus) which acts as a full-fledged messaging infrastructure.
- **Web services binding:** Supports WSDL 1.1 and Service Registry based on UDDI 3.0, and uses SOAP/HTTP or SOAP/JMS with or without WS-Security and WS-Atomic Transaction.
- **Default (SCA) binding:** Used mainly for module-to-module communication, supporting both synchronous and asynchronous communication.
- **EIS binding:** Supports interaction with a wide range of application environments (also known as enterprise information systems), including PeopleSoft, SAP, and Siebel.

If you're familiar with WebSphere MQ, you'll be glad to know that WESB also supports MQ and MQ JMS message bindings.

- **MQ binding:** Similar to JMS binding, allows the use of WebSphere MQ as the messaging infrastructure, instead of the WebSphere Platform Messaging. Both JMS and the native MQ transports are available for the MQ binding.

> **Modules and Mediation Modules**
>
> A regular module, as we know it in WID, is sometimes called a business module to distinguish it from a mediation module. The main difference is that mediation modules have access to the message headers and enable you to change properties, such as service endpoints, at runtime.

From a business integration perspective, when using mediation modules, there are two integration approaches:

- The mediation module is interposed between a service requester and the service provider. The service interfaces are defined using WSDL. The module operates on all service interactions, requests, and responses, as shown in Figure 15.17.

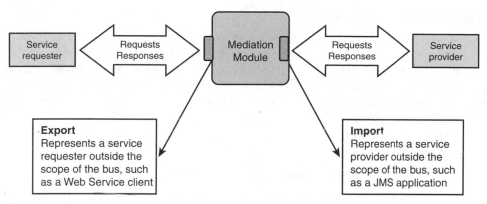

Figure 15.17 Mediation module showing an import bound to JMS and an export bound to a Web service

- In the other approach, the mediation module uses only default binding. Communication with service requesters and providers is moved to separate modules. This allows for "rewiring" a requester to a different provider, thus giving solution administrators more control. Figure 15.18 shows a mediation module with default bindings connected to a pair of modules that interact with a JMS application and a Web service client.

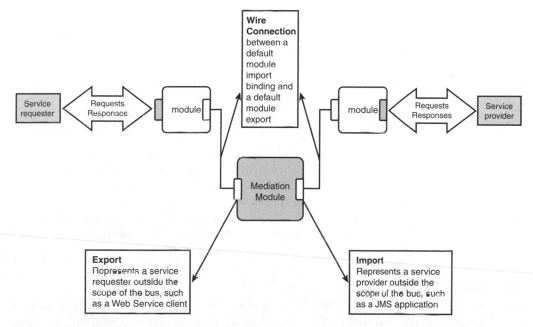

Figure 15.18 Mediation module showing the interaction with connection modules

Mediation Flow Component

This new component type, introduced by WESB to the SCA model, is no different from any other service component. Inside the mediation module, there can be only one mediation flow component that offers one or more interfaces and uses one or more partner references. Along with the mediation flow component, one or more Java components can be created inside a mediation module. Actually, Java components are supported in mediation modules, but custom mediations need not use a separate Java component, because the code can be inline in the mediation flow.

> **WESB Mediation**
>
> WESB mediation flow components can act as "service intermediaries," allowing for separate processing of requests and responses.

Mediation Flow

A mediation flow graphically shows the mediation steps required to perform the desired mediation logic. The different processing steps of a request are shown graphically by distinguishing between a request flow and a response flow. Mediation flows consist of a sequence of processing steps that are executed when an input message is received. A request flow starts with a single input from the source operation and can have multiple callouts. A response flow, on the other hand, starts with one or more callout responses and ends with a single input response. Data that flows through is really message objects.

To elaborate a bit more on Service Message Objects (SMOs), each import and export binding interacts with a specific service provider type. The data from this binding-specific interaction is turned into a common data structure—the SMO. An SMO contains elements such as a business object (BO), binding-specific information by way of headers, and context information. This is a special kind of Service Data Object (SDO) with additional information to support aspects of a messaging subsystem. All SMOs have the same basic structure and are defined by an XML schema. They have three major sections: body, header, and context.

You can use the context section of the message to store a property that mediation primitives can use later in the flow. The data to be contained in the context must be defined in a single BO. Two context elements can be used to pass properties in a flow. *Correlation context* makes the property persist throughout the duration of the flows. It is used to pass values from the request flow to the response flow. *Transient context* makes the property available for the duration of the current flow (request or response). It is used to pass values between mediation primitives in the same flow.

Mediation Primitive

Mediation primitives are the smallest building blocks in WESB. They accept messages that are processed as SMOs. They are wired and configured inside mediation flows. A request flow begins with a single input node followed by one or more mediation primitives in sequence.

A response flow begins with a callout response node for each target operation, followed by one or more mediation primitives in sequence. When developing WESB artifacts in WID, the following mediation primitives are available in the tooling:

- **Custom:** Enables you to execute custom mediation logic implemented in Java
- **Database Lookup:** Used to augment a message with data retrieved from a database
- **Endpoint Lookup:** Enables you to perform dynamic routing of messages based on service endpoint information stored in WSRR
- **Event Emitter:** Enables you to emit business events (Common Base Events), which can then be monitored
- **Fail:** Used to terminate a mediation flow and generate an exception
- **Message Element Setter:** Enables you to set, copy, and delete elements from the SMO
- **Message Filter:** Allows you to selectively route messages
- **Message Logger:** Used to store or log messages in a database
- **Stop:** Terminates the mediation flow silently
- **XSLT:** Transforms messages based on transformations defined in an XSL style sheet

One last thing to know about mediation primitives is that they can have three types of terminals: Input terminal, Output terminal, and Fail terminal. The Input terminal can be wired to accept a message. One or more Output terminals can be wired to propagate a message. And when there is an exception, the Fail terminal propagates the original message along with the exception information. Figure 15.19 gives you a perspective of the various WESB structures.

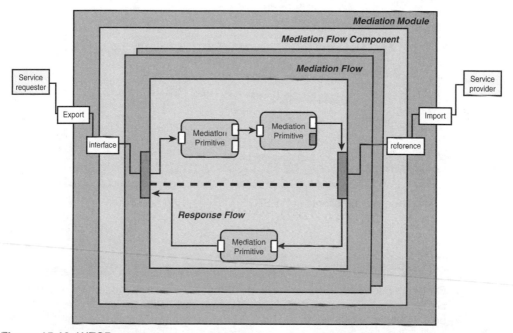

Figure 15.19 WESB structures

Installing WESB

As shown in Figure 15.16, when you install WebSphere Process Server, the capabilities of both WAS Network Deployment and WESB get installed. For that reason, we have not devoted a separate section to installing WESB as a stand-alone product. We will use the WPS instance to demonstrate some of the WESB topologies and functionality. Nonetheless, if you wanted to install WESB as a stand-alone product, the steps to do so are very similar to those for installing WPS. This is described in Appendix A, "WebSphere Process Server Installation." With WESB, you get three service clients that are also available with WebSphere Process Server:

- IBM Message Service Client for C/C++
- IBM Message Service Client for .NET
- IBM Web Services Client for C++

Figure 15.20 shows the Message service clients installation description. It indicates how these clients extend the messaging and Web services capabilities of WESB to non-Java environments—a critical element of any ESB.

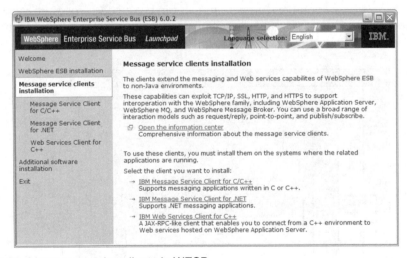

Figure 15.20 Message service clients in WESB

> **Service Client Installation**
>
> On the Windows platform, we have found that it is best to choose the custom installation option and select your own installation folder. By default, all these clients are installed in the C:\Program Files\IBM\... folder.

Working with WESB

WESB uses Service Component Architecture (SCA) as its basic programming model, and it shares the SCA runtime with WebSphere Process Server. With that in mind, we can use the same WebSphere Administrative Console that we have used before for WPS to access and administer WESB-related components in the WebSphere software stack. Bring up the administrative console as we did before (http://*HOST_NAME*:9060/admin). From the navigation pane, select **Applications** > **Enterprise Applications**. You should see *ESBSamplesGallery* in the list of enterprise applications with a running status, as shown in Figure 15.21. This is one indication that the WESB runtime is installed and available for use.

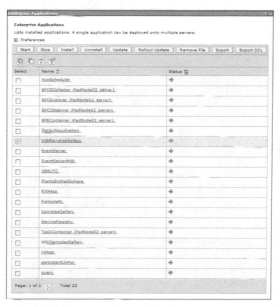

Figure 15.21 *ESBSamplesGallery* enterprise application shown in the administrative console

Use the same default server, named *server1*. Select **Service integration** > **Buses**. You see the two service integration buses that are created during installation: SCA.APPLICATION and SCA.SYSTEM. When a mediation module is installed into WESB, the module is deployed onto a member of the SCA.SYSTEM bus with a set of bus destinations getting created on a member of that bus. We will do this in the next section.

WESB and WID

A.15.6

If you followed the directions in Appendix B, "WebSphere Integration Developer v6.0.2 Installation," on how to install WID, you should have two profiles: *wps* and *esb*. All the tooling required to create WESB-related components should be available. One of the ways to verify this is to look at the Servers pane. You should see the test WebSphere ESB Server v6.0 listed, as shown in Figure 15.22.

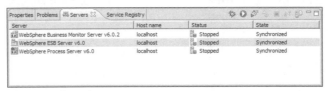

Figure 15.22 WESB test server in WID

Creating a Mediation Module

With the *BookSample* project open in the Business Integration perspective in WID, go to the Business Integration view, and right-click. Select **New > Project**, and then select **Mediation Module**. In the ensuing screen, shown in Figure 15.23, enter the Module Name CreditCheckMM, make sure that the Target Runtime is WebSphere ESB Server v6.0, and accept all the other default settings. You could click **Finish**, but for illustrative purposes click **Next**.

Figure 15.23 Creating a new mediation module

You then can select one or more shared libraries that you want to refer to within the mediation module. In this case, we selected *BookSampleLibrary*. Shared libraries included in this step are deployed as part of the module. As soon as you click **Finish**, a new project is created. You should see it in the navigation pane, as shown in Figure 15.24.

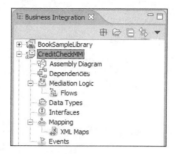

Figure 15.24 A mediation module project folder in WID

There are some subtle differences in the contents of a mediation module compared to those of a business module. In a mediation module, you have a folder called Mediation Logic that contains the Mediation Flows; it does not exist in a business module. A business module, on the other hand, has Business Logic.

Deploying the Mediation Module

There is no implementation yet, but we want to show you the steps of deploying the newly created mediation module. It involves two steps: exporting the application from WID as an enterprise archive (EAR) file, and installing the EAR file on the server:

1. In the Business Integration view of the Business Integration perspective, highlight the *CreditCheckMM* project. Right-click, and select **Export**. From the export choices, select **EAR file**. Click **Next**.

2. On the EAR Export screen, shown in Figure 15.25, select CreditCheckMMApp as the EAR project. Enter a destination with a filename of .ear. By habit, as developers, we chose to export the source files; however, we recommend that you not export source files.

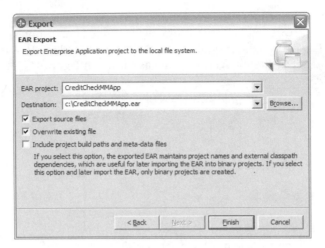

Figure 15.25 EAR Export screen

> **Exporting EAR Files**
>
> When exporting Enterprise Application projects to be installed in a pro-
> duction environment, you should not export source files. You do not
> want to expose source code, and you also want to keep the size of the
> application as small as possible. The option to export source files is
> more for developers who might want to modify source code.

3. When you click **Finish**, the project is packaged as an EAR.

4. Bring up the WebSphere Administrative Console, and log in as an administrator. In
   the navigation pane, select **Applications > Install New Application**.

5. Specify the path to the export EAR file on the local file system, as shown in Figure
   15.26. Click **Next**.

Figure 15.26 Specifying the path to the new application

6. Click **Next** on the next six screens, accepting all the default settings. Make sure that the application is installed on server1. If you receive any warnings, continue. On the Summary screen, make sure the installation options are correct, and then click **Finish**.

7. At the end of the deployment process, look for the message "Application CreditCheckMMApp installed successfully."

8. Save the changes to the master configuration.

9. In the navigation pane, select **Applications** > **Enterprise Applications**. You see *CreditCheckMMApp* listed. Select the application and start it.

Checking the Bus

The easiest way to check whether this mediation module and all other business integration modules are deployed is to check the SCA modules section in the WebSphere Administrative console. The other way is to look under the bus!

You have to go a long way to see this in the WebSphere Administrative Console. In the navigation pane, select **Service integration** > **Buses**. From the listed buses, click **SCA.SYSTEM.*CELL_NAME*.Bus**. In the Configuration tab, under Topology, click **Bus members**. Click the bus member name, and then click the messaging engine (ME). On the Configuration screen, under Message points, click **Queue points**. The recently added CreditCheckMM is listed as a queue point, as shown in Figure 15.27.

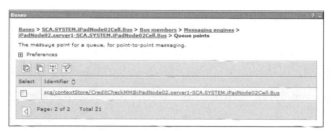

Figure 15.27 A message point for a queue

This short section did not do justice to the versatility and power of WESB. We suggest you look at the product InfoCenter to understand what you can do with WESB to help architect a complete SOA solution. One of the main functions of ESB is to access header information and do things such as dynamic routing based on information in WSRR. You can't do this in business modules. Mediation modules can be used to iron out any low-level technical details and to hide business modules from the details of bindings and application-specific business objects.

Closing the Link

This chapter talked about two components that have become central to any SOA. An ESB especially completes the story on business integration, with all its mediation capabilities. It is no longer an architectural concept.

WSRR and WESB are stand-alone products that come with their own comprehensive product InfoCenters with lots of examples. A service repository helps you store and reuse service artifacts, which should save enterprises precious time and money. An ESB will give enterprises a good return on investment (ROI) on their existing legacy applications because of the standards-based mediations it offers. WebSphere MQ and WebSphere Message Broker are considered part of the Advanced ESB offering from IBM.

In closing, the message we want to get across is that business logic is to be handled in business modules. Low-level technology integration and mediation logic should be handled in mediation modules.

With a good understanding of products such as WebSphere Business Modeler, WebSphere Process Server, WebSphere Enterprise Service Bus, WebSphere Service Registry and Repository, WebSphere Business Monitor, and WebSphere Integration Developer, you know what technologies go into building a Business Integration solution. Now we can truly close the link.

Links to developerWorks

A.15.1 www.ibm.com/developerworks/library/ar-servrepos/

A.15.2 www.ibm.com/developerworks/podcast/spotlight/st-070307btxt.html

A.15.3 www.ibm.com/developerworks/websphere/library/techarticles/0609_mckee/0609_mckee.html

A.15.4 www.ibm.com/developerworks/websphere/library/techarticles/0702_badlaney/0702_badlaney.html

A.15.5 www.ibm.com/developerworks/websphere/techjournal/0610_reinitz/0610_reinitz.html

A.15.6 www.ibm.com/developerworks/websphere/techjournal/0701_flurry/0701_flurry.html

Appendix A

WebSphere Process Server Installation

WebSphere Process Server (WPS) can be installed on Windows 2000, Windows 2003, Windows XP Professional, AIX®, Linux on distributed platforms and Linux on zSeries®, HP-UX, z/OS®, and Solaris on SPARC and Solaris on x86-64. Refer to the product specifications for the exact versions of the operating systems. This appendix illustrates the steps taken to install WPS v6.0.2 on a Windows XP machine. We then talk about the profile creation wizard to create a custom profile. Finally, we discuss "silent" installation.

Installing WebSphere Process Server

You can use the graphical interface or the command-line facility to install WPS. We normally use the graphical installation wizard for development servers, and we normally use the command-line facility for quality assurance (QA) and production servers. Either way, before installing the product, make sure you have at least 2 GB of free space. In this scenario, we install WPS on a system that already has an instance of WPS.

1. From the Disk 1 folder of the WPS product CD, invoke **launchpad.exe**. This brings up the Launchpad Welcome screen. Choose the language of your choice, and then click the **WebSphere Process Server installation** option.

2. Click the link to **Launch the Installation Wizard for WebSphere Process Server for Multiplatforms** (see Figure A.1). The installation wizard starts.

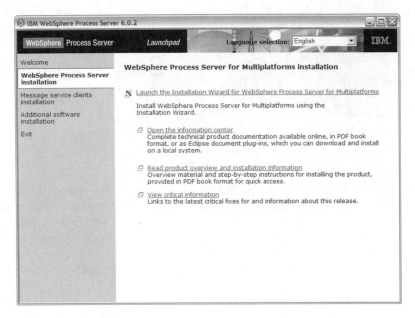

Figure A.1 WPS Launchpad Welcome screen

3. On the Welcome screen, click **Next**. Then accept the software license agreement, and click **Next**.

4. The wizard checks the system for prerequisites. If all the prerequisites are successfully met, click **Next**.

5. If the wizard detects an existing instance of WPS, it lets you know and gives you three options, as shown in Figure A.2. Note that we think the word "instance" should be used instead of "copy."

   • Install a new copy of WebSphere Process Server for Multiplatforms 6.0.2
   • Add features to an existing copy of WebSphere Process Server for Multiplatforms 6.0.2
   • Launch the Profile Wizard for an existing instance of WebSphere Proces Server for Multiplatforms 6.0.2

   Choose the option to **Install a new copy**, and click **Next**.

   If you are installing on a system that has an existing instance of WebSphere Process Server, you are informed about choosing different port values and a different cell if applicable.

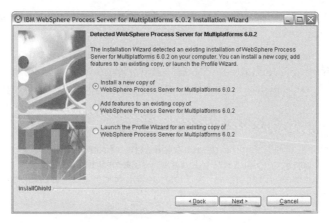

Figure A.2 Options on an existing instance of WPS

6. The wizard looks for an instance of WebSphere Application Server Network Deployment (WAS ND) and gives you the choice to either install a new copy or use an existing installation of WAS ND Version 6.0, as shown in Figure A.3. This comes into play when you install multiple instances of WPS to create a cluster.

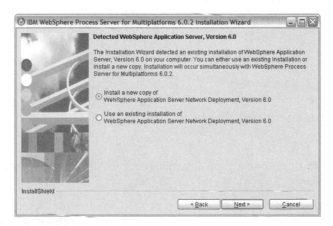

Figure A.3 WAS ND option

WPS Installation

There is an option to install a new copy of WAS ND, but you do not get an option to install a new copy of base WAS, because WPS requires WAS ND extensions.

7. Similar information about sharing port values, this time related to WebSphere Application Server, is displayed.

8. You then have to choose the installation root directory for WPS, as shown in Figure A.4. The default directory on the Windows platform is C:\Program Files\IBM\WebSphere\ProcServer. Enter the installation directory, and click **Next**.

WPS Installation Directory

Do not install WPS in the default folder. The recommendation is that you not use long pathnames and that you avoid directories with spaces in their names. A recommended installation folder is C:\WebSphere\ProcServer.

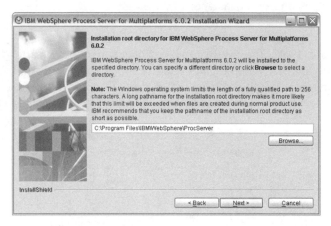

Figure A.4 Choosing the installation folder

9. Next you must choose a type of installation, as shown in Figure A.5. The choices are as follows:

  • **Complete:** Everything needed to run WPS is installed or created, including a default profile, a sample Business Process Container, the Common Event Infrastructure (CEI) , and all the sample applications. This is good for single-node installations, either for testing or demonstration use. If you choose this option, the next screen is the Summary screen.

  • **Custom:** This is the recommended option, because it gives you control over which components you want installed. For instance, on the next screen, you can choose not to install the sample applications or the Public API Javadocs to conserve disk space.

- **Client:** This is a partial installation of WPS, which allows other applications such as WebSphere Portal Server to interact with WPS. If you choose this option, the next screen is the Summary screen. If you are installing the client, the recommended installation folder is C:\WebSphere\WPSClient.

Choose the **Custom** option, and click **Next**.

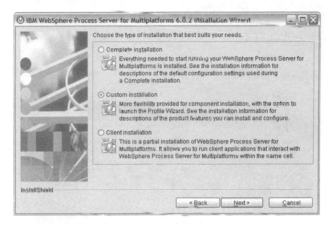

Figure A.5 Choosing the type of installation

10. After you make your choices, and when the Summary screen is displayed, click **Next** to begin the installation process. Then, when you see the "Installation complete" message, click **Finish**.

Remember the following:

- If you choose the Complete installation option, the wizard creates a WPS profile named *default*.

- If you choose the Client installation, you have nothing more to do.

- In the case of a Custom installation, you have the option to create a profile. You can do this immediately by launching the profile wizard, or you can do it later.

Creating a Profile

A WebSphere profile is a runtime environment. You can have multiple WPS profiles on a system, but all profiles on a machine share the same set of product binaries. And at least one profile must exist for you to have a functional installation. You can launch the Profile Creation Wizard in Windows by selecting **Start** > **Programs** > **IBM WebSphere** > **Process Server 6.0** > **Profile creation wizard**.

1. Make sure that the Welcome screen is titled **Welcome to the WebSphere Process Server 6.0 Profile Wizard** and not **WebSphere Application Server**. Click **Next**.

2. Choose the type of profile you want to create. The options, as shown in Figure A.6, are

   • Deployment manager profile

   • Custom profile

   • Stand-alone profile

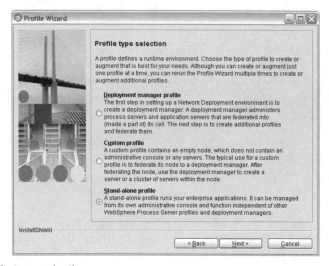

Figure A.6 Profile type selection

3. No matter which kind of profile you create, the name has to be unique. Because this is not a clustered environment, you choose **Stand-alone profile**. If this were the first profile on the system, the wizard would suggest ProcSrv01 as the name. The suffix is incremented by 1 for all subsequent profile names. You do have the choice to give the profile whatever name you want. Choose the default profile name.

4. You may choose to designate this profile as the default profile by checking the box, as shown in Figure A.7. But we did not choose that option. Click **Next**.

> **Profile Creation**
>
> The first profile created on a system is designated as the default profile. Any subsequent profile that is created has the option to be designated as the default one. If you plan to integrate another client software product such as WebSphere Portal with WPS, the integration is done with the profile that is designated as the default profile.

Figure A.7 Naming a profile

5. The Profile directory screen, shown in Figure A.8, asks you to choose the profile installation directory. The recommendation is to accept the default location, which is *WPS_HOME*\profiles*PROFILE_NAME*. Click **Next**.

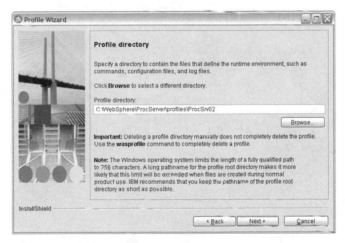

Figure A.8 Choosing the profile directory

6. Specify a **Node name** and **Host name** for the profile, or accept what the wizard picks up. Remember that the node name has to be unique within a WebSphere cell and that the hostname can be either the fully qualified hostname or the IP address.

7. The installation wizard displays the port values assigned to the profile that is being created. If the default ports are not being used, our recommendation is to make a note of the ports that will be used.

Windows Service

Do not run the WPS as a Windows service. Although that option is offered (to be compliant with Windows software guidelines from Microsoft®), we have found that making WPS a Windows service leads to accidental starts. By not making it a Windows service, you also have full control over when to start WPS.

8. Because this is a custom installation, you have to configure the Service Component Architecture (SCA). You also have the choice of configuring the System Integration (SI) Bus in a secured mode. In production environments, you might prefer to have the SI Bus communicate in a secured mode. You don't have to decide this right now, because you can enable security afterward via the WebSphere Administrative Console.

9. The next step is Common Event Infrastructure (CEI) configuration. As shown in Figure A.9, you have to supply a user ID and password, along with the WebSphere server name, to configure CEI. Finally, you have to choose a database where all the Common Base Events (and CEI metadata) may be stored. From the database drop-down list, choose **DB2 Universal V8.2**, and then click **Next**. As of this writing, Cloudscape, IBM DB2, and Oracle are the supported databases.

Figure A.9 Configuring CEI

10. If you choose a database other than Cloudscape, you have to create the CEI database. In production environments, you should use either DB2 or Oracle. Provide the database name and the credentials required to access it. Then click **Next**. Table A.1 shows the fields you have to provide values for when using DB2 or Oracle.

Table A.1 Fields Required When Configuring the Database

DB2	Oracle
Database name	Database instance name (SID)
User ID to authenticate with the database	User ID to create in the database
Password for database authentication	Password for the created user ID
Location of JDBC driver class files. It looks for db2jcc.jar.	User ID with SYSDBA authority
JDBC driver type	Password for User ID with SYSDBA authority
Database server name	Location of JDBC driver class files. It looks for classes12.zip or ojdbc14.jar.
Database server port. The default is 50000.	

11. In the BPC Configuration screen, shown in Figure A.10, check the box to **Configure a sample Business Process Choreographer**. We recommend specifying a password. Then click **Next**.

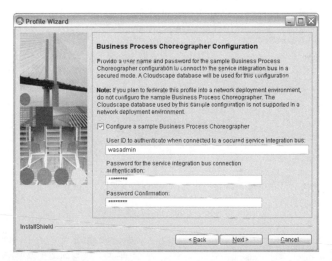

Figure A.10 Configuring the sample Business Process Choreographer container

12. Make sure the installation wizard chooses the correct server for use with the Application Scheduler.

13. The common WPS database is named WPRCSDB. On the database configuration screen, you can specify whether you want to create a new database or use an existing one. Except with Cloudscape, the database can be remote if you choose DB2, Oracle, Informix®, or Microsoft SQL Server.

14. Finally, the summary screen is displayed. Before clicking **Next**, make sure the profile characteristics are correct. After the installation process is complete, look for the message "Profile creation is complete." Then click **Finish**.

WPS should now be installed, with a profile created and ready for use.

Installing WPS Silently

In a large distributed environment, you may be asked to perform a "silent" or background installation wherein you cannot use a graphical user interface such as the wizard. That is possible via the command line using the *install* executable. It is found on CD1 of the product in the WBI folder. The silent installation requires a file to obtain all the responses, which is aptly called the response file. A sample response file is provided. Actually, four sample response files are provided: one for base WPS installation and three for profile creation.

Figure A.11 shows the files in the *WPS_PRODUCT_CD1*\WBI folder. The response files are shipped with default values. So be sure to make a copy of the response file, and then edit and use the copy. Note that you cannot perform a silent installation if an instance of WPS or the WPS Client is already installed on the system.

Figure A.11 Contents of the WBI folder of WPS product CD1

Response File Editing
The best method of preparing the response file is to edit the file on the target operating system. And do not forget to change the license acceptance statement to `true`.

To have an operational WPS environment, you must have a profile. To launch the profile wizard silently at the end of the installation process, remember to change the value of these two options: `-W summaryPanel_InstallWizardBean.launchPCAW` to `true` and `-W pcawResponseFileLocationQueryAction_InstallWizardBean.fileLocation` from `""` to the location of the profile response file. Remember to copy and edit the appropriate profile response file. The filenames match the profile types.

Assuming that you have edited the copy of the base response file and have saved it as *myresponsefile.wps.txt*, the install command is

```
install -options myresponsefile.wps.txt -silent
```

Check the contents of the *log.txt* file found in the *WPS_HOME*\logs\WBI folder to determine the result of the silent installation. If the last line of the file contains the word INSTCONF-SUCCESS, the component you selected was installed successfully.

Creating Additional Profiles Silently

There is also a "silent" option for creating additional profiles. This is done using the *pct* utility via the command line. You can open a command prompt and navigate to the *WPS_HOME*\bin\ProfileCreator_wbi directory. There you will find a batch or shell file (whose name is platform-dependent) that can be used to start the profile creation wizard.

For example, on the Windows platform, you invoke *pctWindows* and use the interactive wizard to create your profile. But if you do not want to use the graphical user interface (GUI), you can use the same *pctWindows* command with the `-silent` option:

```
pctWindows -options myresponsefile.txt -silent
```

Of course, you need to provide all the necessary parameters for the profile creation in the options file indicated by *myresponsefile.txt*. Fortunately, the same directory *profileCreator_wbi* contains an example of a complete options file for each of the three profile types. It is recommended that you make a copy of the supplied sample file, make the necessary changes to suit your environment, and then use it as the input option with the *pct* command.

WPS Installation Folder

Figure A.12 shows the folders where WPS has been installed—the *WPS_HOME* directory. The subfolders of particular interest are _uninstwbi, bin, logs, ProcessChoreographer, and profiles, because more often than not you will need to access contents from these subfolders.

Figure A.12 Contents of the WPS installation directory

The profiles subfolder contains all the profiles that have been created on that instance of WPS. And each profile has its own set of log files in the logs subfolder.

Uninstalling WPS

If you look in the *WPS_HOME* directory structure, you see two folders: _uninst and _uninst-wbi. If you want to uninstall WPS, you should invoke the *uninstall* script from the *WPS_HOME*_uninstwbi folder. Follow the prompts of the uninstallation wizard to remove the WPS instance from your system, and delete all the profiles.

Profile Removal

To uninstall or delete a profile, you have to run the *wasprofile* utility, found in the *WPS_HOME*\bin folder. First you have to unaugment the profile, and then you may delete it. The exact syntax is

```
wasprofile -unaugment -profileName PROFILE_NAME
```

```
wasprofile -delete -profileName PROFILE_NAME
```

The other options available with *wasprofile* are create, augment, deleteAll, listProfiles, getName, getPath, validateRegistry, validateAndUpdateRegistry, and help.

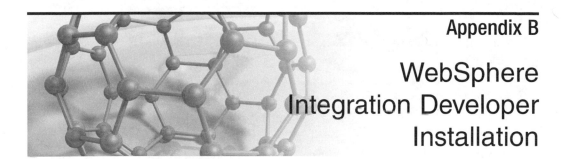

WebSphere Integration Developer Installation

W ebSphere Integration Developer (WID) can be installed on Windows 2000, Windows 2003, Windows XP Professional, Red Hat Enterprise Linux, and SUSE Linux Enterprise Server. Refer to the product specifications for the exact versions of the operating systems. Here, we illustrate the steps to install WID v6.0.2 on a Windows XP machine.

Installing WebSphere Integration Developer

You can use the graphical interface or the command-line facility to install WID. Either way, before installing the product, make sure you have defined an environment variable TEMP and that it points to a valid temporary directory with at least 1 GB of free space. We normally use the graphical installation wizard.

From the Disk 1 folder of the WID product CD, invoke **launchpad.exe**. This brings up the Launchpad, as shown in Figure B.1. Click the option to **Install IBM WebSphere Integration Developer V6.0.2**.

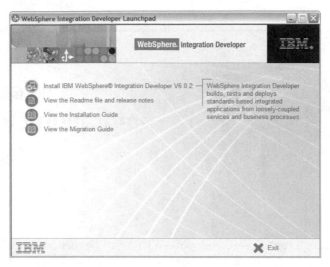

Figure B.1 WID Launchpad screen

1. The rest of the installation screens are easy to follow. On the Welcome screen, click **Next**. Then accept the software license agreement, and click **Next**.

2. Choose a short installation directory, as shown in Figure B.2. On Windows, we do not recommend using the default path of C:\Program Files\IBM. Artifacts running in the test server may hit the 256-character path length limit imposed by the IBM JDK v1.4.2 for Windows, which is used by WID.

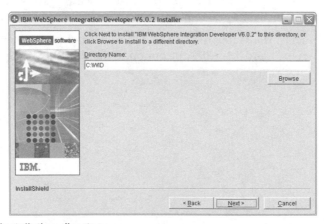

Figure B.2 WID installation directory

3. Make sure you install the WebSphere Process Server test environment so that you can test the software components you create inside WID's test server(s). See Figure B.3.

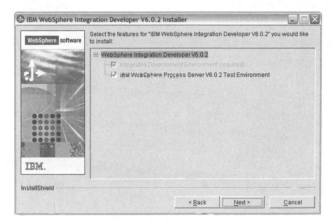

Figure B.3 Choosing the WPS test environment

4. Notice on the profiles screen, shown in Figure B.4, that you can use WID to test WebSphere Process Server (WPS) applications and WebSphere Enterprise Service Bus (WESB) applications. If you intend to create, deploy, and test both types of applications, choose both profiles. We highly recommend doing so. You will notice later that a profile named *wps* gets created for WPS and another named *esb* is created for WESB.

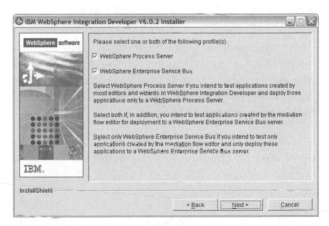

Figure B.4 Choosing the type of profile to install

5. The Summary screen is displayed. Click **Next** to begin the installation process. The installation process takes some time to configure everything. The goal is to get the screen shown in Figure B.5.

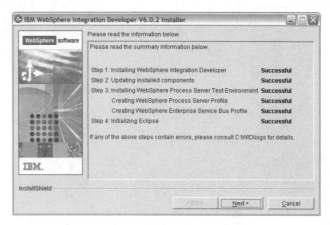

Figure B.5 Summary information for the WID installation process

> ### WID User ID
>
> During the installation of WebSphere Process Server to be used as a test server, a user ID *wid* with a password *wid* is created automatically. This is required for the initial configuration of the Business Process Choreographer and the Common Event Infrastructure.

6. After the installation process is complete, you have the option to launch the Rational Product Updater (RPU). You may choose to use that option if you want to apply maintenance patches to WID. We recommend that you choose the RPU option to make sure you are at the latest available release level. Then click the **Finish** button to complete the installation.

7. Click **Exit** on the Launchpad screen to terminate the launchpad.

WebSphere Integration Developer should now be ready for use.

WID Usage

Start WID and open a workspace to make sure things are working.

1. When you bring up WID, the Welcome Screen is displayed after a new installation, as shown in Figure B.6. After you open a workspace and work with it, you are taken directly to the workbench. If you want to view the Welcome Screen later, simply select **Help** > **Welcome** from WID.

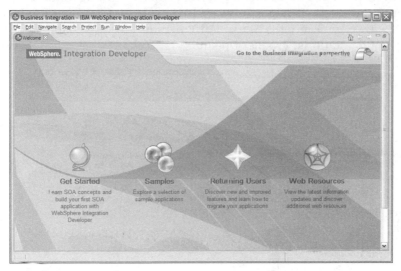

Figure B.6 WID Welcome screen

2. Click the **Go to the Business Integration perspective** arrow in the top-right corner. The workbench should open in a four-pane layout, as shown in Figure B.7.

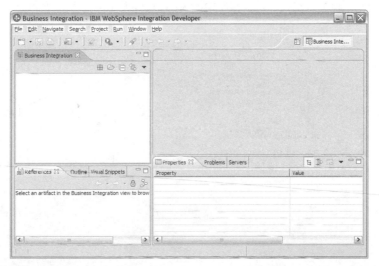

Figure B.7 WID's default four-pane layout

Updating WID

After WID is installed, you can bring up the Rational Product Updater (RPU), shown in Figure B.8, to check for and install new features or to update existing features. You can access RPU from WID by selecting **Help** > **Software Updates** > **IBM Rational Product Updater**. Or, from Windows, you can select **Start** > **All Programs** > **IBM WebSphere** > **Integration Developer V6.0.2** > **Rational Product Updater**.

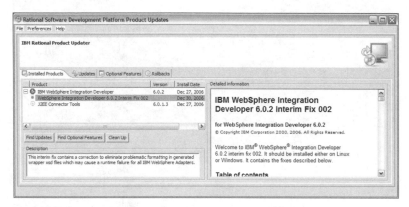

Figure B.8 Rational Product Updater

Running the RPU over the network takes some time. It is highly recommended that you download the update plug-in files to your local hard drive and do your updates locally. You specify the local site by selecting **Preferences** > **Update Sites** and entering the path to the new policy file. Figure B.9, for example, shows the folder where the WSRR update files are stored.

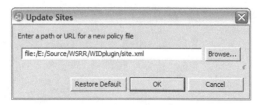

Figure B.9 Specifying a local update site

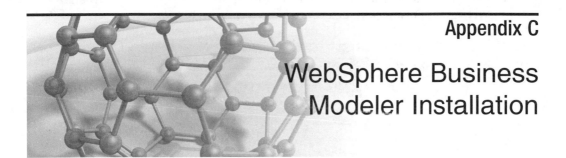

WebSphere Business Modeler Installation

There are two editions of WebSphere Business Modeler v6.0.2: Basic and Advanced. A Publishing Server also is available for Business Modeler, which allows business models to be published and shared on the Internet for collaboration purposes. This appendix shows you how to install the Advanced edition of WebSphere Business Modeler, because it offers simulation and dynamic analysis capabilities. Both the Basic and the Advanced versions can be installed either as a stand-alone Eclipse-based tool or as a plug-in to the WebSphere Integration Developer (WID). As a stand-alone component, WebSphere Business Modeler can be installed only on the Windows 2000 or Windows XP platforms.

WebSphere Business Modeler Installation

Business analysts like to use Business Modeler in its stand-alone mode because it does not have a large footprint. Technical folks who are used to working with Java and Eclipse-based tooling prefer using Modeler as a plug-in to WID.

Installing WebSphere Business Modeler

The following sections describe how to install WebSphere Business Modeler.

Stand-alone Installation

The assumption here is that you are logged in as a user with administrative authority on the Windows system. From the source CD, invoke **setup.exe**.

1. On the product Launchpad screen, shown in Figure C.1, click **Install IBM WebSphere Business Modeler Advanced Version 6.0.2.**

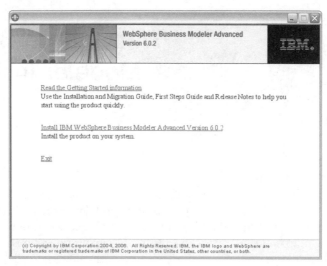

Figure C.1 WebSphere Business Modeler product Launchpad screen

2. The install wizard starts, as shown in Figure C.2. Click **Next**.

Figure C.2 WebSphere Business Modeler Advanced installation wizard Welcome screen

3. Accept the Software License Agreement. On the following screen, shown in Figure C.3, specify the installation directory. Do not use long directory paths or directory names with spaces in them.

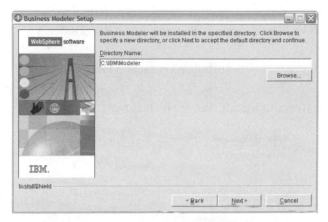

Figure C.3 Specify the WebSphere Business Modeler installation directory

4. On the Summary screen, shown in Figure C.4, click **Next** to begin the installation process.

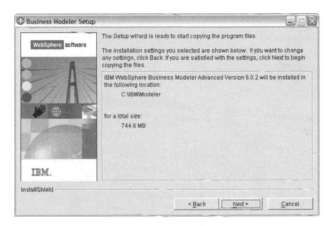

Figure C.4 Summary screen

5. After the installation process is complete and successful, you can run the business modeling tool. Click **Finish** to end the installation process.

The WebSphere Business Modeler v6.0.2 Advanced Edition should now be ready for use.

WID Plug-in Installation

The assumption with this installation process is that you are logged in as a user with administrative authority on the Windows system. WID v6.0.2 must already be installed.

1. Start WID by selecting **Start** > **Programs** > **IBM WebSphere** > **Integration Developer V6.0.2** > **WebSphere Integration Developer V6.0.2** with any workspace.

2. From WID, select **Help** > **Software Updates** > **Find and Install**.

3. You should see the Feature Updates screen, as shown in Figure C.5. Select **Search for new features to install**, and then click **Next**.

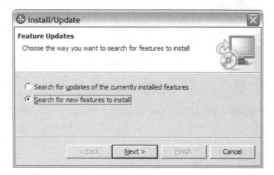

Figure C.5 WID Feature Updates

4. You have the option to select an update site. Click **New Local Site**, and choose the location of the WebSphere Business Modeler software CDs. Specifically, select the folder **WB-Modeler-advanced** under UpdateManager, as shown in Figure C.6. Click **OK**.

Figure C.6 Browsing for a local update site

5. On the Update sites to visit screen, shown in Figure C.7, you should see the inclusion of the local site that points to the source CD image of WebSphere Business Modeler v6.0.2.

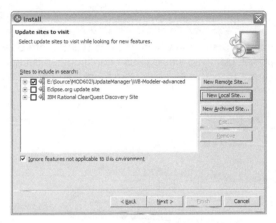

Figure C.7 Update sites screen

6. Check the box to select the path to the WB-Modeler installation software (the local site), and then click **Next**.

7. After a quick search of the local site, the features available for update are listed, as shown in Figure C.8. Click **Select All**, and then click **Next**.

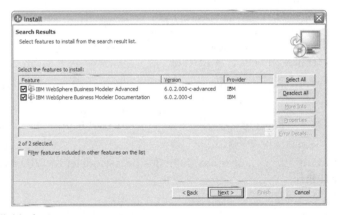

Figure C.8 Available features screen

8. Accept the Feature License agreement, and click **Next**. You are asked for the Install Location, as shown in Figure C.9. Choose *WID_HOME*\sdpisv\eclipse. Click **Finish** to proceed with the updates.

WebSphere Business Modeler Location

Do not create a new folder in which to place WebSphere Business Modeler plug-ins. Doing so would cause configuration issues that could stop WebSphere Business Modeler from functioning properly.

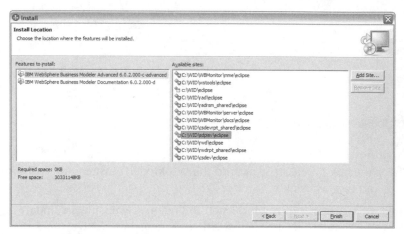

Figure C.9 Feature installation location

9. At the start of the installation process, you must confirm that you want to install unsigned features by clicking **Install**.

10. At the end of the installation, when you are asked to restart the workbench, click **Yes**.

WebSphere Business Modeler v6.0.2 Advanced Edition should now be configured in WID v6.0.2.

You may choose to install/upgrade WebSphere Business Modeler in WID using the Rational Product Updater (RPU).

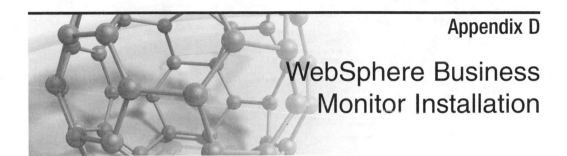

WebSphere Business Monitor Installation

WebSphere Business Monitor v6.0.2 has three installation options: Basic, Advanced, and Integrated Test Environment. This appendix discusses the Basic installation. The Basic installation option is possible only on the Windows platform. However, Windows XP Professional is not recommended in production environments. It is to be used only for application design, development, and unit test environments. Basic installation enables all the WebSphere Business Monitor-related components, including databases, to be installed on a single machine, but with limited flexibility. Many of the installation parameters are preconfigured and require minimal user interaction.

Installing WebSphere Business Monitor

The assumption of this installation process is that you have the IBM DB2 database product and the corresponding business intelligence product, DB2 Cube Views, already installed on the system. Those are some of the prerequisites for WebSphere Business Monitor. From the WebSphere Business Monitor source CD, invoke the **Launchpad** program. The installation has two parts: installation of the Monitor Server and installation of the Dashboard Server. The first few screens of the installation wizard deal with Monitor Server.

1. On the Welcome screen, shown in Figure D.1, click **Install**.

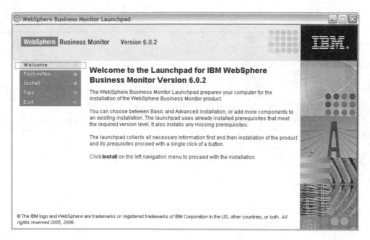

Figure D.1 WebSphere Business Monitor Launchpad Welcome screen

2. Accept the Software License Agreement, and choose the installation type, as shown in Figure D.2. Because all the software components are installed on a single machine, for the Installation Type, choose **Basic**, and then click **Next**. You can also use the **Advanced** option to install everything on a single machine.

> **Monitor Prerequisite Software**
>
> The recommended approach is to let Launchpad install and configure all the required software components.

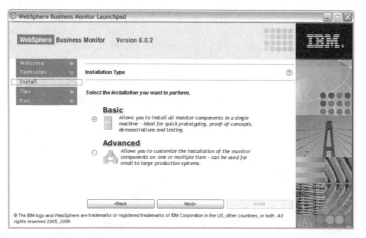

Figure D.2 Installation Type choices

3. If you have more than one instance of any software component, click the **more** icon, shown in Figure D.3, and choose the instance you want to use. Also pay attention to the messages between the input fields. For example, you might see a message that says, "The process server profile (wbmonitor) must use DB2 database as the repository."

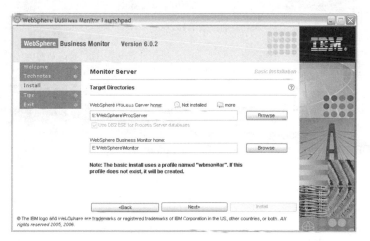

Figure D.3 Specify target directories for supporting components of Monitor Server.

4. Edit the target directories where you want WebSphere Process Server and WebSphere Business Monitor to be installed, and then click **Next**.

Business Monitor Installation

The WebSphere Process Server (WPS) that is installed by the Business Monitor Launchpad (only for use with WebSphere Business Monitor) does not include the Business Process Container. If you want to have the Business Process Container on the same WPS as the WebSphere Business Monitor Server, you must install your own licensed copy of WPS outside the Business Monitor Launchpad.

---

5. If DB2 is already installed on the system, the Launchpad should detect it, as shown in Figure D.4. The hostname and port are also filled in. However, you have to enter the DB2 username and password. Click **Next**.

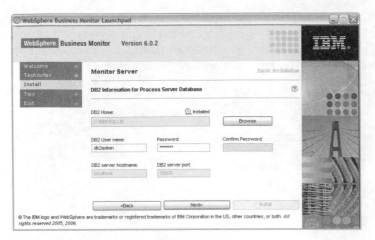

Figure D.4 DB2 Information for Process Server Database

6. Enter the WebSphere Process Server username and password, as shown in Figure D.5. This is for the process server instance that is used by WebSphere Business Monitor. By default, **wasadmin** is used. This username must exist as a user in the local operating system. Click **Next**.

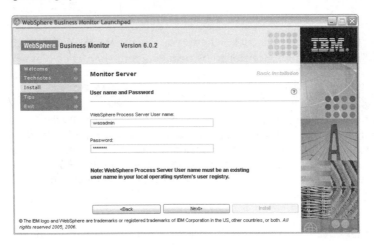

Figure D.5 Screen requiring WPS username and password

7. The Launchpad then checks for existing products. The wait time is proportional to the number of products already installed on the system.

After the Launchpad checks for existing products, you have to set the installation details for the Dashboard Server. Most of the information should be filled in already, but you should verify the values:

8. Edit the target directories where you want WebSphere Application Server, WebSphere Portal, and the DB2 Alphablox products to be installed, as shown in Figure D.6. Click **Next**.

Figure D.6 Specify target directories for supporting components of Dashboard Server.

WebSphere Product Directory

A recommended directory structure for the WebSphere products is shown in Figure D.7.

Figure D.7 Recommended WebSphere product directory structure

9. As shown in Figure D.8, enter the WebSphere Application Server administrator ID, WebSphere Portal administrator ID, DB2 Alphablox administrator ID, and the respective passwords. These values are for the products involved in presenting the Monitor dashboard web pages to end users. The figure shows the default user IDs to use. Click **Next**.

Figure D.8 Screen requiring usernames and passwords for the Portal-related components

10. As part of the databases setup, enter the DB2 username and password, as shown in Figure D.9. You have the option to create the DDL scripts without executing them. This would be useful if your environment requires that only a Database Administrator (DBA) is authorized to execute DDL scripts. Click **Next** without checking the **Create DDL scripts only** box.

Figure D.9 Database setup for Dashboard Server

11. Edit the target directories for DB2 backup and table spaces. We recommend accepting the defaults shown in Figure D.10. Then click **Next**.

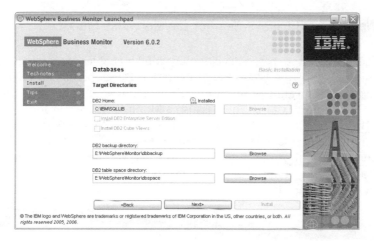

Figure D.10 Specify DB2 target directories for Dashboard Server.

12. On the Summary screen, click **Install** to start the installation process. You are asked to load the subsequent source CDs for the various software components and are asked for the location, which would be your CD drive.

13. The installation process finishes installing the WebSphere Business Monitor artifacts and returns the results. You should then see **Successful** next to all the artifacts, as shown in Figure D.11. At this point, you can click **Finish**. If you get an installation **Failure** against any artifact, you can retry the installation with the correct inputs.

Figure D.11 The WebSphere Business Monitor installation results screen

You should now have an instance of WebSphere Business Monitor v6.0.2.

Installing WebSphere Business Monitor Development Toolkit

As you have seen, the Eclipse-based development toolkit enables users to develop and test a monitoring model within the WebSphere Integration Developer (WID) environment. The tooling component for creating monitor models, which is a set of Eclipse plug-ins, is called the Monitor Model Editor (MME). There is also a Monitor Test Server for testing the monitor models. This test server is equivalent to the standard Monitor Server, but without the Adaptive Action Manager and the Replication Manager. For this installation of the WebSphere Business Monitor Development toolkit, we assume that you already have WID v6.0.2 installed. From the Monitor Development Toolkit source CD, invoke the setup command to start the Launchpad.

> **Monitor Development Toolkit**
>
> The WebSphere Business Monitor Development Toolkit does not support the Cloudscape database.

1. The first screen is the Welcome screen, as shown in Figure D.12. Click the **Install** option in the navigation menu.

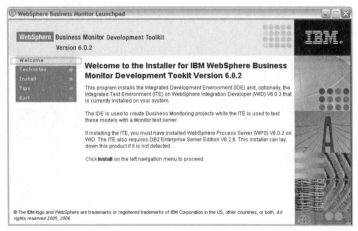

Figure D.12 The WebSphere Business Monitor Development Toolkit Launchpad Welcome screen

> **Monitor Development Toolkit Installation Tip**
>
> The Monitor Development Toolkit cannot be installed on a system that already has a Monitor Server. If you have uninstalled WebSphere Business Monitor, but the Launchpad still finds an existing installation of Monitor Server, go to the C:\Windows folder and rename/delete the **install.vlf** file.

2. On the Installation Options screen, shown in Figure D.13, the Integrated Development Environment (IDE) is required. It is also advisable to select the Integrated Test Environment (ITE). Click **Next**.

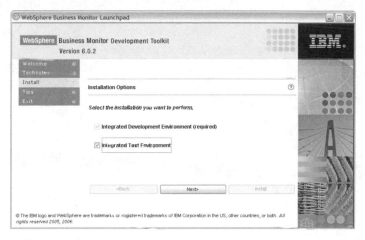

Figure D.13 Installation options

3. As shown in Figure D.14, Launchpad should display the WebSphere Integration Developer v6.0.2 installation folder, which is C:\WID (if you followed our recommendations in Appendix B, "WebSphere Integration Developer Installation") on the Windows platform. Notice that it says it is installed. Accept the target directories for WebSphere Business Monitor and Monitor Model Editor Plugins. Click **Next**.

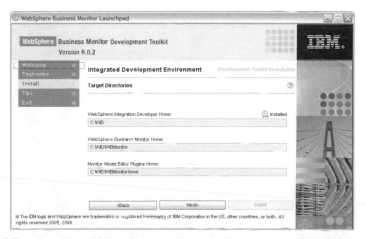

Figure D.14 IDE target directories

4. The next screen asks for target directories related to the Integrated Test Environment (ITE), as shown in Figure D.15. Given that DB2 is already installed and the WebSphere Process Server runtime should be configured in WID, the Launchpad should pick the corresponding directories. A new profile named wbmonitor is created in *WID_HOME*\pf folder. Click **Next**.

Figure D.15 ITE target directories

5. Figure D.16 shows the next screen. It requires the username and password for DB2 and WPS underlying the Monitor ITE. Note the constraints on the WPS username. After entering the values, click **Next**.

Figure D.16 Database and Process Server credentials for the ITE

6. Finally, the Summary screen is displayed. Click **Install**.

7. After the installation is done, look at the results. Both the IDE and ITE should be successfully installed. Click **Finish**.

You should now have the WebSphere Business Monitor Development Toolkit v6.0.2 configured inside your WID v6.0.2.

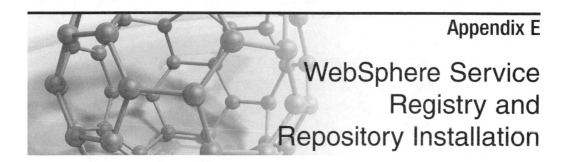

WebSphere Service Registry and Repository Installation

WebSphere Service Registry and Repository (WSRR) v6.0.2 can be installed in three different modes: GUI, Console, or Silent. The installer simply copies the relevant files onto the file system. After that, you have to run the deployment script to create the databases and deploy the applications to the application server where WSRR will run.

Installing WSRR

For this installation, we assume that you have the IBM DB2 database and either WebSphere Application Server or WebSphere Process Server (WPS) already installed on your system.

1. From the WSRR source CD, invoke **setup.exe**. On the Welcome screen, shown in Figure E.1, click **Next**.

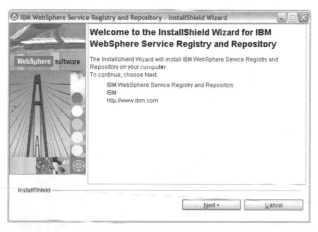

Figure E.1 The WSRR InstallShield Welcome screen

2. By default, on the Windows platform the installation directory is C:\Program Files\IBM\WebSphereServiceRegistry, as shown in Figure E.2. Our recommendation is to install WSRR in C:\IBM\WSRR. Click **Next**.

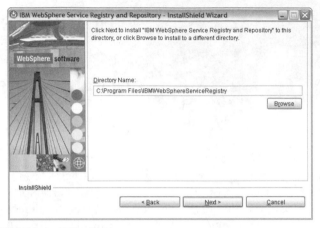

Figure E.2 The WSRR installation folder

3. On the Summary screen, shown in Figure E.3, click **Install** to start the installation process.

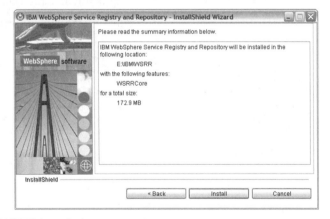

Figure E.3 The WSRR installation summary screen

4. When the installation process finishes, you see a message reminding you to run the deployment scripts, as shown in Figure E.4. Click **Next**.

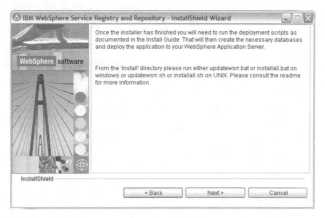

Figure E.4 The WSRR installation message about deployment scripts

5. After the success message appears, click **Finish**. At this point you should have a folder (C:\IBM\WSRR) with all the WSRR-related files. The next steps involve setting up the environment and running the installation scripts.

6. In a command window, go to the *WSRR_HOME*\install folder. Edit the *setenv* script, and then run it to set up the environment. We recommend that you set WAS_HOME and DB_HOME environment variables before running setenv.bat.

> **WSRR Installation Script**
>
> Be sure you check the values in the *setenv* script found in *WSRR_HOME*\install, because it comes pre-loaded with default values. You may have to modify the values to suit your environment.

7. You may run the various installation scripts one at a time or simply run the *installall* script to install all the WSRR applications. Ensure that WPS is stopped, and then enter the **installall** command, as shown in Figure E.5. Remember to substitute the values to match your environment.

```
C:\IBM\WSRR\install>installall -was-password wasadmin -db-password password -was
-profile ProcSrv01 -soap-port 8887 -bootstrap-port 2811 -was-user wasadmin -db-u
ser db2admin
Installing Xmeta
Output is being logged to C:\IBM\WSRR\install\\installxmeta.log
Installing ServiceRegistry
Output is being logged to C:\IBM\WSRR\install\\installsr.log
Installation complete
```

Figure E.5 Running the *installall* script

The deployment scripts create two databases named SOR and XMETA1. If you look in the WebSphere Administrative Console, as shown in Figure E.6, you will notice two enterprise applications: *RXMeta* and *ServiceRegistry*. In addition, if you select **Service integration** > **Buses**, you will notice two new buses that support notification: *ServiceRegistryBus* and *xmeta_defaultBus*.

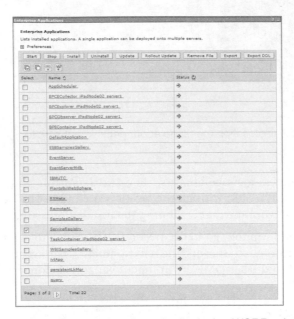

Figure E.6 The WebSphere Administrative Console displaying WSRR-related applications

You should now have WebSphere Service Registry and Repository configured with WebSphere Process Server.

Installing the WSRR Eclipse Plug-in in WID

WSRR comes with an Eclipse-based plug-in. The steps of installing that plug-in into WebSphere Integration Developer (WID) are similar to the initial steps of installing the WebSphere Monitor Development Toolkit, which is described in Appendix D, "WebSphere Business Monitor Installation." The assumption here is that WID v6.0.2 is already installed and running.

1. Select **Help** > **Software Updates** > **Find and Install**.

2. On the Features Updates screen, select **Search for new features to install**.

3. Choose **New Local Site**, and select *WSRR_SOURCE*\Eclipse. This location gets added to the list in the wizard, as shown in Figure E.7.

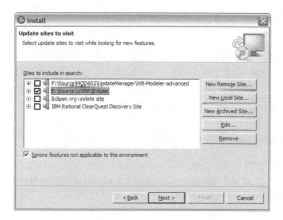

Figure E.7 The WSRR eclipse plug-in site

4. Select all the features. In this case, there is only the service registry core feature. Accept the Feature License agreement, and click **Next**.

5. You are asked for a location. Select *WID_HOME*\eclipse as the installation folder, as shown in Figure E.8. Click **Finish** to install the plug-in.

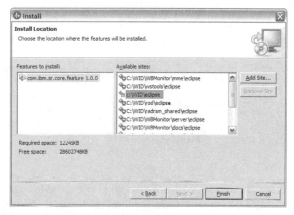

Figure E.8 The installation location of the service registry feature

6. At the start of the installation process, you must confirm that you want to install unsigned features by clicking **Install**.

7. At the end, when you are asked to restart the workbench, click **Yes**. Before you can use the plug-in, you need to configure it. You do this via the preferences settings. From WID, select **Windows** > **Preferences**.

8. Expand **Service Registry**, and highlight **WSRR Locations**. In the window that appears, click **Add**.

9. Specify an Alias, the Host name (which can be either the fully qualified hostname or the IP address) and the JNDI port number, as shown in Figure E.9. The default port number is 2809. Leave the security at **none**, because security is not enabled in this instance of WebSphere Process Server. Click **OK**.

> **Plug-in Installation**
>
> In the Add Service Registry Preferences dialog box, if WebSphere global security is enabled, you have to choose *sas.client.props* from the Security drop-down list and specify its location.

Figure E.9 Adding service registry preferences

10. On the preferences screen, you see the *myWSRR* alias name, as shown in Figure E.10. By clicking **OK**, you search for and publish documents to the specified instance of the registry.

11. Open the Service Registry by selecting **Window** > **Show View** > **Other**. In the Show View dialog, shown in Figure E.11, expand the Service Registry folder, and select **Service Registry**. Click **OK**.

Figure E.10 Applying the WSRR location

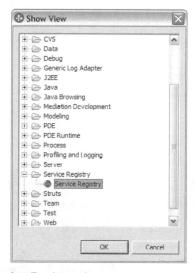

Figure E.11 Enabling the Service Registry view

12. The Service Registry view opens in the bottom right of the WID workbench.

You now have the WSRR Eclipse plug-in installed in WID and configured to talk to the WSRR instance.

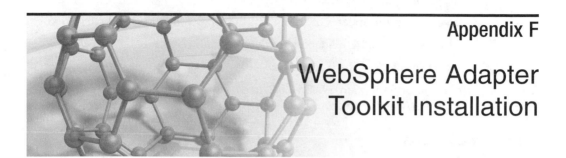

WebSphere Adapter Toolkit Installation

The WebSphere Adapter Toolkit (WAT) is an add-on product that you need if you plan to create custom adapters. It is actually an Eclipse-based plug-in that gets installed in WebSphere Integration Developer (WID)—in this case, WID v6.0.2.

Installing WebSphere Adapter Toolkit

You need to have WebSphere Integration Developer already installed on your system on top of Rational Application Developer before starting the WebSphere Adapter Toolkit installation. That is best done via the Rational Product Updater (RPU).

Using RPU

The recommendation is to use the Rational Product Updater (preferably using a local update site) and to follow these instructions:

1. Start WebSphere Integration Developer.

2. Launch the Eclipse Update Manager by selecting **Help** > **Software Update** > **Find and Install**.

3. For new users of WebSphere Adapter Toolkit:

    a. Select Search for new features to install, and click **Next**.

    b. Create a New Remote Site. Set the Name to IBM WebSphere Adapter Toolkit update site and the URL to http://download.boulder.ibm.com/ibmdl/pub/software/websphere/wat.

For current users of WebSphere Adapter Toolkit:

    a. Select Search for updates of the currently installed features, and click **Next**.

    b. Select IBM WebSphere Adapter Toolkit.

4. Click **Next**, and follow the instructions.

You can get more information on WAT v6.0.2 from www.ibm.com/developerworks/websphere/downloads/wat/wat602.html.

Using Product CDs

For this installation, we assume that you are using the Windows platform and that Rational Application Developer (RAD) and WID exist in C:\WID.

1. From the WAT source CD, go to the ESD folder, and invoke **setupwin32.exe**. Then follow the installation wizard prompts.

2. On the Welcome screen, shown in Figure F.1, click **Next**.

Figure F.1 The WAT InstallShield Welcome screen

3. Accept the Software License agreement.

4. By default, on the Windows platform, the installation directory is C:\Program Files\IBM\ResourceAdapters\AdapterToolkit, as shown in Figure F.2. Our recommendation is to install it in C:\IBM\ResourceAdapters\AdapterToolkit. Click **Next**.

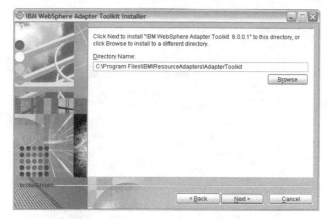

Figure F.2 The WAT installation folder

> **WAT Installation**
>
> With the suggested installation folder, you can then store all the resource adapters in C:\IBM\ResourceAdapters.

5. On the summary information screen, click **Next** to launch the installation process.

6. When the installation process is complete, look for the success message. Click **Finish** to close the installation wizard.

You should now have the WebSphere Adapter Toolkit configured in WID.

Verifying the WAT Eclipse Plug-in in WID

Bring up WID, and open any workspace. Create a new project by selecting **File** > **New** > **Project**. In the ensuing window, you should see **Adapter Toolkit** as one of the options. To create a new adapter project, actually called Connector Project, you have to expand the Adapter Toolkit folder and choose **J2C Resource Adapter Project**, as shown in Figure F.3. Click **Next**, and follow the prompts to create the new Connector Project.

Figure F.3 Choosing a JCA adapter project

You now have the WAT Eclipse plug-in installed in WID, which you can use to create custom resource adapters.

Index

Symbols

* (wildcard character), 332

A

Access Services, 4
accessing
    databases, 208-209
    EJB, 240
action bar
    assembly editor, 57
    process editor, 54
actions (empty), 109
activities
    assigning, 105
    BPEL
        definition, 29
        Fault Activities, 32
        Service Activities, 30
        Structured Activities, 30-32
    choice, 106-107
    correlation sets, associating, 119
    monitor models, 309
    receive choice, 116-117
ad hoc human tasks, 167-168
adapters
    application, 252
    architecture
        CCI, 255
        Enterprise Discovery, 256
        inbound processing, 256
        outbound processing, 255
        RAR files, 257
        SPIs, 255

communicating with WPS, 253
customizing, 268-271
definition, 252
e-mail, 266
flat file, 266
FTP, 266
JCA, 252-253
JDBC
    assembly diagram, 264
    build path settings, 260
    creating, 258-259, 263-264
    dependencies, 260
    discovery agent settings, 261
    enterprise service resource adapters,
        selecting, 260
    objects for discovery, selecting, 262
    properties, 262
    RAR file, importing, 259
    testing, 264-265
    tree structure, 263
legacy, 252
resource, 253, 260
SAP, 266-267
Siebel, 267-268
technology, 252
Add Service Registry Preferences dialog box,
    390
addNode utility, 82
administration of business rules, 149
    decision tables, 149-150
    installing, 149
    Publish and Revert link, 151

Administrative Console
   business process container setting, 192
   business rules, exporting, 151
   CEI monitoring, 192
   human task container setting, 192
   WESB, 343
   WID, 69
   WPS, 85
administrative human tasks, 167
administrative roles, 204
administrators, 204, 325
agents
   discovery, 261
   nodes, 83
ALE (Application Link Enabling), 266
alerts (dashboards), 302
APIs (application program interfaces)
   business flow manager, 238-239
   business processes, initiating, 239
      EJB access, 240
      input messages, 240
      local interface, 239
      process template, querying, 240
      remote interface, 239
   client applications, packaging, 241
   Human Task Manager, 242
   J2EE security, 206
   service invocation, 224
Application Link Enabling (ALE), 266
Application-Specific Business Object
   (ASBO), 23
applications
   adapters, 252
   client, packaging, 241
   enterprise, 299
   integration, 2
   order processing, 99
      activities, assigning, 105
      BackOrderProcess, 101
      business rules, administering, 149-151
      choice activities, 106-107
      correlation sets, 117-120
      CreateOrderProcess, 99-102
      CreditCheckingServiceInputBO, 131
      CreditCheckInterface, 129-130
      decision tables, 144-148
      empty actions, 109
      events, 120-122
      fault handling, 114-115
      faults, defining, 107-108
      human tasks, 109-111
      long-running processes, 108
      mapping, 129-131
      partner operations, invoking, 104-105
      receive choice activity, 116-117

   reference partners, adding, 103
   rule groups, creating, 144-145, 148
   scopes, adding, 114
   ShipOrderProcess, 101
   VerifyCreditAndProcessOrderProcess,
      101
   while loop, 111-112
   user, tracing, 212-213
   WPS, not starting, 210
architecture
   adapters
      CCI, 255
      Enterprise Discovery, 256
      inbound processing, 256
      outbound processing, 255
      RAR files, 257
      SPIs, 255
   BPC Explorer, 183
   high-level, 305
   logging, 189
   logical
      Business Monitor, 301
      monitor models, 303
   SCA (Service Component Architecture)
      assembly diagrams, 18-19
      capabilities, 14
      components. See components
      definition, 7-8
      overview, 16-18, 24-25
      relationship with BPEL, 38
   SOA (Service-Oriented Architecture), 4-5
   WPS architectural model, 17
as-is business models, 275
ASBO (Application-Specific Business
   Object), 23
Assemble phase (SOA), 6
assembly diagrams
   BSMs, 164
   JDBC adapters, 264
   modules, 43
   SCA, 18-19
assembly editor (WID), 57
   action bar, 57
   binding types, 59-60
   canvas, 57
   palette, 58-59
   properties view, 57
Assign activity, 30, 55
assigning
   activities, 105
   administrative roles, 204
asynchronous invocation, 20
asynchronous invocation with callback, 20
asynchronous service invocation, 225-226

attributes
  business items, 283-284
  nested business objects, 50
  simple business objects, 47-48
authentication, 199
authorization, 199
automation (process), 2, 12

B

background installations (WPS), 358-359
BackOrderProcess interface, 101
  correlation sets, 117-120
  events, 120-122
  fault handling, 114-115
  receive choice activity, 116-117
  scopes, adding, 114
BAM (Business Activity Monitoring), 296.
  See also Business Monitor
BAPI (Business Applications Programming
  Interface), 266
BFM APIs, 238-239
BGs (business graphs), 22
bindings
  types, 59-60
  WESB, 338
BMD, installing, 298-301, 380-383
  database/process server credentials, 382
  IDE target directories, 381
  installation options, 381
  properties, 299
  related enterprise applications, 299
  test monitor server, 300
  welcome screen, 380
BOChangeSummary, 16
BOCopy, 16
BODataObject, 16
BOEquality, 16
BOEventSummary, 16
BOF (business object framework), 232
  BOChangeSummary, 16
  BOCopy, 16
  BODataObject, 16
  BOEquality, 16
  BOEventSummary, 16
  BOFactory, 16
  BOType, 16
  BOTypeMetaData, 16
  BOXMLDocument, 16
  BOXMLSerializer, 16, 244
  data abstractions, 15
  maps. *See* business object maps
  overview, 13-14
BOFactory, 16
bottom-up approach (assembly diagrams), 18
BOType, 16

BOTypeMetaData, 16
BOXMLDocument, 16
BOXMLSerializer, 16, 244
BPC (business process choreographer),
  78, 181
  Event Collector, 193
  Explorer, 183
    architecture, 183
    components, 183
    definition, 182
    initial screen, 185
    installing, 182-184
    launching, 183
    navigation pane, 185
    process instances, starting, 185-186
    processes, viewing, 187-188
    tasks, 186
  Observer (BPCO), 193
    initial screen, 196
    installing, 194-195
    logging, enabling, 195
    navigation pane, 196
    overview, 196
    reports, 196
  security roles, mapping, 206-208
  WPS, 78, 81
BPCO (Business Process Choreographer
  Observer), 193
  initial screen, 196
  installing, 194-195
  logging, enabling, 195
  navigation pane, 196
  overview, 196
  reports, 196
BPEL (Business Process Execution
  Language), 4
  activities
    definition, 29
    Fault Activities, 32
    monitor models, 309
    Service Activities, 30
    Structured Activities, 30-32
  BPEL4People, 35
  Business Modeler mapping, 289
  business rules, 142
  CEI logging, enabling, 307-308
  Compensation Handlers, 34
  correlation sets, 33, 117-120
    activity associations, 119
    creating, 118
  definition, 28
  Event Handlers, 34
  events, 120-122
  expression language, 33
  extensions, 35

Fault Handlers, 33, 114-115
interaction model, 28
order processing application, 99
 activities, assigning, 105
 BackOrderProcess, 101
 business rules, administering, 149-151
 choice activities, 106-107
 CreateOrderProcess, 99-102
 CreditCheckingServiceInputBO, 131
 CreditCheckInterface, 129-130
 decision tables, 144-148
 empty actions, 109
 faults, defining, 107-108
 human tasks, 109-111
 long-running business processes, 108
 mapping, 129-131
 partner operations, invoking, 104-105
 reference partners, adding, 103
 rule groups, creating, 144-145, 148
 ShipOrderProcess, 101
 VerifyCreditAndProcessOrderProcess, 101
 while loop, 111-112
partnerLinks, 29
partners, 29
process illustration, 28-29
processes, versioning, 216-217
receive choice activity, 116-117
relationship with SCA (Service Component Architecture), 38
scopes, 33, 114
selectors, 152
supported standards, 28
variables, 29
versioning, 37-38
definition, 8
BPEL4People, 35
BRGs (business rule groups), 142
BRM (Business Rules Manager), 149
decision tables
 saving, 150
 values, entering, 150
 viewing, 149
installing, 149
Publish and Revert link, 151
BSMs (business state machines), 155
assembly diagram, 164
creating, 159-163
 completing, 163
 correlation property, 159
 invoke definition, 162
 names, 159
 references, adding, 161
 skeleton, 160
 variables, initializing, 162

definition, 155
deploying, 165
editor, 160-161
interface, 158
state diagrams, 156-158
template, 165
buses (WESB), 347
Business Activity Monitoring (BAM), 296
business analysts, 13
Business Application Services, 4
Business Applications Programming Interface (BAPI), 266
business drivers, 275
business graphs, programming
change summary, 236-237
instances, creating, 234
objects, customizing, 235
printing, 235-236
business integration
application integration, 2
business graphs
 change summary, 236-237
 instances, creating, 234
 objects, customizing, 235
 printing, 235-236
business object framework
 BOChangeSummary, 16
 BOCopy, 16
 BODataObject, 16
 BOEquality, 16
 BOEventSummary, 16
 BOFactory, 16
 BOType, 16
 BOTypeMetaData, 16
 BOXMLDocument, 16
 BOXMLSerializer, 16
 data abstractions, 15
 overview, 13-14
business objects, programming, 232-233
challenges, list of, 2
cheat sheet, 43
connectivity, 2
IBM's vision of business integration, 2
integration broker scenario, 12
overview, 1
patterns
 Disconnected Object pattern, 22
 Event pattern, 22-23
 overview, 11, 21
 Plain Business Object pattern, 22
process automation, 2, 12
programming model, 7
requirements, 3
separation of roles, 13

WID solution
  libraries, 44
  mediation modules, 43
  modules, 43
business items, 275, 282
  attributes, 283-284
  creating, 282
  exporting, 288-290
  importing, 284-285
business measures, 281, 290-291, 303
Business Modeler. *See also* business modeling
  advanced version, 279
  BPEL constructs, 289
  business items, 282
    attributes, 283-284
    creating, 282
    exporting, 288-290
    importing, 284-285
  business measures, 290-291
  catalogs, 280
  editions, 367
  installation, 274
    stand-alone installation, 367-369
    WID plug-in installation, 369-372
  launching, 276
  projects
    creating, 277
    layouts, 278
    modeling modes, 279
    naming, 280
  Quickstart wizard, 277
  welcome screen, 276
  workspaces, 276
business modeling
  as-is models, 275
  business drivers, 275
  business items, 275, 282
    attributes, 283-284
    creating, 282
    exporting, 288-290
    importing, 284-285
  business measures, 281, 290-291
  Business Modeler
    advanced version, 279
    BPEL constructs, 289
    catalogs, 280
    installing, 274
    launching, 276
    layouts, 278
    modeling modes, 279
    naming projects, 280
    projects, creating, 277
    Quickstart wizard, 277
    welcome screen, 276
    workspace storage, 276

business processes, 285
business rules, 275
business simulation, 291-292
  error checking, 287
  map nodes, 287
  process diagrams, 280-281, 286
  resources, 275
  subtypes, 275
  tasks, creating, 285-286
Business Monitor
  components, 296
  high-level architecture, 305
  installing, 298, 373-379
    dashboard server, 378
    DB2 usernames/passwords, 375
    installation types, 374
    portal components, 377
    target directories, 375-377
    welcome screen, 373
    WPS usernames/passwords, 376
  instrumentation, 301
  logical architecture, 301
business monitoring
  dashboards, 302-303
  data mart models, 304
  KPIs, 302
  monitor models
    BPEL activities, 309
    counters, 311-313
    creating with MME, 308-310
    dashboard, 317
    deploying, 316
    dimensions, 314
    KPIs, 315
    logical architecture, 303
    measures, 314
    metrics, 313-314
    monitor EAR files, 316
    monitoring context, 304
    naming, 308
    testing, 317
    triggers, 310-311
Business Object Editor, 47
business object framework. *See* BOF
business object maps
  creating, 132-134
    Business Object Map Editor, 133
    input/output business objects,
      choosing, 132
    links, 134
    names, 132
  editing, 133
  order processing application, 129-131
  WPS, 78

business objects
  CustomerBO, 131
  input/output, choosing, 132
  nested, 49-50
  programming, 232-233
  simple
    attributes, 47-48
    creating, 46-49
business process choreographer. *See* BPC
Business Process command (New menu), 54
business process container setting
    (Administrative Console), 192
Business Process Execution Language.
    See BPEL
business processes
  business process choreographer. *See* BPC
  business process execution language.
    See BPEL
  correlation sets, 117-120
    activity associations, 119
    creating, 118
  creating, 54
  definition, 3, 23, 27-28
  events, 120-122
  fault handling, 114-115
  illustration, 28-29
  initiating with APIs, 239
    EJB access, 240
    input messages, 240
    local interface, 239
    process template, querying, 240
    remote interface, 239
  long-running, 214
    creating, 108
    definition, 35
    empty actions, 109
    human tasks, 109-111
    transactions, 36-37
    while loop, 111-112
  order processing application, 99
    activities, assigning, 105
    BackOrderProcess, 101, 114-120
    business rules, administering, 149-151
    choice activities, 106-107
    CreateOrderProcess, 99-102
    CreditCheckingServiceInputBO, 131
    CreditCheckInterface, 129-130
    decision tables, 144-148
    empty actions, 109
    faults, defining, 107-108
    human tasks, 109-111
    long-running business processes, 108
    mapping, 129-131
    partner operations, invoking, 104-105
    reference partners, adding, 103

  rule groups, creating, 144-145, 148
  ShipOrderProcess, 101
  VerifyCreditAndProcessOrderProcess,
    101
  while loop, 111-112
process automation, 2, 12
receive choice activity, 116-117
scopes, adding, 114
selectors, 152
short-running
  activities, assigning, 105
  choice activities, 106-107
  creating, 102
  definition, 35
  faults, defining, 107-108
  partner operations, invoking, 104-105
  reference partners, adding, 103
  transactions, 36
versioning, 37-38
  BPEL, 216-217
  WID, 214-216
viewing BPC Explorer, 187-188
business rules, 142
  administration, 149-151
  BPEL, 142
  business modeling, 275
  decision tables, 143
  exporting, 151
  externalized, 142
  groups, 142
  inheritance, 143
  managing, 149-151
  rulesets, 143
  selectors, compared, 152
  WID, 142
  WPS, 78
Business Rules Manager. *See* BRM
Business Services
  assembly editor, 58
  definition, 5
business simulation modeling, 291-292
business state machines. *See* BSMs

C

callbacks, 225-226
canvas
  assembly editor, 57
  process editor, 54
catalogs (Business Modeler), 280
Catch activity, 32
Catch All activity, 32
CBEs (Common Base Events), 190-191
CCI (Common Client Interface), 255
CDs (installation WAT), 394-395

CEI (Common Event Infrastructure), 190
    Common Base Events (CBEs), 190-191
    configuration, 356-357
    enabling, 191-192
    logging, 306-308
    monitoring, 192
    WPS, 77
cells
    definition, 83
    WPS, 83-87
cheat sheets (business integration), 43
Cheat Sheets command (Help menu), 43
checkCredit method, 223
choice activities, 106-107
    process editor, 55
    Visual Snippet Editor palette, 63
choosing
    Business Modeler project layouts, 278
    discovery objects, 262
    enterprise service resource adapters, 260
    workspaces, 42
claiming tasks, 186
classes
    ClientObjectWrapper, 241
    ServiceManager, 19-20, 220
classifier catalogs, 280
client applications, packaging, 241
client model components (BPC Explorer), 183
ClientObjectWrapper class, 241
Cloudscape database support, 380
cluster members, 87
clustering
    horizontal, 88
    MEs, 90
    topologies
        multiple-cluster, 94-97
        resources, 97
        single-cluster, 92-93
    vertical, 88
    WPS, 87-89
        cluster members, 87
        components, 89-90
        SI Bus, 90-92
        transaction failovers, 89
        workload distribution, 87
com.ibm.websphere.bo package, 16
command-line utilities. See utilities
commands. See also utilities
    File menu
        Export, 64
        Import, 172
        New, Business Process, 102
        New, Project, Module, 52
    Help menu, Cheat Sheets, 43
    installall, 387

New menu
    Business Process, 54
    Interface, 50
comment node (Visual Snippet Editor palette), 63
Common Activities (process editor), 55
Common Base Events (CBEs), 190-191
Common Client Interface (CCI), 255
Common Event Infrastructure. See CEI
communication of WPS and adapters, 253
compensate activity (process editor), 56
Compensation Handlers (BPEL), 34
components. See also business processes
    BAM, 296
    binding types, 59-60
    BPC Explorer, 183
    Business Monitor, 296
    business service, 58
    CreditCheckTest, 220
        Java reference, 221
        method skeleton, 222
        properties, 222
        qualifiers, 227-228
        reference interface, 221
        service invocation, 223
        service locator, 222
    definition, 19
    developers, 13
    exports, 20
    imports, 20
    invoking, 19-20
    JDBC adapters
        assembly diagram, 264
        build path settings, 260
        creating, 258-259, 263-264
        dependencies, 260
        discovery agent settings, 261
        enterprise service resource adapters, selecting, 260
        objects for discovery, selecting, 262
        properties, 262
        RAR file, importing, 259
        testing, 264-265
        tree structure, 263
    mapping, 128
    mediation flows, 340
    SCA, 212
    SOA Lifecycle, 75
    stand-alone references, 21
    testing, 67
    tracing, 211
    WPS, 76
        clustering, 89-90
        databases, 79-81
    WSDL, 171

concepts, 324
configurator role, 204
configuring
    CEI (Common Event Infrastructure), 356-
        357
    security, 203-205
    test servers, 68
    WPS, 85
connectivity, 2
Connector Import window, 259
consoles
    Administrative
        business process container setting, 192
        business rules, exporting, 151
        CEI monitoring, 192
        human task container setting, 192
        WESB, 343
        WPS, 85
    WID, 69-71
    WSRR, 327
constraints (attributes), 48
Control Activities, 55-56
control structures, 63
correlation property (BSMs), 159
correlation sets (business processes), 33,
    117-118, 120
    activity associations, 119
    creating, 118
counters
    creating, 311-313
    triggers/metrics/KPIs relationships, 306
Create Property dialog box, 118
CreateOrderProcess, 99-101
    creating, 102
    services, invoking, 129
CreditCheckingServiceInputBO, 131
CreditCheckInterface, 129-130
CreditCheckRG, 144
CreditCheckServiceInterface, 130
CreditCheckServiceInterfacePartner, 222
CreditCheckTest
    Java component, 220
        Java reference, 221
        method skeleton, 222
        properties, 222
        reference interface, 221
        service invocation, 223
        service locator, 222
    qualifiers
        defining, 227
        interface, 227
        reference, 228
current-state models, 275
CustomerBO, 131

customizing
    adapters, 268-271
    business graph objects, 235
    logging, 210-212
    mediation primitives, 341
    WPS profiles, 82

D
dashboards
    monitor models, 317
    servers, 378
    views, 302-303
data
    abstractions
        instance data, 15
        services. *See* services
        type metadata, 15
        WebSphere implementations, 15
    catalogs, 280
    exchange patterns
        definition, 21
        Disconnected Object pattern, 22
        Event pattern, 22-23
        Plain Business Object pattern, 22
    integrity, 200
data maps. *See* business object maps
data mart models, 304
databases
    CEI (Common Event Infrastructure),
        356-357
    Cloudscape, 380
    lookup mediation primitives, 341
    WPS
        access, 208-209
        components, 79-81
decision tables, 143-144
    BRMs, 149-150
    creating, 145, 148
    dimensions, 146
    expanding, 147
    template conversion, 147
    values, adding, 147
default (SCA) bindings, 338
deleting WPS profiles, 360
dependencies
    JDBC adapters, 260
    modules, 52-53
    serviceDeploy zip files, 66
Deploy phase (SOA), 6
deploying
    BSMs, 165
    libraries, 44
    mediation modules, 43, 345-347
    modules, 43
    monitor models, 316

destinations
    partitioning, 92-93
    rule groups, 148
development manager profile (WPS), 82
Development Services, 5
diagrams
    dashboards, 302
    SCA (Service Component Architecture)
        assembly diagrams, 18-19
dialog boxes
    Add Service Registry Preferences, 390
    Create Property, 118
    Import, 172
    Interface Selection, 110
    New Rule Group, 144
    Select Operation, 110
dimensional views (dashboards), 303
dimensions, creating, 314
directories
    target
        Business Monitor, 377
        dashboard servers, 378
    WPS_HOME, 359-360
Disconnected Object pattern, 22
discovery agents, 261
distributing workloads, 87
documents (WSRR)
    governance, 329-330
    loading, 327
    searching, 331-332
drivers (business), 275

E

EAR files
    exporting, 64, 346
    monitor, 316
Eclipse 3.0 framework, 41, 72
Eclipse plug-ins
    WAT (WebSphere Adapter Toolkit)
        definition, 393
        installation, 393-395
        online documentation, 394
        verifying, 395-396
    WSRR (WebSphere Service Registry and
        Repository) plug-in, 388-391
Eclipse Update Manager, opening, 393
editing response files, 358-359
editors
    assembly editor (WID), 57
        action bar, 57
        binding types, 59-60
        canvas, 57
        palette, 58-59
        properties view, 57

Business Object Editor, 47
Human Task Editor, 110
Interface Map Editor, 135
Monitor Model Editor. *See* MME
process editor (WID), 54-56
Relationship Editor, 139-141
Visual Snippet Editor, 61-64
    choice activities, 107
    palette, 63
    visual snippets, 243-248
    Visual snippets view, 62
EIS bindings, 60, 338
EJB, accessing, 240
Email adapters, 266
EMD (Enterprise Metadata Discovery), 256
empty actions
    business processes, adding, 109
    process editor, 55
    replacing with human tasks, 109
Empty activity, 30
emulators (integration test client), 71
enabling
    BPCO logging, 195
    CEI, 191-192, 306-308
    governance, 329
    security, 200-202
    tracing, 211
endpoint lookup mediation primitives, 341
enterprise applications, 299
Enterprise Metadata Discovery (EMD), 256
Enterprise Service Bus (ESB), 4, 335
Enterprise Service Discovery (ESD), 256
error checking business modeling, 287
Error-Handling Activities (process editor), 56
ESB (Enterprise Service Bus), 4, 335
ESD (Enterprise Service Discovery), 256
Event Collector, 193
event emitter mediation primitives, 341
Event pattern, 22-23
events
    business processes, 120-122
    handlers (BPEL), 34
    integration test client, 71
    monitor models, 309
    sequencing, 229-231
expanding decision tables, 147
Export command (File menu), 64
export reference (assembly editor), 58
export values (dashboards), 303
exporting
    business items, 288-290
    business rules, 151
    definition, 20
    EAR files, 346

mediation flows, 153
modules as, 64
    EAR files, 64
    PI files, 66
    zip files, 65-66
expressions
    language, 33
    Visual Snippet Editor palette, 63
Extensible Markup Language (XML), 28
Extensible Stylesheet Language (XSLT), 128
extensions (BPEL), 35
externalized business rules, 142

F

fail mediation primitives, 341
failovers (transaction), 89
Fault Activities (BPEL), 32
Fault Handler activity, 32
faults, 33
    defining, 107-108
    handling
        BPEL, 33
        business processes, 114-115
    interfaces, 51
File menu commands
    Export, 64
    Import, 172
    New, Business Process, 102
    New, Project, Module, 52
files
    EAR
        exporting, 64, 346
        monitor, 316
    flat file adapters, 266
    monitoring, 289
    PI, 66
    RAR, 257-259
    response files, editing, 358-359
    serviceDeploy zip, 66
    WPS installation log, 213
    WSDL, publishing to WSRR, 334
    XSD, 327
    zip, 65-66
flat file adapters, 266
Flow activity, 32
follow-on tasks, 168
for each control structure (Visual Snippet
    Editor palette), 63
free-form layout (Business Modeler projects),
    278
FTP adapters, 266
functional content (WPS), 77-79

G

Gartner Group, 3
gauges (dashboards), 303
GBO (Generic Business Object), 23
getURI method, 246
global security, enabling, 201-202
global transactions, 37
governance, WSRR documents, 323-325
    enabling, 329
    notification, 329-330
    state, transitioning, 330
groups
    business rules (BRGs), 142
    rule
        creating, 144-145
        multiple destinations, 148

H

handlers
    Compensation Handlers, 34
    Event Handlers, 34
    Fault Handlers, 33, 114-115
Help menu commands, Cheat Sheets, 43
high-level architecture (Business
    Monitor), 305
horizontal clustering, 88
HTM (Human Task Manager), 242
human task activity, 55
Human Task Editor, 110
human tasks
    ad hoc, 167-168
    administrative, 167
    assembly editor, 58
    container setting, 192
    empty action replacement, 109
    inline, 110, 167
    long-running business processes,109-111
    originating, 166
    participating, 166
    properties, 110
    pure, 166
    stand-alone, 110, 167
    user interfaces, 168-170

I

IBM's vision of business integration, 2
IDE target directories (BMD), 381
identity relationships, 127
impact analysis (WSRR), 328
implementation qualifiers, 24
Import dialog box, 172
Import menu command (File menu), 172
import reference (assembly editor), 58
Import/Export/Stand-alone References, 58

importing
  business items, 284-285
  definition, 20
  inline WSDLs, 177
  JDBC adapter RAR files, 259
  mediation flows, 153
  WSDLs, 172-175
    expanded file listings, 174
    as HTTP resources, 172
    options, 173
    as WSDL/Interface, 174
inbound integration (JCA adapters), 253
inbound processing (adapters), 256
Information Services, 4
infrastructure (WPS), 79-81
Infrastructure Services, 5
initializing variables, 162
inline human tasks, 110, 167
inline WSDLs, 177
input
  business objects, 132
  messages, 240
  Web services, 172
install utility, 359
installall command, 387
installall script, 387
installation
  BMD, 298-301, 380-383
    database/process server credentials, 382
    installation options, 381
    properties, 299
    related enterprise applications, 299
    target directories, 381
    test monitor server, 300
    welcome screen, 380
  BPC Explorer, 182-184
  BPCO, 194-195
  BRM, 149
  Business Modeler, 274
    stand-alone installation, 367-369
    WID plug-in installation, 369-372
  Business Monitor, 298, 373-379
    dashboard server, 378
    DB2 usernames/passwords, 375
    installation types, 374
    portal components, 377
    target directories, 375-377
    welcome screen, 373
    WPS usernames/passwords, 376
  SAP adapters, 267
  Siebel adapters, 268
  WAT (WebSphere Adapter Toolkit), 393
    with product CDs, 394-395
    with RPU (Rational Product Updater),
      393-394
    verifying, 395-396

WESB, 342
WID (WebSphere Integration Developer),
  41, 361-364
WPS (WebSphere Process Server), 85, 349
  Installation Wizard for WebSphere
    Process Server for Multiplatforms,
    349-353
  log files, 213
  silent installations, 358-359
  WPS_HOME installation directory,
    359-360
WSRR (WebSphere Service Registry and
  Repository), 324-325, 385-391
Installation Wizard for WebSphere Process
  Server for Multiplatforms, 349-353
instances
  business graphs, 234
  business measures, 303
  business objects, 232-233
  data, 15
  metadata, 15
  processes, starting, 185-186
instrumentation, 301
integration broker scenario, 12
integration buses (WESB), 343
Integration Module Export window, 64
integration specialists, 13
integration test client (WID), 67, 70-71
integrity of data, 200
interaction model (BPEL), 28
Interaction Services, 4
Interface command (New menu), 50
Interface Map Editor, 135
interface maps, 127
  assembly editor, 59
  creating, 135-137
    Interface Map Editor, 135
    names, 135
    output, 137
    parameters, 136
  WPS, 78
interface partners, 29
interface qualifiers, 24
Interface Selection dialog box, 110
interfaces
  APIs
    business flow manager, 238-239
    business processes, initiating, 239-240
    client applications, packaging, 241
    Human Task Manager, 242
    J2EE security, 206
    service invocation, 224
  BackOrderProcess
    correlation sets, 117-120
    events, 120-122
    fault handling, 114-115

receive choice activity, 116-117
   scopes, adding, 114
BAPI, 266
BSM, 158
CCI, 255
creating, 50-51
faults, adding, 51
qualifiers, 227
request-response operation, adding, 51
SPIs, 238, 255
SQI, 266
user interfaces, 168-170
WSRR user interface, 324
invocation model (SOA), 7
invocation styles, 219
Invoke activity, 30, 55
invokeAsyncWithCallback API, 225
invoking
   components, 19-20
   partner operations, 104-105
   services
      asynchronously, 225-226
      with SCA, 220-223

J

J2C authentication aliases, 209
J2EE security, 205-206
Java, 33
   assembly editor, 58
   JVM logs, 210
   references, service invocations, 220-223
   snippets, variable initialization, 162
   version 2 security, 202
   Visual Snippet Editor palette, 63
JCA adapters, 252-253
JDBC adapters
   creating, 258-259, 263-264
      assembly diagrams, 264
      build path settings, 260
      dependencies, 260
      enterprise service resource adapters,
         selecting, 260
      objects for discovery, selecting, 262
      properties, 262
      RAR file, importing, 259
      tree structure, 263
   discovery agent settings, 261
   testing, 264-265
JMS bindings, 60, 338
Join activity session qualifier, 227
JSF components (BPC Explorer), 183
JVM logs, 210

K–L

KPIs (Key Performance Indicators), 302
   creating, 315
   dashboard view, 303
   definition, 302
   KPI context, 304
   triggers/counters/metrics
      relationships, 306

launching. *See also* starting
   BPC Explorer, 183
   Business Modeler, 276
layouts (Business Modeler projects), 278
LDAP servers, security, 203-205
legacy adapters, 252
libraries
   contents, 46
   creating, 44-46
   definition, 44
   deploying, 44
   WID business integration solution, 44
licenses (WPS), 84
lifecycles
   governance of WSRR, 323-325
      enabling, 329
      notification, 329-330
      state, transitioning, 330
   SOA, 6, 273
links
   BO maps, 134
   Publish and Revert (BRM), 151
listings
   asynchronous service invocation, 225-226
   business graphs
      change summary, 236-237
      instances, creating, 234
      objects, customizing, 235
      printing, 235-236
   business object instances, creating,
      232-233
   business processes, initiating
      EJB access, 240
      input messages, 240
      local interface, 239
      process template, querying, 240
      remote interface, 239
   callbacks, 225-226
   HTM API local interface reference, 242
   Java snippet for variable initialization, 162
   method skeleton, 222
   service invocations
      API, 224
      SCA, 223

service locators for
rule groups, 222
WSDL references, 224
XPath expression for shipper names, 314
logging
BPCO, 195
CEI, 306-308
customizing, 210-212
file storage, 210
JVM logs, 210
process logs, 210
WID, 71
WPS
architecture, 189
installation log files, 213
logical architecture
Business Monitor, 301
monitor models, 303
long-running business processes
creating, 108
definition, 35
empty actions, 109
human tasks, 109-111
state, 214
transactions, 36-37
while loop, 111-112

M

Manage phase (SOA), 6
Management Services, 5
map nodes (business modeling), 287
maps, 126
business object, 127
Business Object Map Editor, 133
creating, 132-134
input/output business objects,
choosing, 132
links, 134
names, 132
WPS, 78
components, 128
interface, 127
creating, 135-137
Interface Map Editor, 135
names, 135
output, 137
parameters, 136
WPS, 78
mediation modules, 128
relationship, 78, 127-128
security roles, 206-208
Markets in Financial Instruments Directive
(MiFID), 210
MC (monitoring context), 304
ME (messaging engine), 90, 96

measures, creating, 314
mediations, 153
flows, 126
editing, 154
exports/imports, 153
Mediation Flow editor, 154
WESB, 340
WPS, 77
modules, 43, 153
creating in WID, 344-345
definition, 43
deploying, 43, 345-347
mapping, 128
WESB, 337-339
primitives, 154
endpoint lookup mediation
primitives, 341
event emitter mediation primitives, 341
fail mediation primitives, 341
message element setter mediation
primitives, 341
message filter mediation
primitives, 341
Message Logger mediation primitive,
213-214
stop mediation primitives, 341
WESB, 340-341
XSLT mediation primitives, 341
WESB, 337
WID, 153
message element setter mediation
primitives, 341
message filter mediation primitives, 341
message logger mediation primitive,
213-214, 341
messages
input, 240
WPS, 79, 208-209
messaging engine (ME), 90, 96
methods
checkCredit, 223
getURI, 246
onRetrieveCreditRatingResponse, 226
printOrderBG, 235-236
skeletons, 222
metrics
creating, 313-314
triggers/counters/KPIs relationships, 306
microflows. See short-running business
processes
MiFID (Markets in Financial Instruments
Directive), 210
MME (Monitor Model Editor), 303
CEI logging, 306-308

monitor model
    BPEL activities, 309
    counters, 306, 311-313
    creating, 308-310
    dashboard, 317
    deploying, 316
    dimensions, 314
    KPIs, 306, 315
    measures, 314
    metrics, 306, 313-314
    monitor EAR files, 316
    naming, 308
    testing, 317
    triggers, 306, 310-311
Model phase (SOA), 6
modules
    assembly diagrams, 43
    creating, 52-53
    definition, 43
    dependencies, 52-53
    deploying, 43
    exporting as, 64
        EAR files, 64
        PI files, 66
        zip files, 65-66
    mediation, 43, 153
        creating in WID, 344-345
        definition, 43
        deploying, 43, 345-347
        mapping, 128
        WESB, 337-339
    structure, 53
    testing, 67
    WID business integration solution, 43
monitor EAR files, 316
Monitor Model Editor. *See* MME
monitor models
    BPEL activities, 309
    counters, 311-313
    creating with MME, 308-310
    dashboard, 317
    deploying, 316
    dimensions, 314
    KPIs, 315
    logical architecture, 303
    measures, 314
    metrics, 313-314
    monitor EAR files, 316
    monitoring context, 304
    naming, 308
    testing, 317
    triggers, 310-311
monitor role, 204
Monitor Toolkit. *See* MME

monitoring
    BAM, 296
    BMD, 298-301
    Business Monitor
        components, 296
        dashboard server, 378
        DB2 usernames/passwords, 375
        high-level architecture, 305
        installing, 298, 373-379
        instrumentation, 301
        logical architecture, 301
        portal components, 377
        target directories, 375-377
        welcome screen, 373
        WPS usernames/passwords, 376
    CEI, 192
    data mart models, 304
    integration test client, 71
    monitor models
        BPEL activities, 309
        counters, 306, 311-313
        creating with MME, 308-310
        dashboard, 317
        deploying, 316
        dimensions, 314
        KPIs, 306, 315
        logical architecture, 303
        measures, 314
        metrics, 306, 313-314
        monitor EAR files, 316
        monitoring context, 304
        naming, 308
        testing, 317
        triggers, 306, 310-311
    observing, compared, 189
monitoring context (MC), 304
monitoring files, creating, 289
MQ bindings, 338
multiple-cluster topologies, 94-97

N

names
    BO maps, 132
    BSMs, 159
    Business Modeler projects, 280
    interface maps, 135
    monitor models, 308
    relationships, 138
    visual snippets, 243
navigation pane
    BPC Explorer, 185
    BPCO, 196
nesting
    business objects, 49-50
    scopes, 121
network deployment configuration (WPS), 85

New Business Object window, 47
New Business Process wizard, 102
New Decision Table window, 145
New Interface Wizard, 50
New menu commands
    Business Process, 54
    Interface, 50
New Module wizard, 52
New Rule Group dialog box, 144
New, Business Process command (File
    menu), 102
New, Project, Module command (File
    menu), 52
nodes
    agents, 83
    definition, 83
    Deployment Manager, federating, 82
    map, 287
    Visual Snippet Editor palette, 63
    WPS, 83-85
nonidentity relationships, 127
notification framework (WSRR governance),
    329-330

O

OASIS, 8
objects
    ASBO (Application-Specific Business
        Object), 23
    business graphs
        change summary, 236-237
        customizing, 235
    business objects
        CustomerBO, 131
        input/output, choosing, 132
        nested, 49-50
        programming, 232-233
        simple, 47-49
    business object framework
        BOChangeSummary, 16
        BOCopy, 16
        BODataObject, 16
        BOEquality, 16
        BOEventSummary, 16
        BOFactory, 16
        BOType, 16
        BOTypeMetaData, 16
        BOXMLDocument, 16
        BOXMLSerializer, 16, 244
        data abstractions, 15
        maps. See business object maps
        overview, 13-14
    GBO (Generic Business Object), 23
    ProcessTemplateData, 240
    SDOs (Service Data Objects), 8

Observer, 193
    initial screen, 196
    installing, 194-195
    logging, enabling, 195
    navigation pane, 196
    overview, 196
    reports, 196
observing, 189
one-way operations, 101
onRetrieveCreditRatingResponse method, 226
ontology, 326
operations
    one-way, 101
    partners, invoking, 104-105
    request-response, 51
    two-way, 101
operator role, 204
Order BSM
    assembly diagram, 164
    BSM editor, 160-161
    creating, 159-163
        completing, 163
        correlation property, 159
        invoke definition, 162
        names, 159
        references, adding, 161
        skeleton, 160
        variables, initializing, 162
    deploying, 165
    interface, 158
Order process, 156-158
order processing application, 99
    activities, assigning, 105
    BackOrderProcess, 101
        correlation sets, 117-120
        events, 120-122
        fault handling, 114-115
        receive choice activity, 116-117
        scopes, adding, 114
    business rules, administering, 149-151
    choice activities, 106-107
    CreateOrderProcess, 99-102
    CreditCheckingServiceInputBO, 131
    CreditCheckInterface, 129-130
    decision tables, 144-148
    empty actions, 109
    faults, defining, 107-108
    human tasks, 109-111
    long-running business processes, 108
    mapping, 129-131
    partner operations, invoking, 104-105
    reference partners, adding, 103
    rule groups, creating, 144-148
    ShipOrderProcess, 101
    VerifyCreditAndProcessOrderProcess, 101
    while loop, 111-112

OrderBG
    change summary, 236-237
    creating, 234
    objects, customizing, 235
    printing, 235-236
OrderBO, 131, 232-233
organization catalogs, 280
organizational view (dashboard), 303
originating human tasks, 166
outbound integration (JCA adapters), 253
outbound processing (adapters), 255
output
    business objects, 132
    interface maps, 137
    Web services, 172
OWL (Web Ontology Language), 326

P

packaging client applications, 241
palettes
    assembly editor, 58-59
    BSM editor, 160-161
    process editor, 55-56
    Visual Snippet Editor, 63
Parallel activity, 32, 56
parameters (interface maps), 136
participating human tasks, 166
partitioning destinations, 92-93
Partner Services, 4
partnerLinks (BPEL), 29
partners
    BPEL, 29
    operations, 104-105
    reference, 103
passwords (Business Monitor), 376
patterns
    Disconnected Object pattern, 22
    Event pattern, 22-23
    overview, 11, 21
    Plain Business Object pattern, 22
pct utility, 359
pctWindows utility, 359
PI (project interchange) files, 66
Pick activity, 31
Plain Business Object pattern, 22
plug-ins
    Eclipse
        WAT, 393-395
        WSRR, 388-391
    installation, 369-372
primitives (mediations), 154
    endpoint lookup mediation
        primitives, 341
    event emitter mediation primitives, 341
    fail mediation primitives, 341

message element setter mediation primi-
    tives, 341
message filter mediation primitives, 341
Message Logger mediation primitive,
    213-214
stop mediation primitives, 341
WESB, 340-341
XSLT mediation primitives, 341
printing business graphs, 235-236
printOrderBG method, 235-236
privacy, 200
process automation, 2, 12
process catalogs, 280
process component (assembly editor), 58
process diagrams, 280-281, 286
process editor (WID), 54-56
    action bar, 54
    business processes, 54
    canvas, 54
    palette, 55-56
    properties view, 55
    trays, 55
process logs, 210
processes
    business process choreographer. See BPC
    business process execution language.
        See BPEL
    correlation sets, 117-120
    creating, 54
    definition, 3, 23, 27-28
    events, 120-122
    fault handling, 114-115
    illustration, 28-29
    initiating with APIs, 239-240
    long-running. See long-running business
        processes
    order processing application. See order
        processing application
    process automation, 2, 12
    receive choice activity, 116-117
    scopes, adding, 114
    selectors, 152
    short-running, 35-36, 102-108
    versioning, 37-38, 214-217
    viewing BPC Explorer, 187-188
ProcessTemplateData object, 240
profiles
    creating, 83
    WPS (WebSphere Process Server) profiles,
        82-83
        creating, 353-359
        deleting, 360
programming
    business graphs
        change summary, 236-237
        instances, creating, 234

objects, customizing, 235
    printing, 235-236
business integration, 7
business objects, 232-233
SCA
    qualifiers, 227-228
    services, invoking, 220-223
    WESB, 343
    WSDL references, 223-226
visual snippets
    BOXMLSerializer Service, choosing, 244
    creating, 243-248
    getURI method, 246
    inherited methods, 247
    Java method, 244
    methods, typing/wiring, 247
    naming, 243
Project Explorer view (WID), 259
project interchange (PI) files, 66
projects (Business Modeler)
    creating, 277
    layouts, 278
    modeling modes, 279
    naming, 280
properties
    BMD, 299
    correlation, 159
    custom adapters, 269
    human tasks, 110
    Java references, 222
    JDBC adapters, 262
    XSD files, 327
properties view
    assembly editor, 57
    process editor, 55
Publish and Revert link (BRM), 151
publishing WSDL files, 178-179, 334
pure human tasks, 166

Q

QoS (qualifiers), 23-24, 227
qualifiers, 227
    definition, 23, 227
    event sequencing, 230-231
    implementation qualifiers, 24
    interface qualifiers, 24, 227
    Join activity session, 227
    QoS, 23-24, 227
    reference qualifiers, 24, 228
    Security permission, 227
query catalogs, 280
querying
    templates, 240
    WSRR, 332
Quickstart wizard (Business Modeler), 277

R

RAR (Resource Adapter Archive) files, 257-259
Rational Product Updater (RPU), 393
Receive activity, 30, 55
receive choice activity
    business processes, 116-117
    process editor, 56
reference architecture (SOA), 4-5
reference partners
    definition, 29
    short-running business processes, 103
reference qualifiers, 24
references
    BSMs, 161
    Import/Export/Stand-alone, 58
    Java, 220-223
    qualifiers, 228
    WSDL, 223
        asynchronous service invocation, 225-226
        callbacks, 225-226
        service invocation API, 224
        service locator, 224
Relationship Editor, 139-141
Relationship Manager, 141-142
relationship maps (WPS), 78
relationships, 126
    creating, 138
        names, 138
        Relationship Editor, 139-141
        Relationship Manager, 141-142
        types, 139
    identity, 127
    maps, 127-128
    model, 138
    nonidentity, 127
repeat control structure (Visual Snippet Editor palette), 63
Reply activity, 30, 55
report catalogs, 280
reports
    BPCO, 196
    dashboards, 303
request-response operation, 51
Resource Adapter Archive files (RAR), 257-259
resource adapters, 253, 260
resource catalogs, 280
resources
    business modeling, 275
    clustering topologies, 97
response files, editing, 358-359
Re-throw activity, 32, 56
return node (Visual Snippet Editor palette), 63

roles
administrative, 204, 325
business analysts, 13
component developers, 13
definitions, 127
integration specialists, 13
security role mappings, 206-208
separation of, 13
solution deployers, 13
user, 325
root governance records, 330
RPU (Rational Product Updater), 393-394
rule group component (assembly editor), 58
rules
business rules, 142
administration, 149-151
BPEL, 142
business modeling, 275
decision tables, 143
exporting, 151
externalized, 142
groups, 142
inheritance, 143
rulesets, 143
selectors, compared, 152
WID, 142
groups
creating, 144-145
multiple destinations, 148
rulesets, 143

S

SAP adapters, 266-267
SAP Query Interface (SQI), 266
Sarbanes-Oxley Act (SOX), 210
saving decision tables, 150
SCA (Service Component Architecture)
architecture, 16-18, 24-25
assembly diagrams, 18-19
bindings, 60
capabilities, 14
components. *See also* business processes
definition, 19
exports, 20
imports, 20
invoking, 19-20
stand-alone references, 21
tracing, 212
definition, 7-8
invocation styles, 219
qualifiers, 227-228
relationship with BPEL, 38
runtime, 77
services, invoking, 220-223
Java reference, 221
method skeleton, 222

properties, 222
reference interface, 221
service invocation listing, 223
service locator, 222
WESB, 343
WSDL references, 223
asynchronous service invocation, 225-226
callbacks, 225-226
service invocation API, 224
service locator, 224
scaling up ME, 96
SCDL (Service Component Definition Language), 16
scenarios for business integration, 12
Scope activity, 31
scopes
BPEL, 33
business processes, 114
nesting, 121
process editor, 56
scripts, 387
SDOs (Service Data Objects), 8
searching WSRR documents, 331-332
security, 199
administrative roles, 204
authentication, 199
authorization, 199
BPC, 206-208
configuring, 203-205
enabling, 200-201
global, enabling, 201-202
integrity, 200
J2EE, 205-206
Java 2, 202
overview, 200
privacy, 200
security stack, 201
single sign-on, 200
WPS
applications not starting, 210
database access/messaging, 208-209
Security permission qualifier, 227
Select Operation dialog box, 110
selectors, 126
assembly editor, 59
BPEL, 152
business integration solution, 152
business rules, compared, 152
separation of roles, 13
sequence activities, 31, 56
sequencing events, 229-231
Server Overview window, 68-69
servers
dashboard, 378
LDAP, 203-205

test
    WESB in WID, 344
    WID, 68-69
test monitor, 300
WebSphere process server. *See* WPS
Service Activities (BPEL), 30
Service Component Architecture. *See* SCA
Service Component Definition Language
    (SCDL), 16
Service Data Objects (SDOs), 8
service locators
    rule groups, 222
    WSDL references, 224
Service Message Objects (SMOs), 213
Service-Oriented Architecture. *See* SOA
Service Provider Interfaces (SPIs), 238, 255
Service Registry in WID (WSRR), 332-335
    retrieval, 332-333
    WSDL files, publishing, 334
serviceDeploy utility, 65-66
serviceDeploy zip files, 66
ServiceManager class, 19-20, 220
services. *See also* SOA
    Access Services, 4
    BOChangeSummary, 16
    BOCopy, 16
    BODataObject, 16
    BOEquality, 16
    BOEventSummary, 16
    BOFactory, 16
    BOType, 16
    BOTypeMetaData, 16
    BOXMLDocument, 16
    BOXMLSerializer, 16, 244
    Business Application Services, 4
    Business Services, 5
    callbacks, 225-226
    definition, 3, 15
    Development Services, 5
    ESB (Enterprise Service Bus), 4, 335
    Information Services, 4
    Infrastructure Services, 5
    Interaction Services, 4
    invoking with SCA, 220-223
        asynchronously, 225-226
        Java reference, 221
        method skeleton, 222
        properties, 222
        reference interface, 221
        service invocation listing, 223
        service locator, 222
    Management Services, 5
    Partner Services, 4
    SCA (Service Component Architecture)
        architecture, 16-18, 24-25
        assembly diagrams, 18-19

capabilities, 14
components. *See* components
definition, 7-8
relationship with BPEL, 38
SDOs (Service Data Objects), 8
SOA Lifecycle, 75
Web
    input/output, 172
    technologies, 171
    WSDLs, 171-179
WESB, 336
    administrative console, 343
    buses, checking, 347
    installing, 342
    integration buses, 343
    mediation flows, 340
    mediation modules, 337-339, 344-347
    mediation primitives, 340-341
    mediations, 337
    SCA, 343
    service endpoint interaction
        support, 336
    test server in WID, 344
    WebSphere platform, 336
WPS, 76
WSRR, 322
    administrators, 325
    concepts, 324
    console, 327
    document searches, 331-332
    documents, loading, 327
    functionality, 334
    governance, 329-330
    governance lifecycle, 323-325
    impact analysis, 328
    installing, 324-325
    ontology, 326
    querying, 332
    semantic metadata support, 323
    Service Registry in WID, 332-335
    taxonomies, 326
    user interface, 324
    user role, 325
    XSD files, 327
setenv script, 387
shell sharing (WID), 72
ShipOrderProcess process, 101
short-running business processes
    activities assigning, 105
    choice activities, 106-107
    creating, 102
    definition, 35
    faults, defining, 107-108
    partner operations, invoking, 104-105
    reference partners, adding, 103
    transactions, 36

SI Bus, clustering, 90-92
Siebel adapters, 267-268
silent installations (WPS), 358-359
-silent option (pctWindows command), 359
simple business objects
    attributes, 47-48
    creating, 46-49
simulation snapshots, 291
single-cluster topologies, 92-93
single-server topologies, 92
single sign-on (SSO), 200
skeletons, 222
SMOs (Service Message Objects), 213
snapshots, 291
Snippet activity, 33, 55
snippets
    editing. See Visual Snippet Editor
    visual
        BOXMSerializer Service, choosing, 244
        creating, 243-247
        getURI method, 246
        inherited methods, 247
        Java method, 244
        methods, typing/wiring, 247
        naming, 243
        viewing, 248
SOA (Service-Oriented Architecture)
    Access Services, 4
    advantages, 9
    Business Application Services, 4
    business processes, 3
    Business Services, 5
    Development Services, 5
    Information Services, 4
    Infrastructure Services, 5
    Interaction Services, 4
    invocation model, 7
    lifecycle, 273
        Assemble phase, 6
        components, 75
        Deploy phase, 6
        illustration, 5
        Manage phase, 6
        Model phase, 6
        services, 75
    Management Services, 5
    overview, 3-4
    Partner Services, 4
    popularity, 3
    reference architecture, 4-5
solution deployers, 13
SOX (Sarbanes-Oxley Act), 210
SPIs (Service Provider Interfaces), 238, 255
SQI (SAP Query Interface), 266
SSO (single sign-on), 200

stand-alone configuration (WPS), 85
stand-alone human tasks, 110, 167
stand-alone installation (WebSphere Business Modeler), 367-369
stand-alone profile (WPS), 82
stand-alone references
    assembly editor, 58
    definition, 21
starting. See also launching
    business processes, 185-186, 240
    test servers, 68
    WID, 42, 364-365
    WPS, 86
state diagrams (Order process), 156-158
state machine component (assembly editor), 58
Stateless Session EJB bindings, 60
states (WSRR governance), 330
stop mediation primitives, 341
stopping WPS, 86
storing
    Business Modeler workspaces, 276
    workspaces, 42
    WPS logs, 210
Structured Activities (BPEL), 30-32
structures
    JDBC adapters, 263
    modules, 53
subtasks, 168
swimlane layouts (Business Modeler project), 278
Switch activity, 31
synchronous invocation, 20

T

tables (decision), 143
    BRM, 149-150
    creating, 145, 148
    dimensions, 146
    expanding, 147
    template conversion, 147
    values, adding, 147
target directories
    BMD, 381
    Business Monitor, 375-377
    dashboard servers, 378
tasks
    business modeling, 285-286
    claiming, 186
    human
        ad hoc, 167-168
        administrative, 167
        assembly editor, 58
        container setting, 192
        empty action replacement, 109

inline, 110, 167
long-running business processes,
   109-111
originating, 166
participating, 166
properties, 110
pure, 166
stand-alone, 110, 167
user interfaces, 168-170
working on, 186
taxonomics, 326
technology
   adapters, 252
   Web services, 171
templates
   BSMs, 165
   decision table conversion, 147
   querying, 240
Terminate activity, 32, 56
test configurations, 71
test monitor servers, 300
test servers
   WESB in WID, 344
   WID, 68-69
testing
   business modeling, 287
   JDBC adapters, 264-265
   monitor models, 317
   WID
      components, 67
      integration test client, 70-71
      modules, 67
      WSDLs, 175-177
Throw activity, 32, 56
throw nodes (Visual Snippet Editor palette),
   63
tokens, 292
toolkit. See WAT
top-down approach (assembly diagrams), 18
topologies (WPS)
   multiple-cluster, 94-97
   single-cluster, 92-93
   single-server, 92
tracing
   components, 211
   SCA components, 212
   user applications, 212-213
transactions
   coordinators, 37
   failovers, 89
   global transactions, 37
   in long-running processes, 36-37
   in short-running processes, 36
transitioning WSRR state, 330
trays (process editor), 55

tree structures (JDBC adapters), 263
triggers
   counters/metrics/KPIs relationships, 306
   creating, 310-311
troubleshooting
   business modeling, 287
   WID, 72
   WPS applications not starting, 210
two-way operations, 101
type metadata, 15
types
   binding, 59-60
   Business Monitor installation, 374
   relationships, 139

U

UML (Unified Modeling Language), 156
uninstallation of WPS (WebSphere Process
   Server), 360
updating WID (WebSphere Integration
   Developer), 366
user applications, tracing, 212-213
user interfaces
   User Interface Generator, 168-170
   WSRR, 324
user role (WSRR), 325
usernames (Business Monitor), 376
utilities
   Deployment Manager node, federating, 82
   install, 359
   pct, 359
   pctWindows, 359
   serviceDeploy, 65-66
   was profile, 360

V

validating WSDLs, 175-177
variables
   BPEL, 29
   initializing, 162
VerifyCreditAndProcessOrderProcess process,
   101
verifying WAT (WebSphere Adapter Toolkit)
   installation, 395-396
versioning
   BPEL processes, 37-38
   business processes
      BPEL, 216-217
      WID, 214-216
vertical clustering, 88
viewing
   business graphs change summary, 236-237
   business processes (BPC Explorer), 187-188
   dashboards, 302-303, 317
   decision tables, 149

logs, 71
properties
    assembly editor, 57
    process editor, 55
visual snippets, 62, 248
WID
    Console, 71
    Project Explorer, 259
visual programming, visual snippet creation,
    243-247
    BOXMLSerializer Service, choosing, 244
    getURI method, 246
    inherited methods, 247
    Java method, 244
    methods, typing/wiring, 247
    naming, 243
    viewing, 248
Visual Snippet Editor, 61-64
    choice activities, 107
    palette, 63
    visual snippets
        BOXMLSerializer Service, 244
        creating, 243-247
        getURI method, 246
        inherited methods, 247
        Java method, 244
        methods, typing/wiring, 247
        naming, 243
        viewing, 62, 248
visual snippets
    BOXMLSerializer Service, choosing, 244
    creating, 243-247
    getURI method, 246
    inherited methods, 247
    Java method, 244
    methods, typing/wiring, 247
    naming, 243
    viewing, 62, 248

W

Wait activity, 31, 56
wasprofile utility, 360
WAT (WebSphere Adapter Toolkit), 268
    adapters, customizing, 268-271
    definition, 393
    installation, 393
        with product CDs, 394-395
        with RPU (Rational Product Updater),
            393-394
        verifying, 395-396
    online documentation, 394
WBIA (WebSphere Business Integration
    Adapters), 252
Web Ontology Language (OWL), 326

Web services
    bindings, 60, 338
    for BPEL. *See* BPEL
    input/outputs, 172
    technologies, 171
    WSDLs
        components, 171
        importing, 172-175
        inline, importing, 177
        publishing, 178-179
        schemas, 171
        validating, 175-177
Web Services Description Language
    (WSDL), 28
websites
    CBE specification document, 190
    clustering topologies resources, 97
    Eclipse framework, 41
    WPS documentation, 97
    WSDL, 171
    XSLT, 128
WebSphere Adapter Toolkit. *See* WAT
WebSphere Business Integration Adapters
    (WBIA), 252
WebSphere Enterprise Service Bus. *See* WESB
WebSphere Integration Developer. *See* WID
WebSphere Process Server. *See* WPS
WebSphere Process Server 6.0 Profile Wizard,
    353-358
WebSphere Service Registry and Repository.
    See WSRR
WESB (WebSphere Enterprise Bus), 336
    administrative console, 343
    buses
        checking, 347
        integration, 343
    installing, 342
    mediations, 337
        flows, 340
        modules, 337-339, 344-347
        primitives, 340-341
    SCA, 343
    service endpoint interaction support, 336
    test server in WID, 344
    WebSphere platform, 336
While activity, 31
while control structure (Visual Snippet Editor
    palette), 63
while loop
    long-running business processes, 111-112
    process editor, 56
WID (WebSphere Integration Developer), 41
    administrative console, 69

assembly editor, 57
   action bar, 57
   binding types, 59-60
   business service components, 58
   canvas, 57
   Import/Export/Stand-alone References, 58
   Interface Map and Selector, 59
   palette, 58
   properties view, 57
BPEL constructs of Business Modeler, 289
business integration solution, 43-44
business rules, 142
components, testing, 67
Console, 71
help, 43
installation, 41, 361-364
integration test client, 70-71
   emulators, 71
   events, 71
   modules/components, testing, 67
   monitors, 71
   test configuration, 71
interfaces, 50-51
libraries, 44-46
logs, viewing, 71
mediation modules, 153
   creating, 344-345
   deploying, 345-347
modules
   creating, 52-53
   dependencies, 52-53
   exporting, 64-66
   structure, 53
   testing, 67
Monitor Toolkit. *See* MME
nested business objects, 49-50
process editor, 54-56
   action bar, 54
   business processes, creating, 54
   canvas, 54
   Common Activities, 55
   Control Activities, 55-56
   Error-Handling Activities, 56
   palette, 55-56
   properties view, 55
   trays, 55
processes, versioning, 214-216
Project Explorer view, 259
relationships, creating, 138
   names, 138
   Relationship Editor, 139-141
   Relationship Manager, 141-142
   types, 139
shell sharing, 72

simple business objects
   attributes, 47-48
   creating, 46-49
starting, 42, 364-365
test servers, 68-69
troubleshooting, 72
updating, 366
User Interface Generator, 168-170
Visual Snippet Editor, 61-64
WAT (WebSphere Adapter Toolkit) Eclipse
   plug-in, 395-396
WESB test server, 344
Workspace Launcher screen, 42
workspaces, 42
WSDLs
   importing, 172-175
   inline, importing, 177
   publishing, 178-179
   validating, 175-177
WSRR (WebSphere Service Registry and
   Repository)
   Eclipse plug-in, 388-391
   retrieval, 332-333
   WSDL files, publishing, 334
wildcard character (*), 332
windows
   Connector Import, 259
   Integration Module Export, 64
   New Business Object, 47
   New Decision Table, 145
   Server Overview, 68-69
wizards
   ESD, 256
   Installation Wizard for WebSphere Process
      Server for Multiplatforms, 349-353
   New Business Process, 102
   New Interface, 50
   New Module, 52
   Quickstart, 277
   WebSphere Process Server 6.0 Profile
      Wizard, 353-358
   WPS installation, 85
workload, distributing across cluster
   members, 87
Workspace Launcher screen (WID), 42
workspaces
   Business Modeler, 276
   WID, 42
WPS (WebSphere Process Server), 75
   administrative console, 85
   architectural model, 17
   BOF, 232
   BPC, 78, 81
   business rules, 78
   CEI, 77

cells, 83-87
clustering, 87-89
    cluster members, 87
    components, 89-90
    horizontal, 88
    SI Bus, 90-92
    transaction failover, 89
    vertical, 88
    workload distribution, 87
communicating with adapters, 253
components, 76
    clustering, 89-90
    databases, 79-81
database access, securing, 208-209
documentation website, 97
event sequencing, 229-231
functional content, 77-79
infrastructure, 79-81
installation, 85, 349
    Installation Wizard for WebSphere
        Process Server for Multiplatforms,
        349-353
    silent installations, 358-359
    WPS_HOME installation directory,
        359-360
licenses, 84
logging
    architecture, 189
    customizing, 210-212
    installation files, 213
    JVM logs, 210
    process logs, 210
    storing, 210
maps, 78
mediation flows, 77
messaging, 79, 208-209
network deployment configuration, 85
nodes, 83-85
overview, 76
profiles, 82-83
    creating with pct utility, 359
    creating with WebSphere Process Server
        6.0 Profile Wizard, 353-358
    deleting, 360
SCA runtime, 77
security
    configuring with LDAP server, 203-205
    enabling, 200-201
    global, 201-202
    security stack, 201
services, 76
stand-alone configuration, 85
starting/stopping, 86

topologies
    multiple-cluster, 94-97
    single-cluster, 92-93
    single-server, 92
troubleshooting, 210
uninstallation, 360
usernames/passwords, 376
WPS_HOME directory, 359-360
WS-BPEL. See BPEL (Business Process
    Execution Language)
WSDL (Web Services Description
    Language), 28
    components, 171
    files, publishing to WSRR, 334
    inline, 177
    references, 223
        asynchronous service invocation,
            225-226
        callbacks, 225-226
        service invocation API, 224
        service locator, 224
    Web services
        components, 171
        importing, 172-175
        inline, importing, 177
        publishing, 178-179
        schemas, 171
        validating, 175-177
    website, 171
WSRR (WebSphere Service Registry and
    Repository), 322
    administrators, 325
    concepts, 324
    console, 327
    documents
        loading, 327
        searching, 331-332
    Eclipse plug-in, 388-391
    functionality, 334
    governance
        enabling, 329
        lifecycle, 323-325
        notification, 329-330
        state, transitioning, 330
    impact analysis, 328
    installation, 324-325, 385-388
    ontology, 326
    querying, 332
    semantic metadata support, 323
    Service Registry in WID, 332-335
        retrieval, 332-333
        WSDL files, publishing, 334
    taxonomies, 326
    user interface, 324

user role, 325
XSD files, 327

X–Z

XML (Extensible Markup Language), 28
XML Schema, 28
XPath (XML Path Language), 28, 33, 219
XPath expressions, 314
XSD files, 327
XSLT (Extensible Stylesheet Language
  Transformation), 128
XSLT mediation primitives, 341

zip files, exporting modules as, 65-66

BOOKS ONLINE

ENABLED

THIS BOOK IS SAFARI ENABLED

INCLUDES FREE 45-DAY ACCESS TO THE ONLINE EDITION

The Safari® Enabled icon on the cover of your favorite technology book means the book is available through Safari Bookshelf. When you buy this book, you get free access to the online edition for 45 days.

Safari Bookshelf is an electronic reference library that lets you easily search thousands of technical books, find code samples, download chapters, and access technical information whenever and wherever you need it.

TO GAIN 45-DAY SAFARI ENABLED ACCESS TO THIS BOOK:

- Go to **http://www.prenhallprofessional.com/safarienabled**
- Complete the brief registration form
- Enter the coupon code found in the front of this book on the "Copyright" page

If you have difficulty registering on Safari Bookshelf or accessing the online edition, please e-mail customer-service@safaribooksonline.com.

PRENTICE HALL